Powerful Patriots

OXFORD
UNIVERSITY PRESS

Oxford University Press is a department of the University of Oxford.
It furthers the University's objective of excellence in research, scholarship,
and education by publishing worldwide.

Oxford   New York
Auckland   Cape Town   Dar es Salaam   Hong Kong   Karachi
Kuala Lumpur   Madrid   Melbourne   Mexico City   Nairobi
New Delhi   Shanghai   Taipei   Toronto

With offices in
Argentina   Austria   Brazil   Chile   Czech Republic   France   Greece
Guatemala   Hungary   Italy   Japan   Poland   Portugal   Singapore
South Korea   Switzerland   Thailand   Turkey   Ukraine   Vietnam

Oxford is a registered trademark of Oxford University Press
in the UK and certain other countries.

Published in the United States of America by
Oxford University Press
198 Madison Avenue, New York, NY 10016

CIP data is on file at the Library of Congress.

ISBN: 978–0–19–938755–7 (hbk.); 978–0–19–938756–4 (pbk.)

3 5 7 9 8 6 4 2
Printed in the United States of America
on acid-free paper

CONTENTS

LIST OF ILLUSTRATIONS

Figures

Tables

ACKNOWLEDGMENTS

I am deeply grateful to those who helped me bring this book to fruition. I started this project while a graduate student at the University of California, San Diego, where I began my journey as a political scientist and China scholar under the tutelage of David Lake and Susan Shirk. As co-chairs of my dissertation committee, they provided invaluable mentorship, support, and feedback at critical points along the way. At UCSD I was also privileged to work with Branislav Slantchev and benefited from stimulating conversations with Lawrence Broz, Richard Madsen, Tai Ming Cheung, Sam Popkin, Miles Kahler, Steph Haggard, Peter Gourevitch, and Eddy Malesky. Jean Oi, my undergraduate advisor at Stanford, provided encouragement from afar and an early introduction to field research in China.

I am especially indebted to the many individuals in China who trusted me with their thoughts and reflections. I would name them individually but doing so would betray their confidence. Many Japanese and American officials also generously spoke with me at length. In China, Qin Yaqing at the China Foreign Affairs University and Chu Shulong at Tsinghua University helped make possible my extended stays in 2006 and 2007. I also benefited from the support and feedback of my fellow travelers in China, particularly Greg Distelhorst, Rachel Stern, and Chad Futrell. Diao Ying provided invaluable assistance, friendship, and moral support.

As I turned my dissertation into this book, I benefited enormously from the Princeton-Harvard China and the World Program and a postdoctoral fellowship at Princeton University. Jack Snyder, Tom Christensen, Iain Johnston, and Ken Scheve generously read and commented on an earlier version of the manuscript at my book workshop in 2010. I am especially grateful to Tom Christensen, Iain Johnston, Margaret Pearson, Allen Carlson, Yinan He, Taylor Fravel, Ezra Vogel, and Kay Shimizu for detailed feedback on various chapters. Pierre Landry, Deborah Davis, Ellen Lust, Susan Hyde, Nikolay Marinov, Alex Debs, and Judith Kelley are due special thanks for comments on the article-length version of the argument that was published in *International Organization*. Comments from colleagues and audiences at Columbia, Stanford, Harvard, Michigan, Ohio State, Duke, Princeton, Berkeley,

Chicago, Cornell, the University of Washington, University of Virginia, University of Oxford, London School of Economics, and National Committee on U.S.–China Relations Public Intellectuals Program helped stimulate and deepen my thinking. I would also like to thank the political science department and Mershon Center at Ohio State, where a productive and enjoyable sabbatical in 2011–2012 enabled me to devote myself fully to the manuscript.

I am especially grateful to Kacie Miura, Lizzie Shan, and Koichiro Kawaguchi for their enthusiastic and unstinting research assistance. A number of other students also provided valuable help, including Dong Yan, Flora Tsang, Morgan Ramsey-Elliott, Rachel Wang, Liu Wenqi, Liu Yu, Yinan Song, Yuke Li, Tianhao Yang, Ashley Wu, and Helen Gao. My research would not have been possible without funding from the National Science Foundation, the Institute on Global Conflict and Cooperation at the University of California, the U.S. Department of Education Fulbright-Hays Program, the Bradley Foundation, and the MacMillan Center for International and Area Studies at Yale.

My editor at Oxford University Press, David McBride, has been nothing short of wonderful to work with. He and Alexandra Dauler have ensured that the gears have turned rapidly and smoothly, and I am very grateful for their timely support and effort.

My parents, Noel Weiss and Chu Chen, have always been an inspiration: dedicating themselves to scientific inquiry as well as family and the arts. I am thankful for the example they have set and their willingness to consider political "science" good enough for their daughter. My close friends in New Haven, Valarie Kaur and Ellie Powell, have helped me keep perspective.

Finally, Jeremy Wallace has contributed in more ways than I can name to this book. As my friend, he was an early and effective advocate for graduate training in political science. As my partner, he galvanized me to move quickly through graduate school so that we could do research in China at the same time. As my husband and closest colleague, he has read every word of every chapter, often multiple times. Yet he has managed to preserve and reignite my excitement about research and our many intellectual adventures to come. It is to him that I dedicate this book.

Powerful Patriots

1

Introduction

In regard to China-Japan relations, reactions among youths, especially students, are strong. If difficult problems were to appear still further, it will become impossible to explain them to the people. It will become impossible to control them. I want you to understand this position which we are in.

—Deng Xiaoping, speaking to high-level Japanese officials, June 28, 1987[1]

This book examines China's management of nationalist, antiforeign protests—both those that occurred and those that were prevented—and their diplomatic consequences between 1985 and 2012. In China, anti-American protests were allowed in 1999 after NATO planes accidentally bombed the Chinese embassy in Yugoslavia but were repressed in 2001 after a U.S. reconnaissance plane and Chinese fighter jet collided. Anti-Japanese demonstrations were repressed throughout the 1990s and late 2000s but erupted in 1985, 2005, 2010, and 2012. When the United States invaded Iraq in 2003, antiwar demonstrations broke out in countries as far flung as Egypt, Russia, and Indonesia. Yet Chinese authorities banned antiwar demonstrations, only to relent two weeks later.[2] Popular demonstrations have never been allowed over the issue of Taiwan, perhaps the issue of greatest concern to Chinese nationalists.

Explaining this pattern sheds light on an important debate about the role of nationalism and public opinion in China's foreign relations. Can China's unelected leaders ignore popular sentiment in handling foreign affairs? Or are China's authoritarian leaders so dependent on nationalism that they must appease domestic calls for a more assertive foreign policy, inhibiting rational diplomacy? This book takes a middle position between these two extremes, arguing that the degree of popular influence on Chinese foreign policy is affected by the government's management of nationalist, antiforeign protest. Does the government let angry citizens take to the streets and organize demonstrations outside foreign embassies and consulates? Or do the authorities shut down calls for protest as they begin to circulate online, bring activists in to "drink tea," and disperse crowds shortly after they materialize?

The central argument of this book is that the decision to allow or repress nation-alist protests helps signal an authoritarian government's intentions and shapes its room for diplomatic compromise. Just as an American president can say that his hands are tied by Congress and domestic opinion, so can Chinese leaders claim that they cannot give in to foreign demands that "hurt the feelings" of over a billion Chinese people. Such rhetoric is more credible when the streets of Chinese cities are filled with antiforeign protests that may turn against the government, particu-larly if it appears weak in defending the national interest. Without visible evidence of popular mobilization, foreign observers are more likely to dismiss such state-ments as "cheap talk."

There is wide variation in how authoritarian governments handle antiforeign protest, ranging from suppression to encouragement to containment. The Jordanian government suppressed pro-Iraqi demonstrations in 1996 and all protests in 1998 after signing a peace treaty with Israel and strengthening ties with the United States. In Syria, thousands demonstrated in October 2005 against the UN inves-tigation into the assassination of former Lebanese prime minister Rafik Hariri, shouting anti-American slogans and carrying photographs of Syria's president. Schoolchildren who participated in the rally "were told when they arrived at school that their classes were canceled and that they would be 'spontaneously demonstrat-ing today in support of President Assad.' "[3] A month earlier in Iran, Islamic student associations protested outside the British embassy, formed human chains around Iran's nuclear reactors, and demanded that Iran's leaders resume uranium enrich-ment. The demonstrations turned violent when protesters began throwing grenades and attempted to enter the embassy. Although the police used tear gas to disperse the crowd, the police chief reportedly told a circle of students that had gathered around him:

> Damn those who cause the police to confront the students. A number of people had obtained permits to demonstrate here, and we cooperated with them. We have certain feelings as you do. I'm sure that you didn't have any intention of hurting the system. And we never wanted to clash with Hezbollah students.[4]

His words illustrate several critical features of antiforeign protest in authoritarian states. First is the risk that nationalist protests will escalate beyond their anticipated scope, potentially causing a diplomatic incident and bringing protesters into con-flict with the regime. Once begun, protests can trigger the sudden realization that taking to the streets is acceptable, even safe, leading more and more people to join the protest. Citizens who join an antiforeign protest may discover common cause against the regime itself, particularly if the government fails to take a tough diplo-matic stance. Once unleashed, protests become more difficult for the government to restrain. Even strong authoritarian governments may have difficulty reining in protests that are widely seen as patriotic and legitimate. State security may disobey orders to curtail antiforeign protests with force, as the Shah of Iran discovered during the 1979 revolution.

China's leaders are keenly aware of the threat posed by nationalist mobilization. Indeed, the last two Chinese regimes—the Kuomintang government in 1949 and the Qing dynasty in 1912—fell to popular movements that accused the government of failing to defend the nation from foreign predations. Given the risk that protests might get out of hand and turn against the regime, why have China's Communist leaders been willing to allow nationalist protests? Two common explanations focus on the Chinese Communist Party's eroded domestic legitimacy, following the disasters of the Great Leap Forward and Cultural Revolution under Mao Zedong, as well as the repression of pro-democracy demonstrations in 1989. With the move away from Communist ideology, a prominent argument holds that China's authoritarian rulers have become so dependent on patriotism for their legitimacy that they cannot risk defying nationalist pressures. Another common view argues that China's leaders benefit from nationalist protests as a distraction from domestic grievances or a relatively safe outlet for pent-up anger.

While compelling, these arguments have difficulty accounting for the variation in China's management of nationalist protests. Existing studies have focused on nationalist protests that have occurred but not those that have been repressed: paying greater attention to the "ones" than the "zeros." Selecting on the dependent variable may bias our conclusions, leading us to overlook the Chinese government's ability to mitigate the impact of popular nationalism on foreign policy. The regime is worried about grassroots nationalism, but it is not uniformly paralyzed. As in democratic states, there is a political process that sometimes amplifies and sometimes mutes the impact of public opinion. Both protesters and government authorities have agency. China's authoritarian leaders are most constrained by popular sentiments when protesters are in the streets. But the Chinese government is not feeble. When it chooses to mount the effort, it is usually capable of curtailing popular mobilization through dissuasion and censorship. Nonetheless, the costs of curtailment and the risk that repression will fail create incentives for the government to take a tough foreign policy stance, easing domestic pressures and persuading protesters to desist.

To be clear, this should not be characterized as state manipulation of popular protest, but as state management of protests that are costly to repress but also risky to allow. "Red light, green light" is a useful analogy to describe the management of nationalist protest in authoritarian regimes. Protesters are in the driver's seat, motivated by sincere grievances as well as anger that has been stoked by patriotic propaganda and inflammatory media coverage. As activists and protesters rev their engines, the government signals when to go, when to stop, and when to exercise caution. But the government does not control protesters, though it may try to enforce speed limits. Once protests gain momentum, it is difficult for the government to stop them without evidence of progress toward their demands. It is because nationalist protests are difficult to control and can easily turn against the government that nationalist protests constrain the government's diplomatic options. If nationalist protesters were "puppets," this constraint would not be real—nor would it be credible to foreign observers.

This framework builds on existing explanations that balance the risks of allowing protest against the costs of repression. Allowing protests may be beneficial as a "safety valve" for citizens to vent their domestic grievances. Yet citizens harboring domestic grievances may seize the opportunity to mobilize under the protective cloak of patriotism. Competing elites may also utilize street protests to strengthen their hand in internal power struggles. Although nipping protests in the bud avoids the risks that accompany mobilization, repression is also costly, exacerbating resentment against the regime's high-handed suppression of patriotic sentiments. These trade-offs suggest that domestic factors are important but often indecisive as the government considers how to respond to nationalist mobilization. Given these domestic dilemmas, the government's diplomatic motivations often tip the scales toward allowing or repressing nationalist protest.

Diplomatic objectives are an important and understudied part of the government's management of nationalist protests. I argue that when the Chinese government wants to signal its resolve—using public sentiment to "teach foreigners a lesson"—it has been more willing to tolerate nationalist street demonstrations. On the other hand, when the Chinese government wants to reassure foreign audiences, defuse a potential crisis, and preserve its diplomatic options, it has been more willing to keep nationalist protests in check, despite the domestic costs of defying popular sentiment.

In diplomacy, nationalist mobilization can be an asset as well as a liability. Domestic constraints make international cooperation more difficult but can also provide negotiating leverage. Demonstrations of popular anger can be helpful when the leadership seeks to signal resolve and demonstrate its commitment to defending the national interest. Provided that foreign observers can tell the difference between sincere and manufactured protests, the government conveys greater resolve when protests are allowed to erupt and greater reassurance when protests are kept in check.

Because nationalist protests are costly to repress and can spiral out of control, triggering domestic or diplomatic instability, nationalist protests both convey and exacerbate an authoritarian government's vulnerability to domestic pressure. As protests gain momentum, they generate additional pressure on the government to stand firm in diplomatic negotiations, raising the domestic cost of backing down. Because it is easier for the government to curtail street demonstrations before they have grown in size and spread to multiple cities, the escalation of street protests ties the government's hands, making it more likely that the government will stand firm in diplomatic negotiations and risk an international standoff rather than confront mobs in the streets. A democratic president or prime minister can point to Congress or Parliament and say, "I'm pinned." With antiforeign protesters in the streets, the autocrat can retort: "You might lose a few points at the polls, but I could be thrown into exile or much worse. You may have Congress, but I have mobs!" In short, visible protests provide unelected leaders a means of showcasing domestic pressure as leverage in diplomatic negotiations, a form of brinkmanship that conveys resolve and commitment to an unwavering stance.

But authoritarian leaders do not always seek to demonstrate resolve and tie their hands in diplomatic disputes. Often, foreign policymakers seek to preserve room for maneuver, defuse potential crises, and insulate diplomatic relations from nationalist opposition. When the government seeks to reassure foreign governments that cooperative initiatives and bilateral commitments will not be hijacked by domestic extremists, it has diplomatic incentives to keep nationalist protests in check. Nationalist protests are costly to repress, creating resentment and leaving the government vulnerable to charges of selling out the nation. Because the act of nipping protests in the bud is costly, doing so sends a credible signal of reassurance, demonstrating to outside observers that the government is willing to defy domestic demands for the sake of international cooperation. The decision to stifle antiforeign protests demonstrates the government's willingness to spend domestic capital to restrain domestic voices that might reduce diplomatic flexibility and prevent cooperation.

My argument does not imply that international incentives are primary in the management of antiforeign protests, only that they are a critical and often omitted factor in existing analyses. In addition, domestic factors are critical to understanding the diplomatic consequences of nationalist protest. Nationalist protests are only effective if they appear to be domestically costly for the government to repress; otherwise, they will be dismissed as "cheap talk." Whether the government allows or stifles popular mobilization, the sincerity of nationalist anger must be apparent in order to be credible.

Foreign perceptions of China's motivations and constraints are crucial. At the diplomatic level, whether nationalist sentiments are actually spontaneous or state led matters less than whether foreign negotiators expect Chinese leaders to be constrained by domestic sentiments or pay a high political price for defying popular opinion. An important task is to identify the observable characteristics that make nationalist protests more or less credible. I argue that the specter of nationalist mobilization is more convincing when protests appear costly to repress and potentially destabilizing. Government efforts to channel nationalism and thereby mitigate the danger to the regime and diplomatic relations run a different risk: that nationalist opinions will be dismissed by foreign observers as manufactured. If foreign observers believe that the government can manipulate Chinese mass opinion at will, even raucous street protests will have little diplomatic sway. If protests are seen as "safety valves" for domestic discontent, releasing popular anger and then subsiding with no impact on foreign policy, foreigners have less inducement to offer concessions, because they expect China's leaders to be able to show flexibility soon thereafter. Outside observers often fail to recognize that diverting domestic grievances toward foreign policy issues does not strengthen the government's legitimacy if it cannot claim diplomatic victory or point to tough countermeasures that the government has taken to protect the nation's interest. Likewise, the repression of protests only signals reassurance when outside observers understand that the abortive demonstrations were genuinely antiforeign rather than a cover for antiregime dissent.

One may wonder why foreign governments should make concessions if the risks of nationalist mobilization are primarily borne by the Chinese government. Nationalist mobilization enables authoritarian leaders to play the "good cop" in the "good cop, bad cop" routine. Even prickly leaders appear moderate when compared with angry demonstrators in "the street." Many external actors—from governments to multinational enterprises to international investors—have a stake in the stability of China and many other authoritarian states. Provided that foreign leaders prefer the status quo to instability, nationalist protests give foreigners an incentive to make concessions and give the authoritarian leadership more slack.[5] By making diplomatic accommodations, foreign decision-makers ease the domestic pressure on the government to adopt tougher policies. Faced with a hawkish or unstable alternative, foreign governments may see concessions as a wise hedge against a worse fate. Often, it is the moderate autocrat whom foreign governments seek to bolster against conservative competitors who might gain influence with the eruption of nationalist protests.

As these risks make clear, antiforeign protest is hardly a one-size-fits-all instrument for diplomatic wrangling. Like a short-range missile, protests are but one weapon in a large arsenal and better suited to certain missions than others. Nationalist protests are only credible when they appear genuine, not state directed—rooted in sincere anger against foreign acts of perceived aggression or humiliation, not manufactured by the state to distract attention from domestic grievances. Nationalist protests are also a blunt instrument, ill suited for delicate negotiations where fine-grained compromises are inevitable. When diplomatic and domestic considerations have counseled flexibility and restraint, authoritarian rulers have often sheathed the "double-edged sword" of nationalism.

Finally, the management of nationalist protests may be a tactical asset in the short run but a strategic liability in the long run. Domestically, the government may find it increasingly difficult to preserve domestic stability as the cycle of nationalist mobilization repeats. State control and legitimacy may erode as protesters gain experience with political participation and domestic observers become cynical toward the government's selective tolerance. Internationally, foreign observers may become inured to nationalist protests, discounting them as "crying wolf," while others become more convinced that China's leaders are in fact "riding the tiger" of popular nationalism. This polarization of foreign perceptions may make it more difficult for China to facilitate a smooth rise and defuse acrimonious debates over China's long-term intentions.

Method and Approach

To my knowledge, no study has systematically evaluated the pattern of nationalist, antiforeign protest in China, examining the causes and consequences of protests that occurred as well as protests that were preemptively stifled. Indeed, the phenomenon of antiforeign protest has not been systematically studied by social scientists, with protests against foreign targets typically excluded from widely used cross-national data sets on internal unrest.[6] China is a substantively important as well as appropriate setting in which to assess the plausibility of the theoretical framework. In different respects, China is both a tough and easy case for the general theory.

As a strong authoritarian state, China is tough case. Because the Chinese government demonstrated its willingness and ability to put down nationwide demonstrations on June 4, 1989, foreign observers may doubt that popular protests pose a real risk to state control or are costly for the government to curtail.[7] As two international relations scholars note, "Tiananmen Square should serve as a cautionary tale for those peddling ideas about the weakness of single-party regimes."[8] If we still observe domestic and foreign concerns about China's vulnerability to nationalist protests and the difficulty of defying popular opinion, we should increase our confidence in the theory's general applicability to other authoritarian regimes. On the other hand, as a country with a long history of nationalist protest and mass revolution, China is a relatively easy case. Foreign officials may be more willing to believe that Chinese leaders are vulnerable to popular nationalism than authoritarian leaders that do not depend so heavily on nationalism for their legitimacy.

Indeed, resistance to foreign domination has been a central tenet in Chinese political discourse since the mid-nineteenth century. A key point of reference is the so-called Century of National Humiliation (*bainian guochi*), beginning with China's defeat in the first Opium War in 1842 and ending with China's victory on the side of the Allied Powers in 1945. During this period, the Qing dynasty was forced to sign several hundred "unequal treaties" that gave foreign powers treaty port rights and territorial concessions. Particularly galling was Japan's victory in the Sino-Japanese War of 1894–95, which resulted in the loss of control over Taiwan. The Boxer Rebellion was one of several forms of antiforeignism to emerge as a response to the increasingly pervasive feeling that China was being carved up by foreign powers. Other forms of resistance included the anti-American boycott of 1905, organized in response to anti-Chinese immigration laws and mistreatment of Chinese workers in the United States. Indeed, it was out of the need to defend the nation from foreign encroachments that Chinese intellectuals such as Sun Yat-sen first began to use the phrase

"Chinese nation" (*zhonghua minzu*) in the early 1900s, replacing the culturally based view of China as a civilization with the Western (Westphalian) concept of China as a territorial nation-state.[9] By 1911, the Qing rulers were forced to step down.

The victory of Chinese nationalists in overthrowing the Qing did not spell the end of China's subjugation to foreign powers. During World War I, Japan seized German-held territories in Shandong province and presented China with additional demands, giving Japan extensive economic and military rights in Manchuria and Inner Mongolia. At the end of the war, Chinese delegates to the conference at Versailles were shocked to learn that Britain, France, and Italy had signed a secret agreement awarding Germany's territorial holdings in China to Japan. This perceived betrayal sparked a series of antiforeign demonstrations in cities across China, beginning with Beijing on May 4, 1919. The May Fourth movement, as it came to be known, was both patriotic and self-critical: seeking to strengthen China against foreign imperialism while attacking Chinese traditionalism as inferior to Western political, intellectual, and scientific practice. Many of China's rising political leaders were active in the May Fourth demonstrations, including Zhou Enlai and close colleagues of Mao Zedong.[10]

The Japanese invasion and occupation of mainland China caused further national trauma, beginning with Manchuria in 1931 and the Chinese heartland in 1937. During the war, Japan attacked or occupied much of China, with its army following a brutal and indiscriminate policy of "kill all, burn all, and destroy all" in Communist-controlled areas of northern China. In Manchuria, Unit 731 of the Japanese army set up several biological and chemical warfare research centers, whose field trials included Chinese military and civilian subjects.[11] According to official Chinese estimates, 300,000 were killed in the 1937 Nanjing Massacre. It was against this backdrop that Mao Zedong and the Chinese Communist Party came to power in the civil war that followed China's liberation at the end of World War II. With the founding of the People's Republic of China in 1949, Chairman Mao declared: "Ours will no longer be a nation subject to insult and humiliation. We have stood up."[12]

Under Mao, mass antiforeign rallies were commonplace, organized and sanctioned by the government. The Communist Party assumed the mantle of anti-imperialism, consistent with the international Communist effort as well as China's nationalist struggles against foreign exploitation. The United States was the primary target—for entering the Korean War, intervening in the Taiwan Strait, and rearming Japan—but protesters also rallied against India, Britain, Vietnam, Indonesia, and the Soviet Union following the Sino-Soviet rift in 1960. In 1960 alone, the *People's Daily* reported 283 anti-American demonstrations, 99 anti-Soviet demonstrations, and 54 other antiforeign demonstrations.[13] Antiforeign fervor reached its zenith during the Cultural Revolution, when Chinese mobs attacked foreign embassies and consulates, even burning the British embassy.

In the 1970s, the waning of the Cultural Revolution and increased fears of Soviet expansionism created the background conditions for rapprochement and normalization of relations with the United States and Japan. Prioritizing diplomatic recognition and cooperation against the Soviet Union, China agreed to relinquish claims that Japan provide war reparations.[14] It was not until the 1980s that this "benevolent amnesia" began to fade, as the Soviet threat waned and China grew more concerned about Japan's rearmament under the U.S.-Japan alliance.[15] China also launched a new wave of education and propaganda efforts to buttress the Party's legitimacy and discredit Western-style liberalization after the pro-democracy protests of 1989 and the fall of Communist regimes throughout the Soviet bloc, reviving the narrative of "national humiliation" through new textbooks, films, and commemorative museums.

China's remembered humiliation at the hands of foreign powers—both real and reinforced through patriotic propaganda—has provided ample kindling for nationalist mobilization in the post-Mao era. Although many foreign powers played a role in China's "Century of National Humiliation," since the 1970s almost all antiforeign protests in China—whether realized or stillborn—have targeted Japan. Chinese citizens also sought to mobilize anti-American protests in two high-profile crises with the United States. France bore the brunt of nationalist protests after President Nicolas Sarkozy publicly contemplated a boycott of the Beijing Olympics in 2008. Anti-Indonesian protests were repressed in response to violence against ethnic Chinese in Indonesia in 1998.

An important advantage of a single-country study is the ability to identify and analyze the "dogs that did not bark"—in this case, nationalist protests that the government preemptively repressed. The appendix catalogues all observed episodes in which antiforeign protests were allowed or prevented in China between 1985 and 2012. Including stillborn protests provides the "universe of cases" in which the argument is relevant: episodes where popular mobilization prompted a government response. I have undoubtedly missed some episodes, particularly small or remote events that went unnoticed or unreported by foreign and domestic sources. By definition, however, unobserved episodes do not impact foreign perceptions, so their absence is less troubling for the study of nationalist protest in China's foreign relations. The fact that there are nearly as many observations of repression as tolerance, even when the size of aborted protests is very small, also gives confidence that this list provides a plausible universe of cases.

I define antiforeign protest as a public manifestation by a group of people, containing hostile feeling toward a foreign government or people, and rooted in advocacy or support for the nation's interests, especially to the exclusion or detriment of other nations. I follow Haas in defining nationalism as an ideology that makes "assertions about the nation's claim to historical uniqueness, to the territory that the nation-state ought to occupy, and to the kinds of relations that should prevail between one's nation and others."[16] Throughout the book, I use the terms *nationalist*

protest and *antiforeign protest* interchangeably, recognizing that many different currents of nationalism flow beneath the surface of these demonstrations.[17] There is no
single Chinese nationalism, with distinct and competing visions articulated by state
propaganda, liberal and conservative intellectuals, and grassroots activists, making
it all the more difficult for the Chinese Communist Party to harness nationalism in
support of its rule.

It is particularly important to distinguish the phenomenon of what I call "antiforeign protest" from official rallies or other state-organized demonstrations. Official
rallies are organized under government or party auspices and attended by a select
group of prescreened participants. State-organized mass demonstrations, such as
those in North Korea or in China during the Mao Zedong era, are not very costly
for the government to curtail, nor do they carry the same risk of turning against the
regime.[18] In contrast, grassroots antiforeign protests—including demonstrations,
petitions, marches, and strikes—may receive official permission but are organized
and attended by individuals acting in a private capacity or as part of an independent,
unofficial organization.[19]

Nationalist, antiforeign mobilization in the post-Mao era has typically followed a recurrent cycle, beginning with efforts by students or dedicated activists to stage a peaceful demonstration or protest march, attracting the notice and
participation of bystanders, and at some point precipitating government efforts
to rein in and disperse protesters. What has varied is the government's response
at the outset of the protest cycle, ranging from preemptive repression to acquiescence to facilitation. Repression includes preemptive efforts to stifle grassroots
mobilization (removing calls for protest and dissuading activists in advance of
rumored protests or important dates) as well as rapid containment (confiscating
protest banners, removing online petitions, and dispersing crowds as soon as they
materialize). Tolerance includes tacit acquiescence (allowing calls for protest to
circulate and providing passive security as demonstrations grow in size and geographic spread) as well as facilitation (preapproving protest routes and slogans
presented by grassroots organizers as well as using party structures to organize
protests and provide logistical support). The government's willingness to repress,
tolerate, or facilitate nationalist mobilization has not strictly corresponded
with the anticipated or realized size of protest demonstrations. Both small- and
large-scale protests have been prevented as well as allowed, ranging from a dozen
activists to thousands of participants.

To explain why China has allowed or repressed nationalist protest and to evaluate the diplomatic consequences of this variation, in the remaining chapters I trace
China's management of antiforeign protests against Japan and the United States.
While these relationships are not representative of China's foreign relations, the
scarcity of grassroots mobilization against China's other counterparts to date lessens
the empirical sacrifice. It is crucial to note that all of Chinese diplomacy is not under
the scope; grassroots mobilization restricts the set of cases in which the repression

or tolerance of nationalist protest is informative and potentially constraining. The government has many other tools of pressure, including official demarches, suspension of high-level exchanges, economic threats, and military mobilization. Given these possibilities, this book does not seek to provide a comprehensive history or analysis of Sino-Japanese or Sino-American relations, nor does it assess all of the difficult negotiations and disputes these governments have confronted. Rather, I limit my scope to those issues over which Chinese citizens attempted to stage street demonstrations against Japan and the United States, requiring the Chinese government to respond and foreign observers to interpret Chinese actions. In the conclusion, I return to the issue of generalizing to China's other diplomatic relations and authoritarian regimes more broadly.

To trace the links between perceptions, motivations, actions, and reactions, I draw upon data gathered over 14 months of field research, including memoirs of high-ranking officials and senior leaders, party histories, yearbooks, and diplomatic records, policy analysis published by government-affiliated think tanks, nationalist bulletin boards and discussion forums online, and more than 170 interviews with nationalist activists, students, protesters, journalists, analysts, and diplomats in China, Japan, the United States, France, and Taiwan.

Plan of the Book

The remainder of the book is divided into eight chapters. Chapter 2 develops the logic of nationalist protest in authoritarian regimes, first identifying the domestic and international factors that make authoritarian leaders more or less likely to tolerate antiforeign protest, and then developing the mechanisms by which protest tolerance and repression affect foreign perceptions. Chapter 3 assesses the management of anti-American protests in the context of two "near crises" in U.S.-China relations. Chinese leaders viewed the 1999 bombing of the Chinese embassy in Belgrade as a deliberate test of China's resolve. By permitting anti-American protests, the Chinese government communicated its determination to stand up to U.S. bullying as well as the domestic demands it faced to take a tougher foreign policy stance. In contrast, Chinese diplomacy was aimed at reducing the perception that China posed a threat to the United States when the 2001 EP-3 collision occurred, shortly after President George W. Bush took office. By repressing nationalist protests, the Chinese government helped defuse the crisis, sending a costly signal of its intent to maintain friendly relations despite domestic accusations that the Chinese government was being too soft on the United States. The chapter also illustrates that the domestic character of nationalist protests influences their diplomatic credibility. After the Chinese government took visible measures to stage-manage the second, third, and fourth day of anti-American demonstrations in 1999, foreign incredulity reduced their diplomatic impact beyond the initial signal of resolve.

Chapters 4, 5, 6, and 7 turn to China's management of anti-Japanese protest between 1985 and 2012. Chapter 4 examines Sino-Japanese relations in the 1980s, assessing China's lenience toward anti-Japanese protests in 1985 and their contribution to political instability and Japanese concessions. The first anti-Japanese protests in the post-Mao era broke out on September 18, 1985, condemning Japanese prime minister Yasuhiro Nakasone's official visit to Yasukuni Shrine, where 14 A-class war criminals are enshrined. The anti-Japanese protests helped convince Nakasone that his visits to Yasukuni were undermining China's policy of engagement and reform, illustrating that foreign governments often have incentives to bolster embattled moderates in light of popular unrest. It would be 11 years before another Japanese prime minister visited the shrine. Nakasone's concessions were unable to prevent the downfall of his friend and counterpart, General Secretary Hu Yaobang, however. As protests spread, demonstrators accused the government of selling out the nation's interests and demanded political reform. The anti-Japanese protests helped set the stage for the pro-democracy protests of 1986 and 1989, the most severe crisis of legitimacy that the Communist Party has faced in the reform era—underscoring the risk that nationalist protests may galvanize a broader movement for change.

Chapter 5 examines Sino-Japanese relations in the 1990s, when China restrained anti-Japanese protests amid tensions over the Diaoyu/Senkaku Islands. Anti-Japanese protests were repressed throughout the 1990s despite efforts to bolster national unity after the Tiananmen crackdown. China launched a patriotic education campaign with materials that often featured Japan as the central villain in China's history of national humiliation, but attempts to shore up the regime's legitimacy did not translate into a more permissive attitude toward nationalist protest. As China sought to break free of its post-Tiananmen economic isolation, the government courted Japanese assistance and restrained anti-Japanese mobilization between 1990 and 1994. Japan's continuing interest in stabilizing China in the early 1990s produced a new "honeymoon" in bilateral relations. Despite the emergence of grassroots activism and civilian demands that the Japanese government make amends for its wartime atrocities, the Chinese government repressed protests on several occasions: in 1990, when a dispute erupted over the islands in the East China Sea, in 1992, during the Japanese emperor's first historic visit to China, and in 1994, when Japanese prime minister Hosokawa visited China. When right-wing activists from Japan built a lighthouse on one of the disputed islands in 1996, China again prevented anti-Japanese protests, concerned about impending revisions to the U.S.-Japan alliance and trying to mitigate the diplomatic fallout of Chinese nuclear tests and military exercises in the Taiwan Strait. China's restraint helped defuse the crisis with Japan, eliciting assurances that the Japanese government would not officially recognize the lighthouse. The 1990s illustrate that China has not always been forced by public opinion and a crisis of domestic legitimacy to allow protests; the government was willing to suppress grassroots nationalist protest for the sake of reassuring foreign audiences and promoting bilateral cooperation.

Chapter 6 assesses the softening of China's attitude toward anti-Japanese protests during the 2000s, including the large-scale anti-Japanese protests that erupted in 2005. Following Japanese prime minister Junichiro Koizumi's repeated visits to Yasukuni Shrine, China began to tolerate small-scale anti-Japanese demonstrations and Internet petitions. But it was not until Japan's bid for a permanent seat on the UN Security Council gained momentum that the Chinese government allowed large-scale anti-Japanese protests to support its diplomatic campaign to undermine Japan's candidacy and head off a vote in the General Assembly. Petitions and protests in dozens of cities helped the Chinese government signal resolve against Japan's candidacy and mobilize third-party support for China's position. At the bilateral level, Chinese pressure also elicited symbolic Japanese concessions.

Chapters 7 and 8 address China's management of anti-Japanese protests between 2006 and 2012, including two crises over the Diaoyu/Senkaku Islands. Chapter 7 demonstrates that the Chinese government is still capable of restraining large-scale nationalist protests, even with the spread of the Internet and social media. In 2010, when Japan arrested a Chinese fishing captain after a collision near the islands, China initially restrained anti-Japanese protests, expecting Japan to follow precedent and release the captain. China did not take more severe countermeasures until the Japanese government extended the captain's detention and continued to insist that domestic law be used to handle the case. As China escalated pressure on Japan to recognize the territorial dispute, no nationwide effort was made to prevent anti-Japanese protests, which erupted in two dozen cities. Although Japanese observers credited China's efforts to cool down nationalist protests during the crisis, the uneven management and appearance of domestic grievances amid anti-Japan protests fueled foreign skepticism about their sincerity and credibility as a constraint on Chinese foreign policy. The lessons of 2010 played a role in shaping Japanese resolve and perceptions two years later, when a new crisis escalated in the East China Sea.

Chapter 8 traces China's lenience toward the most widespread anti-Japanese protests to erupt in post-Mao China over Japan's purchase of three of the Diaoyu/Senkaku Islands. After a right-wing Japanese governor campaigned to purchase and develop infrastructure on the islands, the central Japanese government declared its intent to bring the islands under state control. China sought to prevent what it perceived to be an adverse shift in the legal status quo but also preserve plans to commemorate the fortieth anniversary of normalized relations. Seeking to display resolve without jeopardizing bilateral cooperation, China tolerated anti-Japanese street protests and showcased the landing of Hong Kong activists on the islands to assert Chinese sovereignty. China escalated after Japan announced that it would proceed with the purchase, satisfying domestic demands to take a tougher stance and banking the fires that it had helped light. Despite growing signs of China's opposition, Japan discounted Chinese resolve and believed that Chinese authorities would curtail anti-Japan protests before they could become constraining or destabilizing. Japanese observers largely viewed the protests as a convenient distraction from domestic concerns rather than as a credible signal of the Chinese government's willingness to retaliate.

Chapter 9 considers the continuing struggle for credibility amid China's evolving management of nationalist protests. The increasingly viral mobilization of protests and local variation in the government's response has made it more difficult for outside observers to interpret the government's intentions. The chapter also reflects on the prospects for nationalist spillover to democratic dissent, highlighting the connections between anti-Japanese protest and pro-democracy movements in the 1980s and considering whether a more democratic and developed China would be more or less nationalistic. The chapter concludes by discussing the role of nationalist sentiment in other policy areas, including the South China Sea, Taiwan, and Tibet, as well as in other authoritarian regimes.

2

Nationalist Protest and Authoritarian Diplomacy

The authorities did not clearly express support, but the government did not unduly interfere, which implies its "consent" (*ren tong*).
—Tong Zeng, activist and founder of the China Federation for Defending the Diaoyu Islands[1]

To speak plainly, the government uses us when it suits their purpose. When it doesn't suit them, it suppresses us. This way the government can play the public opinion card. After all, Japan is a democracy and respects public opinion. Even in a nondemocratic country like China, the government can still point to the public's feelings.
—Anti-Japanese activist and website founder[2]

In China, as in most authoritarian states, there are no institutional channels for popular input on foreign policy. Members of the Politburo do not answer to mass electoral constituencies; their success is judged by others within the Party elite. Yet the extent to which public opinion influences Chinese foreign policy remains a subject of great speculation, particularly when nationalist protesters take to the streets over international issues or Chinese diplomats refer to the "hurt feelings" of the Chinese people. What are the consequences of antiforeign nationalism, and why does the Chinese government sometimes allow and sometimes suppress, encourage, or tolerate nationalist street demonstrations?

This chapter develops a framework for understanding the management of antiforeign protests in authoritarian regimes like China.[3] As authoritarian leaders weigh the domestic benefits and risks of nationalist protest, they also calculate the international consequences. Nationalist mobilization, if sincere, can be a diplomatic boon. When allowed, nationalist protests give unelected leaders a way to point to public opinion and credibly claim that diplomatic concessions would be too costly at home. By allowing antiforeign protests, autocrats can signal their resolve to stand firm, demonstrate the extent of public anger, and justify an unyielding bargaining stance. When repressed, nationalist mobilization enables authoritarian leaders to play "good cop" to the hawkish voices in society that might undermine cooperation and destabilize the status quo if given free rein. By stifling antiforeign protests, autocrats can signal reassurance and their commitment to a more cooperative, flexible diplomatic stance.

The Domestic Politics of Authoritarian Diplomacy

For many years, scholars and observers of politics viewed the relatively monolithic, opaque character of autocracies as an advantage for diplomacy. Unlike democrats, autocrats could conduct state affairs with secrecy, without fear of domestic debates being "overheard" by foreign observers. Autocracies could maintain a steady course rather than being blown about by the winds of particularistic interests and faddish public opinion. Recently, the very features that once seemed to put democracies at a disadvantage, particularly transparency, have been viewed as benefits to credible commitment and communication. Only in the last few years has the pendulum begun to swing back. Certain types of autocracies—whose leaders are vulnerable to punishment by other elites if not popular elections—are now seen as performing on par with democracies in international conflict.[4] The arguments developed here follow in this vein, viewing domestic vulnerability and the ability to communicate that vulnerability to foreign observers as a potential advantage in international bargaining.

Authoritarian leaders are no exception to the "two-level game" of strategic interaction between international and domestic politics.[5] Although autocrats are not held accountable to the citizenry via open and competitive elections, they are nevertheless accountable to a certain "selectorate" or "winning coalition."[6] Just as U.S. politicians seek re-election, authoritarian leaders strive to retain power.[7] Leaders may have other goals, including ideological or policy objectives, but holding office makes it easier to achieve those goals.[8] The process of rising to power also tends to favor those who have an appetite for it, weeding out those who do not.[9] Once in power, autocrats may have even stronger incentives than democrats to stay in office, given the irregular and violent manner in which autocrats are often removed.[10] In ordinary times, authoritarian leaders may be accountable to the military, the bureaucracy, or some other constellation of powerful actors. I argue that antiforeign protests also give importance to the voice of ordinary citizens normally outside the selectorate or winning coalition. The decision to allow or repress protests alters the potential costs that the authoritarian regime must pay to restore order to the streets and signals its vulnerability to popular sentiment, akin to a "revolution constraint" on foreign policy.[11]

I develop two analytically distinct mechanisms by which the management of nationalist protests serves as a potentially credible diplomatic signal and an endogenous constraint on foreign policy. The first incorporates the risk that protests pose to regime stability, akin to Thomas Schelling's "threat that leaves something to chance."[12] Nationalist protests can get out of hand and undermine authoritarian stability in a number of ways: providing a protective umbrella for domestic dissent, giving citizens experience with political mobilization, and generating populist fuel for intra-elite competition. Because nationalist protests can get out of hand, the decision to allow such protests signals resolve.

The second mechanism captures the escalating cost of repression, or the difficulty of putting the genie back in the bottle. As protests materialize and gather momentum, they become increasingly difficult and costly for the government to curtail, changing the government's incentives. Rather than restore order by force, which is costly, the government has an incentive to take a tough diplomatic stance in order to appease nationalist protesters and persuade them to disperse peacefully. On the other hand, the decision to nip protests in the bud can signal the government's ability and willingness to cooperate and defuse international tensions. In either case, the decision to allow or suppress nationalist protests enables foreign observers to learn about the regime's diplomatic intentions. In cases where the regime is too weak to curtail nationalist mobilization, street protests reveal information about the degree of popular opposition to compromise or conciliation.

Because governments have strategic incentives to misrepresent their resolve in international bargaining, credible communication is difficult.[13] Although governments prefer to avoid the escalation of tension and open conflict, each wants to ensure the best possible terms of any tacit or negotiated agreement. To signal resolve, states must take actions that distinguish their statements from bluffs. One way to demonstrate resolve is to take actions that increase the risk of bargaining failure.[14] An influential body of literature has argued that public posturing is one way for leaders to send a costly signal of resolve.[15] By going public before domestic audiences, the government increases the potential costs of subsequently backing down. These "audience costs" make it harder for the government to offer concessions, increasing the risk that the government will be locked into a position it cannot yield. The decision to go public signals resolve; the ensuing threat of domestic punishment ties the government's hands.

The microfoundations of audience costs have generated significant controversy.[16] In a seminal article, Fearon suggests that domestic audiences punish leaders who back down for betraying the "national honor."[17] Audience costs are assumed as an exogenous parameter; the public does not actually have the opportunity to act. This raises two questions about the credibility of audience costs. First, is it rational for citizens to punish their leaders for backing down? Second, under what conditions are citizens able to impose punishment? Most work on the microfoundations of audience costs has focused on why citizens would punish their leaders. Smith argues that backing down reveals incompetence. If failure to follow through with past commitments reflects poorly upon a leader's competence, then voters may rationally punish leaders for backing down despite being content with the outcome, that is, having avoided war or some other form of "foreign entanglement."[18] Nevertheless, as Schultz points out, it is unclear why citizens would punish their leaders for getting caught bluffing, since bluffing can be an optimal strategy.[19] An alternative line of argument suggests that being caught bluffing destroys a country's reputation for honesty.[20] In this view, voters have incentives to remove leaders who back down in order to restore the nation's credibility. Survey experiments by Tomz indicate that U.S. respondents indeed disapproved more strongly when the president failed to follow through with a threat than when the president stayed out of the crisis altogether.[21] Yet others argue that citizens care less about holding leaders to their word than about choosing appropriate policies under the circumstances.[22]

Despite these debates, audience costs have been marshaled to explain international cooperation, crisis behavior and outcomes, compliance with trade agreements, monetary policy credibility, and even democratic consolidation.[23] Moreover, the conventional wisdom suggests that the probability that authoritarian leaders will be punished for appearing incompetent or weak on foreign policy is small, even though the magnitude of the punishment may be large in the event of a coup or other irregular turnover.[24] Which effect dominates is moot if the domestic costs of backing down are invisible to outsiders. Unless authoritarian leaders can convince foreign negotiators *ex ante* that the adverse consequences are real and are not part of a bluffing strategy, these audience costs will have no bite. The king's hands may be tied, but the bonds are invisible. One of the few dissenting voices in this literature argues that many autocrats are able to invoke audience costs because they are vulnerable to punishment by other elites within the regime, particularly in single-party and hybrid autocracies, and politics are stable enough that outsiders can detect this potential punishment.[25]

Yet we still lack a mechanism by which authoritarian leaders can demonstrate *ex ante* their vulnerability to domestic pressure, which is likely to vary across different issues and crises. Departing from the conventional focus on institutions and regime type as determinants of political vulnerability, I turn to the strategic interaction of citizens and leaders in nondemocratic states.

The decision to allow or repress antiforeign protests enables authoritarian leaders to signal their diplomatic intentions and determine the degree to which their hands are tied by popular nationalism. First, because protests can spiral out of control, the decision to allow protests is analogous to a "threat that leaves something to chance."[26] Even if the government allows protests in the first place, there remains some probability, however small, that protests get out of hand.[27] Antiforeign protests may turn against the government, grow too large for the state security apparatus to disperse, or generate such popular support that state insiders are tempted to defect and disobey orders to suppress the protests. Second, by raising the specter of mobs that will figuratively storm the palace gates if the government betrays the national interest, the government can more credibly refuse to make international concessions. In bargaining terms, the decision to allow antiforeign protest represents a credible commitment to stand firm as well as a costly signal of resolve.

In determining whether to allow or repress a particular occurrence of nationalist protest, autocrats weigh the potential risk to regime stability against the cost of repressing protests before they can materialize or gather steam. Any given instance of nationalist protest varies along these two dimensions.

The Risk of Instability

Nationalist protests pose a risk to domestic as well as diplomatic instability. Antiforeign protests may trigger an international incident if mobs overrun diplomatic compounds and injure or even kill foreign nationals, jeopardizing diplomatic relations as well as foreign trade and investment. Moreover, nationalist protests pose a risk to authoritarian stability for several reasons identified in the literature:

> *Demonstration effects, tipping points, and information cascades*: Protests, once begun, can trigger the sudden realization that protest is acceptable, even safe, leading more and more people to join the protest. Once a critical mass has gathered in the streets and authorities have not suppressed the protest, the protest can rapidly swell to a size unimaginable the day before.[28]

> *Resource mobilization*: Protests beget protests by lowering the costs of collective action for other groups that have fewer resources, activating new networks and facilitating the spread of protest techniques and repertoires from hard-core activists to previously passive groups and individuals.[29]

> *Elite splits*: Protests may expose weaknesses in the government that may not have been widely apparent, revealing sympathetic allies among the elite and potential regime-threatening fissures between hardliners and moderates.[30] As Ithiel de Sola Pool notes, "The kind of unity and cohesion created by [authoritarian] methods is fragile. Whenever the structure of controls breaks down, the apparent unanimity collapses quickly."[31]

Nationalist protest is especially risky because it has the potential to shake the foundation of state legitimacy, particularly those that rely upon nationalist myth-making to bolster their credentials with the public.[32] Nationalist protests have broad appeal and pose a greater threat than movements that advocate more particularistic interests.[33] Nationalist protests advance goals that may challenge the foundation of the government's legitimacy, such as "the historical mission of the nation, ranging from quiet self-perfection to conquest or the restoration of some golden age," as Haas puts it.[34] Nationalism promotes love of the nation, not love of the government, meaning that nationalist protest can easily escalate to demands for revolution if the

public feels that the government has failed to defend the nation from foreign depredations. As Snyder notes, "Often, nationalists claim that old elites are ineffective
in meeting foreign threats and that a new, popular government is needed to pursue
national interests more forcefully."[35]

How often have antiforeign protests spun out of control to such an extent that
autocratic incumbents lost their grip on power? The Archigos data set on political
leaders from 1875 to 2004[36] documents 573 instances in which leaders lost power in
an irregular manner but were not deposed by a foreign state. Of these, popular protests pushed leaders out of office in 29 cases. Using Lexis-Nexis and the sources cited
by Archigos, I found evidence to suggest that four of these 29 leaders were ousted
by protests that were at least partly antiforeign: the 1956 revolution in Hungary,
where an anti-Soviet uprising caused the government to collapse (and also precipitated a Soviet invasion); the 1979 revolution in Iran, where anti-American protesters deposed the shah; the 1972 riots in Madagascar against neocolonial agreements
with France, which pushed President Tsiranana out of office; and the 1992 ouster
of Azerbaijani president Mutalibov, during which protesters demanded tougher
action by the government against Russia and Armenia in Nagorno-Karabakh. In
2014, nationalist protests in Ukraine forced President Yanukovych to flee the country, galvanized in large part by his deference to Russia and rejection of greater ties
to the European Union.

In these examples, protests were the proximate cause of irregular leadership turnover,[37] but there are undoubtedly many more cases where antiforeign protests created
instability that provided a pretext for a military coup or foreign takeover. It is also
important to note that there are selection effects working against these outcomes, as
governments tend not to allow high-risk protests. When they do, moreover, government officials are likely to take actions—such as adopting a more hawkish foreign
policy stance—that will mollify protesters and prevent a popular backlash.

The Cost of Repression

Protests are easier to nip in the bud than to suppress after they have begun.
Repression is always costly, but dispersing an amassed crowd is more costly than
hauling away a few "early risers" at the scene or warning off activists on the eve
of protest. The cost of curtailment also increases as protests attract domestic and
international scrutiny. The larger and more prominent the protest, the more likely
international and domestic observers are to condemn the government for quashing
political freedoms. Even members of the public who disagree with the protesters'
demands may be spurred to defend the right to protest, varying with the extent to
which other observers view the protests as legitimate.

Nationalist protests are especially costly to suppress because doing so appears
unpatriotic, a betrayal of the national myth. Nationalism provides a layer of protection against government suppression, raising the cost of using force to disperse

protests. Clever protesters seeking to gain sympathy and avoid suppression have often used this to their advantage. In China, for example, nationalist protesters often chant the slogan, "Patriotism is not a crime!" (*aiguo wuzui*). The very attempt to repress nationalist protests may backfire if security forces side with the protesters. In Iran, the 1979 revolution succeeded in large part because of support from elements in the military who turned against the pro-American shah.[38]

Protestors may participate for many different reasons, including thrill-seeking and blowing off steam, but many are also purposive, seeking to effect policy change. Because one individual's decision to participate can increase the likelihood that others join in, the private risk and cost of action also diminish as demonstrations grow in size, providing relative safety in numbers. Although some participants will satisfy their appetite for protest after a short period of participation, others in the crowd will find that the experience has whetted their appetite for protest, stirring them and others to continue pressing their demands.[39] That protestors act instrumentally holds even if nationalist protest is insincere, a mask or outlet for anti-government grievances. In an insincere protest, protesters are still unlikely to disperse without achieving their objectives, in this case domestic concessions rather than foreign policy demands.[40]

The Regime's Domestic Dilemma

In deciding to allow or repress grassroots efforts to mobilize nationalist protests, the government must weigh both the domestic and international costs and benefits. At the domestic level, the government faces a dilemma: prevent citizens from gathering in the street and pay a certain cost of repression, or allow protests and accept an increased risk of domestic and diplomatic instability. As Johnston and Stockmann note, the government has to "walk a fine line between allowing public expressions of negativity (thereby boosting its nationalist credentials but risking large-scale protests that might turn against the regime and harm its international image) and constraining popular anger (thereby maintaining public order and protecting its external image but threatening the regime's internal legitimacy)."[41]

All else equal, the greater the domestic risk that protests will get out of hand, the less likely the government is to allow protest. Protests over issues that are integral to the government's nationalist credentials and draw sympathy from diverse groups in society pose a greater risk to stability than those that are more peripheral and appeal to a narrow group of ultranationalists. Nationalist protests that appear insincere or primarily a cover for antiregime dissent are also relatively risky and more likely to be suppressed. Vietnam, for example, has taken pains to shut down protests against Chinese actions in the South China Sea, imprisoning several activists and bloggers on charges of working with overseas dissident groups and "conducting propaganda against the state."[42] Conversely, the lower the risk to domestic stability, the more likely the government is to tolerate a given protest. When the risk is low enough, such protests may have a salutary effect on domestic stability by allowing citizens to air their grievances and blow off steam, particularly if tight security measures ensure that the "venting" effect dominates the "mobilization" effect, aided by restrictions on protest participation, predetermined time limits on protest duration, and police cordons to prevent passers-by from joining hard-core activists.

The government's willingness to tolerate antiforeign protest is also likely to vary with the cost of repression, depending on the state's coercive capacity (including police discipline, training, and surveillance resources) and the magnitude of grass-roots mobilization (including the salience and resonance of the issue with the broader public). Different regimes are likely to vary in their ability and willingness to repress protests. Relative to democrats, authoritarian leaders have greater moti-vation and capacity to repress nationalist protest. Nationalist protest is both riskier for regime survival and less costly to repress in autocracies than democracies, where laws and norms protecting freedoms of speech and assembly are stronger. Moreover, democratic protests are less likely to escalate to demands for regime change, often feeding into the electoral process. As Tarrow notes, "The ease of organizing opinion in representative systems and finding legitimate channels for its expression induces many movements to turn to elections."[43]

Figure 2.1 illustrates a stylized universe of possible protests defined by the risk of instability and the cost of repression. The dashed line represents the cutoff between protests that the government is willing to allow and protests that the government is likely to repress.

Below the dashed line, the risk to stability is low relative to the cost of repression, making it likely that the government will tolerate protests. Above the dashed line, the risk to stability is high relative to the cost of repression, making it more likely

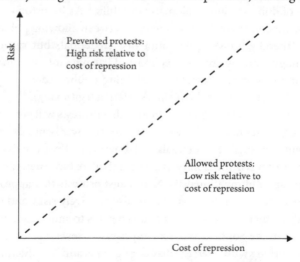

Figure 2.1 The Authoritarian Regime's Domestic Dilemma

that the government will squelch protests. Along the line are cases in which the government is uncertain or indifferent between tolerance and repression, where the choice to allow or prevent protest is not obvious.

Empirically, most potential protests will cluster around this line, since the factors that affect the risk to stability are also likely to affect the cost of repression. For example, the level of discipline and training among riot police is likely to affect both the risk that a protest spins out of control as well as the ease with which the government can disperse protesters without bloodshed. Likewise, the public salience and resonance of the issue affect the risk that a protest will undermine regime legitimacy as well as the cost of repressing potential protesters.

Yet one can imagine cases both above and below the line. Above the line, the risk to stability exceeds the cost of repression. The anniversary of June 4, 1989, is a focal point for dissent in China. Every year, on that date, a number of individuals attempt to walk toward Tiananmen Square by themselves or in groups to commemorate the movement and its tragic end. Such actions do not pose a great risk on an individual basis, but a gathering crowd could set in motion a chain of events with unpredictable and destabilizing consequences. Thus far, the Chinese government has faced little difficulty in shutting down these small-scale acts of resistance. When one writer who participated in the 1989 demonstrations attempted to approach the square on June 4, his journey was cut short by security officials who detained him en route. Surveillance cameras and facial recognition software had flagged him as a potential troublemaker. Such anecdotes illustrate cases in which the government represses protests because the potential instability is greater than the cost of additional surveillance and police resources to prevent a demonstration from forming at Tiananmen Square.

Other instances of protest might fall below the line, where the government decides to tolerate protest because the cost of repression is high relative to the risk of instability. In November 2006, for example, Chinese police cordoned off but did not disperse a crowd of several hundred dog owners who gathered in front of the Beijing zoo to protest restrictions banning the ownership of dogs taller than 35 centimeters and limiting families to one dog per household. Although it would have been costly to repress a protest at such a visible location (on a major arterial in central Beijing), the protest took place outside the Beijing zoo, not a location with political importance. Moreover, the protest demands were specific to height restrictions on dog ownership in Beijing and relatively unlikely to escalate to appeals for systemic political reform or spread to other cities, many of which have less strict regulations on dog ownership.[44] Based on location and demands alone, Chinese security officials may have concluded that the risk of instability was insufficient to warrant the costs of repression.

My purpose here has been to create a simplified representation of the domestic calculus against which the government must weigh the international consequences. Next, I argue that the set of protests that the government is willing to allow expands

or contracts depending on the government's diplomatic objectives and the anticipated international consequences of nationalist protest. Put differently, the diplomatic repercussions of nationalist protest may lead the government to allow some
protests that it would otherwise prevent, and prevent some protests that it would
otherwise allow.

Protest Management as a Diplomatic Signal

The decision to allow antiforeign protest is a coercive tactic, like limited war: "a
risky engagement, one that could develop a momentum of its own and get out
of hand."[45] Some portion of the risk to domestic and diplomatic stability is independent of the government's actions on foreign policy, that is, it is exogenous to
the international negotiations, determined by the "fragility" of the authoritarian
system and security apparatus. This element of risk renders antiforeign protests
analogous to Schelling's "threat that leaves something to chance."[46] The innova-
tion here is that the potential for disaster is political instability and antiforeign
violence rather than mutually assured nuclear exchange. Whereas traditional
models require actions that increase the risk of war to signal resolve,[47] I suggest
that actions that increase the risk of domestic and diplomatic instability can also
serve this purpose.

Because antiforeign protests may escalate to anti-government protests, the government's willingness to run this risk differentiates it from a government that is only
bluffing about its concern over the disputed issue.[48] As Thomas Schelling notes,
"international relations often have the character of a competition in risk-taking,
characterized not so much by tests of force as by tests of nerve."[49] Antiforeign protests provide a mechanism for authoritarian leaders to communicate resolve under
conditions of incomplete information and incentives to bluff.

The risk to domestic and diplomatic stability need not be deliberately embraced
in order to help convince foreigners of the need to compromise or stand down.
States do not send troops to the border in order to heighten the risk of an unintended
skirmish, nor do they develop nuclear weapons in order to increase the likelihood
of a nuclear accident. Yet the increased risk of confrontation may still weigh heavily
on foreign calculations of whether to strike a compromise and prevent unwanted
escalation. If the government is unable to prevent protests, their occurrence signals
the government's vulnerability to domestic pressure.

The decision to allow protests that pose a risk of getting out of hand and constrain
the government's diplomatic options is not as crazy or irrational as it may sound.
By allowing nationalist protests, the government avoids appearing unpatriotic
and conserves the political capital it would have spent to repress demonstrations.
Tolerating protests may be a judicious choice, particularly when the government
desires to take a tough stance against foreign demands. The government can

also calibrate the risk of instability through measures such as police cordons and prenegotiated protest routes and time limits.

Ironically, the prospect of antiforeign mobilization also offers a cooperative function. Because it is costly for authoritarian leaders to nip protests in the bud, although not as costly as suppressing protests once they have gained steam, the decision to repress protests sends a costly signal of reassurance to foreign observers, telegraphing its willingness to cooperate even in the face of domestic criticism. By stifling demonstrations before they can grow large, dispersing crowds as soon as they gather or detaining activists on the eve of a rumored protest, governments generate resentment among would-be protesters and leave themselves vulnerable to charges of being soft on foreign policy. These preemptive actions, if apparent to outside observers, send a costly signal of the government's interest in international cooperation.[50]

The threat of domestic and diplomatic instability gives foreign governments an incentive to show leniency under certain conditions. To be effective, the threat that leaves something to chance requires that the threatened outcome—regime instability and possible regime turnover—be worse than the status quo. Even if the foreign government desires regime change, believing that a new government would be more moderate or democratic than the incumbent regime, the transition costs may be too high. In the context of economic interdependence—including "mutually assured financial destruction" in contemporary U.S.-China relations—stability is often a key priority. Nontraditional security threats, such WMD proliferation, terrorism, and piracy, often give foreign governments a vested interest in the stability and governance of small and weak states, not just large and powerful states. Stability may also trump the desire for regime change in the context of geostrategic objectives such as the Middle East peace process and the containment of radical Islamism. Indeed, the desire for authoritarian stability continued to guide U.S. policy toward Egypt even after Hosni Mubarak's fall, evidenced by the Obama administration's reticence to call the ouster of democratic president and Muslim Brotherhood leader Mohamed Morsi a "military coup" in 2013.

Large-scale protests can alter the balance of power between hardliners and doves within the reigning elite, pushing the regime to a more hawkish stance. If nationalist protests are perceived to be more hawkish than the government's position, then foreign governments may conclude that making compromises in the short run will bolster a friendly autocrat in the long run. For example, according to a senior Chinese expert on Sino-Japanese relations, "The gap between the people and the government is really large on Japan. For example, the Chinese government definitely doesn't support the boycott of Japanese goods. Japan is very important to China's economic development. But the public feels more strongly than the government about Japan."[51] In fact, if China were to become more democratic, said a prominent nationalist author, "It would obviously be more hard-line. Right now, foreigners have special privileges that would not be allowed in a democracy."[52]

The specter of domestic instability need not equal revolution or even a titular change of leadership. Nationalist protests must be more hawkish than the status quo or more impatient in pressing their demands than government diplomats[53] in order to elicit concessions from foreign actors with a vested interest in stability. An implication is that authoritarian governments with the capacity to prevent pro-foreign protests—those that are more closely aligned with the foreign negotiator's position—are likely to nip such efforts in the bud. Dovish or pro-foreign protests are domestically disruptive but provide the government with no extra leverage in diplomatic negotiations. Pro-foreign protests may even reduce bargaining leverage, giving foreign negotiators an incentive to stand firm and hope that regime instability will bring a friendlier government to power.[54]

As the extremism of nationalist demands vary, so does the perceived risk to the status quo. The more radical the voices in the street, the more convincingly the government can play the role of "good cop," a bulwark against the seething masses. But radical voices are also more difficult for the government to placate. To calibrate the perceived danger to the status quo, the government may selectively permit or channel protests in a moderately hawkish direction, whose demands still put pressure on the government to revise the status quo but are easier to appease with a tough foreign policy stance and evidence of incremental diplomatic progress.

Protest Management as a Diplomatic Constraint

Under ordinary circumstances, authoritarian leaders have a relatively free hand to shape foreign policy. While bloggers, netizens, and commentators may express discontent with the government's foreign policy stance, foreign observers may conclude that domestic opposition is limited to a vocal minority and is unlikely to influence foreign policy. Even if official pronouncements declare that foreign transgressions have hurt the "feelings of the people", as Chinese diplomats often claim, it is difficult for outsiders to determine whether this is "cheap talk" or grounds for a stiffer foreign policy.

Once citizens begin to mobilize, however, the domestic costs of ignoring or defying public opinion become visible. If the government chooses to nip nationalist protests in the bud, it can reduce its vulnerability to hawkish demands. The government can also signal its willingness to preserve diplomatic flexibility and cooperation by spending physical resources on suppressing demonstrators and accepting the damage to its patriotic credentials. In Jordan, for example, the government suppressed pro-Iraqi demonstrations in 1996 and all protests in 1998, following the decision to sign a peace treaty with Israel and strengthen Jordan's ties to the United States. According to Marc Lynch, "the regime's strategic decision to curtail its relations with Baghdad as part of its renewed alignment with the United States and Israel... contributed directly to the crackdown on public freedoms in that period."[55] When protests are kept in check, foreign observers are more likely to conclude that the government is able and willing to spend domestic political capital in order to prevent domestic extremists from derailing international cooperation.

If protests are allowed to gain momentum, however, the credibility of a hawkish foreign policy stance grows with the domestic costs of suppression. By raising the public salience of the international dispute,[56] protests increase the "audience costs" of backing down and make a tough stance on foreign policy more attractive, effectively constraining the government's diplomatic options. Vacillating or vague statements are likely to fan the flames of popular ire, whereas a tough diplomatic stance or escalatory measures may placate protest demands. Foreign concessions are the most effective at assuaging nationalist demands, but even a more hawkish diplomatic stance may satisfy protesters that their demands have been heard.

Nationalist protests do not guarantee that a government will get its way in international disputes. Antiforeign protests constrain a government's ability to compromise, shifting the burden of concession to the other party if the two sides are to reach a deal. But like other "lock-in" tactics, antiforeign protests increase the likelihood that relations will become strained and talks will collapse. As in the classic game of chicken, throwing away one's steering wheel makes it more likely that the other driver will swerve. If he does not, a crash will almost certainly ensue. But the probability that the other driver swerves is not 100 percent, as he weighs the potential destruction of his car against the damage to his reputation.

The utility of protests as a commitment tactic also depends on their credibility. The foreign government is unlikely to make concessions if it believes that the authoritarian government can easily repress or "turn off" nationalist protests. Likewise, if foreign observers believe that state media can brainwash citizens into believing that the government has wrought victory from defeat, protests are unlikely to be regarded as credible constraints. In the chicken game, the other driver must believe that one's steering wheel is not just temporarily absent or easily replaced in order to have an incentive to swerve.

Observable Implications

Two sets of predictions follow. One set of predictions addresses the government's management of nationalist protest. A second set of predictions concerns their consequences for foreign perceptions and diplomatic bargaining. To the extent that authoritarian governments are forward-looking decision-makers, these predictions are linked. That is, authoritarian governments anticipate the consequences of their decisions in selecting which protests to allow or repress, seeking to maximize their expected utility at the domestic and international level.

The diplomatic utility of allowing or preventing antiforeign protest depends on the balance of resolve and reassurance the government wishes to strike. As signals of resolve, protests are useful during the stage of negotiations when parties are trying to reveal preferences, establish reservation levels, and locate a bargain. Once the government has tied its hands and demonstrated resolve by allowing antiforeign protests, the burden of conciliation falls to the foreign government. However, the nature of strategic interaction means that the ultimate outcome depends on the resolve and actions of the other parties. Diplomatic talks may also collapse, leading to escalation or simply a lack of cooperation. If the foreign government concedes or both parties strike a compromise, subsequent antiforeign protests may jeopardize the implementation of an implicit or explicit agreement. When reassurance and compliance are the primary diplomatic objective, antiforeign protests cease to be useful, while restraining nationalist mobilization can help the government communicate its commitment to cooperation.

The diplomatic stakes concern not only the material or symbolic value of the dispute but also the government's reputation for resolve: its willingness to hold out for a better bargain even at the expense of failure at the negotiating table. In this way, the diplomatic stakes reflect the extent to which foreigners underestimate the government's willingness to stand firm as well as the importance of the underlying issue. If the government places great value on the outcome of the diplomatic dispute, but the government's resolve is already evident to foreign negotiators, then there is little diplomatic advantage to be gained by allowing nationalist protests. We should thus expect the government to allow protest only when it believes it will gain leverage or a reputation for resolve that it would not otherwise have. When there is no gap between the government's actual and perceived level of resolve, there is little international benefit to offset the domestic risk of allowing protests.

The perception gap can also work in the opposite direction, giving authoritarian governments an incentive to repress protests in order to combat the perception of excess resolve. Such circumstances arise when a government feels that it is perceived to be more belligerent than it actually is, exacerbating the security dilemma and impeding cooperation. Sometimes, a tough image can be an advantage, encouraging deference. But a tough image may be also be counterproductive, galvanizing a countervailing coalition and making it difficult for the government to maintain a low profile.

The government's willingness to allow nationalist protests is also affected by its readiness to stand firm if the target escalates. Antiforeign protests are like a strategic bet, whose expected return depends on the reaction of the opponent: will she fold, call, or raise? All else equal, the government is unlikely to allow protests when the target government is unlikely to back down and the government is unwilling to risk further escalation by standing firm. When the government is not prepared to placate protesters with a tough stance or diplomatic concessions, it is more likely to nip protests in the bud.

A variety of factors are likely to affect the foreign government's perceived resolve, some more readily observable than others. For example, the balance of military power and economic interdependence are observable components of resolve. Yet structural

Citizens

		Mobilize	Not Mobilize
Government	Allow	Sincere protests	Manufactured protests
	Not Allow	Stifled protests	No protests

Figure 2.2 Sincere versus Manufactured Protests

factors may be less informative than new signs of the foreign government's willingness to deploy these assets and bear the cost of escalation and strained relations. Indeed, most crises arise when observable components of resolve fail to deter new challenges.[57] As a dispute unfolds, the authoritarian government is likely to pay as much attention to other signals that might reveal foreign resolve, including statements by opposition leaders, military deployments, and indications of popular support for a tough stance. The contours of foreign public opinion are important, particularly if the foreign state is democratic. Antiforeign protests may affect the foreign government's resolve indirectly by increasing the foreign public's appetite for conflict. On the other hand, if the foreign electorate or business lobby groups are relatively dovish, the foreign government may face pressure to respond to protests with concessions.

Under what conditions will nationalist protest be successful in compelling foreign governments to make concessions, and under what conditions will it backfire? The theoretical framework has thus far assumed complete information, where the government and foreign observers share a common assessment of the risk to stability and the costs of repression. In reality, these are subjective judgments that may not be held in common. Convincing foreigners of the risk to stability and the cost of repression is a critical task for the government that seeks to use nationalist protest for bargaining leverage. In particular, the success of this tactic depends upon foreigners being able and willing to distinguish between "sincere" and "manufactured" protests, illustrated in figure 2.2.

In sincere demonstrations, participants are self-motivated, self-chosen, and largely self-organized, even if their plans have been vetted or pre-approved by government authorities. Continue to mobilize and demonstrate until the government responds to their demands or forcibly curtails their activities. In manufactured protests, participants are selected, organized, and motivated by the government (whether by monetary reward or compulsory mandate). Sincere protests are often described as "spontaneous" protests by government spokesmen and protest organizers, both of whom wish to differentiate their protests from "rent-a-crowd" mobs, whose participants are not personally motivated to demonstrate. Sincere protests, unlike manufactured protests, carry a risk to stability and a cost of repression that is not present in manufactured protests, which are likely to be discounted or dismissed as "cheap talk." In reality, sincere and manufactured protests are not cleanly divided. For example, governments often stage protests in order to co-opt and steal the thunder of grassroots activists, who are then compelled to stay at home or remain on the fringe of official activities. Stage-management reduces but does not eliminate the potential for protests to get out of hand, as participants or bystanders may defy the authorities.

The success of repression as a signal of reassurance also depends upon outside observers being able to distinguish between protests that did not occur because the government nipped them in the bud and protests that did not occur because there was no grassroots mobilization. In both instances, foreigners must be able to see inside the regime with enough clarity to draw conclusions about the extent of popular interest and support for nationalist protest. The regime must be open enough that foreigners can "overhear" grassroots sentiment and discern popular attempts to mobilize.

Given the subjective nature of these assessments, foreign observers may over- or underestimate the risk to regime stability and the cost of repression. Indeed, the government may even privately take actions that reduce the risk that protests get out of hand or become difficult to curtail. With hidden action, such as the infiltration of plainclothes police into protest marches or wiretapping activists' phones, the government may minimize the actual risk of instability relative to the perceived risk that protests get out of hand. Such actions are distinct from visible measures to reduce risk, such as police cordons, riot trucks, and buses to transport protesters. Such visible measures telegraph to participants and observers the extent to which the government is willing to allow protest—signaling the possibility of forceful suppression should protesters go too far. However, because such measures are also apparent to international observers, they also dampen the signal of resolve sent to outsiders.

Given the possibility of hidden action, foreigners may also become skeptical and discount the actual risk that the government runs by allowing protest and the cost of curtailment. The government may have "cried wolf" too often. Take Syria, for example. Marc Lynch writes: "In the lead-up to the second Gulf War, for example, anti-war rallies in Syria were authorized and coordinated by the Syrian government, reducing their authenticity as expressions of public opinion."[58] Having facilitated protests in the past, authoritarian governments give foreigners reason to distrust the sincerity of popular participation and the risk to stability.

Foreign observers may become similarly jaded about the difficulty of repression. If the authoritarian government has allowed nationalist demonstrations but then curtailed them without first achieving a diplomatic victory or taking other measures to satisfy protesters, such actions may indicate that the government is willing and able to crack down on its citizens, creating the perception that the cost of repression is low and undermining the credibility of the government's commitment to a tough bargaining stance. By prematurely cracking down on protesters, the government may have revealed that it was bluffing when it claimed that the costs of repression tied the government's hands.[59]

Foreign governments may also discount nationalist protests that appear to be a cover for anti-government dissent or a distraction from domestic grievances. When outside observers have difficulty discerning the weight of domestic and foreign policy grievances in motivating street protests, they may underestimate the degree to which the government is diplomatically constrained. If ostensibly antiforeign protests are purely a cloak for antiregime dissent and have no diplomatic agenda, foreigners have little incentive to show lenience if those concessions cannot be used to placate protests and reduce the risk of instability. However, protests intended to divert attention from domestic grievances may still require the government to deliver on its foreign policy gambit.

Table 2.1 summarizes the observable implications of the argument. Some may be less readily observable because decision-makers may unconsciously incorporate or purposefully conceal these perceptions and motivations. Highly certain implications are unequivocal; the theory is falsified if no evidence of the predicted outcome is found. Many predictions are probabilistic, however, meaning the theory cannot be ruled out even if the implied outcomes are not observed.

A detailed tracing of events is the most appropriate method of assessing whether decision-makers acted and reacted in a manner consistent with the theorized mechanisms. As difficult as it is to discern motives in the democratic decision-making process, it is even more so in autocracies, particularly during crises defined by a limited time frame for response and a typically circumscribed set of participants in the decision-making process. Without records of internal deliberations, observations by officials and analysts with privileged access can serve as reasonable proxies, recorded in oral interviews, written analysis, and personal memoirs. Ideally, we seek government statements that its intention in allowing protests was to justify an unyielding diplomatic stance and signal the government's vulnerability to popular nationalism. But government leaders are unlikely to make such statements publicly. The more the government appears to have stirred up antiforeign protests, the more foreign observers should discount their sincerity. To the extent that government leaders publicly refer to protests, we expect them to emphasize the spontaneity and sincerity of popular protests.

Different types of evidence help shed light on the government's motivations and how foreign leaders perceived its actions, increasing confidence in the specified mechanisms. To infer motivations, the evidence should show that diplomatic factors were important in the government's calculus to allow or repress protests. We should find evidence that the government understood the domestic risks and costs of nationalist protest and sought to reveal these domestic constraints to foreign observers. To trace the diplomatic impact of nationalist protests, we should also find that foreign decision makers updated their beliefs about the government's domestic constraints and the risk of escalation.

Table 2.1 **Observable Implications**

Hypothesis	Observable Implications	Degree of Certainty
General argument: Because nationalist protest poses a risk to the status quo and makes compromise domestically difficult, the management of grassroots mobilization enables authoritarian governments to signal their diplomatic intentions and determine the degree to which their hands are tied internationally.	Foreign and government diplomats refer to popular sentiment during negotiations.	*Low*: Popular sentiment may affect negotiations and diplomatic positions even if officials do not refer to it.
	Government officials cite effect on diplomatic relations as motivation to allow or prevent protests.	*Low*: Government officials have strategic incentives to hide their role in allowing protests (but emphasize their role in curtailing protests when signaling reassurance).
Signaling resolve: Nationalist protests demonstrate a "threat that leaves something to chance," signaling resolve and the government's vulnerability to popular nationalism.	Government officials understand risks that nationalist protests pose to the domestic and diplomatic status quo.	*High*: If government officials are unaware or dismissive of risks, or see risks as unconnected to foreign policy choices, protests do not signal resolve.
	Foreign leaders express concern about dangers posed by nationalist protests.	*Low*: Foreign leaders may recognize risks but not voice explicit concern.
	Subsequent, similar interactions are influenced by information revealed about government's vulnerability to popular nationalism.	*High*: If decision-makers regard situations as similar but protests have no effect on subsequent interactions, then signal of resolve was unsuccessful; however, foreign leaders may not refer to previous situation but still utilize information revealed, including the decision to avoid actions that might arouse nationalist anger and precipitate another dispute.

Table 2.1 **Continued**

Hypothesis	Observable Implications	Degree of Certainty
Hawkish commitment: Nationalist protests raise the government's cost of concession, increasing the credibility of an unyielding diplomatic stance.	Government leaders consider the costs of defying protesters in setting foreign policy.	*High*: If government officials are unaware or dismissive of the domestic costs of backing down and having to repress protests, protests do not credibly commit the government to a hawkish stance.
	Foreign leaders are more inclined to make allowances for the government in light of popular protests.	*Low*: Although protests may enhance hawkish credibility, foreign government may counterescalate; on *average*, protests make the terms of diplomatic compromise more favorable.
	Foreign perceptions of the government's domestic constraints diminish once protests end or are controlled.	*High*: If foreign leaders see government as identically constrained in presence and absence of protests, the theory fails; protest curtailment reduces, but does not necessarily eliminate, the government's perceived constraints.
Credible reassurance: Stifling nationalist protests sends costly signal of reassurance and makes diplomatic flexibility easier.	Government leaders incur popular resentment by preventing street protests.	*High*: If curtailment of protests is not domestically costly, repression does not send credible signal of reassurance.
	Foreign leaders acknowledge difficulty of stifling popular anger and quelling street protests.	*Low*: Foreign leaders may recognize but not verbally acknowledge government's efforts to curtail protests.
	Foreign leaders link repression of protests to desire for diplomatic flexibility in pursuing cooperation.	*High*: If foreign leaders believe government repression of antiforeign protests is driven purely by domestic considerations, curtailment of protests does not send a signal of reassurance.

Alternative Views

The framework builds upon three strands in the existing literature on Chinese nationalism, which has largely focused on domestic drivers of nationalist protest:

> *State incapacity in the face of sincere popular grievances against a foreign provocation or transgression.* Nationalist protests occur because the government is unwilling to prevent nationalist protests, or because protests erupt before the government can contain them. Even if the government has sufficient warning and physical resources to stifle protests before they can draw large crowds, the cost to the government's legitimacy of appearing unpatriotic may be prohibitively high. In some cases, it may be "too hazardous for the government to try to disallow student protests altogether."[60] At other times, "unable to suppress the protestors, authorities were forced to plead with them for calm."[61]
>
> *Elite or factional competition.* Nationalist protest reflects conflict within the inner circle of the authoritarian leadership, where elites jockeying for influence give a green light to nationalist protests, hoping to use public opinion or the threat of instability to gain the upper hand in internal power struggles. Hawkish elites, seeking to strengthen their position and put pressure on their moderate rivals to take a tougher stance, may encourage antiforeign protests without the knowledge or consent of the top leadership.[62]
>
> *State-sponsored mobilization of nationalistic protest to divert public attention from domestic ills and bolster popular support.* Authoritarian leaders gin up antiforeign sentiment to rally support for the regime and allow nationalist demonstrations to provide an outlet for pent-up grievances in society, as "a foil to distract public attention from other, far more serious problems within those societies"[63] or "to channel the increasing agitation of Chinese society by whipping up extreme nationalist feelings [for] self-preservation."[64]

These views contain important insights but do not attempt to explain the variation in the government's management of nationalist protest. They can explain why protests occur, but they have difficulty explaining why protests are at other times prevented by the government. In the state-sponsored view, protests are beneficial to the government, providing a "safety valve" or diversionary scapegoat for domestic grievances. In the bottom-up view, protests occur because the government is unable to prevent protests or unwilling to appear unpatriotic. By themselves, neither can account for the repression of protest. The bureaucratic or factional view also has difficulty explaining the pattern of protest over time because it does not specify why hawkish elites only sometimes mobilize popular sentiment, yet are unable or unwilling to do so at other times. Elite discord may better capture the difficulty of reining in protests once begun, as street demonstrations tempt officials to reach out and avail themselves of the populist mantle.

Woven together, these explanations provide greater analytic leverage than their individual parts. Whether protests occur depends on the interaction of government objectives and societal demands: a top-down decision by an authoritarian government confronted with bottom-up mobilization. The government faces a dilemma in deciding how to respond to grassroots mobilization: spend political capital to repress protests and appear illegitimate, or allow protests and run the risk that they snowball and jeopardize domestic and diplomatic stability. Indeed, one of the chief risks that nationalist protests pose is the temptation for hawkish elites to split with the government and ally with demonstrators.

If one only looks at cases in which nationalist protests occur, the implications of my argument point in the same direction as existing explanations. Nationalist protests constrain the government's diplomatic objectives, help divert attention from domestic problems, and require the government to satisfy domestic demands in order to avoid becoming the target of protesters' wrath. But there are selection effects at work here: protests are often kept in check, facilitating diplomatic flexibility and eschewing the temptation to distract citizens with diplomatic saber rattling. To draw a fuller picture of the role nationalist sentiment plays in Chinese foreign policy, we must look at variation in how China has responded to and managed nationalist protest.

Although domestic factors are important inputs to the management of popular nationalism, the role of diplomatic considerations and incentives has not been systematically analyzed. At the same time, the domestic character of nationalist protests—whether they appear sincere, diversionary, or manufactured—affects their diplomatic consequences. I develop this line of argument, arguing that the domestic and international levels are inextricably linked. In suggesting that China's diplomatic objectives partly influence how the government manages nationalist sentiment and popular protest, I develop a "second-image reversed" argument, whereby the international environment influences domestic outcomes.[65]

Many scholars have acknowledged that playing the "nationalist card" may be diplomatically advantageous,[66] although few have given the diplomatic consequences of nationalist mobilization a central place in the government's decision-making. I develop this intuition, arguing that the diplomatic benefit of allowing nationalist protest depends on the balance of resolve and reassurance that the government wishes to signal. Moreover, the government's response to nationalist mobilization largely determines the degree of domestic constraint on its foreign policy. The existing literature has not differentiated the level of constraint on Chinese foreign policy, implying that popular anger reduces flexibility whether protests are in the streets or nationalist mobilization online is permitted or censored.

Most scholars of Chinese nationalism and public opinion take a "second image" approach: examining the impact of domestic factors on international outcomes.[67] To the extent that nationalism affects Chinese foreign policy, its impact has largely been seen as detrimental to rational foreign policy and cooperation. For these scholars, the yardstick of diplomatic success is cooperation per se, not the terms of agreement. They rightly acknowledge that domestic constraints may reduce the set of acceptable agreements, thus reducing the likelihood of cooperation.[68] While cooperation may be the long-term goal, a rational government may nonetheless choose short-term delay or escalation over cooperation on unfavorable terms. As the two-level games literature points out, if the foreign negotiator understands that nationalist opinion has reduced the government's "win set," the foreign negotiator is more likely to offer concessions to salvage an agreement and avoid conflict. Demonstrating that one is unable or unwilling to make concessions helps shift the burden of compromise to the other party. Domestic constraints may improve a government's chances of achieving a favorable outcome, even if the likelihood of bargaining failure is higher.

In China, it is common to refer to nationalism as a "double-edged sword" (*shuang ren jian*)—a weapon that can wound oneself as well as one's opponent. The analogy appropriately underscores the domestic and diplomatic consequences of nationalist protest. Beyond this intuition, we must also ask when this weapon will be most effective and hence most likely to be employed by those governments that have the option to wield it. By making explicit the diplomatic-domestic trade-offs, we stand to gain a better understanding of China's management of nationalist protest—illuminating the government's motivations for sheathing as well as wielding this double-edged sword.

What if we no longer assume that authoritarian leaders have the capacity to choose whether to allow or prevent popular protests? Most authoritarian regimes are neither omniscient nor omnipresent actors with the ability to anticipate and respond to every development in society. In the very weakest regimes, the government may lack the wherewithal to choose whether or not nationalist protests occur. Even in relatively strong regimes, a large protest might erupt before the government has time to coordinate a response, especially if there are divisions within the government elite over the appropriate course of action. What are the implications of state weakness and elite fragmentation? Consistent with the theory, I argue that even if protests occur without a deliberate decision by the government, the constraint on authoritarian diplomacy remains. After examining the effects of state incapacity and elite fragmentation, the last section considers the potential diversionary benefits of nationalist protest.

State Incapacity

The weaker the state, the less ability the government has to choose whether to allow or repress antiforeign protest. Indeed, a protest may happen without the government's knowledge or ability to prevent it. This observational equivalence means that when outsiders observe antiforeign protest, they may not know whether to infer that the government valued the international outcome highly enough to allow protest despite the risk to regime stability, or whether the government was simply unable to prevent protest. The diplomatic consequences are similar, however. Whether the government allowed the protest or was caught by surprise, the government still has incentive to take a more hawkish position to placate protesters. The weaker the government, the less it can afford to suppress protests. State weakness makes the signal of resolve fuzzier, but the commitment mechanism operates more strongly.

Selection effects make it difficult to observe the true risk and suppression cost associated with nationalist protests.[69] The larger the risk to the government, the less likely the government is to allow protests; the greater the cost of suppression, the more likely the government is to choose placation (via a tough foreign policy stance). In both cases, high observed values of risk and suppression costs are likely to be censored because they are "off the equilibrium path." However, selection effects are weaker when state capacity is low. Governments that are too fragile to repress protests must take a tough bargaining stance to placate the public. Strong governments, by contrast, face greater difficulty convincing foreigners that their hands are tied. The stronger a government appears, the greater the size and scope of nationalist protests required to demonstrate vulnerability.

In this way, we should expect variation in the degree to which nationalist protests convey the diplomatic intentions of authoritarian regimes. Perceptions of state capacity influence which mechanism—signaling resolve or hawkish commitment—is likely to dominate. Protests are more likely to be interpreted as signals of resolve in strong states, whereas protests are more likely to be interpreted as a sign of fragility and a credible justification for a tough bargaining stance in weak states. As Shibley Telhami writes of Jordan's decision to stay out of the U.S.-led coalition in the first Gulf War:

> Governments such as Jordan that had responded to our earlier calls for political democratization, and that thus had to be more responsive to public opinion, were inclined to oppose U.S. policies. . . . The fact that America's ally in the region, King Hussein of Jordan, found himself opposing the American-led coalition against Iraq in 1991 was a function of his assessment that he would not otherwise be able to overcome the anger of his public.[70]

Because feeble or liberalizing autocrats are less capable of suppressing protests, such governments are more quickly locked into a tough bargaining stance, having little choice but to placate protesters by adopting their foreign policy demands.

Indeed, scholars who emphasize the Chinese government's fragility tend to give public opinion and nationalism the greatest weight.[71] Summing up the field,

Christensen, Johnston, and Ross write that "most agree that on some issues—such as the relationship with Japan—mass, not just elite, opinion has prevented the leadership from exploring ways of downplaying the history question."[72] Particularly with the spread of the Internet and other technologies that facilitate rapid communication, often beyond the government's ability to censor or control, public opinion is said to hinder the government's ability to conduct diplomacy with discretion and flexibility. As Xu argues: "in times of diplomatic crisis, such as the spy-plane collision in 2001 and the embassy bombing in 1999, people's spontaneous online responses might complicate the situation and impede a smooth resolution in China's interest."[73] For these scholars, even though nationalist sentiment may stem from legitimate popular grievances, popular pressures are nonetheless seen as a constraint on rational, effective diplomacy, often leading to suboptimal diplomatic outcomes.

Those who emphasize the Chinese government's role in stoking popular sentiment through patriotic propaganda also attribute substantial foreign policy influence to nationalist sentiment. For many of these scholars, however, the diplomatic repercussions are unintended consequences. Leaders become constrained by nationalist rhetoric and mythmaking that they themselves encouraged to buttress their domestic legitimacy and rally the public.[74] As He writes: "Elite mythmaking shapes negative public opinion, but public opinion can later constrain leaders when they consider policy change. . . . the public holding negative emotions and perceived intentions will pressure the government to adopt hard-line policies on specific bilateral issues."[75] In this view, Chinese leaders who would otherwise favor international cooperation become constrained by their domestic stratagems for political survival.

My framework extends this line of argument by pointing out that the degree of domestic constraint is endogenous to the government's management of nationalist mobilization. In the presence of protests, the theory predicts the same outcome as the "bottom-up" theory of unwanted pressure: a tougher diplomatic stance. When protests are repressed, however, government officials should have greater leeway in diplomatic negotiations, and foreign governments should be sensitive to these differences, interpreting tolerance as resolve and repression as a gesture of reassurance. Protest curtailment reduces, but does not necessarily eliminate, foreign perceptions of the government's domestic constraints.

Empirically, the theory is agnostic about the timing of escalatory steps and nationalist protests. The government may toughen its diplomatic stance before or after protests occur. Protests may strengthen the credibility of existing demands as a signal of resolve or appear to tie the government's hands by forcing the government to take a tougher stance. So long as there is evidence that the government anticipated nationalist mobilization and allowed demonstrations to occur, either sequencing is consistent with the strategic framework. Indeed, a canny government may "lead from behind," thus emphasizing its vulnerability to nationalist pressure and emphasizing the spontaneity of public protests. In contrast, arguments about unwanted pressure require the government to escalate only after protests occur.

Elite Conflict

What are the diplomatic implications of nationalist protests that occur without the consent of the top leadership, instigated by rival elements within the elite who seek to bolster their position and interests? In building the framework, I cited divisions within the elite, some of whom might be tempted to seek common cause with the street, as one of the primary risks associated with protests in the authoritarian context. But elite divisions may be a cause as well as a consequence of nationalist protest. As Fewsmith and Rosen note, "a high degree of elite cohesion sharply limits the impact of public opinion."[76] In a similar vein, Reilly argues that public mobilization is most likely when elites are divided and diplomatic relations are tense, but once the dangers of popular mobilization become apparent, elites tend to unite around a consensus to cool down popular anger. Reilly suggests that public opinion does not constrain the long-term direction of Chinese foreign policy, and even its short-term effects are reversible given a top-level consensus.[77] At the same time, Fewsmith and Rosen note that public mobilization may also cause elite conflict and thereby have a more direct effect on policy.[78]

When elite divisions are apparent, there is again more "noise" in what protests reveal about the government's resolve, but the diplomatic consequences are similar. So long as rival elites responsible for the antiforeign protests are themselves more hawkish than the incumbent, the top leadership still has an incentive to take a more hawkish position: to seize the high ground, protect their flank, and steal their rivals' thunder. Second, if foreigners suspect that unfriendly elements in the regime are responsible for the protests, then foreign negotiators have greater incentive to bolster the position of the embattled incumbent, whose vulnerability to hawkish rivals is more credible in light of nationalist protests.

Diversionary Benefits

An influential set of arguments and conventional intuitions focuses on the domestic benefits of allowing nationalist protest to divert public attention from domestic grievances and enable citizens to vent pent-up anger. As the *Washington Post* wrote after the anti-American protests in 1999, the Chinese government "generated precisely the response it wanted: a frenzy of nationalistic protests that distract people from their domestic discontents while, the regime hopes, increasing China's leverage abroad."[79] The diversionary logic often implies two distinct mechanisms: allowing citizens to blow off steam and rallying the public against an external scapegoat.

In the "pressure valve" view of nationalist protest, aggrieved citizens derive satisfaction from the act of protesting, regardless of the diplomatic outcome. This view implies that neither China nor the foreign government need accommodate protest demands, because the government can easily restore order once the public has vented its spleen. In the "rally round the flag" view, citizens reflexively support the government when the country is challenged by an external threat.

On the one hand, a short-term boost in popular support may give the government more diplomatic room to maneuver. Others argue that the Chinese government can shape nationalism at will, using it for domestic purposes without hindering the government's strategic calculations. For example, Simon Shen calls Chinese nationalism "a chicken with no eggs," writing that "contemporary Chinese nationalism exists more vividly in official rhetoric than actuality [and] is unlikely to become the new Chinese foreign policy framer in the future."[80]

Yet public opinion may also turn against the regime if the government seems to be appeasing or abetting the enemy. Nationalist protests may boost the government's popularity, but protesters must see progress toward their demands. The domestic benefits of protest are contingent on the diplomatic outcome. Once the government has diverted domestic attention toward its performance on the international stage, the government must deliver evidence of diplomatic victory. If the government does not satisfy public demands, the government's diversionary gambit fails, adding the crime of "being soft on foreign policy" or "selling out the nation" to the list of domestic grievances against the regime. Swift curtailment risks a popular backlash unless the government takes escalatory steps or the foreign government makes concessions, enabling the government to disperse protests peacefully.

Conclusion

Understanding the management of nationalist protest advances our knowledge of authoritarian regimes in international relations, joining a stream of research that has sought to move beyond the "black box" or "residual category" of autocracy.[81] A large body of scholarship has emphasized the advantages of democracy for the conduct of international relations, with only a few cautionary counterarguments. The drive to find theories that can both explain the democratic peace and generate new testable implications has encouraged scholars to study democracies in international relations. Given that the vast majority of interstate wars are fought in autocratic and mixed dyads, illuminating the foreign policy decision-making of authoritarian leaders is important to improving our understanding of conflict and international relations more broadly.

Whereas regular elections enable democratic publics to remove leaders at relatively little cost, citizens in autocracies are assumed to be nearly powerless to punish leaders that act against the national interest. Although autocratic leaders may face harsher punishments in the event of a coup or other irregular change of leadership, this probability is often assumed to be either very small or not visible *ex ante* to foreign decision-makers.[82] Antiforeign protests provide a visible mechanism by which domestic politics affect international bargaining. Unlike institutional and elite-based mechanisms of accountability, antiforeign demonstrations give potential force to protestors and ordinary citizens outside the elite, providing a visible, costly signal of the leadership's resolve and commitment to stand firm. At other times, repressing such protests sends a costly signal of reassurance and preserves diplomatic flexibility. The strategic logic of nationalist protest is thus sensitive to the trade-offs between enhancing credibility and maintaining flexibility.[83] When decision-makers seek to preserve room for maneuver, they can repress nationalist protests and signal their interest in avoiding conflict.

The double-edged sword of nationalist protest represents a useful bargaining tactic, not in spite of—but because of—the risk of instability and the cost of defying public opinion. If antiforeign protests are credible signals in international bargaining, then it is not necessarily the case that democracies have the advantage in utilizing domestic politics as diplomatic leverage. If both regime types utilize public opinion to reveal information and communicate credibly, other factors must explain the democratic peace.

3

Anti-American Protest and U.S.-China Crisis Diplomacy

The U.S. should respect China's national sovereignty and territorial integrity, respect China's national core interests and the people's feelings.
—Premier Wen Jiabao to Secretary of State
Hillary Clinton, September 4, 2012[1]

In 1999, U.S. planes mistakenly bombed the Chinese embassy in Yugoslavia during a NATO air strike, killing three Chinese journalists and wounding 20 others. In 2001, a Chinese fighter jet and a U.S. EP-3 reconnaissance plane collided, killing the Chinese pilot and forcing the American plane to make an emergency landing on Hainan Island, China's southernmost province. In both cases, Chinese citizens sought to protest American actions. Yet the government only allowed anti-American protests after the embassy bombing. After the spy plane incident, would-be Chinese protesters were quickly escorted away by police. Official media were instructed to tone down the negative rhetoric in covering the incident. Why did the Chinese government allow anti-American protests in 1999 but stifle them in 2001? How did this choice affect U.S. perceptions of Chinese resolve?

These crises are considered the only "major conflicts" to have tested U.S.-China relations other than the issues of Tiananmen and Taiwan since the two nations established diplomatic relations in 1979.[2] Comparing the embassy bombing and plane collision offers insight into China's management of nationalist protest during international crises, where the stakes are higher and the time frame for response is shorter than in typical diplomatic negotiations. Both incidents were seen as violations of Chinese sovereignty. The bombing destroyed Chinese diplomatic property during an air campaign that China had opposed on the principle of noninterference in the sovereign affairs of another country.[3] The collision took place while a U.S. reconnaissance plane conducted surveillance along China's coastline, entering Chinese airspace without permission to make an emergency landing.[4] Both the embassy bombing and plane collision were "unforseen by either side, without intent of warfare," according to one Chinese scholar.[5] Because both sides perceived "a threat to basic values and a finite period for response but not an increased probability of military hostilities,"[6] the two episodes have been labeled "near crises" by the International Crisis Behavior Project. At no time was the use of force explicitly threatened in either crisis, and escalation to military conflict appeared unlikely.[7]

An important feature of crisis diplomacy is the belief that the outcome will have lasting consequences for the nation's credibility and reputation.[8] Chinese leaders were convinced that their response to the embassy bombing and plane collision would shape international perceptions of China's willingness to defend its sovereignty. As Jiang Zemin said in his remarks to the Politburo Standing Committee on May 8, 1999, "This incident is extremely important and urgent. Whether we respond and handle it properly will have significant influence on the overall situation of the party, country and international affairs."[9] In his memoir, Foreign Minister Tang Jiaxuan drew a comparison between the two crises, writing: "I couldn't help but recall the incident on May 8, 1999, when the U.S.-led NATO bombed our embassy in Yugoslavia. Now, not two years later, this 'plane collision' once again harmed Chinese life and property."[10] Like the embassy bombing, China's leaders regarded the EP-3 collision as a "serious, sensitive emergency" involving "major matters of principle, including national sovereignty, territorial integrity, and national dignity" in which "U.S.-China relations would again be put to a severe test."[11]

Although daily interactions and negotiations affect state reputations, crises concentrate the attention of both governments and publics, often leaving a stronger and more lasting impression. The Chinese word for "crisis" (*weiji*) connotes both "danger" (*wei*) and "opportunity" (*ji*). A controversial reading of "opportunity" suggests that China has precipitated international crises in order to gain power and influence, although scholars have pointed out that this exaggerates the meaning of the Chinese term.[12] A more neutral reading of the character *ji* denotes a "incipient moment" or "crucial point."[13] "Crisis management is the way and means to avoid the danger of conflicts, and to seek and realize a favorable turn," notes Xia Liping, vice president of the Shanghai Institute for International Strategic Studies.[14] Crises are opportunities insofar as they provide a focal point for altering foreign perceptions and changing the course of diplomatic relations. As such, the diplomatic gain may be cooperative as well as conflictual. As Xia notes: "It may also be the last ladder leading to war, or the last mountain to overcome to realize the long-term peace."[15]

Crisis diplomacy thus brings into greater relief the tension between demonstrating a willingness to defend the nation's interests and the desire to prevent unwanted escalation.[16] Demonstrating resolve is critical to warding off challenges to the nation's sovereignty, yet signaling one's commitment to cooperation may also be necessary to defusing tensions. As then-Vice Premier and former foreign minister Qian Qichen notes in his memoir: "We should address ourselves to struggle as well as development and cooperation. These two tactics are equally significant."[17]

Such signals need not be mutually exclusive. Resolve and reassurance exist along a continuum, with governments employing a mix of both threats and assurances.[18] The appropriate balance between resolve and reassurance depends not only on the stakes at hand but also on the government's larger strategic objectives. If a government is concerned that its image is too frail, inviting future challenges, it may seek to signal strength and resolve. On the other hand, a government that wants to mitigate foreign suspicion and perceptions of aggressive intent may want to emphasize its commitment to cooperation.

The embassy bombing and plane collision took place against different diplomatic environments in U.S.-China relations, affecting the balance of resolve and reassurance the Chinese government sought to signal. The diplomatic stakes were asymmetrical across the two crises: higher for China in 1999 and higher for the United States in 2001. In 1999, China's leaders primarily sought to combat the perception that China could be "bullied" in the international arena, ranging from NATO intervention outside the auspices of the UN Security Council to the terms of China's accession to the World Trade Organization. In China's view, the embassy bombing was the third in a series of provocations meant to probe China's mettle. First was the U.S.-led war in Kosovo, which in China's view set a troubling precedent for intervention in secessionist disputes.[19] The second was President Clinton's refusal to sign an agreement on China's entry into the WTO during Premier Zhu Rongji's visit to Washington.

In 2001, by contrast, China sought to reassure the new Bush administration that China should not be regarded as an enemy. When the plane collision occurred, China's leaders were concerned about jeopardizing the fragile relationship with the hawkish new Bush administration. Taking U.S. resolve into account, China was also more concerned that protests would backfire in 2001 than in 1999. Responsibility for the embassy bombing clearly lay with the United States, which U.S. officials acknowledged from the outset of the crisis, even if the initial level and solemnity of U.S. apologies were deemed insufficient by the Chinese side. In 2001, by contrast, the United States was convinced that the Chinese pilot was at fault on technical grounds and concerned for the EP-3 crew. Having begun to establish a positive footing with Washington, Chinese diplomacy was aimed at reducing the perception that China posed a threat to the United States. In short, Chinese leaders appeared more concerned about demonstrating resolve and signaling strength in 1999 than in 2001, creating incentives for the Chinese government to allow anti-American protests in 1999 but not in 2001.

Although China's diplomatic priorities in the broader context of U.S.-China relations differed across the two crises, the embassy bombing and plane collision are comparable in many ways. Jiang Zemin was China's paramount leader during both crises. Less than two years separate the incidents, allowing us to control for the balance of power between the United States and China. Both crises arose suddenly, yet neither appeared likely to escalate to the use of force.

Given the low likelihood of military conflict in both cases, it is important to assess the role of nonmilitary signals of resolve and reassurance. According to many Chinese analysts, China's leaders "no longer regard force as an effective tool for achieving limited political gains in a crisis," taking military action only when alternative measures have failed.[20] Crises often tempt states to use nonmilitary means to showcase their resolve. Even in military confrontations, the material balance of power is not necessarily the most important factor. A country's willingness to risk escalation and endure the costs of military, economic, or diplomatic retaliation is just as important. As Swaine notes, "Chinese leaders tended to believe that a strong show of resolve was necessary in part to compensate for relative weakness."[21]

The management of nationalist sentiment may play a compensatory role in signaling resolve when one side is otherwise disadvantaged. For example, one Chinese scholar describes the utility of domestic factors in signaling resolve, drawing upon Schelling:

> Risk and cost are the defining characteristics of a crisis. In fact, crises are a kind of competition in accepting risk. The greater the ability to accept risk, the stronger the display of resolve (*juexin*). . . . Pointing to domestic factors, such as the political system, the orientation of public opinion, and popular attitudes can increase one's ability to accept risk and show one's determination to prevail in the crisis.[22]

Yet public sentiment is not always a credible diplomatic card, requiring grassroots mobilization to create the popular pressure that makes the management of nationalist protests a costly signal. Under Mao Zedong, mass demonstrations against the United States were government-organized. Kuang-sheng Liao notes that these were "government-directed protest rather than a spontaneous mass movement. . . . few of them can slip out of control and be turned against the central authority."[23] From a diplomatic standpoint, such protests should be considered cheap talk, organized for primarily domestic purposes.

In reform-era China, popular attempts to mobilize protests against the United States have been sparse relative to protests against Japan.[24] In 1993, the United States interdicted the Chinese freighter ship *Yinhe* (Milky Way) and forced an inspection based on faulty intelligence that its cargo contained chemical weapons bound for Iran. No protest attempts were reported in mainland China, even though Chinese officials invoked popular will in denouncing American actions.[25] Not long after, Beijing narrowly lost the competition to host the 2000 Olympics. American actions stoked popular anger and increased Chinese suspicions that the United States sought to "hold China down."[26] The U.S. Congress had held hearings and passed a nonbinding resolution opposing Beijing's bid on human rights grounds in the months leading up to the International Olympic Committee's decision.[27] Amid rumors that students were planning protests at the U.S. embassy if Beijing lost, Chinese authorities reportedly increased campus security.[28] Two years later, student anger was confined to campus posters and assemblies over the U.S. visit of Lee Teng-hui, which precipitated the Taiwan Strait Crisis. Students were also reportedly denied permission to protest against the U.S.-led mission at the outset of the Kosovo war in March 1999.[29] In March 2003, students were allowed to hold campus assemblies to condemn the U.S. invasion of Iraq, but Chinese authorities prevented protest marches that would have taken place at locations around Beijing, including the U.S. ambassador's residence.[30] As these anecdotes make clear, the Chinese government in the post-Mao era has stifled anti-American demonstrations more often than it has allowed them.

The embassy bombing and protests have been assessed in detail, and both the embassy bombing and EP-3 incident have been analyzed from the perspective of crisis management.[31] Yet why protests were allowed in 1999 but prevented in 2001 has not been explicitly examined. Revisiting these crises enables us to trace the logic of protest management to the government's diplomatic and domestic objectives as well as to assess the impact of domestic decisions on foreign perceptions. In both episodes, the domestic management of public opinion appeared to influence foreign perceptions of Chinese resolve and diplomatic intent. By allowing anti-American protests in 1999, the Chinese government communicated its determination to stand up to the United States as well as the domestic demands it faced to take a tougher foreign policy stance. By repressing nationalist protests in 2001, the Chinese government sent a costly signal of its intent to keep U.S.-China relations on an even keel. Despite domestic accusations that the government was being too soft, Chinese leaders signaled that the incident should not impede progress in bilateral relations. The repression of nationalist protests in 2001 demonstrates that Chinese leaders have not always been forced by popular nationalism to take a tougher stance against their will.

Tracing the stage management of protests after the embassy bombing also demonstrates the role of risk and credibility. Protests that appeared spontaneous and volatile on the first day of the crisis were more credible than protests that appeared stage-managed thereafter. Orchestration reduced the amount of information sent by prolonged protests and the perceived constraints imposed by public opinion. Nonetheless, the signal of resolve and the government's vulnerability to nationalist opinion persisted, shaping U.S. perceptions during the 2001 crisis.

The 1999 Embassy Bombing

At 5:45 a.m. on Saturday, May 8, 1999 (Beijing time), two U.S. B-2 bombers dropped five precision-guided bombs on the Chinese embassy in Yugoslavia, killing three Chinese journalists and wounding 20 Chinese citizens. The bombing occurred during a NATO air strike, part of Operation Allied Force in Kosovo, which sought to compel an end to Serb atrocities in Kosovo. As news of the embassy bombing reached China on the morning of May 8, university students in Beijing began putting up posters critical of the United States and applied for permission to demonstrate outside the U.S. embassy.[32] After the Chinese leadership convened an emergency meeting to decide how to handle the crisis, Vice Foreign Minister Wang Yingfan summoned U.S. ambassador James Sasser to lodge China's strongest protest against the bombing, demanding an immediate halt to NATO air strikes in Yugoslavia.[33] Ambassador Sasser, who had contacted the Chinese Ministry of Foreign Affairs upon learning of the bombing from the White House, expressed his condolences for the "terrible mistake."[34] At noon, the Chinese government released a statement, carried by Xinhua and CCTV, which condemned the bombing in harsh terms: "U.S.-led NATO brazenly (*hanran*) used three missiles to attack the embassy of the People's Republic of China in the Federal Republic of Yugoslavia from different angles."[35]

That afternoon, tens of thousands of students took part in anti-American demonstrations in dozens of cities across China. As protests raged, the residence of the consul general in Chengdu was set on fire. CIA director George Tenet and defense secretary William Cohen issued a joint statement, saying, "we deeply regret the loss of life and injuries," calling the bombing an "error" and stating that "there is no such thing as risk free military operations."[36] A few hours later, at 2:35 a.m. Beijing time, President Bill Clinton called the bombing a "tragic mistake" during remarks to reporters at an Oklahoma tornado site, even as he defended the Kosovo mission. Just before midnight, U.S. secretary of state Madeleine Albright personally delivered a letter of apology to the Chinese embassy in Washington, D.C., stating her "sincere apologies and condolences."[37]

On Sunday, May 9, protests grew as more organized demonstrations took place and word spread that protests had official support. The *People's Daily* featured a front-page photograph of the Beijing protests and stated that the demonstrations had been approved by the Public Security Bureau. The statements of regret by U.S. and NATO officials were not mentioned. Back in Washington, President Clinton apologized both on camera and in a letter to Chinese president Jiang Zemin in which he stated his "apologies and sincere condolences."[38] That afternoon, the government began to take measures to rein in the protests. On the six o'clock evening news, Vice President Hu Jintao stated that the government "firmly supports and protects" all "legal protest activities," yet urged that "we must prevent overreaction, and ensure social stability by guarding against some people making use of the opportunities to disrupt the normal public order."[39]

The next day, on Monday, May 10, the Chinese government announced that it was suspending talks with the United States on human rights and nonproliferation.[40] Foreign Minister Tang Jiaxuan met with U.S. ambassador James Sasser and demanded that the United States make an open and public apology, investigate the bombing, promptly publicize the results, and severely punish the perpetrators. Protests continued to take place in front of the U.S. and British embassies, but the demonstrations were more orderly. Universities and work units were instructed to wind down the protests.[41] According to Ambassador Sasser, "The situation has stabilized somewhat and we feel like we can last the siege through." White House press secretary Joe Lockhart stated that "it is considerably calmer at this point."[42] Speaking from the White House on May 10 (U.S. time), Clinton said, "I apologize, I regret this," and reaffirmed his commitment to strengthen U.S.-China relations.[43] Clinton also tried unsuccessfully to reach Jiang by phone.

On Tuesday, May 11, the Chinese media reported on the apologies by President Clinton, NATO secretary-general Solana, and Secretary Albright.[44] The official media urged citizens to return to their normal duties. Jiang Zemin praised the "great patriotism of the Chinese people" but stated that "the whole country is now determined to study and work harder, so as to develop the national economy continuously, enhance national strength, and fight back with concrete deeds against the barbaric act of U.S.-led NATO."[45] Xinhua quoted a model student: "We believe the party and the government can appropriately handle the current situation, and we college students should redouble our efforts to gain knowledge and master skills. This is true patriotic conduct."[46]

Protests outside the U.S. embassy and consulates dwindled to a fraction of the preceding three days, even as thousands of protesters marched in Hong Kong.[47] Ambassador Sasser told the reporters, "We may go to bed early and get a good night's sleep."[48] The crisis continued to de-escalate over the next several days. The streets were quiet on May 12, which Ambassador Sasser had called "a critical day" because of concerns that a new wave of protests would be sparked by the repatriation of the remains of the Chinese journalists killed in the bombing.[49] That day, the U.S. embassy and consulates lowered their flags to half mast in respect for the dead. On May 13, President Clinton signed the official book of condolences brought to the Oval Office by Ambassador Li Zhaoxing. On May 14, President Clinton and President Jiang spoke directly by telephone, during which Clinton expressed his regrets for the tragic bombing, promised an investigation into the matter, and reaffirmed his commitment to bringing bilateral relations back to normal.[50]

On June 16 (Beijing time), presidential envoy and Undersecretary of State for Political Affairs Thomas Pickering presented the results of the U.S. investigation into the bombing. Ambassador Li responded that China had "taken note of the apology" but rejected U.S. explanations for the "so-called mistaken bombing" as "anything but convincing."[51] On July 30, the two governments reached an agreement whereby the United States would pay $4.5 million in compensation to the victims of the bombing and their families. By September, relations between the two governments were "back on track," in the words of U.S. national security adviser Samuel Berger.[52] In December, China agreed to pay $2.8 million to the United States for damages to U.S. diplomatic facilities caused by the protests, and the U.S. government agreed to pay $28 million to China for damages to the Chinese embassy in Belgrade caused by the bombing.[53]

To Allow or Not Allow Protest: Chinese Motivations

Faced with popular anger and requests for permission to protest, the government faced a difficult dilemma. Allowing nationalist protests would be risky because the embassy bombing occurred less than a month before the tenth anniversary of June 4, 1989. The embassy bombing protests marked the first time that university students in Beijing had taken to the streets en masse in the 10 years after Tiananmen.[54] Moreover, 10,000 Falun Gong supporters had gathered two weeks earlier outside the leadership compound in Beijing. By all accounts, the Falun Gong demonstration took the government by surprise, sending the Chinese leadership into a state of high anxiety. [55] Social movements based in religious and spiritual practices have historically posed challenges to Chinese rule. Like nationalism, sectarian movements facilitate mobilization by cutting across social cleavages, demonstrated by the Falun Gong's extensive organizational apparatus and ability to recruit adherents across the country, including Party cadres.[56] Jiang Zemin's remarks to the Politburo Standing Committee reflected the deep anxiety among the Chinese leadership after the Falun Gong protest:

> This incident is the largest mass incident in Beijing since the 1989 political crisis. . . . A sensitive time is approaching. We must immediately take effective measures to guard against a similar incident. . . . We have repeatedly stressed the importance of "nip it in the bud" (*fangwei dujian*) and the request for instructions and reporting of information for significant incidents.[57]

When the Chinese embassy was bombed two weeks later, some within the leadership feared that the West was trying to cause instability in China by demonstrating the feebleness of the Communist Party as defender of the national interest.[58] Zong Hairen, the pseudonym for an elite insider, has also published an account of this period with the assistance of Columbia professor Andrew Nathan. In Zong's account, even the reform-oriented Li Ruihuan—once put forward as a potential Chinese "Gorbachev"[59]—reportedly said: "The possibility cannot be excluded that this was a premeditated plot of the United States to create chaos in China, to have China's young people vent their hatred of the United States on the Chinese government."[60]

If anti-American protests posed such a great risk due to the timing of the embassy bombing in 1999, why did the government not stifle them preemptively? A number of scholars and observers have pointed to the prohibitive cost of repression. After the bombing had created "visible martyrs," it would have been "too hazardous for the government to try to disallow student protests altogether," notes Elizabeth Perry.[61] "Unable to suppress the protestors, authorities were forced to plead with them for calm,"[62] writes Peter Gries. The intensity of popular feeling aroused by the embassy bombing made repression a very costly option, likely to stoke popular resentment and lead to accusations that the regime was unwilling to defend the national interest.

To this day, most Chinese, both elites and ordinary citizens, still believe the bombing was intentional.[63] Chinese media fed this belief by portraying the bombing as a brazen, wanton act rather than an accidental strike. Even the liberal *Nanfang Zhoumo* (Southern Weekend) quoted a military expert as saying the bombing was intended "to probe the Chinese government's reaction to international crises, especially sudden accidents, as well as its mass reaction, public opinion, and related policies."[64] A *Beijing Review* editorial declared that few people believed the bombing was an accident because "NATO, armed with high-tech weapons, always knows which targets it is going to hit." The editorial continued:

> The raid on the embassy is just a signal that U.S.-led NATO is speeding up the pace of its strategy of containing China. The bombing is deliberately designed. For Washington's politicians and NATO generals, Belgrade is an ideal place to send that signal to China. You can't drop bombs on Tiananmen Square in Beijing, because you have no excuse. But it sounds like a good idea to launch missiles on the Chinese Embassy in Belgrade under the cloak of an accidental strike.[65]

Many Chinese who sought information from other sources also arrived at similar conclusions, including students residing in the United States.[66] In Beijing, one student from Tsinghua University told Hong Kong's *Mingpao Monthly* that he had searched the Internet after hearing of the bombing from a classmate. He concluded that the purpose of the bombing was to "test our nation's strength," declaring that if China's "response is not strong enough, the American devils (*guizi*) will further meddle in our internal affairs."[67]

Given the degree of popular outrage, the Chinese government faced a dilemma in responding to popular mobilization. To forbid protests would foster resentment and undermine regime legitimacy, but to allow protests might invite dissent and instability on the eve of the tenth anniversary of the Tiananmen Square crackdown. Ruan Cishan, editor-in-chief of Hong Kong–based Phoenix Television, noted, "If the government's foreign attitude was too feeble, it would face domestic popular pressure, but if it restrained demonstrations, popular sentiment could change direction and target the government."[68] Both the risk of allowing protests and the repercussions of trying to prevent them worried senior Chinese leaders. "The Chinese government was actually very concerned about the possibility of losing control if it allowed a large-scale anti-U.S. demonstration to break out,"[69] Dingxin Zhao writes, but "because of the seriousness of the incident in the minds of most Chinese, most PRC leaders worried that the students would turn against the government if anti-U.S. demonstrations were not permitted."[70]

Faced with this dilemma, the government gambled on a middle road: channeling protests so that popular anger would target the United States rather than the government. Allowing protests while providing guidance through party and student organizations would mitigate the risk to stability while eschewing the need for repression, enabling the leadership to claim its "support and leadership of the righteous voice and actions of mass protests against NATO."[71] At the meeting on May 8, the top leadership anticipated that "after we make public the news that our embassy was attacked, there will inevitably arise a strong reaction among the people, as everyone's patriotism will necessarily rise."[72] The leadership decided upon "a policy of persuasion rather than coercive prevention,"[73] with relevant security departments issuing a circular "to intensify reporting on domestic public opinion, to give guidance to the youth and students, and to prevent chaos or the loss of control." [74] Although Party-led student associations were instructed to co-opt unofficial demonstrations as soon as they arose, spontaneous protests outnumbered university-organized protests on the afternoon and evening of May 8.[75] According to a report later released by the graduate student association at Beijing University, only five of the 11 major demonstrations by Beijing University students were legally registered.[76]

Diplomatic Intent: Signaling Resolve

The desire to signal resolve as well as mitigate the domestic consequences played a role in tipping the scales toward allowing nationalist protests. With the risk to stability and the cost of stifling protest appearing equally unattractive, the international benefits of demonstrating China's mettle appear to have favored a decision to allow protests. Rather than creating additional resentment against the regime, anti-American anger could be harnessed to serve China's diplomatic objectives. As Foreign Minister Tang Jiaxuan noted:

> When news of the embassy bombing and the resulting Chinese casualties spread across China, there was an immediate and vehement reaction. Large numbers of people held street demonstrations, severely condemning the American atrocity. Wave upon wave of increasingly indignant protests put great popular pressure on the United States and NATO.[77]

The embassy bombing occurred at a time of deteriorating relations with the United States, after a set of snubs that left China's leaders looking weak on the international stage. Although Presidents Bill Clinton and Jiang Zemin had declared their intent to build a "strategic partnership" at a presidential summit in 1997, by mid-1999 diplomatic relations had worsened dramatically. In March, NATO began bombing Yugoslavia over the objections of China and Russia. Although the West viewed the Kosovo campaign as part of a humanitarian mission to end Serb atrocities, for the Chinese government

this represented a violation of Yugoslavian sovereignty and "an extremely perilous precedent" for Western intervention in secessionist disputes, with implications for China's difficulties with Tibet, Xinjiang, and Taiwan.[78] Li Peng drew a stark parallel to China's historical humiliation, describing NATO's intervention as that of an "eight-nation alliance" (*baguo lianjun*), the same phrase used to describe the foreign army sent to suppress the Boxer Rebellion at the turn of the last century. In Li Peng's words, NATO's "attack on 'this disobedient, sole Communist regime in Europe' created a precedent (*xianli*) of making war on a sovereign nation without UN authorization."[79]

The embassy bombing also closely followed on the heels of a second perceived humiliation. During Premier Zhu Rongji's visit to Washington in April 1999, President Clinton refused to sign an agreement on China's entry into the WTO. Zhu had expressed reluctance to seek a WTO deal at a time when anti-China sentiment was running high in the United States. Wen Ho Lee, a nuclear scientist at Los Alamos National Laboratory, had been accused of espionage. Influential members of Congress escalated their opposition to Chinese membership in the WTO.[80] Despite his unease, Zhu Rongji traveled to Washington and offered significant concessions that surprised his U.S. counterparts.[81] But the package was turned down by Clinton on the advice of his domestic advisers and then published on the website of the U.S. Trade Representative.[82] When the concessions became public, Zhu came under attack in internal Chinese discussions.[83] Opponents of China's entry to the WTO renewed their criticism, and industry leaders who had not known the extent of the deal expressed their outrage. Accusations that Zhu was a "traitor" to the nation filled Internet forums.

Two weeks later, NATO planes bombed the Chinese embassy in Belgrade. U.S. investigators later concluded that the CIA's targeting maps and no-hit lists had not been updated to reflect the relocation of the Chinese embassy. But Chinese observers noted that the building was the only target nominated by the CIA, many foreign diplomats had visited the Chinese embassy at its new location, and the only portion of the building hit by U.S. precision-guided bombs was that of the Chinese military attaché, whose office was suspected of feeding Milosevic intelligence.[84] Widespread suspicion that the bombing was intentional or the result of a clever conspiracy led many in the Chinese government to treat the crisis as a test of China's mettle.[85] As Jiang Zemin told the Politburo Standing Committee,

> They attacked the embassy with not one but many missiles, from different angles. . . . Seen in the international context, the U.S.-led NATO attack on our embassy in Yugoslavia was definitely not an accident, definitely not innocent (*juebu shi ouran de, qiebuke tianzhen*). . . . We must speak with the force of justice and make known to U.S.-led NATO: the Chinese people will not be humiliated! The Chinese nation will not be bullied![86]

As recounted by Zong Hairen, most of the top Chinese leaders at the May 8 meeting expressed a conviction that the bombing was an intentional plot to

probe China's resolve: to "find out to what degree we might react to its hegemonic interference in China's internal affairs" (Qian Qichen); to sound out "our reaction to, and stand on, international crises and conflicts" (Jiang Zemin); "with the intention of feeling out our attitude" (Wei Jianxing); and with the intention of "sounding out our position" (Wan Li).[87] Several opponents of China's entry into the WTO also suggested that China's willingness to negotiate concessions had encouraged American aggression. Li Peng reportedly said: "The United States' choice to bomb the embassy is also related to our eagerness to join the WTO. It is because the United States has this bargaining chip that it dares to brandish this big stick against our heads."[88] He and Wei Jianxing speculated that the United States had singled out China because Russia had already softened its opposition to the Kosovo war.[89] Whatever the U.S. motivation, even Zhu Rongji concurred on the importance of a strong response, according to Zong's account: "This was a deliberate action by the United States. Its purpose is to see China's reaction. If we submit to this humiliation without a protest, the United States will become even more unbridled in the future."[90]

How the government responded to the crisis was regarded as setting an important precedent for future encounters. As Foreign Minister Tang Jiaxuan wrote in his memoir: "How to deal with this bolt from the blue was a critical test of the Chinese government's capacity, and also proved to be an important issue for China's development, as well as for world peace and stability."[91] As one Chinese scholar noted, "Once the embassy bombing had been defined as a 'premeditated government action' and judged to be a far-reaching anti-China conspiracy, the strongest response became necessary to stop the insatiable United States, that is: 'only if the United States recognizes that China cannot be violated will China avoid being the next Yugoslavia.'"[92]

Limited by China's "military weakness and economic dependency on the West,"[93] Beijing sought alternative measures to demonstrate that China could not be bullied. Given rising popular anger, street demonstrations would signal resolve and demonstrate popular support for the government's diplomatic position without risking military escalation or irreparable damage to the international climate for China's development. Popular outrage and the delicacy of managing domestic sentiment were important considerations in China's response, but the top leadership also stressed the importance of watching the American response and adjusting as needed. As Jiang Zemin told the Politburo Standing Committee: "We must strongly condemn the U.S.-led NATO and continue to watch carefully what attitude they adopt, reserving the right to take future actions."[94]

Diplomatic Impact: Signaling Resolve with Limited Leverage

To evaluate the diplomatic impact of the protests, it is useful to identify three phases of the crisis and its resolution: the first day and half of spontaneous, volatile protests, after which the government took the upper hand in stage-managing the demonstrations on the evening of May 9; the next three days in which protests were choreographed and then curtailed on May 12; and the aftermath of the crisis, including negotiations with the United States over China's entry into the WTO, which culminated in a November agreement.

A close tracing of events illustrates the correspondence between the perceived risk and cost associated with anti-American protests and the credibility of the signal. Overall, the protests were effective in conveying China's resolve during the first phase. Despite government efforts to channel popular sentiment and provide logistical support, including buses, the sincerity of public anger and the government's vulnerability to domestic outrage was apparent to U.S. observers. With evidence on the streets, the government's vulnerability to public opinion could not be easily dismissed, giving credibility to President Jiang's later claim that "the outrages of 1.2 billion people are beyond any possible containment."[95] As the government grew more concerned about the danger to domestic stability and more satisfied with American attentiveness to Chinese concerns, including U.S. apologies and recognition of Chinese resolve, authorities took visible measures to reduce the risk that protests would get out of hand. After four days, the government curtailed protests entirely. Without angry mobs in the streets, the government's hands were no longer tied. As protests appeared more manipulated and less costly to curtail, U.S. officials increasingly discounted the protests and warned China that the United States would not make concessions on China's entry into the WTO or negotiations over Kosovo.

First Phase: Spontaneous, Volatile Protests

On the day that news of the Belgrade bombing reached China, Chinese protests appeared spontaneous and volatile. Besieged inside the U.S. embassy, Ambassador Sasser told CBS's *Face the Nation* by telephone: "The problem. . . is that this whole thing could spin out of control. We're just hoping that the police can continue to control them."[96] U.S. officials recognized the Chinese government's complicity in steering the protests but also understood that popular anger was strong and volatile enough to pose a nontrivial risk to domestic and diplomatic stability. As a senior diplomat in the U.S. embassy recalled:

> This thing got out of control. The government and the Foreign Ministry did not realize how determined and angry these people were. . . at the United States, but also, as it went on, partially directed at the Chinese government. That's when I think the government decided that the better part of wisdom was to join the students and try to bus them over there to the American embassy. Because who knows? They might have stopped in Tiananmen and said bad things about the government.[97]

According to a senior White House official at the time, the U.S. embassy in Beijing was nearly overrun. Sensitive documents were destroyed as a precautionary measure. If Chinese security forces did not intervene, U.S. officials warned, the Chinese government would have an international incident on their hands.[98]

Despite statements of regret by President Clinton and U.S. cabinet officials, including a letter of apology from Secretary Albright, the crisis escalated. The Chinese media did not publicize the Albright apology or Clinton's remarks, apparently because China's leaders were outraged at what they deemed an insufficient display of American remorse. As Tang Jiaxuan wrote in his memoir, "The U.S.-led NATO tried to evade responsibility, alleging that the bombing had been a 'mistake.'"[99] According to Li Peng, "The United States tried to shift blame to the NATO command in order to relieve the U.S. government of responsibility."[100] The initial statement by CIA director George Tenet and Secretary of Defense William Cohen said that "We regret any loss of civilian life or other unintended damage, but there is no such thing as risk-free military operations."[101] A few hours later, Clinton expressed his regrets during a tornado site visit. Clinton called the bombing a "tragic mistake" but also rejected the Chinese description of the bombing, stating: "Well, it wasn't barbaric. What is barbaric is what Mr. Milosevic has done. It's tragic. It's awful. But it's a tragedy, and it was an accident."[102]

To many Chinese analysts, Clinton's remarks at the tornado site reflected a lack of concern commensurate with the severity of the incident. Tsinghua University's Yan Xuetong noted that Clinton and Albright "seemed to think that killing Chinese was no important matter, for a long time showing no indication of compensation, apology, or comfort, as seen by the tone of their language, casually saying 'sorry' (*dui bu qi*) as if those three words could solve all problems."[103] Another Chinese scholar notes that Ambassador Li Zhaoxing became angry with State Department officials for first expressing concern about the safety of American diplomatic personnel in China and only then offering regrets and apologies.[104] According to Wu Xinbo, "Washington's insistence on continued air strikes against Yugoslavia and criticism of the Chinese position on the Kosovo issue made the Chinese government feel that the United States was not taking the issue of the embassy bombing seriously enough."[105] Although Albright's letter of apology was considered "a more serious step in U.S. efforts to apologize, it still fell short of addressing the Chinese concern over how the U.S. government would handle the issue."[106]

Protests gained momentum on the second day as fear of repression diminished with official signals of lenience and encouragement. Media coverage of the protests served as a green light to those who had been apprehensive about participating.[107] In Beijing, one student at Tsinghua University told me that he had been reluctant to participate on the night of May 8, when hundreds of Beijing University students had come to mobilize students, shouting, "Come out and join us—don't be chicken!" The next day, however, he and other student association leaders were deputized to organize a protest at the embassy, choosing students to fill the quota for his department and arranging for food and water.[108]

Despite signs of government complicity in allowing the anti-American protests, U.S. observers understood the risk that protests posed and the difficulty the Chinese government faced in managing popular sentiment. Asked whether the Chinese government could turn the demonstrations off at will, Orville Schell, a prominent commentator and longtime China hand, stated that there were "two risks": one to Sino-American relations and one to domestic stability. As Schell put it, "Anti-foreign bias could easily well up in a way that would be very inchoate, very hard to control, and could gather to it all sorts of other grievances. And dare I say the anniversary of the June 4th demonstrations and massacre is almost upon us."[109] Douglas Paal, senior director for Asian affairs at the National Security Council under George H. W. Bush, reminded American viewers that "in the last century prior to the establishment of the People's Republic of China—every government that fell, fell in large part because it didn't react strongly enough to a sense of injury by foreigners. So they know that they have to go through at least some psychodrama publicly."[110]

As protests continued for a second day, U.S. officials also recognized that their initial statements had been insufficient to assuage Chinese anger. As then-Deputy Assistant Secretary of Defense Kurt Campbell concluded, "these carefully framed apologies only served to enrage the Chinese people further. . . . Washington would clearly need to do more to satisfy the Chinese demands for an apology, an investigation, compensation, and punishment for those responsible."[111] Campbell noted that "the overriding desire initially inside the National Security Council was not to lose momentum or international support for the Kosovo campaign. . . [U.S.] policy makers likely underestimated how intensely China would respond to the attack."[112] The protests helped focus U.S. attention on the "Chinese dimension" of the Kosovo mission, with an interagency working group "recommend[ing] that U.S. leaders show more remorse in public and spare no effort in establishing an off-line communication channel with Chinese leaders at the highest levels in order to head off the crisis."[113]

On May 9, Clinton apologized in a formal letter and unsuccessfully attempted to reach Jiang by phone. The Clinton-Jiang phone call ultimately took place on May 14. Although one U.S. official called the delay "inexplicable,"[114] the Chinese side appeared reluctant to use the hotline until the terms of the phone conversation had been agreed upon in advance.[115] Only after Clinton's apology in a letter to President Jiang Zemin and a May 13 signing of a book of condolences did the Chinese side relent. "Considering the change of attitude by the United States, President Jiang Zemin accepted Clinton's request and a telephone conversation took place on May 14," Tang Jiaxuan concludes.[116] Likewise, the decision not to publicize Clinton's initial remarks in the domestic media appeared to stem from dissatisfaction with the level and solemnity of U.S. regrets and apologies. As Wu Xinbo notes,

Although Clinton's comment represented a response from the highest level in the U.S. government, it was regarded as insincere and inadequate by the Chinese given the fact that it was delivered in an informal way, without an apology. Moreover, his words justifying the NATO air strike against Yugoslavia served only to further anger the Chinese as they believed Clinton was trying to pass the buck to Milosevic.[117]

Publishing Clinton's initial remarks might have inflamed rather than pacified domestic anger, particularly if protesters concluded that the United States was trying to get away with the bombing without taking full responsibility or that the Chinese government was so ineffectual that it was willing to trump up these token regrets. One protester implied as much, saying:

> Could Clinton's statement even be called an apology? The government was right not to report it (*meiyou fabiao*). Even though it wasn't reported, we saw it on the Internet. Had it been reported, it would have been like throwing oil on the fire—then things would really have gotten out of control (*shikong le*).[118]

While some have accused China of belatedly reporting American apologies in order to exploit the crisis as a domestic diversion and to extract greater concessions from the United States, China's behavior is also consistent with fear of domestic criticism and a sincere determination to signal resolve rather than risk appearing complacent.

Second Phase: Stage Management, Diminished Risk, and U.S. Skepticism

Growing concern that nationalist protests might get out of hand became a primary focus of the top leadership as it met again on the afternoon of May 9.[119] With U.S. officials now recognizing the seriousness of China's concerns, fears of instability appeared to outweigh the marginal benefit of allowing protests to continue unabated. On the one hand, China's leaders voiced satisfaction with the diplomatic results. "A powerful political force against the U.S.-led NATO atrocity is taking shape, fully demonstrating (*chongfen xianshi*) the might of our Party, nation, and people,"[120] Jiang Zemin told the Politburo Standing Committee. "The vehemence of China's series of responsive acts over the embassy bombing surprised the U.S. government," wrote Tang Jiaxuan. "Forced by China's firm stance and diplomatic pressure, by increasingly vehement domestic protests and international criticism, the United States was forced to change its attitude and apologized to China."[121]

On the other hand, the risk of diplomatic and domestic instability began to weigh more heavily.[122] Noting that protesters had smashed the U.S. embassy windows, Li Peng recalled: "If it continued this way, some actions could go too far (*chuge de xingwei*)."[123] After commending the patriotic actions of students and citizens, Jiang warned the Politburo Standing Committee of hostile elements that might "fish in troubled waters" and cause havoc, jeopardizing foreign investment and commerce.[124] He stressed that

> we must display the vehemence and strength of the whole nation's anger toward a common enemy. But we must also show the world a civilized image of our Chinese nation and grand country. So protest activities must be civilized, rational, and orderly, preventing extreme actions that do not help our larger struggle against U.S.-led NATO's savage act [or] the maintenance of social stability. We must be especially alert and guard against hostile forces that seek to take advantage of the situation and sow chaos.[125]

On television that evening, Vice President Hu Jintao stressed that "we must prevent overreaction, and ensure social stability" while acknowledging that the government "firmly supports and protects" all legally approved demonstrations.[126] Working through Party organizations on campus, the government increasingly stage-managed the demonstrations. Students in uniforms followed a seven-block route, carrying preprinted school banners. Security around U.S. diplomatic buildings noticeably increased as orderly protests continued for the third and fourth days.[127]

As the government asserted more control, the perceived risk and pressure on the government diminished. Stage-management dampened the signal of resolve, reducing the information that foreigners could glean from the ongoing protests. The effect was palpable to U.S. observers. On May 10, the White House press secretary said that "it's considerably calmer than it was yesterday. The embassy personnel, both in Beijing and around the country, are able to move in and out of the embassy."[128] On May 11, Ambassador Sasser told reporters: "We may go to bed early and get a good night's sleep."[129] As orderly protests continued, U.S. alarm that the situation might get out of control faded to suspicions that the protests were manufactured. U.S. officials were quoted as saying that the anti-American protests were intentional and had to stop. Secretary of State Albright noted that the demonstrations had received government approval, saying: "The vice president of China made a statement in which he in fact said that the demonstrations could be carried on within legal means. That is definitely an indication of their support."[130]

Congressional voices from both parties condemned the government's hand in the protests. "What is happening in Beijing and throughout China today is intentional," said Democratic senator Joseph Lieberman. "This is, unfortunately, going to be a very serious test of our relationship, whether the Chinese exploit this terrible accident."[131] Republican senator and presidential candidate John McCain told reporters that "it is clear that the Chinese are orchestrating this for some political reason. It should stop immediately."[132] A *Washington Post* editorial accused China of having "whipped people into a fury with inaccurate and incomplete reporting. Newspapers have failed to report U.S. explanations or apologies."[133]

Chinese officials attempted to defuse American skepticism, aware of the struggle for credibility with a U.S. audience. On PBS *NewsHour*, Ambassador Li Zhaoxing rebuffed Jim Lehrer's suggestion that the protests were mobilized, saying:

> This question was put in the wrong context, in the wrong way. Do you sincerely believe, think they believe that the Chinese people and the Chinese students had to be mobilized by the government to demonstrate and to condemn the U.S.-led NATO atrocities? No. If anyone should believe that, they are underestimating. . . the people of China, the students of China.[134]

Likewise, Jiang Zemin emphasized the sincerity of the protests when he spoke with Bill Clinton on May 14, stating: "The assault on the Chinese embassy seriously hurt the feelings of the Chinese people. After the incident, Chinese people took actions of their own accord to express their indignation in various forms, and a wave of strong protests spread across the nation. This was only natural."[135]

At the meeting of the top leadership on May 11, Jiang set the stage for the complete curtailment of protests. Noting that the tensions in U.S.-China relations "cannot be completely resolved in a short period of time," Jiang emphasized that the demonstrations had successfully conveyed the strength of China's resolve against foreign aggression while warning that "hostile foreign forces are eager to see China in chaos, using chaos to Westernize and split the country."[136] The protests also appeared to have served their purpose in achieving China's immediate objectives vis-à-vis the United States. As Tang Jiaxuan notes,

> The biggest gain for us was the lesson we taught the United States: that today's China and its people cannot be bullied and will not be scared by evil forces. They are ready to fight for the defense of national sovereignty and dignity at all costs.[137]

The government took a series of steps to meet protester demands, consistent with the hawkish commitment mechanism. The Chinese media finally broadcast U.S. apologies along with China's diplomatic measures, including the halting of bilateral talks. These measures appeared to defuse a degree of popular anger. One Tsinghua University protester noted, "I believe the government's decision to break off talks on business, human rights, and proliferation was completely correct. You are hoodlums, riding over our heads and shitting on us. How can we talk to you? Whether we negotiate later will depend on your attitude."[138] As a Chinese scholar concluded: "The demonstrations got results. . . the United States apologized, and the government could show this to the students. They weren't satisfied, but it was enough."[139]

Despite the publication of U.S. apologies and China's diplomatic actions, the curtailment of protests was not costless. In one case, officials had to threaten a group of students with disciplinary action to prevent them from continuing to the U.S. embassy, suggesting that repression would have been even costlier without diplomatic satisfaction. Dingxin Zhao notes that many students were outraged when told by officials that demonstrations were now illegal. According to Zhao, Party officials detained a group of several hundred university students en route to protest at the U.S. embassy. First university officials and then a high-level city official threatened students with disciplinary action for participating in a demonstration that had not been approved by the security authorities. Although half the group of students was persuaded to return to campus via buses provided by the government, several student union leaders became defiant and told students to ignore the officials.[140]

Third Phase: Crisis Aftermath and Negotiations

Given their swift curtailment, the anti-American protests offered limited diplomatic leverage. Indeed, U.S. officials and congressional leaders warned China not to take advantage of the crisis and voiced suspicions about the Chinese government's role in fomenting the protests. American officials stated that there would be negative consequences if China tried to "exploit" the incident and refused to make further concessions beyond a formal apology and compensation for loss of life and damages. Secretary of Defense Cohen told a Senate committee that there is "a distinction between righteous indignation and calculated exploitation and I think we have to be very concerned about that."[141] Republican congressman Christopher Cox stated, "Barely disguised stage management of the riots and demonstrations displays the manipulative nature of the Chinese government."[142] The atmosphere in Washington was further poisoned by investigations into illegal Chinese campaign contributions and the May 25 release of the Cox Commission report, which contained detailed allegations of Chinese theft of nuclear weapons secrets.[143] As a former State Department official noted, "Washington has seemed a parallel universe, one of equal fury and indignation. . . . Mirroring Beijing, a group of leading congressmen sent a letter to the president urging a pause in relations with China."[144]

With U.S. resolve stiffening, the short-lived embassy bombing protests did not provide China with much leverage during negotiations over Kosovo or China's entry into the WTO. Both issues were settled on terms that favored China's position, but neither involved significant American concessions. On Kosovo, China's diplomatic stance gradually became more pragmatic once NATO airstrikes ended. In the aftermath of the embassy bombing, China had threatened to obstruct a UNSC vote to authorize a peacekeeping mission as long as the air campaign continued.[145] The other permanent UNSC members were not swayed. Undersecretary of State Thomas Pickering dismissed China's objections as a "temporary setback," noting, "It doesn't seem to me in light of where the Chinese have been that they would veto a peace settlement."[146] Even Russia, who stood with China in calling the bombing a "barbaric action," sent an envoy to Beijing with the message that the incident should not derail the Kosovo negotiations.[147]

In June, when the matter was put to a Security Council vote, China abstained and let the resolution pass. NATO and Yugoslavia had reached an agreement on the withdrawal of forces, satisfying Russian and Chinese demands that Yugoslavia consented to any settlement.[148] The "important point," Li Peng noted, was that "NATO had stopped the bombing and recognized Yugoslavian sovereignty and territorial integrity."[149] The decision to abstain was a "wise move," one Chinese scholar noted, since NATO airstrikes had formally stopped and the resolution conformed to China's wishes in affirming the Security Council's role in maintaining peace and security.[150] Whereas the "United States and its NATO allies had denied Beijing a voice on Kosovo by launching air attacks without seeking approval from the United Nations," Michel Oksenberg noted, "now that the emerging Yugoslav settlement includes a strong role for the United Nations, Washington can no longer ignore Beijing's view."[151]

On the WTO, China refused to resume negotiations for several months. With U.S. officials warning that China should not exploit the embassy bombing for leverage in the WTO, Chinese leaders decided to delink the two issues, allowing the domestic fallout of the April humiliation and May embassy bombing to subside before reopening the talks. In November, the two sides finally reached an agreement that was not markedly different from the terms discussed before the bombing. However, the final agreement was better for China in one sector deemed critical to national security: telecommunications.[152] Whereas the April deal would have allowed a controlling 51 percent foreign ownership, the final agreement allowed only 49 percent in basic telecommunications services and 50 percent in value-added services, such as data storage and processing.[153] According to then-Deputy Assistant Secretary of State Susan Shirk, the November agreement contained "somewhat worse terms" for the United States,[154] even though U.S. negotiators worked strenuously to ensure that the November deal could be considered "roughly as strong"[155] as the package discussed in April.

As with the Kosovo negotiations, it is difficult to ascertain how much of the difference in outcome was due to the embassy bombing and protests or other factors. It is also challenging to assess the counterfactual, because the terms discussed in April were not final.[156] Barshefsky herself pondered this point in hindsight, recounting: "Even had the talks continued even in Washington, I think by the time the talks ended, he probably would have had to pull back on the 51."[157] Comparing the November agreement on China's WTO entry with the counterfactual, one might conclude that the embassy bombing had relatively little impact other than delaying the agreement. Barshefsky was able to "rebalance the package,"[158] as she put it: obtaining Chinese concessions in other areas and ensuring that the overall agreement could still be considered "essentially the same."[159] Yet U.S. perceptions of Chinese resolve were altered by the demonstrations, reinforcing American concerns about the vulnerability of China's moderate leaders and their inability to meet

U.S. demands. While stage-managed and quickly curtailed, the demonstrations increased U.S. receptivity to assertions that certain compromises would be domestically untenable for Chinese leaders, requiring greater flexibility on the U.S. side in order to reach an agreement.

Initially, the U.S. side was focused less on China's domestic constraints than on opposition within the United States. During Zhu Rongji's April visit, U.S. negotiators were determined that the Clinton administration not rush "prematurely" toward a deal. On the counsel of his economic advisors, Clinton told Zhu that there would be no agreement during his visit to Washington. The day after the terms of the would-be agreement were posted online, Zhu emphasized the mounting anger in China and the risk to his position should he agree to greater concessions. At a dinner banquet, Zhu told his American audience:

> Our current controversy with the American side lies in our insistence on maintaining controlling shares. . . . At present, I have no way of persuading the ordinary man in the street in China. You have a Congress, and so do we. . . . We have already made very big concessions, but the American side wants us to make even bigger concessions. It is not that I am afraid of losing my position. What I fear is that even if I do sign the agreement, our Chinese people will probably not agree to it. . . . I can only say these things here. If I said them in China, I might lose my job.[160]

During Senate hearings on April 13, several senators commented on Zhu's extraordinary efforts and voiced concern that the deal was "slipping by," noting that the "Chinese public" and "the Chinese leaders" were outraged by Clinton's rebuff and the USTR's decision to post the terms online.[161] Yet U.S. negotiators gave no indication of relenting. Two senators pressed Barshefsky on the likelihood of the deal falling apart in light of anger within the Chinese public and leadership. Barshefsky responded: "My major concern in these talks has always been to find a means to capture progress made, to arrest any Chinese backsliding [and] also not to do an agreement under the press of a deadline because of the visit, when what they were offering in certain areas was not adequate."[162]

After the embassy bombing, China announced the suspension of bilateral talks on human rights and nonproliferation, but the WTO talks were not mentioned. Privately, Jiang Zemin told an internal meeting on May 9:

> We will never give in to the harsh, unreasonable demands they have made on China's accession to the WTO; we must resolutely refuse them. . . . Can China survive another ten years of absence from the WTO's membership list? Yes, and we might even be living a better life. . . . We must have this resolve. With such resolve, we will have enough courage. In short, we will never be cowards.[163]

The next day, Minister for Foreign Trade and Economic Cooperation (MOFTEC), Shi Guangsheng, told the European Trade Commissioner: "I don't think the talks will be cancelled, but do not expect us to make any concessions; in theory, politics and business should not mix, but it is hard to separate the two."[164] His remarks left the impression that China expected concessions on the WTO in order to get relations back on track.[165] "The Chinese leadership hopes the moral high ground it has attained after the embassy accident might strengthen its hand at the WTO negotiation table," said a diplomatic source in Beijing. "Beijing hopes Washington would not be pushing too hard on a number of trade concessions."[166]

Consistent with expectations that stage management and curtailment limited China's bargaining leverage, Western officials warned that China should not link protests against the embassy bombing to the WTO negotiations. "To link [the attack] to the WTO is the beginning of the end," said Sergio Marchi, Canada's trade minister.[167] On May 12, the day that anti-American protests in China were "turned off," American trade officials explicitly warned China against pressing for concessions. U.S. Trade Representative Barshefsky stated:

> It is very dangerous for China, in any way, to link the tragic events in Yugoslavia with WTO accession. . . . The only possible rationale in China's mind for the notion that leverage has shifted. . . is that U.S. negotiators will feel guilty. Negotiations don't involve guilt.[168]

By the end of May, negotiations over the WTO had not resumed. U.S. negotiators suggested that further Chinese concessions might be required. Barshefsky warned China that time was running out, stating that the talks would "take as their starting point the concessions agreed by China in early April and will go further."[169] Testifying before the Senate, Assistant Secretary of State for East Asian and Pacific Affairs Stanley Roth reiterated that China should not attempt to use the bombing as leverage on other issues. Roth linked his warnings to suspicion about the authenticity of the anti-American protests, stating:

> I think the way it was handled and managed and orchestrated makes it clear that this was a decision [sic] to use for their own purposes. . . . The nationalist card is being played. . . the hard question is, how much and how permanent is it?. . . There are those who undoubtedly speculate, both in China and the United States, that perhaps the crisis of the last few weeks, this trough in the U.S.-China relationship, represents an opportunity for China to press for concessions from the U.S. on issues such as the terms for China's WTO accession, human rights, Tibet, and non-proliferation. These speculators are dangerously mistaken.[170]

Recognizing that the United States was unlikely to yield and might retaliate if China linked the embassy bombing to the WTO negotiations, the Chinese government decided to suspend the WTO negotiations until the crisis was resolved. According to a Chinese scholar who has extensively researched the 1999 crisis, Roth's testimony

> gave an indirect hint that the United States would see this is a negotiable opportunity for China, and hoped that China would not misuse this opportunity. And he gave the example of WTO. This message was received by China's leaders and the Chinese public: "If I overreact, you will hold the WTO up." So China's response was to separate these two negotiations—a very smart tactic—to prevent the United States from using the WTO to soften the Chinese position on the embassy bombing.[171]

As Wu concluded in his analysis of the incident, "The Chinese government was wise to temporarily suspend the negotiations with the United States on China's accession to the WTO [and] to impress its domestic audience by not sacrificing its principles."[172]

Delinking the two issues, Vice Minister of Foreign Trade and Economic Cooperation Long Yongtu stated that the WTO talks would not be resumed until the United States had made a "thorough and complete" explanation of the embassy bombing. Long said that the embassy bombing had "damaged the whole atmosphere" of the WTO talks, declaring: "If our negotiating partners are determined to push us further, we will have to say: 'Sorry, we are not in a hurry, we will wait.' China can survive without the WTO."[173] State Councilor Wu Yi, who had helped draft the April deal, told reporters that state-owned telecom enterprises would be consulted, and "if people thought that. . . the United States demanded too much from us, we could give up the idea."[174]

The hardening of China's position and refusal to restart negotiations along the lines of the April deal continued through the fall. Even when talks began in September, the Chinese side cut discussions short after itemizing a list of disagreements with the list posted in April. Chief negotiator Long Yongtu did not accompany the "more conservative" MOFTEC head Shi Guangsheng to Washington, furthering speculation that the embassy bombing had further eroded the position of moderate elites and Jiang Zemin's willingness to push forward on a WTO deal.

U.S. observers acknowledged the vulnerability of China's moderates. As one American scholar noted, "Jiang was not in the political position to respond to U.S. efforts to restart the negotiations. It was only several months later, with public emotion significantly cooled and broader steps taken to repair the rift in Sino-U.S. relations, that Jiang took the steps noted earlier to produce an agreement."[175] Another expert wrote: "with the U.S. bombing of the Chinese embassy in Belgrade, these voices became both strident and difficult to ignore. Jiang was, in the immediate aftermath of the embassy bombing, in a very difficult situation."[176]

In November, when negotiations resumed in earnest, U.S. negotiators acknowledged the domestic difficulties facing the Chinese side and accepted Zhu Rongji's inability to agree to the April terms. Zhu Rongji told the American delegation that the embassy bombing had changed the domestic atmosphere, requiring him to stand firm on the telecom issue. According to official Chinese records, Zhu told Barshefsky:

> One or two percentage points do not mean much, practically speaking. But why we do insist? It is not that we are going back on our word. It is because the environment has changed, because first of all you should not have bombed our embassy. The entire environment changed after that. You have Congress and public opinion. We also have the National People's Congress and the Chinese People's Political Consultative Conference. We also have public opinion. Even if it's not in the newspapers, it's on the Internet and extremely influential. . . . Chinese people have always believed that telecommunications and insurance are vital industries. They think if I agree to 51 percent, I am selling out China's interest, even if I don't think that way. . . . To face the nation, I now insist on this. So I am happy that you no longer emphasize the "two 51 percents" [in telecommunications and pension insurance]. Although it means little in practice, you have done me a personal favor.[177]

Zhu Rongji's predicament had become clear to American officials. As Barshefsky recounted: "The April deal had foreign ownership of telecom at 51 percent. [But in November] we settled at 50. I kept saying to Zhu, 'Come on, it's just one percentage point. Let's go back to 51.' He couldn't do it. There was no way he could do it."[178] Recognizing the extent of domestic opposition within China, American negotiators relented. As Shirk notes: "The Chinese claimed their pound of flesh for the April humiliation by retracting a number of previous commitments. . . . After throwing away the WTO agreement in April, we retrieved it in November by the skin of our teeth, and on somewhat worse terms."[179]

The 1999 embassy bombing demonstrations illustrate that nationalist protests can be an effective signal of resolve even when leverage is limited. Anti-American protests in dozens of cities conveyed the depths of Chinese anger and resolve. In allowing protests, China demonstrated to the United States that China could not be bullied, its embassy bombed with only token regrets. Early American statements of "regret" were dismissed as insufficient remorse for what many believed was a conspiracy to test China's mettle. Clinton's initial condolences were given in remarks to reporters during a tornado site visit and emphasized the need to "stay the course" in Yugoslavia. At stake for China was not whether the United States would say "sorry" but the level and sincerity of those apologies, symbolizing U.S. recognition of the importance of China's interests. After the protests on May 8 and 9, Clinton apologized in a formal letter and unsuccessfully attempted to reach Jiang by phone.

With limited access to internal deliberations, it is difficult to assess China's motivations conclusively. We know that the Chinese leadership decided to allow protests; anti-American demonstrations did not erupt across the nation in 1999 without the government's knowledge and forbearance. Nationalist protests were initially sincere rather than ginned up; the government's actions were primarily reactive rather than proactive. The majority of protests on the first day arose spontaneously, as Party and university authorities scrambled to co-opt and guide them. After the first day and a half of protests, the government recognized that out-of-control sentiment presented a liability for its domestic and international objectives.

Heavy-handed orchestration mitigated the risk to stability posed but also reduced the diplomatic impact of nationalist protests and heightened American skepticism. The staged appearance and curtailment of the protests reduced any additional leverage the Chinese government might have gained had the protests appeared more spontaneous. As U.S. Trade Representative Barshefsky noted:

> There was always this feeling on my part that the protests were orchestrated, simply because of the way in which they started, and then the way in which they abruptly ended. That made for very good theater and also increased bargaining leverage somewhat, though it's easy to misgauge by how much, because the U.S. was contrite almost immediately. But the protests demonstrated that China would stand up to the U.S.—period. China understood where its national interests lay, and if it meant collision with the United States, particularly under such circumstances, then so be it.[180]

Barshefsky's remarks underscore that resolve and leverage are distinct and separable.

Although orchestration limited the extent to which China gained leverage, the protests helped China signal its resolve to stand up to U.S. interference in the sovereign affairs of another country and its determination to prevent external involvement in a future scenario concerning China's own struggles with national unity. Asked why the Chinese government had encouraged the anti-American demonstrations, Jim Woolsey, CIA director during Clinton's first term, suggested that China meant to demonstrate resolve against U.S. intervention in a potential Taiwan scenario. Woolsey remarked:

> I think they're laying down this marker particularly with regard to Taiwan. I think they want to let us know that this province of Serbia into which we are intruding ourselves by way of trying to protect the human rights of the Kosovars is not some analogy in the future they would like to see for our helping protect Taiwan.[181]

The 2001 EP-3 Incident

On the morning of April 1, 2001, an American EP-3 reconnaissance plane and a Chinese F-8 fighter collided over the South China Sea, about 70 nautical miles to the southeast of Hainan Island, China's southernmost province. At 9:33 a.m., the U.S. aircraft made an emergency landing at a military airstrip in Hainan. The Chinese fighter and pilot were lost at sea. The U.S. Pacific Command (PACOM) released a statement on its website requesting that the Chinese government "respect the integrity of the aircraft and the well-being and safety of the crew."[182] U.S. embassy officials attempted to reach their counterparts in the PRC Ministry of Foreign Affairs, but their phone calls were for the most part not answered or returned.[183]

At 9:30 p.m., approximately 12 hours after the collision, Assistant Foreign Minister Zhou Wenzhong met with U.S. ambassador Joseph Prueher. Zhou stated that a sudden turn by the U.S. aircraft was the direct cause of the collision and demanded that the United States take full responsibility. Prueher requested a meeting with the crew and stated that the Chinese version of the events was "physically impossible"[184] given the relative speed and maneuverability of the EP-3 plane and Chinese fighter jet. At 10:00 p.m., the Chinese Foreign Ministry released its first public statement regarding the collision, asserting that responsibility for the incident lay "entirely with the U.S. side."[185] PACOM chief admiral Dennis Blair refuted the Chinese version of events at a press conference in Hawaii, saying that it was "pretty obvious as to who bumped into whom" and that Chinese fighters had been intercepting U.S. aircraft in a pattern of "increasingly unsafe behavior."[186]

The following day, April 2, Ambassador Prueher told reporters in Beijing that "it is inexplicable and unacceptable and of great concern to the most senior levels of the U.S. government that the air crew has been held incommunicado for over 32 hours."[187] That evening, Assistant Foreign Minister Zhou called an emergency meeting with Prueher and told him that U.S. officials could meet with the EP-3 crew the next day.[188] Zhou also demanded that the United States accept full responsibility and apologize for the collision. Back in Washington, President Bush released a public statement demanding "immediate access" to the EP-3 crew and saying that "failure of the Chinese government to react promptly to our request is inconsistent with standard diplomatic practice, and with the expressed desire of both our countries for better relations." He also stated that the U.S. military was ready and willing to help in the search and rescue effort for the Chinese pilot and aircraft.[189]

On April 3, Jiang Zemin released a statement demanding that the U.S. side bear responsibility for the incident and halt surveillance flights near China.[190] Foreign Ministry spokesman Zhu Bangzao reiterated that the United States should apologize (*daoqian*). After learning that American officials had gained access to the aircrew, President Bush took a tougher public stance, stating: "We have allowed the Chinese government time to do the right thing. But now it is time for our servicemen and women to return home."[191] Later that day, Secretary of State Colin Powell for the first time mentioned his "regret" for the loss of the Chinese pilot in a press briefing.[192] The next morning, Jiang reiterated that the United States should apologize and do something to "benefit the development of U.S.-China relations, rather than making statements that confused right with wrong." Because Jiang's remarks came as he departed for a scheduled two-week visit to Latin America,[193] however, many observers concluded that the storm would blow over.[194]

Following Jiang's statement, Secretary Powell again used the term "regret" in his remarks to reporters and a letter to Vice Premier Qian Qichen. Powell told reporters: "We regret that the Chinese plane did not get down safely, and we regret the loss of the life of that Chinese pilot. But now we need to move on and we need to bring this to a resolution."[195] The Powell-Qian letter formed the basis of a five-step plan to resolve the crisis that Prueher and Zhou drafted on April 5. The first step would be to publish a paragraph from Powell's letter expressing regret for the loss of the Chinese pilot; the second would be a formal letter from Ambassador Prueher expressing regret for the loss of life and U.S. intrusion into Chinese airspace; the third would be the release of the EP-3 crew; the fourth would be a meeting to discuss the prevention of future accidents; and the fifth would be the return of the aircraft.[196]

Between April 5 and April 11, American and Chinese diplomats held a series of consultations over the wording of the formal letter, compromising on the term "sorry" in lieu of a formal apology. On April 8, Secretary Powell used the word "sorry" for the first time. Speaking on a Sunday morning news program, Powell said: "We have expressed regrets and we have expressed our sorrow, and we are sorry that the life was lost."[197] On April 11, Ambassador Prueher delivered a letter to Chinese foreign minister Tang Jiaxuan that twice stated that the United States was "very sorry," once for the loss of life and aircraft, and once for the unapproved entering of China's airspace. Tang then told Prueher that the U.S. aircrew was free to leave. On the morning of April 12, the U.S. aircrew left China aboard a chartered American plane. Meetings to discuss responsibility for the collision, how to prevent future incidents, and the return of the U.S. aircraft began on April 18 in Beijing. On July 3, the EP-3 left China in five pieces aboard a Russian cargo plane.

To Allow or Not Allow Protest: Chinese Motivations

As in 1999, the government again faced a dilemma. Allowing anti-American protests would accept some risk that protests might get out of hand, creating a diplomatic incident or turning against the government. Yet repressing protests would stoke domestic resentment and accusations that the government was tough at home but weak on the international stage. On the one hand, the risk to stability after the plane collision was somewhat less than after the embassy bombing, as there were no sensitive anniversaries immediately approaching. Concerns about Falun Gong had also subsided with the government's continuing crackdown. Public opinion had turned against the "evil cult" after several self-immolations in Tiananmen Square were widely covered in the Chinese media.[198] Some officials also congratulated themselves on the improved public security situation. A district chief of the Beijing Public Security Bureau noted that between 1998 and 2001, "the situation became more stable, and the number of criminal cases stabilized and fell.... The deepening strike-hard campaign promoted overall stability in the public order."[199]

On the other hand, the number of "mass incidents" had risen from approximately 30,000 in 1999 to 50,000 by 2002, according to the Ministry of Public Security.[200] Many Chinese observers also noted that public anger at the United States could easily turn against the Chinese government. According to Lianhe Zaobao, the collision "aroused the anger of Chinese Internet users, but the target of many people's discontent was not the United States but the Chinese government, demanding that it not be 'weak' and that it 'must teach the United States a lesson.'"[201] With the embassy bombing having "resulted in a clear rise of anti-American sentiment among the Chinese public" and left an "unhealed scar on the Chinese body politic," as several Chinese analysts put it, the EP-3 collision reopened these "psychological wounds."[202] Surveys of Beijing residents indicated that feelings of amity toward the United States had recovered by a few degrees after the embassy bombing, but popular attitudes cooled further after the plane collision.[203]

The disappearance of the Chinese fighter jet and pilot, blamed on a "sudden turn" by the U.S. aircraft in China's initial statements, aroused widespread anger. As Foreign Minister Tang Jiaxuan recounted:

> In the days that followed, all across the country the masses further expressed their resentment and condemnation of the U.S. reconnaissance plane's collision with our military aircraft.... The U.S. attitude and manner made us furious and naturally provoked a strong reaction within the Chinese public. Cadres, masses, and soldiers were filled with righteous indignation, extremely dissatisfied with the U.S. refusal to take responsibility. Online, many people proposed a protest demonstration at the U.S. embassy, even demanding that the Chinese government put the U.S. crew on trial.[204]

Along with calls for protest, netizens vented their anger on Internet forums and called for a boycott of U.S. products. Patriotic hackers defaced U.S. government websites.[205]

Given popular outrage and calls for protest after the plane collision, why did the government choose to repress anti-American demonstrations? On the one hand, allowing protests may have been less risky in 2001 than in 1999 given the absence of prominent anniversaries surrounding the plane collision and Falun Gong's diminished stature in mainland China. Another possibility is that repression was less costly in 2001. If popular anger was less intense or widespread than in 1999, the government may have been less concerned about its ability to repress protests without triggering a popular backlash. On the other hand, public anger was partially tempered by doubts about what had caused the collision. Particularly among Chinese elites and intellectuals who accessed international news reports, there was greater doubt about which side was responsible for the EP-3 collision than the embassy bombing. One Chinese journalist who had participated in the 1999 demonstrations as a university student in Beijing described the difference between the two crises, recalling: "These two incidents weren't the same. There were lots of unanswered questions about the plane collision. Why would the U.S. plane run into the Chinese plane?. . . By 2001, we could go online and access a lot of reports from overseas media, so we could see both sides of the dispute."[206]

In assessing the degree of domestic anger and the difficulty of repressing protests, it is also important to note that both were partly endogenous to domestic media coverage. From the outset of the EP-3 crisis, the domestic media were instructed to report the incident in a relatively restrained manner. On April 2, People's Daily ran a single story on the fourth page with the headline: "Foreign Ministry Spokesman Comments on Crash of U.S. Reconnaissance Plane into Chinese Military Aircraft."[207] On April 3, the Chinese leadership met and "issued clear guidelines, policies, and objectives for the handling of the incident. . . to engage in a resolute struggle against the erroneous behavior on the part of the United States as well as [to] strive for an early resolution of the event."[208] After the meeting, the Propaganda Department issued a series of guidelines to the domestic media regarding coverage of the collision. The *Beijing Youth Daily*, which had been given an award by the Propaganda Department for its extensive coverage of the embassy bombing in 1999, had by April 3 carried only two short syndicated Xinhua stories.[209] The *People's Daily* further stressed that citizens should concentrate on their work and trust the government to handle the situation.[210]

Despite quieter treatment in the domestic media, students still sought to mobilize protests at dozens of universities. Acting on instructions from the top leadership and Ministry of Public Security, Beijing security authorities stepped up preventive measures to handle mass attempts to march toward the U.S. embassy.[211] According to one report, "On the second day of the collision incident, students in more than 50 mainland Chinese universities in nine cities—including Beijing, Shanghai, Nanjing, Guangzhou—asked to protest, but the CCP authorities issued a circular calling on them not to hold large-scale marches. Many students at military universities also made the same request, but the Central Military Commission told them that 'teachers and students may gather and discuss on campus, but not hold large-scale demonstrations in public.'"[212]

Diplomatic Intent: Signaling Reassurance

Both the cost of repression and the risk of allowing protests were somewhat less in 2001 than in 1999, suggesting that the government's optimal domestic response to anti-American mobilization after the EP-3 collision was again not obvious. The diplomatic context favored reassurance, however, tipping the scales toward repression. Although both the embassy bombing and plane collision were deemed serious tests of China's response to sudden crises, three features of the diplomatic context in 2001 gave China's leaders greater incentive to demonstrate reassurance than resolve.

First, China's overall diplomacy toward the United States was focused more on smoothing relations with the new Bush administration than on demonstrating that China could not be pushed around. In 2001, China faced a surplus rather than a deficit of perceived resolve vis-à-vis the United States. On the campaign trail, George W. Bush had criticized Clinton for being too soft on Beijing, calling China a "strategic competitor." With the Cold War over and the attacks of September 11 still to come, Beijing feared that the new administration might cast China as America's next enemy, particularly given hawks like Dick Cheney and Donald Rumsfeld in Bush's cabinet.

Less than two weeks before the midair collision, Vice Premier Qian Qichen went to Washington to "give Bush and his new team a correct understanding of U.S.-China relations, to institute a positive and pragmatic China policy in order to benefit the healthy and stable development of relations between the two countries," according to Tang Jiaxuan.[213] Qian's visit was hailed positively. As former ambassador Wu Jianmin notes, "The visit was successful. Afterward, the U.S. side replaced the aggressive formulation 'strategic competitor' with 'not strategic partners, but not irreconcilable enemies.'"[214] President Bush told Qian: "I am going to look you in the eye and tell you we can have good relations with China."[215] Qian's visit led to cautious optimism that U.S.-China relations might weather the new Bush administration. "People [thought] for a time that the Bush administration would make a great change in U.S. policy toward China and that Sino-U.S. relations would retrogress," wrote a professor at the Central Party School. With Qian's visit, however, "the relations between the two countries finally continued to move forward."[216]

When the midair collision occurred, Chinese officials emphasized the importance of protecting this fragile warming of relations. Allowing anti-American protests would have antagonized the Bush administration at a time when the Chinese government was more interested in establishing a positive footing. As a senior Chinese expert on U.S.-China relations noted:

> In contrast with the embassy bombing, the midair collision occurred shortly after Bush had taken office. Qian Qichen had visited the United States and things were going all right. China's leaders didn't want the airplane collision to derail U.S.-China relations. They wanted to let a little

frustration out, but they didn't want the incident to escalate and affect the broader relationship.[217]

Faced with popular anger, the Chinese government repressed public displays of outrage in the form of street protests. According to a PLA colonel, "If the university authorities hadn't stopped the students from taking to the streets, there would have been demonstrations everywhere."[218] As another Chinese analyst recalled:

> Before the EP-3 incident, Sino- U.S. relations were improving. In March 2001, Qian Qichen, as special representative of Jiang Zemin, visited DC and met with Bush, Cheney, Powell. He was quite pleased by how he was received. When the collision occurred, there were no demonstrations because students don't have that kind of freedom. To protest, to march— all that requires approval. I think that the school authorities coordinated with the central government. Anti-American protests would have put too much pressure on the government and made it hard for the government to make decisions.[219]

Officials were tempted during the first several days of the crisis to hold large public rallies and take a dramatic public position, but "Jiang was clear from the beginning about not doing anything to negatively impact the long-term relationship with the U.S.," according to a senior Chinese foreign policy advisor.[220] China's leaders sought to walk a fine line: to resolve the crisis on terms that would be domestically palatable once the incident became public without jeopardizing the fragile rapport they had begun building with the Bush administration.

Second, the nature of the incident made it less imperative for the government to show resolve. Even though China publicly blamed the United States for causing the collision, Chinese analysts were less convinced that the incident was meant to test China's mettle. In the immediate aftermath of the crisis, Chinese military officials informed the civilian leadership that the U.S. plane had suddenly veered into the Chinese fighter jet, perhaps to deflect responsibility for the Chinese pilot's actions and the increasingly dangerous pattern of interference the air force had been conducting around American surveillance flights. This version of events became the official Chinese position.[221] After Ambassador Prueher and others American officials refuted this version of events as technically impossible, however, "the Chinese side no longer focused on the collision's cause once the negotiation started, raising a question about the accuracy of the information provided by the PLA," according to Wu Xinbo.[222]

Within China's foreign policy community, more were willing to believe that the midair collision was unintentional.[223] "The majority of international relations scholars believed that the air collision was an accident, not the U.S. fault like 1999," one analyst recalled. "A minority of scholars even criticized the pilot, Wang Wei, for perhaps even causing the accident."[224] The top leadership ultimately concluded that the incident was a byproduct of a sustained pattern of U.S. surveillance rather than an intentional effort to test China's resolve.[225] As Wu notes: "After receiving initial reports on the incident, the Chinese leaders came to a two-point conclusion: first, this was an accident, not a deliberate action (unlike the embassy bombing in 1999); second, the issue should be resolved as soon as possible."[226]

Third, the detention of the EP-3 crew and tough public statements by the U.S. side raised the salience of the crisis among the American public, creating audience costs on the American side that China feared might force the Bush administration to escalate further. The day after the U.S. Pacific Command released a statement about the incident, Ambassador Prueher publicly warned that the crisis could negatively affect U.S.-China relations, telling reporters: "The downside potential, if we do not resolve this well, is fairly high because it can bleed over into some other areas."[227] *Bush's public stance also toughened as the crisis wore on. On April 3, Bush's rhetoric escalated as he stated from the Rose Garden*: "This accident has the potential of undermining our hopes for a fruitful and productive relationship between our two countries. To keep that from happening, our servicemen and women need to come home."[228] On April 4, members of Congress introduced legislation to revoke China's permanent normal trading relations with the United States, stating that China had "failed to promptly release the 24 United States military personnel."[229]

Chinese observers were keenly aware of the domestic anger that the Bush administration had aroused by publicizing the incident and using tough rhetoric. As Zhang Tuosheng notes, "The U.S. military unilaterally made the event public, and President George W. Bush soon spoke publicly about it, making it impossible to find a solution through quiet diplomacy. . . thereby exerting tremendous domestic pressure on the decision-making process of both governments."[230] One Chinese expert blamed the U.S. media for stirring up public anger by accusing China of treating the U.S. crew "inhumanely," which in turn "spurred the Bush administration to pursue a tough policy regarding the incident."[231] Li Xiguang accused the U.S. government, military, and media of "invok[ing] what would most command the attention of the U.S. public: a threat to the safety of Americans" by "focusing the public's attention on the 'aggressive pilot'" and Chinese attempts to steal technology from the surveillance plane.[232] According to Li, Bush's strong stance and decision to dispatch three warships to the waters near Hainan were intended "to show the U.S. electorate that he was an unquestionably competent and strong leader (given errors in the counting of votes, many Americans believed he became president by chance, and had no international experience)."[233]

Chinese officials appeared particularly concerned about growing outrage among the American public, whose concern about the fate of the detained American crew could force the Bush administration to label the situation a hostage crisis if the situation were not resolved quickly. *As Tang Jiaxuan recounts: "According to reports from our embassy in the United States, during that time we received many threatening*

phone calls. Some people even staged protests outside our consulates and embassy. . . .
Our diplomats were waylaid by some people almost hysterically shouting, 'Why don't
you let our people return home?'"[234] In hindsight, some analysts have suggested that
the Chinese side would have been better positioned to negotiate more favorable terms had
it not detained the crew, which only served to arouse American fury. As Wu Xinbo writes:
"since China did not intend to keep the twenty-four U.S. crew members as hostages,
it would have been more helpful to release them early. . . . With the release of the
crew, the U.S. reactions, especially from the public, might have been less intense
and the sense of crisis less strong."[235] With American emotions running high, Bush
toughening his public stance, and internal doubts about the cause of the collision
growing, the Chinese leadership concluded that it was more important to resolve
the crisis quickly than to maintain an unyielding stance.

Fearing that the crisis would escalate if they continued to hold the aircrew, the
Chinese leadership quickly determined that they would release the crew as soon
as the United States apologized. As former ambassador Wu Jianmin writes, "The
central authorities set forth on April 2 the policy of separating crew and plane (*renji
fenli*), mainly because: first, if the 24 Americans were detained in China for too long,
it would arouse strong feelings among the U.S. public; and second, Easter holiday
was approaching, an important holiday in the United States, and if by that time the
U.S. crew were unable to join their families, it would create public animosity toward
China and harm our diplomatic efforts."[236] The importance that Chinese officials
placed on American public opinion is evident in their discussion of Ambassador
Yang Jiechi's interview on CNN. Both Tang Jiaxuan and Wu Jianmin credit this
interview with assuaging U.S. anger and making a diplomatic compromise acceptable to the American public. According to Wu Jianmin:

> Ambassador Yang Jiechi, in an interview with CNN, gave the following
> example: "Imagine that every day a person drives up and uses a telescope
> to 'survey' your house. One day a member of your family drives out of the
> garage and collides with that other person, damaging the vehicle and kill-
> ing your family member, while the other person is mostly unharmed. How
> would you feel then? Is it any wonder that the other person should apol-
> ogize to your family?" In this way, American emotions, which had been
> quite agitated, gradually calmed down.[237]

Tang Jiaxuan continues: "The broadcast interview had a positive impact on U.S. public opinion. According to media reports, following Ambassador Yang's CNN interview, the proportion of Americans in favor of its government apologizing to China
grew by a large margin, from less than 20 percent to above 50 percent."[238]

Yet American officials remained leery of appearing to make public concessions
that could give the impression that the United States had given in to Chinese "bullying." American sensitivity to domestic audience costs was apparent in warnings

to the Chinese government that the handover and signing of the Prueher letter on April 11 must be conducted quietly. If Chinese media were present, U.S. negotiators warned, Ambassador Prueher would leave without giving Tang Jiaxuan the letter or even taking a seat.[239] Although some analysts have suggested that Bush's public statements "put President Jiang 'in a box' that made quick resolution impossible," John Keefe points out that China's initial demands preceded all U.S. remarks except the initial PACOM press release.[240] Had the Pacific Command not issued a public release, perhaps the two sides might have privately resolved the incident without prompting Chinese demands for an apology. Once the incident became public, however, tough U.S. statements and the resulting public outcry impressed upon China the need to resolve the situation quickly.

After the crew's release, the United States conceded on the manner of the aircraft's return, while China compromised on the issue of U.S. surveillance. Although Chinese officials had initially sought to negotiate the reduction or termination of U.S. reconnaissance flights near China, American officials countered that U.S. surveillance flights took place over international waters. Deputy Secretary of State Richard Armitage on April 13 stated on a television program that the United States, along with China, had a right to fly in international airspace and that "six other countries in Asia, including the Chinese, fly reconnaissance flights in international airspace."[241] On May 7, U.S. reconnaissance flights near China resumed. In retaliation, the Chinese side informed the United States that the EP-3 would not be allowed to fly out of China, since "to let the U.S. plane fly home would hurt China's national dignity. . . and the Chinese people would never agree," as one Chinese scholar put it.[242] With American audiences no longer captivated by the plight of the EP-3 crew, the Chinese government determined that it would be safe to stand firm on the manner of the plane's return.[243] On May 17, the American side proposed to disassemble the plane and return it in parts via a commercial plane, and on May 28, Assistant Foreign Minister Zhou Wenzhong agreed to let the dismantled EP-3 return to the United States via a Russian cargo plane.[244]

Diplomatic Consequences

By preventing anti-American protests and restraining domestic media coverage, the Chinese government sent a costly signal of reassurance and made it easier for both sides to show diplomatic flexibility. Chinese officials made clear that the crew would not be released without some form of apology, but the Chinese side ultimately accepted terms that fell far short of its original demands. In the initial aftermath of the collision, Chinese officials demanded that the United States bear full responsibility for the incident and stop reconnaissance flights along China's coast and territorial airspace.[245] As U.S. officials toughened their stance and China became concerned about rising anger in the United States, China reduced its demands to an apology, and even then Chinese negotiators settled for "very sorry." As former ambassador Wu Jianmin notes: "on the wording of the U.S. apology, China had originally demanded *daoqian*, which in English is 'apologize.' But ultimately both sides accepted the word "sorry," or *baoqian*. Given the diplomatic deadlock, with both sides looking for a way out, putting forward a mutually acceptable proposal was wise."[246]

Had China allowed anti-American demonstrations, the Chinese government would have been hard-pressed to compromise on the terms of the crew's release. As Wu Xinbo notes:

> China demonstrated flexibility over the conditions for release of the crew. . . . After it became clear that insistence on those conditions would not lead to an early solution, Beijing reduced its demand to one item: an apology. Then, as the negotiations revealed that the Bush administration had no intention of using the word "apology," Beijing accepted the wording of "very sorry.". . . Such efforts [to repress protests] helped to avoid escalation of the crisis and allowed the negotiations to be conducted in a relatively calm atmosphere.[247]

After President Bush echoed the regrets expressed by Powell but refrained from making a stronger apology, saying: "I regret that a Chinese pilot is missing, and I regret one of their airplanes is lost,"[248] the Chinese media publicized Bush's words of regret "with unusual speed," portraying his statement as a softening in the U.S. stance.[249] President Jiang told reporters in Chile that "when people have an accident, the two groups involved always say 'excuse me.'"[250] This was translated by the Chinese media as *duibuqi*, a more colloquial and ambiguous form of regret than *daoqian*—the more weighty term that the Chinese government had initially insisted upon.[251]

Repressing protests also sent a credible signal of reassurance, which was received by the U.S. side. Western media reported that Chinese police had taken away several protesters attempting to put up anti-American posters in front of the U.S. embassy on April 4 and 5. While demonstrations took place in Hong Kong, mainland Chinese were prevented from staging demonstrations against the United States.[252] According to Dennis Blair (then PACOM chief) and David Bonfili:

> For the first time, it appeared that China was more interested in solving the problem than it was in holding to its version of the collision and attempting to extract an admission of responsibility from the United States. . . . It seemed unlikely to the U.S. side that China intended to drag out the issue long enough to create the perception of a hostage crisis. At the same time, however, there was no initiative coming from the Chinese side. The demand for an apology seemed to be the only Chinese position.[253]

Along with President Jiang Zemin's decision to depart for Latin America as scheduled, the repression of protests reassured the United States that China was amenable to compromise. The moderation of China's stance became apparent to American officials apparent when Ambassador Prueher met with Assistant Foreign Minister Zhou the following morning, on April 5. According to Blair and Bonfili, "It became clear to the U.S. side that an arrangement could be negotiated that would end the impasse."[254]

One of the most striking aspects of the EP-3 crisis is that American officials appreciated the pressure of popular nationalism on the Chinese government in the absence of street demonstrations. U.S. officials understood the difficult position the Chinese leadership was in and credited the government's efforts to rein in public anger. As John Keefe, special assistant to Ambassador Prueher at the time of the EP-3 crisis, recounted:

> We also saw a Chinese government acutely sensitive to public opinion about this incident. The Chinese government repeatedly expressed to us the pressure that the Chinese public was bringing to bear. . . . University students wanted to hold demonstrations to vent their anger. The government forbade them from taking such action [and] repeatedly stressed. . . that this event should not be seen as a major affair in U.S.-China relations.[255]

During the crisis, China conveyed the pressure of public anger without aggravating the situation by allowing physical protests. Although the Chinese media remained relatively muted, many stories lauded the heroism of the martyred pilot. Xinhua opened an online memorial for netizens to leave messages for the pilot's widow and child.[256] In his first meeting with Ambassador Prueher, Assistant Foreign Minister Zhou Wenzhong invoked the anger of the Chinese public, saying: "The Chinese people demand that the United States explain: Why did the U.S. military plane come so close to China? Why did the U.S. plane make a sudden turn, crashing into the Chinese plane?"[257] Foreign Minister Tang Jiaxuan told Ambassador Prueher that China opposed American demands and was unafraid, saying: "The facts over many years have shown that the more pressure that the United States applies, the more you arouse the anger of the Chinese people."[258]

What gave credibility to these remarks was not only China's actions during the crisis, such as hauling off would-be protesters and facilitating online expressions of popular anger, but also the impression left by the embassy bombing protests. Had the 1999 demonstrations appeared wholly manufactured, U.S. officials should have been more dismissive of Chinese efforts to restrain protests in 2001. Instead, American officials recognized that the Chinese government was partially responsible for fanning the flames of nationalist sentiment. Yet those flames were still difficult for the government to tamp down without getting burned.[259] As Bush's national security advisor, Condoleezza Rice, recounted:

The Chinese pilot who'd rammed our plane had been killed in the incident, making him an instant hero in the Chinese press. The Chinese wanted us to apologize for his death, something that we were unwilling to do—particularly once we learned that his hot-dogging had been a prime cause of the accident. But it became a matter of national pride in China. Time and time again we would see this. China would stir up nationalist sentiment in the population through the state-controlled media, diminishing its own room for maneuver as it reacted to the very passions it had created. . . . The crux of the matter was to find a face-saving way out for the Chinese. We could not apologize for what was not our fault. But after several days, the Chinese sent a signal: if Colin would send a letter that said that we were sorry for the loss their pilot's life, we could end the crisis.[260]

As in 1999, U.S. officials understood that popular anger was partly a function of China's propaganda choices. Yet they also appreciated that the Chinese authorities, having nourished popular anger, were also trying "very hard" to keep it leashed. As a former senior U.S. intelligence analyst recalled:

It was never clear that the Chinese government at the highest levels wanted that [EP-3] incident to occur. . . . There was a lot of nervousness on the Chinese side about what direction the administration was going. They knew that Powell was inclined toward a more positive relationship with China, but they knew clearly that Cheney and Rumsfeld and some of the Vulcans[261] had a different view on China. So when the incident occurred, I think they had to be worried that if [their response] were to become overly nationalistic, with students in the streets, it might have shifted the debate within the administration. . . . Recognizing that there was some danger to the nascent relationship with the new Bush administration, they worked very hard to keep that nationalism in check. They orchestrated in 2001 an extremely successful PR campaign [to] mourn the Chinese pilot without bringing people to the streets. . . to allow an outlet for public sentiment without making it overtly anti-American.[262]

The visible curtailment of protests signaled that the Chinese government was willing to spend domestic political capital to defuse the crisis. U.S. officials interpreted China's restraint as evidence of a sincere interest in maintaining stable relations and avoiding conflict with the new Bush administration.

By stifling protests, China also made it easier for the U.S. side to compromise, giving U.S. officials space to use the phrase "very sorry" and refrain from labeling the situation a hostage crisis. According to a senior administration official, "Throughout the week we conditioned the American public for what this would ultimately look like," starting first with Powell's statement of "regret," which

President Bush then repeated, followed by "sorry" and finally "very sorry."[263] China's restraint may have also strengthened the hand of U.S. officials who favored a temperate approach. As Nicholas Lardy noted: "There was some tension—there's no doubt. This is a victory for Secretary Powell and a more realistic, less ideological approach towards dealing with China."[264] One American conservative, Gary Schmitt, complained that "it was only the secretary of state and a few select friends of China who were able to deliberate within the administration, and everybody else was told to shut up."[265]

Although the crisis strained relations, the counterfactual would have been worse. As Zhang notes: "The Sino-American relationship might have suffered more if the two governments had not focused on the overall well-being of their relationship and relatively quickly settled the crisis."[266] Had China allowed anti-American protests while holding the EP-3 crew and plane, both sides would have had more difficulty reaching the face-saving compromise embodied by the "two sorrys" of the Prueher letter. Even without anti-American demonstrations, the Bush administration faced domestic criticism for expressing sorrow and regret over a collision that was seen in the United States as unambiguously the Chinese pilot's fault.[267] Two conservatives called the episode a "profound national humiliation" and warned that "American capitulation will also embolden others around the world." [268] On the Chinese side, with street demonstrations the government would have been hard-pressed to maintain a flexible position, resist calls to prosecute the U.S. crew, and accept the phrase "sorry" in lieu of a formal apology.

Conclusion

China's management of anti-American protests in 1999 and 2001 demonstrates that the government has played a central and deliberate role in shaping the extent to which nationalist sentiment and public opinion constrain its diplomatic options. During the EP-3 crisis, Chinese authorities kept popular mobilization in check, concerned that anti-American demonstrations would put too much pressure on the government's stance toward the United States. During the embassy bombing crisis, in contrast, the government allowed and then facilitated popular protests, seeking to demonstrate resolve in the face of American "bullying" while also mitigating the risk that protests strayed off-message.

This account acknowledges both the genuine, grassroots nature of popular anger[269] as well as the role of state-led, top-down direction.[270] Both elements are critical to evaluating the diplomatic impact of antiforeign protests, not only when demonstrations erupt but also when they are repressed. Indeed, the strength and credibility of the government's signals depends on the visibility and sincerity of grassroots anger and attempts to mobilize nationalist demonstrations. As the embassy bombing protests appeared more and more choreographed, foreign credulity diminished. Yet the credibility of popular nationalism was sufficient to earn the government credit for restraining anti-American demonstrations two years later.

The 1999 protests also reminded U.S. observers of the domestic costs of compromise facing China's moderate elites, who had already been weakened by Clinton's unexpected refusal to accept Zhu Rongji's concessions on the WTO.[271] The protests made clear that the embassy bombing had further undermined the position of Chinese moderates who favored closer ties with the United States, making the government's tough stance in the wake of the embassy bombing more understandable in light of hawkish domestic pressures.[272] As Douglas Paal noted:

> Jiang Zemin and Zhu Rongji, especially, have leaned toward keeping the U.S. relationship open. . . . They've had a series of embarrassments over the last couple of months in handling the U.S., and they're trying to keep themselves from being swamped by the opposition in China who says get a tougher line on the U.S.. So, they're putting up a tough front now—I think—to buy themselves some maneuvering room.[273]

Although protests helped convey the pressure on China's moderate leaders, there is little evidence that hawkish or conservative elites fomented demonstrations without the top leadership's consent in 1999. Even though there is widespread agreement that the embassy bombing prompted internal criticism of Jiang Zemin as too pro-American, leaked documents do not suggest that bureaucratic or factional elements facilitated protests to press Jiang to take a tougher stance.[274] We cannot rule out this possibility, but a simpler explanation is that Jiang allowed protests to show both domestic and international audiences that he could be tough on the United States.

Moreover, the lack of elite cohesion during the EP-3 crisis did not result in anti-American demonstrations. Some U.S. observers have noted that Chinese military officials tried to deflect blame for the collision by claiming that the EP-3 plane was responsible.[275] If the military provided civilian leaders with misinformation, this may explain the discrepancy between China's initial escalation of the crisis and its later decision to resolve the crisis swiftly, once the technical impossibility of a "sudden turn" by the U.S. aircraft became clear. But the civil-military gap did not appear to influence the decision to repress—not allow—protests, despite incentives that PLA officers might have had to encourage protests, perhaps to avoid reprimand from the top leadership.

Finally, the government's management of anti-American sentiment in 1999 and 2001 cannot be captured by simply characterizing nationalist protests as a "safety valve" for domestic grievances. Not only does the analogy downplay the sincerity of grassroots anger at the United States, it also neglects important features of the government's motivations, particularly the danger that protests might get out of hand rather than "safely" regulate domestic pressures. Those who argue that the 1999 protests diverted attention from the Tiananmen anniversary also emphasize the risk to social stability.[276] Moreover, many who participated in the embassy bombing protests became more disillusioned with the Chinese government, not less—angered by the government's curtailment and manipulation of the protests rather than pleased to have vented their frustrations.[277]

Such anecdotes suggest that the domestic benefits of nationalist protest are far from assured, even if the diplomatic outcome is favorable. In 1999, the government helped ameliorate public anger by pointing to U.S. apologies, halting negotiations on the WTO and other issues, and promising an investigation into the bombing. Had the United States been unwilling to make such extensive efforts to pacify Chinese anger and taken a tougher stance—publicly chiding China for supporting Milosevic or giving China an ultimatum on the WTO rather than allowing talks to be postponed—China might have had to soften its stance, absorbing the diplomatic humiliation in order to move forward with other priorities. In this counterfactual, protests would have been domestically damaging rather than beneficial. During the EP-3 crisis, moreover, the Chinese government's desire to defuse the crisis amid fears of U.S. escalation meant that anti-American protests would likely have backfired as a tactic to strengthen the government's nationalist credentials. While nationalist protests are often characterized as a convenient tactic to divert domestic attention, these episodes illustrate that their domestic benefits are also dependent on the diplomatic outcome, meaning that protests will not always be allowed whenever domestic grievances are running high.

4

The 1985 Anti-Japan Protests and Sino-Japanese Relations in the 1980s

On August 15, 1985, Japanese prime minister Yasuhiro Nakasone broke precedent and paid an official visit to Yasukuni Shrine, which commemorates the spirits of 2.5 million war dead and 14 A-class war criminals, including Hideki Tojo. The date marked the fortieth anniversary of Japan's defeat in World War II and the most sensitive day for a Japanese head of state to visit the shrine. On September 18, to mark the anniversary of Japan's invasion of Manchuria, a thousand university students in Beijing marched to Tiananmen Square. Disregarding instructions to stay on campus, the students laid wreaths at the square and denounced Japan's "economic invasion" of China. Over the next several weeks, demonstrations spread to other cities across China, emboldened by the government's tolerant attitude. Protesters began to criticize the government directly, blaming the nation's ills on elite corruption and lucrative deals to secure Japanese economic assistance and investment.

The anti-Japanese protests helped convince Nakasone that his actions were undermining China's policy of international engagement and economic reform. Giving in to Chinese pressure, Nakasone canceled his plans to visit Yasukuni during the autumn festival. Despite Nakasone's concessions, the Chinese government faced difficulty curtailing the protests, which helped seed the ground for pro-democracy protests the following year, setting the stage for the crisis in 1989, the greatest upheaval that the Communist Party has faced in the post-Mao era.

The 1985 anti-Japanese protests illustrate that foreign governments often have incentives to make concessions to embattled moderates, particularly when confronted with the specter of antiforeign mobilization. Nakasone pledged to give up visiting the shrine altogether, hoping to help his friend and reform-minded counterpart, Hu Yaobang. Nakasone's efforts did not save Hu Yaobang, who was purged in the aftermath of the 1986 pro-democracy protests. But it would be 11 years before another Japanese prime minister visited Yasukuni Shrine.

To explain why the Chinese government adopted such a lenient attitude toward anti-Japanese protests in 1985, I first examine the domestic dilemma the government faced in responding to calls for anti-Japanese protest. I then assess the diplomatic context and China's desire to show resolve against Nakasone's efforts to alter the status quo. To evaluate the diplomatic impact of the protests, I turn to Japanese perceptions of the protests and Nakasone's motivations in conceding to Chinese pressure.

Student Mobilization and Government Response

The anti-Japanese protests reflected growing popular resentment against Japan and rising frustration with economic conditions. By 1985, China's trade deficit with Japan had reached $5 billion. A flood of Japanese goods led to accusations that Japan was launching a "second invasion" of China.[1] Anti-Japanese sentiment was further fed by special ceremonies to commemorate the fortieth anniversary of World War II's end and a barrage of media coverage, including a popular television series that dramatically portrayed one family's sufferings during the Japanese invasion and occupation.[2] Author Liu Xinwu noted

> the mass anti-foreign sentiment that had been welling up in the capital for years as rich foreign investors, especially other Asians, flooded into the city and vaunted their superior material lifestyles. . . as well as of the general disquiet people felt towards a government that seemed to be pandering to foreign interests, in particular Japan.[3]

Grievances over living conditions and inflation were also running high. In 1983, there were 36 incidents of campus unrest across the country.[4] In December 1984, over a thousand students demonstrated at Beijing University to protest a lights-out policy to save electricity.[5] In January 1985, students at two campuses in Beijing threatened to strike over high recreation fees, poor food, and shoddy medical care.[6] According to Beijing University Professor Kong Qingdong: "Everyone knows that the 1980s generation of university students, especially those at Beijing University, were pretty crazy. . . they felt that responsibility for the nation rested on their shoulders. Having such high expectations, they often raised a ruckus."[7] In May 1985, concerned about the overheating economy, the government implemented a new round of price reforms, further raising the price of meat and other food stuffs.

After Nakasone's visit to Yasukuni Shrine, these commingled grievances produced calls for anti-Japanese protests to commemorate September 18, the anniversary of Japan's invasion of Manchuria. On September 13, big-character posters appeared at Beijing University calling on students to take action and admonishing them for only being brave enough to protest the school's lights-out policy.[8] Although university authorities took down the big-character posters, which had been banned since the tightening of political freedoms in 1979 and 1980,[9] a new poster appeared the next day, calling the university's actions "traitorous" and suggesting that students hold a demonstration in Tiananmen Square on September 18. A flurry of posters followed, debating how to commemorate the anniversary.

Concerned that protests could get out of control yet also reluctant to suppress student patriotism, the government attempted to appease students with official campus commemorations. Citing "obvious extremist tendencies" among students and a set of important Party meetings from September 16 to 23, the Party leadership instructed university authorities to put a stop to the big-character posters and prevent a demonstration in Tiananmen Square.[10] On September 16, the student unions announced that a campus assembly would take place on September 18. At the ceremony, students would have the opportunity to make speeches, and the student unions would present a proposal to the National People's Congress to designate September 18 a "Day of National Humiliation" along with a letter from the students of Beijing University to Japanese prime minister Nakasone.

Despite these attempts to co-opt and contain student mobilization, new posters continued to appear. One read, "Commemorate the martyrs, overthrow the corrupt cadres, strengthen the nation scientifically, and respect knowledge."[11] Another attacked the student unions for being puppets of the university administration and called the campus assembly "an offer of 'amnesty to rebels'—an attempt to lock our fervor within the small confines of campus and let it run its course." A third poster called for students to gather at Tiananmen Square, proclaiming: "This is our civil right and freedom!" Others condemned the "pro-Japanese faction" in the government and called for students to take action and "sweep away the traitorous running dogs who are selling out our country."[12]

The day before the anniversary, Beijing University president Ding Shisun urged an assembly of 2,000 student cadres to refrain from extreme behavior for the sake of social stability and the approaching Party conferences. Students continued to mobilize, however, with posters appearing on nearby campuses and students making phone calls to rally support from universities in other cities, including Shanghai, Nanjing, and Hefei. On September 18, a large group of students assembled in front of the Beijing University library. When the students attempted to set forth, the university locked the campus gate, separating the students from a crowd gathered just outside. A few students continued to give speeches, accusing the school authorities of acting unconstitutionally by closing the gate and violating their freedom of speech, protest, and assembly. Ding Shisun told students via loudspeaker that the authorities had forbidden any off-campus commemorative activities, and that this decision had been approved by the central and city Party authorities. He urged students to attend the official campus commemoration, warning students to "guard against a small minority of bad people who would take advantage of your patriotism with serious consequences."[13] Meanwhile, several hundred students who had managed to leave campus gathered at Tiananmen Square and refused to leave when security guards told them that a demonstration without government approval was not allowed. After consulting with higher-level city authorities, the security guards allowed the students to march around the square, laying wreaths at the Monument to the People's Heroes before dispersing peacefully.[14]

The government's acquiescence reflected a light hand in comparison with previous incidents. Only a few months before, in May, a soccer riot broke out in Beijing after a match between China and Hong Kong. During the mayhem, the rioters harassed foreigners and shouted antiforeign slogans.[15] According to one Chinese scholar, "What was most remarkable about the riot was that it escaped government control and to a certain extent went against the established order, taking on a fierce and potentially adversarial form."[16] The next day, the city government moved quickly, declaring that the perpetrators would be severely punished and condemning the riot as the gravest incident to take place during a sporting event since the nation's founding in 1949. Nine days later, the national Chinese soccer team was suspended temporarily.

By contrast, authorities sent relatively lenient signals to anti-Japanese protesters in the fall of 1985. Rather than threaten punishment, the government sent top-level officials to university campuses to persuade students through "dialogue" to redirect their patriotism into more productive channels.[17] Government officials appeared to sympathize and defend the sentiments expressed by the student demonstrators. The day after the September 18 protest, the Foreign Ministry spokesman stated that "the Japanese side did not heed our friendly warnings and insisted on paying a formal visit to Yasukuni Shrine, severely hurting the feelings of the Chinese people."[18] On September 28, two high-level officials, Hu Qili and Li Peng, met with students in the leadership compound at Zhongnanhai and "praised the basic motivation behind the demonstration as patriotic and consistent with university tradition."[19]

Between September 28 and October 2, more than one thousand university students participated in anti-Japanese demonstrations in Xi'an, denouncing Nakasone and protesting Japanese imports.[20] Similar protests were reported in other cities across the country, including Kunming and Wuhan. Students from Beijing were active in distributing flyers to other universities, even visiting campuses in other cities to encourage demonstrations.[21] Meanwhile, big-character posters at Beijing University called for a "return to democracy," railing at the university for its dictatorial behavior on September 18. One poster read, "Should the crashing waves of our blood be chilled and frozen, what will we have gotten from all this? Just police and refrigerators!"[22] Another poster said: "In the battle between democracy and dictatorship at Peking University, dictatorship has won. But this is not yet the end. It is now time to hold a burial service for dictatorship."[23]

Although university authorities removed the posters and a former ambassador to Japan was sent to Xi'an to speak with students about self-restraint,[24] the government adopted a relatively lenient attitude toward the protests. Given early indications that the protesters might challenge the government not only for being weak against Japan but also over corruption and the right to demonstrate, why did the government not act more decisively to curtail student mobilization? While calls for protest nominally targeted Japan, the big-character posters also signaled rising anger at campus authorities and corrupt officials for "selling out the nation," suggesting the risk that protests would turn against the regime was not negligible. On the one hand, repressing student protests would hurt the government's nationalist credentials and open the government to accusations of hypocrisy. On the other hand, lenience could be read as a sign of weakness vis-à-vis student mobilization, inviting further transgressions. Yongshun Cai aptly describes the danger of responding tepidly to protests: "The state's failure to demonstrate its actual power or credible threats may trigger regime-threatening actions."[25] Indeed, the government's mixed signals toward anti-Japanese mobilization in the fall of 1985 would feed into pro-democratic mobilization in 1986, as detailed in the concluding section of this chapter. These competing concerns suggest that it was not obvious based on domestic factors alone whether tolerance or repression was the wiser response to anti-Japanese mobilization. How did diplomatic factors weigh upon this dilemma and affect the government's response?

The Diplomatic Context

By ignoring Chinese concerns and visiting Yasukuni Shrine in an official capacity on the sensitive anniversary of August 15, Nakasone challenged the status quo on more than the issue of Yasukuni. The symbolism and stated intentions surrounding Nakasone's visit threatened to upend the pattern of Sino-Japanese relations since 1972, characterized by mutual compromise on territorial and geostrategic issues and Japanese deference to Chinese demands on historical issues and economic assistance. Under Prime Ministers Tanaka, Miki, Fukuda, and Suzuki, Japan had accommodated Chinese desires to include an "anti-hegemony" clause and set aside the territorial issue during normalization and treaty negotiations. Moreover, previous Japanese leaders had bowed to Chinese demands after the cancellation of contracts and textbook revisions in 1981 and 1982. Chinese observers saw Nakasone's actions as upsetting this pattern of compromise and conciliation.

Mutual Compromise over Territorial and Geostrategic Issues

During negotiations over the normalization of relations in 1972 and a Treaty of Peace and Friendship in 1978, both sides had shown a willingness to compromise, at least tacitly, on territorial and security issues. China and Japan had normalized relations amid growing concerns about Soviet activity in Asia and following the swift rapprochement between China and the United States.[26] Negotiations became heated over the issue of war reparations and whether to include an "anti-hegemony clause" committing both parties to countering Soviet influence.[27] Japan feared antagonizing Moscow and claimed that Chinese reparations had been forfeited in the 1952 treaty between Japan and the Republic of China.[28] Both sides ultimately compromised in the joint communiqué of September 29, 1972: China agreed to drop the phrase "right to claims against Japan," and Japan agreed to include the anti-hegemony clause along with the caveat that the normalization of Sino-Japanese relations was "not directed at any third country."[29]

The two governments compromised again when the territorial issue and anti-hegemony clause threatened to derail progress toward a peace treaty. As the Soviet Union pressured Japan to stop talks with China, the anti-hegemony clause became "the major sticking point" for Japan.[30] Japanese parliamentarians demanded that the treaty include Chinese recognition of Japanese sovereignty over the Senkaku (Diaoyu) islands, seen by some in China as setting a "price" on the anti-hegemony clause.[31] In protest, an armed flotilla of roughly 100 Chinese fishing boats sailed to the disputed area in April 1978. Although Chinese vice premier Geng Biao told a Japanese delegation, "I can assure our Japanese friends that we did not consciously or deliberately arrange this,"[32] many observers were unconvinced. Hong Kong's *Ming Pao* suggested that China's actions were likely meant to "put pressure on Japan."[33] One scholar speculated that "Beijing feared that failure to act in some way might have been taken as a tacit recognition of the Japanese claim to the islands."[34] Another suggested that "there is little doubt that the vessels were under formal PLA naval command or that they embarked with Politburo approval."[35]

Following this display, both sides effectively agreed to leave aside the territorial issue and move forward with the treaty negotiations. In May, Deng Xiaoping told reporters that "China believes that the issue will be easy to resolve in the future,"[36] and Prime Minister Takeo Fukuda persuaded his party to begin negotiations.[37] The Treaty of Peace and Friendship, signed on August 12, 1978, contained the anti-hegemony clause and the reassuring "third party" clause. In what would become known in China as the policy of "setting aside" or "shelving" disputes, the territorial issue was left out. During his October 1978 visit to Tokyo, Deng Xiaoping stated at a press conference that "we both agreed not to address this issue. . . . It does not matter if we shelve this issue even for 10 years."[38]

Japanese Economic Assistance and Deference on Historical Issues

With this foundation in place, in the late 1970s Japan began providing enormous economic assistance to China. Japanese businesses also rushed to invest, caught up in what many called a "China fever." When disputes arose over the cancellation of contracts and Japanese history textbooks, Japan accommodated Chinese demands. In 1979, after China suspended two dozen projects with Japanese firms, Prime Minister Masayoshi Ohira pledged the first round of Official Development

Assistance in the form of long-term, low-interest yen loans. According to former Foreign Ministry official Kazuhiko Togo,

> In order to overcome this shock and sustain economic relations between the two countries, the Japanese government decided to mobilize its powerful instrument of economic cooperation. The emerging trend in China towards a market-oriented, stable, and strong economy shown in the policy of "Reform and Opening" was in the interest of Japan, not only from an economic but also from a political point of view. A stable and rational China was in the interest of the security and prosperity of the entire Far East region.[39]

For Japan the loans served multiple purposes: securing Japanese access to raw materials and the Chinese market;[40] supporting China's nascent reform efforts following Mao's death and the end of the Cultural Revolution; and implicitly compensating for Japan's invasion during World War II, sometimes described as "disguised reparations."[41] According to one Japanese scholar, the loans sought "to bring China over to the West [and] help stabilize Sino-Japanese relations and strengthen China's alignment with the West through supporting the reform and liberalization policies of Deng Xiaoping."[42] As one Chinese scholar noted: "Although there were no direct connections between the controversies [that would erupt in the 1980s] and the loans, the Japanese used government loans as goodwill gestures to smooth over the friction and to promote better ties with the Chinese."[43]

Between 1980 and 1982, two controversies arose but were again resolved by Japanese concessions. The first was China's cancellation of a raft of foreign contracts, 60 percent of which were Japanese.[44] Faced with severe fiscal imbalances, China suspended or canceled Japanese contracts worth about 300 billion yen and halted construction of the Baoshan steel plant, a prominent symbol of Sino-Japanese economic cooperation.[45] Despite Japanese anger over "what it saw as China's lack of respect for international business customs,"[46] the Japanese government agreed to China's request for new yen loans to salvage the contracts, particularly the Baoshan project, and provide compensation for others. Allen Whiting attributes Japanese concessions to a combination of calculations about future trade and investment and "a genuine desire to help China develop. . . . Japanese officials asserted, 'We owe it to China. We must help after all the damage we did to them.'"[47] It was with this blend of concern and resignation that Japan "proved responsive to successive Chinese demands as fiscal crises repeatedly threatened key projects," advancing new loans to resolve the crisis and demonstrating to many observers that "the Japanese are, at times, inclined to uncritically accept and accommodate China's expressed preferences and economic requests."[48]

The second controversy arose when Japanese media reported that the Ministry of Education had softened the language used by Japanese history textbooks to describe Japan's actions in World War II, changing the word "invasion" (*shinryaku*) to "advance" (*shinshutsu*).[49] Although Japanese media later corrected their earlier reports, stating that no revisions had yet taken place and that these were only suggestions,[50] the issue had already provoked international outcry. After a few brief reports, beginning in late July the Chinese media unleashed a storm of criticism, detailing Japanese atrocities in lurid detail and warning of resurgent Japanese militarism.[51] *Renmin Ribao* ran 232 articles in two and a half months.[52] Yet China's recriminations were limited to the media and official protests lodged by the government. No street demonstrations took place in mainland China, while thousands of protesters staged anti-Japanese demonstrations in Hong Kong, Seoul, and New York.[53] Chinese officials warned the Japanese side "not to shirk responsibility" for the textbook revisions and "to take necessary measures to redress the Ministry of Education's error."[54] China informed Japan that it was "inappropriate" for Minister of Education Ogawa to visit under the circumstances and warned that Japanese prime minister Zenko Suzuki might have to cancel his upcoming visit to China to mark the tenth anniversary of normalized relations if the textbook issue was not settled first.[55]

Under pressure from Beijing, Seoul and liberal voices inside Japan, Prime Minister Suzuki conceded over the objections of Education Ministry officials and Diet members who decried interference in Japan's internal affairs. Suzuki promised to review the disputed textbooks and resolve the issue "in a manner suitable to China,"[56] declaring that "it is a fact that in China and around the world there is strong criticism and belief that Japan was an invader and it is necessary for our government to recognize that."[57] His cabinet issued a statement reaffirming Japan's "deep remorse" and stated that "from the perspective of building friendship and goodwill with neighboring countries, Japan will pay due attention to these criticisms and make corrections at the Government's responsibility."[58] These concessions facilitated Suzuki's successful visit to Beijing, where Deng Xiaoping reassured Suzuki of "the friendship between Chinese and Japanese people for generations to come."[59] In November, the Japanese Education Ministry issued a statement setting forth the "Asian neighbors clause," whereby Japan stated that "it would be a requirement that sufficient regard be given to international understanding and harmony when dealing with modern historical events that involve neighboring Asian countries."[60]

Nakasone, Yasukuni, and China's "Independent Foreign Policy"

Although Nakasone entered office with a hawkish record and reputation, it was not until 1985 that his actions threatened to overturn the pattern of accommodation in Japan's policy toward China. During his first years as prime minister, Nakasone developed a strong personal rapport with CCP General Secretary Hu Yaobang. Yet many in China harbored deep concerns about Nakasone as a nationalist who would take Japanese foreign policy in a more assertive direction. As Defense Agency director general in 1970 under the Sato administration, Nakasone was the first to release a white paper for defense. Described by one Japanese scholar as "exceptionally hawkish among postwar politicians with regard to security matters," Nakasone's "emphasis on autonomous defense and his demonstration of a strong interest in revising the basic defense policy of Japan brought Chinese criticism of Japanese 'militarism.'"[61] As chairman of the Liberal Democratic Party (LDP) executive council, Nakasone had attempted to stymie the peace treaty negotiations in 1978 by suggesting that the disputed islands should be included in the talks.[62]

As prime minister, Nakasone also improved Japan's relationship with the United States. The Suzuki government had taken a "half step backward" in its reluctance to meet Washington's requests,[63] leading one Chinese commentator to remark that "when Nakasone took office, postwar U.S.-Japan relations were 'at their lowest point.'"[64] After taking office, Nakasone and President Reagan established "close relations" and developed "the U.S.-Japan military alliance one step further," wrote one Chinese scholar.[65] Nakasone was delighted when his remarks were translated as describing Japan as an "unsinkable aircraft carrier" that could be used in an emergency to "completely control the four straits around it."[66] Although Nakasone's language sought to reassure Reagan of Japan's support in a contingency against the Soviet Union, some in Asia saw the Reagan administration tilting toward Japan under Nakasone and away from China.[67] When Nakasone sent a special envoy to China in February 1983, Chinese foreign minister Wu Xueqian warned that Japanese "armed forces should be defensive, of the appropriate size, and not constitute a threat to its friendly neighbors."[68]

Yet there were also signs that Nakasone could be counted on to adopt a friendly stance toward China. During his third visit to China in 1980, Nakasone had remarked that Japan would "as much as possible help China's modernization drive, which is in accordance with Japan's national interest."[69] In Washington, Nakasone had also declared his interest in the "further strengthening of friendly three-way ties among Japan, the United States, and China."[70] Two Chinese scholars pointed out that although Nakasone was the earliest leader in postwar Japan to advocate becoming a "great political power," Nakasone was also "the first Japanese prime minister to clearly recognize that Japan's war against China was a 'war of aggression.'"[71] During Hu Yaobang's visit to Japan in November 1983, relations "reached a new high"[72] when the two leaders agreed to add "mutual trust" as a fourth principle guiding Sino-Japanese relations. Hu reportedly "compared the PRC and Japan to rival heroes in a Chinese classic tale and stated: 'When they fought, both sides were weakened. But when they were united, they were invincible.'"[73] In March 1984 Nakasone paid a return visit to China and pledged over 470 billion yen in a second round of long-term loans and economic assistance.[74] Although Chinese leaders privately urged Japanese officials to speed up the pace of technology transfer and alleviate the trade deficit by giving China greater access to the Japanese market,[75] Japan's ambassador to China remarked that relations were "in the best condition ever."[76]

Beneath the glossy surface of high-level visits and exchanges, Chinese apprehensions about Nakasone's leadership were brewing. Historian Song Chengyou wrote that "since Ohira, each Japanese prime minister has more clearly revealed the objective of becoming a great power."[77] Suzuki had emphasized "Japan's ability, capacity, power and status" in 1981, and Nakasone in 1983 demanded a greater role for Japan's "right to speak" in world politics, not only as an "economic power" but also as a "political power."[78] Another Chinese analyst noted that "Nakasone has very strong nationalist traits," writing that Nakasone has "expressed dissatisfaction with U.S. control over Japan [and] has called for readjusting the U.S.-Japan relationship," including "an equal footing" with the United States and Soviet Union.[79]

During this period, China's strategic rationale for close ties with Japan was also diminishing. Beijing saw the Cold War balance of power tilting away from the Soviet Union, undermining the need to pursue a "united front" with Japan and the United States against the threat of Soviet hegemony in Asia.[80] Beginning in April and May 1982, Chinese pronouncements had reverted to criticizing both superpowers for creating international instability and endangering the Third World. In talks with Prime Minister Suzuki in May 1982, Premier Zhao Ziyang had placed "nearly equal blame" on the two superpowers.[81] The formal statement of this new orientation came in Hu Yaobang's report to the Twelfth Party Congress in September 1982. Observers at the time described these developments as "a major change of attitude in the framing of foreign policy"[82] and a signal of Beijing's desire to "highlight its own independence from both superpowers."[83] In late 1982, two Chinese Politburo members told visiting Japanese lawmakers that "China has never opposed nor supported the U.S.-Japan Security Treaty,"[84] contrasting with Deng Xiaoping's remark four years earlier that "strengthening Japan's defense capability and the U.S.-Japan Security Treaty is a natural course."[85] China also began reaching out to Moscow, initiating a "slow but steady process" of rapprochement.[86] China's new "independent" foreign policy would coincide with Nakasone's new "internationalist" policy, providing the strategic backdrop for the events of 1985.

It was over the issue of Nakasone's decision to pay an official visit to Yasukuni Shrine that these latent concerns erupted. Yasukuni had been the "most important shrine in the State Shinto religion, the chief ideology of militarist Japan."[87] After the war, it was placed in private hands so as not to violate the separation of state and religion set forth in Article 20 of the postwar Japanese constitution. Since then, conservative lawmakers—Nakasone among them—had unsuccessfully sought to reestablish state support for the shrine.[88] Most Japanese prime ministers before Nakasone had visited the shrine, but the norm of visiting in an unofficial capacity began in 1975 when Prime Minister Takeo Miki signed the guestbook without his official title and made an offering with his own money.[89] Following Miki's example, the next three prime ministers—Fukuda, Ohira, and Suzuki—visited Yasukuni in an unofficial capacity.[90] Nakasone began to challenge this norm, making three visits to Yasukuni in 1983 while declining to answer whether his visit was official. Whereas the Suzuki cabinet had stated that it "could not rule out doubts that paying homage [at Yasukuni] constituted a violation of the constitution,"[91] a private advisory council appointed by Nakasone concluded in August 1985 that official visits to Yasukuni did not violate the constitution. Nakasone told an LDP seminar that it was time that the "Japanese state and the Japanese race can walk proudly in the world."[92] As Ijiri notes, visiting Yasukuni was "part of a larger campaign by Nakasone to build a new national spirit"[93] and a symbol of Japan's return to normalcy, whereby the head of government is allowed to pay tribute to those who gave their lives for the nation.

On August 15, 1985, Nakasone and his cabinet ministers broke precedent in paying an official visit to Yasukuni Shrine on the fortieth anniversary of Japan's surrender in World War II. The day before the anniversary, a Chinese Foreign Ministry spokesman had warned that a visit by Nakasone to the shrine would "hurt the feelings" of people around the world who had suffered under militarism, especially in China and Asia.[94] Although Miki had also visited on this sensitive date in 1975, Nakasone was the first prime minister to do so since 14 A-class war criminals, including Prime Minister Hideki Tojo, had been enshrined at Yasukuni in 1978.

China's Reaction to Nakasone's Yasukuni Visit

It was against this diplomatic backdrop that the Chinese government responded tepidly to student-led anti-Japanese protests, with authorities refraining from punitive or coercive measures to forestall or repress protests. Unfortunately, we lack definitive evidence of the government's motivations and decision-making process that might enable us to discriminate among competing explanations for the government's tepid response to anti-Japanese mobilization. One interpretation is that government officials reasoned that tolerating protests would satisfy students while providing welcome diplomatic pressure on Nakasone. While Chinese leaders did not want to derail relations, they also perceived in Nakasone's actions a disregard for Chinese concerns and a troubling precedent for the future. As Xiong Dayun notes, Nakasone "crossed into one forbidden zone after another in postwar Japanese politics," seeking to "promulgate nationalism and 'rouse the national spirit.'"[95] Nakasone's official visit to Yasukuni contradicted the premise of postwar friendship between China and Japan, in which Chinese propaganda blamed Japanese militarism on a few bad elements who had brought catastrophe to the Chinese and Japanese peoples.

Even before students began calling for anti-Japanese protests, Chinese leaders sought to curb what they saw as a potentially dangerous trend in Japanese foreign policy. In the aftermath of Nakasone's visit, Chinese leaders emphasized the friendly basis of relations but also insisted that Japan stop taking actions that hurt the basis of this friendship. Although Whiting notes that China did not immediately lodge an official protest,[96] Rose points out that "China's dissatisfaction was made clear in subsequent meetings."[97] On August 21, a Xinhua editorial noted that this was "the first time since the end of the war" that the Japanese prime minister had paid an "official visit to the shrine" and accused Nakasone of trying "to obscure more or less the wicked nature of the war of aggression unleashed by the Japanese militarists,"[98] actions that "unavoidably arouse the alarm and concern of the peoples in Asia."[99] Politburo member and Secretary of the CCP Secretariat Yao Yilin conveyed the same sentiment a week later, telling Japanese reporters that Nakasone's visit "hurt the feelings" of those peoples who had suffered during the war and "naturally aroused the unease of neighboring countries." Yao also urged greater Japanese investment and technological assistance to rectify the trade imbalance.[100] On August 29, Deng Xiaoping brought up the history issue with a visiting delegation of the Japanese Socialist Party, saying that "the relationship between our countries is still good" but expressing concern about Japanese "militarist elements," stating that he hoped Japanese politicians would take "past experience as a guide to the future" and not forget lessons learned.[101] In an address to a mass rally on September 3, 1985, Chairman of the National People's Congress Standing Committee Peng Zhen stated that although "the era in which Japan's militarism and invasion brought about enmity between the two nations is over, this history must never be repeated."[102]

Numerous articles in the Chinese press criticized Nakasone's official visit to Yasukuni, in contrast with the brief treatment of Suzuki's 1982 visit as a private individual.[103] Official media commentary portrayed Nakasone's visit as a reflection of his stated desire to revitalize Japan as a normal nation and set aside postwar remonstrances in a "total settlement of postwar accounts." On August 16, *Renmin Ribao* quoted a Japanese editorial describing Nakasone's official visit as a dangerous portent of the "beautification of war and negation of the peace constitution."[104] On September 7, a Xinhua editorial cited Japanese reports that the Ministry of Education had mandated the use of the rising sun flag and an anthem "eulogizing the Japanese emperor" during public school ceremonies. Quoting Japanese critics, the Xinhua editorial stated that recent events in Japan have revealed "a dangerous undercurrent towards resuming the system which prevailed before World War II."[105] Although the Chinese media featured some positive stories on Japan, such as a September 1 article in *Renmin Ribao* that described Japanese soldiers who assisted during China's civil war,[106] this coverage was set against a sweeping campaign to commemorate the fortieth anniversary, including a mass assembly of 10,000 children on August 15, 1985, and the designation of new war memorial sites.[107] As Whiting notes, it was this campaign of propaganda and official commemorations that set the stage for the sentiments that would erupt on university campuses in September.[108]

Chinese officials and media commentary also emphasized how controversial Nakasone's actions were within Japan, perhaps anticipating as well as pressuring Nakasone to temper his position on Yasukuni. On August 16, *Renmin Ribao* ran the headline: "Nakasone and Cabinet Members Pay Official Visit to Yasukuni

Shrine; Japanese Opposition Parties and Public Associations Strongly Object."[109] On August 20, Xinhua reported that "the broad masses of the Japanese people do not agree [with] the shouting and trouble-making activities" of a right-wing demonstration outside the Chinese embassy in Tokyo.[110] On August 28, Vice Premier Yao Yilin praised visiting Japanese Socialist Party officials for opposing Nakasone's visit.[111] At the mass ceremony to commemorate the war on September 3, which included Japanese guests,[112] Peng Zhen reminded the audience that "a handful of Japanese are still attempting to revive militarism against the will of both the Chinese and Japanese peoples and to the detriment of friendship between the two countries and world peace.'"[113] Consistent with China's standard narrative of a few "bad elements" causing trouble in the relationship, such comments also reflected the hope that Nakasone might be persuaded to reconsider his visits given domestic criticism and for the sake of bilateral relations.

This interpretation contrasts with the view that protests "forced the Chinese government to take a tougher position" than it desired against Japan.[114] For example, James Reilly argues that "there was little indication that the Chinese government intended to emphasize Nakasone's recent Yasukuni visit in diplomatic relations. This changed only *after* the student protests began."[115] Yet it is not clear that Chinese leaders were pushed against their will by public opinion to take a stronger stance against Japan. Statements by top leaders along with official commentary indicate that China's stance toward Japan was already toughening before big-character posters appeared in mid-September. Protests may have exerted further pressure on China's stance toward Japan, but this pressure may have been desired or anticipated by Chinese leaders in an effort to gain leverage against Japan.[116]

Between these two interpretations is a third view, which suggests that moderate officials were forced to take a tougher stance against Japan because of the pressure generated by popular protests. In one reading of these events, hawkish elements secretly fomented student protests without the approval of moderate leaders, particularly Hu Yaobang, at the top. As Whiting and Xin write, "Demonstrations happen because some faction in the leadership has given its tacit or explicit sanction. And the evidence suggests that opinion within the Chinese leadership has been divided with respect to Japan."[117] In a more modest reading of factional conflict, internal divisions over how to respond to student mobilization prevented the government from responding quickly or coherently to spontaneous protests. As Reilly writes, "While student anger was sincere, officials' tolerance of the protests reflected elite divisions."[118] Although the locus of decision-making is different, such explanations are consistent with diplomatic incentives to allow protest and subsequent pressure on officials to take a tougher foreign policy stance. Hawkish voices who took a more permissive stance may have been motivated by a desire for a tougher policy toward Japan; protests may then have forced moderate officials to take a tougher stance against Japan than they preferred.

If policy preferences motivated conservatives as well as the desire to prevail in domestic power struggles, factional explanations are not incompatible with diplomatic incentives to tolerate or repress protests. Factional explanations are only inconsistent with the broader framework if the internal debate over whether to allow protests was purely domestic. That is, the theory has little purchase if conservatives sought to embarrass Hu Yaobang and his moderate allies by fomenting anti-Japanese protests without actually desiring a tougher stance against Japan. However, most factional interpretations of the 1985 anti-Japanese protests view elite disagreement over Japan policy as genuine rather than a cloak for political intrigue. As Susan Shirk writes, many observers in 1985 saw "signs of divisions within the top elite over two issues that had become intertwined: policies toward Japan and China's political reform."[119] Opposition to China's reliance on foreign capital and rapid inflation gave conservatives cause to utilize popular sentiment as ammunition against Hu Yaobang, whose friendly statements and unauthorized overtures to Japan, such as inviting 3,000 Japanese students to visit China, left him vulnerable to charges of heading a "pro-Japan faction."[120] As Yinan He notes, "elites will mobilize public opinion, often in the name of patriotism, to support their own policy positions vis-à-vis their opponents."[121]

Ultimately, we lack sufficient evidence to determine whether the government's initial tolerance in 1985 was the result of conservative machinations, liberal acquiescence, or a consensus to pressure Japan. Nor can we know the relative weight of foreign policy and domestic preferences. Indeed, without documentation of the internal decision-making process, we cannot rule out alternative conjectures about the dimensions of factional conflict. Although conservatives are typically assumed to have taken a more encouraging or permissive stance toward anti-Japanese protests, moderates may not have objected. Moderate leaders may have judged that Nakasone's actions on Yasukuni were undermining their broader cooperative agenda and hoped that student protests would succeed where official exhortations had not. In addition, moderates may have acknowledged the legitimacy of students' actions and been reluctant to use repression, even if moderate elites did not support the students' sentiment against Japan. Once protests got underway, disagreement over what the protests meant and what they would become may have led to a "logroll" whereby both hawks and moderates were willing to adopt a "wait and see" attitude.[122] Whether internal divisions were actually responsible for the government's lenience toward student mobilization, many Japanese observers viewed the protests in this light, including Nakasone.

Diplomatic Impact and Japanese Concessions

For Nakasone, the protests underscored the vulnerability of China's policy of engagement with Japan. Sensing the fragility of Hu Yaobang's position vis-à-vis conservative elites and hoping to aid his embattled counterpart, Nakasone abandoned further plans to visit Yasukuni. On October 9, Japanese newspapers reported that Prime Minister Nakasone intended to cancel his upcoming visit to Yasukuni during the autumn festival due to his "tight political schedule," including a trip to Washington.[123] Japanese government sources suggested that in light of China's "serious" response, Nakasone meant to calm the waters before Japanese foreign minister Shintaro Abe's visit to Beijing on October 10.[124] During his meetings with the top Chinese leadership, Foreign Minister Abe was repeatedly asked to consider the feelings of the Chinese people, as reflected in the university protests.[125] After raising the trade deficit and pointing out that the transfer of technology from Japan still lagged behind that from the United States and Europe, Deng Xiaoping told Abe that the Yasukuni visit had created "big problems for us." Deng stated:

> We know that the Japanese government has its own explanations, but as far as the people are concerned, not just in China but across Asia—including East Asia and Southeast Asia—there is the issue of people's feelings. In order to continue developing friendly Sino-Japanese relations, I suggest that the Japanese leadership pay attention to this problem. . . . For the Japanese side, there is no harm in not doing these things, and our economic and political relationship can continue developing peacefully and stably.[126]

At the opening ceremony of the Japan-China Friendship Committee for the Twenty-First Century on October 15, Zhao Ziyang reiterated that Japan should "do more things to benefit the two countries' friendship and strive to avoid things that hurt the people's feelings and obstruct mutual trust."[127] In Chengdu, anti-Japanese protesters became violent, stoning Japanese cars and smashing Japanese radios. An editorial in the local Party newspaper, *Sichuan Ribao*, blamed a small group of "lawless elements" for the vandalism and expressed concern that protests were becoming increasingly networked across the country, "establishing ties and exchanging experiences with various localities."[128]

Japanese media reported on October 17 that Nakasone had "side-stepped" the question of whether he would continue to "exercise restraint" on the Yasukuni issue.[129] Nakasone told the Diet that he would consider future visits on a case-by-case basis,[130] but large groups of LDP members visited Yasukuni during the autumn festival from October 17 to 19.[131] On October 18, Hu Yaobang finally spoke, stating in a four-point speech that Japan should "give earnest consideration to the friendly suggestion and reasonable demand of the other side and strive to avoid any action which may hurt the feelings of the people of the other side."[132]

Days later, Japan eased Chinese concerns with two announcements. On October 21, the Japanese Foreign Ministry stated that it would grant China 700 million yen worth of agricultural machinery to help China modernize rice production.[133] On November 5, the Japanese cabinet released a statement indicating that Nakasone had no intention of making official visits to Yasukuni a formal institution and that his objective in visiting Yasukuni was not to rehabilitate Japanese war criminals.[134] Chinese official media publicized and welcomed the Japanese statement. On November 8, *Renmin Ribao* quoted Japanese foreign minister Abe as saying that "paying formal homage to A-class war criminals is inappropriate."[135]

Why did Nakasone abandon his plans to visit Yasukuni Shrine? In his memoir, Nakasone explained his decision as an attempt to bolster Hu Yaobang's fragile position:

> I felt there was a danger that Hu Yaobang would be denounced and would be forced to resign as a result of my visits to Yasukuni Shrine... [so] I commissioned Yoshihiro Inayama, who was going to China on business, to find out what the Chinese really thought about the Yasukuni visits. . . . Party Secretary Gu Mu and Vice-Premier Wan Li called on him looking extremely tense and serious and said, "Remembering the ordinary war dead is fine, but war criminals who invaded China are enshrined in Yasukuni Shrine. Yasukuni Shrine is hurtful to the people of China and damages Japan's image abroad. Furthermore, it has a huge influence on China's domestic politics, and General Secretary Hu Yaobang and we ourselves are put in a very difficult position, so please tell Mr. Nakasone that we would really like him to put an end to it." This suggested that the situation was rather acute. The conservative faction was rallying and it was likely that Hu Yaobang would be their target. If he were to be overthrown it would be a major loss to the world and to Japan. It was with this in mind that [I] stopped my visits to the Yasukuni Shrine.[136]

Nakasone's rationale for canceling further visits to Yasukuni drew criticism from both the right and the left in Japan. As one right-wing LDP member put it, "we should not constantly be thinking of the views of other countries."[137] On the left, one *Asahi Shimbun* editor criticized Nakasone for failing to admit his "regret for failing to anticipate the foreseeable reaction of Asian countries, including China. . . . One gets the unmistakable impression that, by drawing attention to the power struggle in China, Nakasone was above all shirking personal responsibility."[138]

Despite these personal attacks, including assassination threats,[139] Prime Minister Nakasone's decision returned Japanese policy to the previous status quo, whereby Japanese actions aimed to support a moderate, stable, and reform-oriented China. According to CIA briefing materials for President Reagan before his meeting with Nakasone:

> Some in Tokyo are concerned that a radical leadership could reemerge in Beijing. . . . They view support for China's modernization as a way to improve prospects for the survival of a moderate leadership in Beijing, help to reinforce China's "opening to the West," and reduce incentives for a Sino-Soviet rapprochement.[140]

The desire to bolster a stable, reform-oriented government in China had similarly motivated Japanese aid to China and concessions following the cancellation of industrial contracts in the early 1980s. The Japanese Ministry of Foreign Affairs, in particular, believed that economic assistance "should be used to encourage the Hua-Deng leadership's moderate and realistic policy, which was consistent with Japanese interests."[141] One Japanese analyst attributed the cancellation of contracts partly to China's fear of becoming "a second Poland," where rising food prices and fiscal crises gave birth to social unrest and Solidarity movement in August 1980.[142] During Prime Minister Suzuki's visit to China in 1982, Deng stated that "China-Japan economic cooperation should be considered from a political angle" and "we hope to do more in the area of economic cooperation,"[143] remarks that some Japanese analysts regarded as "hinting at his hope for economic assistance from Japan."[144]

Three years later, when high-level Chinese officials appeared on campus to dissuade students from planning further protests in 1985, Whiting notes, "these activities, however, did not convince the skeptics in Japan and elsewhere, who saw them as part of a complicated maneuver to gain leverage against Tokyo."[145] For many Japanese observers, the protests confirmed a long-standing view that China was "counting on support from the sentimentalists in Japan," who remember China's waiver of wartime reparations and "believe that Japan should extend a helping hand as a neighboring country to help China overcome its current hardships."[146] Some analysts criticized the Japanese government for perpetuating a pattern of Japanese concessions. As Ijiri writes:

> Student demonstrations against the Chinese Government are turned into anti-Japanese demonstrations because they are intertwined with the power struggle between the reformers and the conservatives within the Chinese Communist Party leadership. Japan's reaction to these China problems has followed a basic pattern: when a problem occurs, China opposes Japan, and Japan makes concessions in order to remove immediate frictions, but avoids removing serious, long-standing frictions inherent in the basic structure of relations between the two countries. [147]

Nakasone's writings reveal that it was because of Hu Yaobang's vulnerability that Nakasone made concessions in 1985 and 1986, hoping to bolster a friendly government in China. When controversial new textbook revisions were approved in May 1986, China's Foreign Ministry lodged an official protest, urging Japan to honor the pledge by Prime Minister Suzuki in 1982 to heed the concerns of Japan's neighbors.[148] Nakasone ordered a re-examination of the offensive passages, explaining that "After studying the problems pointed out by China and other nations, I have reached the conclusion that certain portions of the textbook should be re-examined."[149] Despite criticism from the right, Nakasone was easily reelected in the summer of 1986. Amid fresh speculation over whether Nakasone would visit Yasukuni on August 15, the chief cabinet secretary clarified that the prime minister had made a "prudent and independent" decision to forgo visiting the shrine and to "give appropriate consideration to the national sentiments of neighboring countries."[150] Nakasone elaborated his reasoning, stating that "in China and other countries" a prime minister's visit to Yasukuni gives "the opposition good material to attack the government.... Governments friendly with Japan will be driven into a corner and Japan's relations with them will deteriorate."[151]

Nakasone's concessions restored a pattern that one Japanese analyst described as Japan adopting a "low posture" and China a "high posture."[152] On August 15, 1986, Hu Yaobang welcomed Nakasone's "wise" restraint on Yasukuni. When Minister of Education Masayuki Fujio remarked that Japan's occupation of Korea and actions during the Nanjing Massacre had been legitimate, Nakasone demanded Fujio's resignation and fired him after his refusal.[153] On September 13, Hu told the Japan-China Friendship Committee for the Twenty-First Century that he "appreciated Nakasone's fresh efforts and contributions in strengthening and developing bilateral relations lately."[154] Chinese officials continued to press Japan for more economic assistance. In September, Deng Xiaoping reminded Japanese economic and commercial delegations that "just as Japan's postwar economic takeoff required assistance, we also hope to receive assistance from all quarters. . . . We have not yet developed, that is China's problem. So China hopes that Japan will provide long-term assistance to help China develop, which will benefit Japan."[155]

From Anti-Japan to Pro-Democracy

Despite Nakasone's concessions on Yasukuni and exhortations by the official Chinese press to "cherish the hard-won friendship between China and Japan,"[156] students continued to mobilize on campuses in 1985 and 1986, now focusing their attacks on the Chinese government. The comingling of anti-Japanese and democratic demands underscored the growing challenge posed by student unrest to political stability. On November 4, 1985, Fang Lizhi, vice president of the Chinese University of Science and Technology in Anhui, gave a lecture at Beijing University, encouraging students to continue fighting for social and political change.[157] Not long after, a circular appeared at Beijing University calling upon students to gather in Tiananmen Square on November 20. Urging students to "save the Chinese nation from its decay," the circular accused high-level officials of inviting the Japanese "wolf to the door" for personal gain.[158] November 20 was chosen because a Sino-Japanese volleyball match and chess game would take place that day, but the purpose of the protest would be to "celebrate 'Democracy '85,' precede commemoration of 'December 9,' and accomplish the unfinished tasks of the 'September 18' gathering."[159]

On November 20, several hundred students gathered at Tiananmen Square, where they demonstrated for two hours before being dispersed by police with bull-horns and jeeps.[160] Afterward, there were rumors of student arrests for the first time since the anti-Japanese demonstrations had begun in September, although the minister of public security later denied that any students had been arrested.[161] At the time, U.S. ambassador Winston Lord wrote in a confidential cable:

> Public security officials are taking student demonstrations very seriously and... one armed police installation, shortly before last week's student demonstration, "looked like it was preparing for a war.". . . The extent to which the public security organs are drawn into controlling students reflects the extent to which the Communist Party has lost the initiative on campus.[162]

Tensions continued to build as the fiftieth anniversary of December 9 approached. Along with May 4, December 9, 1935, marks the anniversary of the largest student demonstrations in Chinese history, when more than a thousand students in Beijing protested the failure of Chiang Kai-shek's Nationalist government to resist Japan's invasion and occupation of Manchuria. Within a year, the movement had spread to most of China's cities and ultimately pushed the Nationalists into an alliance with the Communists.

In preparation for the fiftieth anniversary of December 9 in 1985, Chinese authorities began a campaign to commend student patriotism while stressing the need to follow the Party's leadership. High-level leaders were dispatched to speak with students, and rumors circulated that students who continued to participate in protests would find their career prospects limited.[163] According to one report, "armed guards are now stationed at all entrances to Peking's universities as the Chinese government nervously awaits student unrest planned for December in what diplomats here see as the most serious challenge to the Government's authority since 1979."[164] To counter calls for nationwide demonstrations on December 9, including another protest in Tiananmen Square, the Communist Youth League and other Party organs organized indoor campus commemorations as well as a mass gathering of several thousand high school students in Tiananmen Square.[165]

In this way, the government succeeded in preventing protests on the December 9 anniversary, although some anti-government slogans were reportedly shouted during the official ceremonies.[166] Over the next several months, localized protests continued to occur at campuses across the country, in cities such as Changsha, Taiyuan, Jinan, and Xi'an.[167] Temporarily eschewing antiforeign and pro-democracy slogans, students protested over food quality and campus-specific policies. Beijing alone witnessed 23 protests on various university campuses between the end of 1985 and early 1986, including one in mid-December that drew more than a thousand students at Beijing Agricultural University.[168]

Despite the easing of tensions in Sino-Japanese relations, a new wave of student mobilization calling for democracy forced Hu Yaobang's ouster in January 1987. On December 5, 1986, several thousand students from the Chinese University of Science and Technology in Hefei marched off campus and surrounded local city and provincial offices. This was the university where Fang Lizhi, who had given such stirring speeches to Beijing students in the fall of 1985, was vice president. Decrying the lack of democratic nomination procedures for the local people's congress, the Hefei protesters carried posters with slogans such as "No democratization, no modernization!" and "Give me liberty or give me death!"[169] On the anniversary of December 9, one year after anti-Japanese protests had been quelled, pro-democracy protests sought to take their place. According to Pepper,

> One poster put up at Wuhan University symbolized the merger of the 1985 and 1986 movements: it called among other things for more independent student associations and more student self-government, as well as the celebration of December 9, so as not to repeat the shame of having failed to do so on the 50th anniversary [in 1985].[170]

Within a month, student demonstrations had spread to roughly 150 campuses in cities across the nation,[171] including Tianjin, Nanjing, Kunming, Hangzhou, Suzhou, and Guangzhou.[172] The largest demonstrations occurred in Shanghai and Beijing, with some estimates as large as 30,000 participants.[173] The message Fang Lizhi delivered to Shanghai students in 1986 was the same message that he had delivered at Beijing University in November 1985, according to Kelly: "Fang's now notorious doctrine that 'democracy is something to be struggled for, not conferred from above' was, significantly, aired in the wake of the earlier round of student demonstrations of late 1985."[174]

The government responded by banning demonstrations without written approval, and the media published criticisms of the disruptive protests and appealed for calm. Despite these efforts, several thousand students from Beijing University defied the ban on New Year's Eve and marched to Tiananmen Square. The students carried placards and posters with slogans such as "Freedom of press and speech!" and "Against tyranny!"[175] The police dispersed the crowd and arrested several dozen participants, only to free them when a new wave of student protesters marched to Tiananmen Square to demand their classmates' release.

January 1, 1987, marked the end of the 1986 protests and the beginning of a new campaign against "bourgeois liberalism."[176] At a special meeting of the Politburo on December 30, Deng Xiaoping had attacked Hu for "having failed to control dissident intellectuals and having been unable to prevent the student demonstrations."[177] Fang Lizhi and a handful of liberal intellectuals were expelled from the Communist Party, accused of leading astray the nation's patriotic but impressionable students.

On January 16, Hu Yaobang's resignation was announced on the evening news. As Deng told a visiting African leader on January 20, the protests and change of leadership were the result of a "serious mistake by comrade Hu Yaobang," namely, "unclear leadership" and "weak efforts to oppose the tide of bourgeois liberalization."[178]

To Japanese audiences, however, Deng Xiaoping emphasized that China's open-door policies would not be affected by the recent tumult. LDP member Noboru Takeshita, a leading contender to succeed Nakasone, visited China shortly before Hu Yaobang's resignation was made public. Deng Xiaoping told Takeshita that the 1986 protests "were different from the September 18 protests the year before, when students took to the streets. . . [this time] only a very small portion of students, no more than 2 percent, made trouble."[179] According to Japanese media reports, Deng reassured Takeshita that China's reform policies and structure will never collapse in the wake of demonstrations, even if student involvement rose to 10 percent.[180] Although Deng downplayed the significance of the pro-democratic demonstrations, Deng urged Takeshita to consider that "the Chinese people, particularly young students, are extremely sensitive" to Japan's 1987 budget, which put defense spending over 1 percent of GNP, a symbolic break with the past.[181]

Relations between China and Japan resumed their previous pattern. When a Japanese court ruled that a dormitory for Chinese students belonged to Taiwan in February 1987, the dispute prompted a storm of criticism in the Chinese media. Deng pressured Japanese officials on June 4, 1987, saying that "from a historical perspective, Japan should do more for China's development. Frankly, Japan is the country that owes China the most in the world."[182] On June 28, Deng told several Japanese officials:

> In regard to China-Japan relations, reactions among youths, especially students, are strong. If difficult problems were to appear still further, it will become impossible to explain them to the people. It will become impossible to control them. I want you to understand this position which we are in.[183]

His words prompted a Japanese Foreign Ministry official to call Deng an "old" and "hard-headed" man "above the clouds."[184] Although Japan refused to overturn the dormitory ruling, citing separation of powers, the offending vice minister was forced to apologize and resign. In September 1987, Nakasone pledged an addition 100 billion yen loan to mark the fifteenth anniversary of the Japan-China Friendship Association.[185] Nakasone's successor, Prime Minister Takeshita, pledged an additional loan of 810 billion yen in August 1988, "reaffirming the status quo in relations," Kokubun writes.[186] Summarizing Japan's policy toward China between 1972 and 1989, Matake Kamiya writes: "In all these cases, Japan's reaction followed a discernibly conciliatory pattern. . . . Whenever political disagreements arose, Tokyo attached the highest priority to avoiding serious confrontation, restraining itself from asserting its own position in front of China and making the concessions necessary to diffuse the crisis."[187]

Conclusion

The 1985 anti-Japanese protests illustrate both the danger and diplomatic value of nationalist unrest. Although the protests helped elicit concessions from Japanese leaders interested in bolstering a moderate, engagement-oriented China, Japan's concessions ultimately failed to save Hu Yaobang. Hu was accused of being too friendly toward Japan, yet it is unlikely that he would have been removed so precipitously if pro-democracy protests had not erupted in 1986. As Whiting notes, "Hu was ousted primarily because of how he handled ideological issues and his personal style of operating without collective guidance. The Japan matter had been of lesser importance."[188] Although it is difficult to discern whether Chinese leaders anticipated that nationalist protests could be successfully used to pressure Japan, Chinese leaders nevertheless referred repeatedly to popular anger, urging Japan to "do more" in light of "reactions among youths." As Ming Wan writes, "Emotions evolved to serve foreign policy objectives. Whether the Chinese government knew from the start that the history issue would humble Japan, it did realize that fact down the line and would use it again."[189]

With Deng Xiaoping intent on maintaining China's open-door policies, the leadership shuffle did not upset Japan's renewed commitment to helping China and defusing bilateral disputes when they arose. If anything, the realized threat of instability in China helped confirm Japanese beliefs about the political necessity of its aid and investment. As Ryosei Kokubun and Jie Liu write, "Deng Xiaoping was remarkable. . . . he linked China's stability with the interests of the world [so that] no other country wanted to destabilize China or rock the [CCP] regime."[190] This concern for China's stability would continue to drive Japanese foreign policy toward China after the Tiananmen Incident and into the 1990s, as we see in the following chapter.

5

Protests Repressed

Sino-Japanese Relations in the 1990s

> The Chinese side has taken a restrained attitude in order to avoid nega-
> tively influencing normal Sino-Japanese relations and to avoid causing
> tension in the Asia-Pacific. [We] should use methods of inducement
> (*shudao*) to stop petitions, demonstrations, protests, and other dramatic
> actions by the masses inside China and take necessary steps to prevent
> and ban this type of activity from taking place and developing.
> —CCP Central Propaganda Department circular, 1996[1]

Throughout the 1990s, the Chinese government adopted a more repressive than permissive attitude toward anti-Japanese protest. Although China launched a patriotic
education campaign to bolster the Communist Party's diminished legitimacy, nationalist propaganda for domestic consumption did not translate into permission for
antiforeign street demonstrations. The first few years were characterized by Chinese
efforts to break through the international sanctions imposed after the crackdown on
pro-democracy protests at Tiananmen Square in the early hours of June 4, 1989. Japan
rewarded Chinese restraint with new loans and a historic visit by the Japanese emperor.
Chinese authorities prevented anti-Japanese protests over the Diaoyu/Senkaku Islands
in 1990 and kept activists from staging demonstrations during the Japanese emperor's
historic visit in 1992 and the prime minister's visit in 1994. Cooperative efforts by both
governments ensured that the first few years of the new decade were among the best in
Sino-Japanese relations, according to Japan's ambassador at the time.[2]

By mid-decade, a number of developments caused new tensions in the relationship. Chinese nuclear tests and missile exercises during the Taiwan Strait Crisis in
1995 and 1996 fanned Japanese concerns about China as a growing military threat,
even as Japan's economy sagged under its worst postwar recession. Steps to revitalize the U.S.-Japan alliance prompted Chinese fears that the alliance might be used to
cover contingencies concerning Taiwan. Domestically, both China and Japan witnessed growing popular activism on historical issues, including a grassroots Chinese
movement to seek legal redress and individual compensation for Japanese war

atrocities, as well as the formation of conservative Japanese associations promoting history textbooks that downplayed or omitted references to Japanese aggression in World War II.

During a renewed controversy over disputed islands in the East China Sea in the summer and fall of 1996, China again repressed anti-Japanese protests, seeking to assuage Japanese concerns and mitigate the fallout of the 1995–96 crisis over Taiwan on the eve of revised guidelines governing U.S.-Japan security cooperation. As large-scale protests in Hong Kong and Taiwan underscored the sincerity of the popular sentiments repressed in mainland China, Japanese observers acknowledged China's restraint and costly efforts to stifle anti-Japanese demonstrations. Japan ultimately agreed to return to the status quo ante, discouraging Japanese right-wing associations whose activities had prompted the controversy in the first place. The terms of the revitalized U.S.-Japan alliance remained ambiguous on the issue of Taiwan, moderating some of the language that China had found most objectionable.

The 1990s illustrate the importance of diplomatic objectives in China's management of nationalist protest. Although the regime sought to prop up its legitimacy by launching a patriotic education campaign, this domestic imperative did not prompt the leadership to allow nationalist, anti-Japanese protests. Rather than divert citizen grievances, the Chinese leadership was more concerned that nationalist activities might be used to cloak democratic dissent and challenge the regime. Concern for domestic stability during this period complemented the government's diplomatic objectives, pointing in the same direction: repression.

Breaking Out after Tiananmen: Anti-Japanese Protests Stifled during the 1990 Lighthouse Controversy

On September 29, 1990, Japanese newspapers reported that the Japanese Maritime Safety Agency had recognized a lighthouse on the main Diaoyu/Senkaku island as an "official navigation mark" and allowed members of a right-wing Japanese group to renovate the lighthouse. Despite large street protests in Taiwan and Hong Kong, mainland Chinese authorities prevented demonstrations over the islands. In mid-October, two dozen athletes sailed from Taiwan to place a torch on the island, but Japanese patrol ships turned them away.[3] Thousands of protesters in Taiwan and Hong Kong took to the streets, and Taiwanese activists and opposition politicians organized a flotilla of fishing boats.[4] In mainland China, by contrast, the government rejected applications from students at several Beijing universities for permission to protest.[5] Chinese authorities increased security around the universities and ordered a blackout of news coverage of overseas protests.[6] According to a Hong Kong report, "the CCP issued a circular to local party committees stressing that tensions over 'these economic and strategically insignificant islands should not affect friendly relations between China and Japan.'"[7]

When the 1990 lighthouse controversy erupted, the Chinese government was still trying to end its post-Tiananmen international isolation. With Japan taking the lead in restoring economic assistance to China, anti-Japanese protests would have been detrimental to China's diplomatic and developmental objectives.[8] After pro-democracy protests had ended in bloodshed on June 4, 1989, the Group of Seven (G7) halted billions of dollars in international assistance and lending to China. The most reluctant country to impose sanctions, Japan was the linchpin in China's efforts to break through its isolation and restore high-level exchanges. As Premier Li Peng noted in November 1989: "Some will go first and others later. We'll wait and see which country will make the first move. The country which does so is brave and praiseworthy."[9]

Japan's reluctance to isolate China stemmed from concern about the implications of an unstable China for regional stability, a desire to maintain friendly relations, and a lingering sense of remorse. As one Japanese scholar noted: "Even though Japan is politically a member of the West, it is also an Asian country in close proximity to China... it has to live pragmatically with China and does not wish to have a hostile relationship with Beijing. Moreover, many Japanese still feel a residual guilt."[10] In the fall of 1989, Haruo Suzuki, head of the Japan-China Association on Economy and Trade, suggested that "so long as China is not stabilized, the stability of the rest of Asia and the world cannot be expected.... To help stabilize China, therefore, Japan must give whatever advice and cooperation are required."[11] Yutaka Kawashima, who would become Japan's vice minister of foreign affairs, recalled that "although the Japanese were appalled by the brutality of the incident, there was noticeable hesitation to take measures that might decisively wreck relations with China."[12]

Japanese officials communicated their emphasis on positive relations with China both publicly and privately. Only days after the crackdown at Tiananmen Square, Japanese prime minister Sosuke Uno told Diet members:

> We need to be aware that the Japan-China relationship is totally different from the U.S.-China relationship. We were once at war with China. . . . Today, with China facing domestic uncertainty, we should avoid making any statements about what is right and wrong. We should avoid going too far by defining the event in black-and-white terms.[13]

The following day, Uno added that, "Applying any sanctions will be inconsiderate toward our neighbor. I hope the situation will return to normal as soon as possible, so we will not [openly] condemn them."[14] At international conferences, Japanese officials told Chinese diplomats that Japan sought to maintain friendly bilateral relations and that what had happened was China's domestic affair.[15]

Although Japan was not alone in reaching out, China recognized that Japan's assistance was key to persuading other Western nations to drop sanctions and restore contacts. Amid public shock and grief over Chinese arrests and executions,

American officials also privately emphasized the importance of Chinese cooperation against the Soviet Union. After the June 4 crackdown, President George H.
W. Bush told Margaret Thatcher that he had "issued a modest statement" because
of the "need to preserve the U.S.-China relationship."[16] Just a few weeks later, Bush
sent his national security advisor, Brent Scowcroft, with Deputy Secretary of State
Lawrence Eagleburger on a secret mission to China.[17] Although internal Chinese
reports argued that American fears of driving China back into isolation or toward
the Soviet Union should give China leverage,[18] a second and more public Scowcroft-
Eagleburger mission to China triggered widespread public outrage in the United
States.[19] Members of Congress chastised the Bush administration for "kowtowing to
a repressive Communist government."[20]

Chinese leaders concluded that Japan was more likely than the United States to
advocate moderation and economic engagement. As Vice Chairman of the National
People's Congress Foreign Affairs Committee Lü Congmin writes in his memoir: "As
we looked closely at the Japanese government's attitude toward China back then, we
discovered that Japan did not intend or dare to go to extremes."[21] Qian Qichen, who
was then China's foreign minister, recalls:

> Japan was a reluctant member of the Western bloc of countries that
> imposed sanctions against China. It endorsed the resolution of the G7
> Economic Summit imposing sanctions imply because it wanted to take the
> same position as the other six countries.... China regarded Japan as a weak
> link in the united front of Western countries that had imposed sanctions
> against China—and therefore the best target for attacking such sanctions.[22]

China courted Japanese assistance by adopting a relatively calm attitude toward new
provocations in bilateral relations. In December 1989, for example, Japan gave visas to a
visiting group of Chinese dissidents—including Wu'er Kaixi, who had played a prominent role in the Tiananmen demonstrations before fleeing China. Yet Chinese officials
only expressed regret at Japan's actions, in sharp contrast to China's strenuous demands
that Japan take appropriate action over the dormitory dispute in the late 1980s.[23]

China's restraint was rewarded when Japan took the initiative in July 1990 to persuade the other G7 members to soften their stance on international assistance to
China. As Premier Li Peng noted, "President Bush told Japanese prime minister
Toshiki Kaifu yesterday that the United States would not stop Japan from providing
aid to China: 'Japan is a sovereign state and can make its own decisions.' It looks like
the Western countries have started to adjust their policy toward China."[24] Although
the Bush administration quietly sought to improve relations with China, it was
Japan that publicly declared the unilateral resumption of loans to China, leading the
way in ending China's international isolation.[25]

In addition, the Chinese leadership sought to lay the groundwork for a state visit
by Emperor Akihito. According to Qian Qichen, a visit by the emperor "would not

only break Western countries' ban on high-level visits with China but it would also be of profound significance for Sino-Japanese relations."[26] The symbolism of China's unprecedented invitation was augmented by the date on which Jiang Zemin made it public: July 7, the anniversary of Japan's full-scale invasion of mainland China.[27] According to Japanese sources, Deng Xiaoping had privately issued an invitation for the Japanese emperor to visit after the Treaty of Peace and Friendship was signed in 1978, an invitation that was repeated during the visits of Li Peng and Qian Qichen to Japan in April 1989 and June 1991, respectively.[28]

When the lighthouse dispute arose a few months after Jiang Zemin publicly repeated the invitation, the Chinese leadership was more interested in fostering Japanese goodwill than demonstrating resolve over the territorial issue. When Japanese media reported that the Japanese Maritime Safety Agency was preparing to recognize the lighthouse on the main Diaoyu/Senkaku island as an official navigation mark, Chinese officials did not immediately comment.[29] By contrast, Taiwanese authorities had immediately lodged a diplomatic protest against Japan's actions. Only after being questioned at a press conference did a Chinese Foreign Ministry official comment on the matter, demanding that Japan take appropriate measures to curtail the activities of Japanese right-wing groups and prevent future incidents.[30] Authorities in mainland China stifled protests and news coverage in the domestic media. Repressing protests was not costless, as the government was criticized for selling out the islands for Japanese yen. Yet Chinese leaders were willing to incur domestic resentment for the sake of China's broader objectives, including the resumption of Japanese loans.[31]

For its part, the Japanese government also sought to ensure that the lighthouse controversy would not derail progress in bilateral relations, as well as to reassure China at a moment when the Diet was considering a bill to authorize Japanese troop deployments on noncombatant peacekeeping missions in the Gulf, reawakening long-held Chinese concerns about Japanese militarism.[32] Although the Japanese Foreign Ministry reaffirmed Japan's sovereignty over the islands, Prime Minister Kaifu announced that Japan would "act prudently" regarding the lighthouse application and would not patrol the islands with military vessels.[33] When a group of right-wing Japanese politicians announced their intent the following year to sail to the islands and raise the Japanese flag, the prime minister's office and senior LDP members persuaded them to abandon their plans.[34]

With both governments prioritizing stability and amicable relations over domestic nationalist pressures, the 1990 lighthouse controversy was resolved with mutual restraint and minimal acrimony. Japanese officials continued to emphasize their commitment to fostering a stable China through economic engagement. In December, Prime Minister Kaifu reiterated at a news conference that "to isolate China will not be good for world peace and stability."[35]

Welcoming the Japanese Emperor: Protests Stifled in 1992

As the twentieth anniversary of the September 1972 normalization drew near, both governments sought to downplay actions that might arouse antipathy over territorial and historical issues. In January 1992, Japanese prime minister Miyazawa privately told President Bush that the Japanese emperor intended to visit China,[36] but two developments threatened preparations for the historic visit. In February, the Chinese National People's Congress adopted a new law declaring that PRC territory included "Taiwan and all islands appertaining thereto including the Diaoyu Islands."[37] Chinese officials hastened to reassure Japan that these "legal formalities" simply restated China's existing stance. Japanese diplomats responded mildly, stating that the law was not aimed at any country and there was no need to take countermeasures.[38] A senior Japanese official even said the law was "merely a matter of China's tidying up its domestic legislative institutions."[39] Yet many Japanese conservatives were outraged by China's assertion of sovereignty and Tokyo's restrained response, accusing the Japanese government of neglecting the nation's interests in order to prepare for Jiang Zemin's visit to Japan and the emperor's visit to China.[40]

A second issue threatened to cast a shadow over preparations for the emperor's visit: a grassroots Chinese movement for wartime compensation claims against the Japanese government. With the support of local officials, Chinese activists put forward a proposal to the National People's Congress (NPC) demanding an estimated $180 billion in compensation for damages. The compensation movement had begun in the late 1980s, when two activists, Li Guping and Tong Zeng, began raising awareness about forced labor practices and chemical weapons experiments during the Japanese occupation of mainland China.[41] A few hundred villagers from Shandong Province also submitted a petition to the Japanese embassy demanding compensation for their forced labor.[42] In 1991, Tong Zeng and his supporters in the National People's Congress put forward a bill stating that China's official waiver of war reparations did not preclude individual compensation claims.

The compensation proposal put the Chinese government in a difficult situation. In response to a reporter's question, Foreign Minister Qian Qichen acknowledged that NPC delegates had the right to submit proposals but stated that the 1972 joint communiqué between Premier Zhou Enlai and Prime Minister Kakuei Tanaka had relinquished Chinese claims to war reparations.[43] A week later, Jiang Zemin told reporters on the eve of his visit to Japan that China's position on reparations remained unchanged, emphasizing that he would again invite the Japanese emperor to visit China in order to cement Sino-Japanese friendship and commemorate the twentieth anniversary of normalized relations.[44]

Miyazawa declined to confirm the emperor's visit during Jiang's trip, however.[45] Amid mounting domestic opposition, Miyazawa stated only that the Japanese government would "continue to give serious consideration" to the matter.[46] Any further action by China on the compensation issue "would dash any chance of a visit by Emperor Akihito later this year," according to Japanese analysts.[47]

It was not until August 25 that the Japanese government confirmed that the emperor and empress would visit China in late October.[48] According to Yoshibumi Wakamiya, deputy managing editor of the *Asahi Shimbun*, fears that "Deng Xiaoping's death might throw China into chaos again" contributed to the Japanese Foreign Ministry's belief that it was "wise for the Emperor to visit China while its supreme leader was still alive and well."[49] Japanese observers also recognized China's eagerness to improve Sino-Japanese relations and willingness to restrain domestic nationalism. According to one Japanese scholar, "China tried to show that it enjoyed good diplomatic relations with Japan. To avoid offending Tokyo, Beijing kept silent" when the Japanese Diet authorized the participation of Self-Defense Forces (SDF) personnel in overseas missions.[50]

As the twentieth anniversary of normalized relations drew near, Wakamiya notes, "China's invitations were becoming more insistent" and "in any event, given the major stakes involved in bilateral relations, it appeared to be very risky to continue to snub China's repeated advances."[51] Having communicated the domestic sensitivity of the emperor's visit, the Japanese government received reassurances from China that the emperor would not be embarrassed or harassed during his visit:

> Should stone-throwing or similar incidents occur, this would ignite Japanese nationalism and damage bilateral relations beyond repair. . . . Beijing promised to do nothing that would put the Emperor in an awkward position. China would make no requests regarding statements by the Emperor and was confident that it could control its people's behavior. China would do nothing that could be interpreted as exploiting the Emperor's visit politically.[52]

Once Emperor Akihito's visit was confirmed, a prominent Japanese scholar noted that Chinese security and propaganda authorities had been instructed to tamp down rhetoric and any petitions or demonstrations against Japan.[53] Furthermore, Chinese officials refrained from making critical remarks and indicated that the wording of the emperor's remarks would be left to the Japanese side.[54] When the head of the Japanese Socialist Party raised concerns about the territorial law and civilian reparations in the context of the emperor's visit, "Jiang Zemin denied that any difficult issues would be raised, displaying all possible consideration."[55]

Both domestic and international factors pointed toward restraining anti-Japanese protests in China. As Akihito's visit approached, Chinese students organized a signature campaign demanding Japanese compensation for war damages, a formal apology, and the renunciation of claims to the Diaoyu Islands. "The emperor must in his official capacity and on a public occasion deliver an unambiguous apology to the Chinese people," said one student organizer, who asserted that students planned to submit the petition to the emperor during his visit.[56] But allowing demonstrations might have jeopardized not only domestic stability but also the diplomatic objectives that the Chinese leadership had been working toward for two years: the Japanese emperor's first visit and a breakthrough in China's post-Tiananmen isolation. Anti-Japanese protests would also have put pressure on the Chinese government to demand a formal apology from the emperor, which Japan's deputy foreign minister had publicly ruled out by stating that it was "not an issue between the Chinese and Japanese governments" and Japan had already "made formal apologies on several occasions."[57]

Determined to ensure a smooth visit, Chinese authorities confined commemorations of the September 18 anniversary to university campuses and stepped up security as Akihito's visit drew near.[58] Chinese authorities banned the publication of a *Beijing Review* poll showing that most citizens supported the reparations movement and the demand that the emperor apologize.[59] During the emperor's visit in late October, the authorities repressed anti-Japanese demonstrations altogether. A high-level circular banned protest activities and singled out Tong Zeng and other activists for increased surveillance amid rumors that thousands of victims and their families might travel to Beijing during the emperor's visit.[60] Tong Zeng and one of his associates were told to leave Beijing on "a business trip" during the emperor's visit.[61] A Shanghai activist who had participated in the 1989 democracy movement, Bao Ge, was placed under house arrest after threatening to take more radical measures to demand an apology from the emperor, including a hunger strike and self-immolation.[62] In Hong Kong, over 2,000 protesters urged Emperor Akihito to apologize formally and compensate wartime victims of Japanese aggression. The protests, organized by liberal parties in Hong Kong, also urged mainland authorities not to prevent people from airing their grievances during the emperor's visit.[63]

During his visit, Emperor Akihito stopped short of a formal apology for Japan's wartime actions, instead expressing his "deep sadness" and acknowledging that Japan "inflicted great suffering on the people of China."[64] Chinese officials were pleased with the statement, even if compensation activists—who had been muffled during the emperor's visit—were not. Akihito's speech "wasn't bad at all," Li Peng noted.[65] Qian Qichen suggested that "compared with previous statements made by Japanese leaders," Akihito's statement had "moved one step further by including deep remorse, although it fell short of an apology."[66]

In the two years that followed Emperor Akihito's visit, both governments continued to deepen bilateral engagement and tamp down nationalist pressure. In 1994, Japanese prime minister Morihiro Hosokawa described Japan's actions in World War II as "a war of aggression," echoing Prime Minister Nakasone's earlier words.[67] Hosokawa also removed two senior officials whose remarks downplayed Japanese atrocities in World War II.[68] In China, police detained over a hundred protesters who gathered outside the Japanese embassy to demand compensation during Hosokawa's March 1994 visit.[69] Shanghai activist Bao Ge was detained and sentenced to three years of reform through labor for linking compensation demands to calls for sweeping political reform.[70] Bao had stated that a referendum on war reparations would "open the way to a constitutional democracy" in China, warning that otherwise a June 4–style confrontation between the government and people might arise.[71] Bao also participated in a petition calling for multiparty competition, independent labor unions, and an investigation into the events at Tiananmen Square.[72]

Other Chinese compensation activists sought to mitigate the political sensitivity of their actions by distinguishing between civilian demands for compensation and the national waiver of war reparations.[73] Nonetheless, the government issued a notice stating that the "actions of Tong Zeng and his reparations group are nominally directed against the Japanese government, but their true target is the Chinese government."[74] Police continued to monitor Tong Zeng closely and in August 1995 detained him for organizing an international press conference for war victims.[75] Tong was instructed to stay away from Beijing during an international forum, which had invited him to speak about forced prostitution or "comfort women" during the Japanese occupation. Defiant, he told reporters: "I certainly am not interfering with Beijing's social order. . . . I won't hold marches or demonstrate, but I will go to Huairou to take part in the meeting."[76] Having addressed the conference, Tong Zeng and his deputy were confined at home for the fiftieth anniversary of Japan's surrender on August 15, even as protests in Hong Kong surrounded the Japanese consulate.[77]

Both diplomatic and domestic concerns appear to have motivated the government's repression of anti-Japanese protests during the early 1990s: the desire to elicit Japanese assistance and end international sanctions alongside the fear of potentially destabilizing links between anti-Japanese mobilization and anti-government dissent. Clamping down on activists who were most likely to organize public activities minimized the risk of instability, while permitting war victims to file lawsuits through Japanese courts allowed the most aggrieved citizens an outlet for their discontent. At the same time, repressing anti-Japanese protests gave the government flexibility to pursue its diplomatic agenda. To allow anti-Japanese protests would have antagonized China's most likely source of international support. The Japanese government had already drawn domestic criticism for sacrificing moral principles for the sake of strategic and economic ties with China. Moreover, the Japanese government was already convinced that China's continued economic reform and openness was domestically vulnerable and that Japanese assistance could help stave off the possibility of a Chinese retrenchment into isolation.

Patriotic Education and the Repression of Anti-Japanese Protests

According to a diversionary logic, the early 1990s should have been an opportune time to allow anti-Japanese protests: to distract citizens from the tragedy of 1989 and bolster the government's diminished legitimacy. The decline of communism as China's governing ideology had created a spiritual void, exacerbated by the disillusionment of June 4, 1989, and its aftermath. After a protracted campaign to root out and punish those who had participated and organized demonstrations in 1989, China lifted martial law in January 1990. Anti-Japanese protests could have provided a "safety valve" for citizens to let off steam against a foreign rather than domestic target. Indeed, domestic unrest rose as economic reforms led to massive layoffs of urban state-owned enterprise (SOE) workers.[78] Between 1993 and 1995, the Ministry of Public Security estimated that the number of "mass incidents" per year rose from 8,700 to 11,000.[79]

Yet the Chinese government did not allow anti-Japanese protests to deflect attention and redirect grievances toward a foreign scapegoat. Instead, the Party leadership emphasized patriotism—not nationalist protests—as a means to bolster the regime's legitimacy and rally citizens around the Communist Party. While reaffirming China's commitment to economic reform and openness, embodied in Deng Xiaoping's famous southern tour in early 1992, the government launched a patriotic education campaign. Mandatory coursework, films, and museum field trips educated students of all ages about the "national condition." Local governments designated thousands of "patriotic education bases," where historic sites and relics marked China's suffering at the hands of Japan and Western imperial powers during the so-called Century of National Humiliation (*bainian guochi*).[80] This propaganda and education campaign—which began in 1991, gained prominence in 1992, and climaxed with the fiftieth anniversary of Japan's defeat in World War II in 1995[81]— did not spell permission for street protests against Japan. The emphasis on China's victimization in the past did not extend to permission to lash out at foreigners in the present.

This apparent disconnect illustrates an important difference between allowing nationalist protests and promoting nationalism through propaganda and education. As a strategy to bolster domestic legitimacy in authoritarian regimes, nationalist protests are far riskier than nationalist propaganda. Both protests and propaganda put pressure on the regime to take a tougher stand by raising the salience of foreign provocations and linking international events to the regime's nationalist credentials. But nationalist protests may backfire as a diversionary tactic in two ways.

First, if domestic dissidents use nationalism as a cloak for anti-government mobilization, then nationalist protests may exacerbate—not lessen—the threat to social stability. Prominent efforts by Tong Zeng, Bao Ge, and their associates to petition the National People's Congress, mobilize war victims, and advocate political reform in some cases aroused fears that nationalist demonstrations might turn against the government. Rather than hope citizens would let off steam, "China's leaders were afraid that demonstrations might not only jeopardize the resumption of Japanese lending but also turn into anti-government protests," as Downs and Saunders note.[82] Such fears were not necessarily unfounded, as Bao Ge explicitly recognized that seeking compensation from Japan "perhaps could have become an opportunity to rekindle China's democracy movement."[83]

Second, if the regime is unwilling or unable to fulfill protest demands on the diplomatic stage, then nationalist protests may divert attention from domestic grievances but also highlight foreign policies that appear weak or spineless. Allowing nationalist protests in the early 1990s would only have highlighted the government's willingness to downplay territorial and compensation concerns for the sake of restoring a favorable international climate for China's development instead of demonstrating Chinese sovereignty and demanding Japanese contrition.

It also bears noting that ideological differences of opinion within the top echelons of the Party leadership did not translate into support for anti-Japanese demonstrations in the early 1990s. Elites were divided over the desirability of continued economic reform, given the inflation and macroeconomic imbalances that had given rise to urban unrest in the late 1980s. Conservatives even attempted without success to roll back some of the reforms in 1990 and 1991.[84] The leadership was also divided over the content and pace of the patriotic education campaign.[85] According to Suisheng Zhao, conservatives pressed for more propaganda against the threat of "peaceful evolution" from the West, while moderates warned that such attacks might imperil China's ability to utilize capitalist reforms to promote economic development and improve the people's livelihoods.[86]

Despite these differences, the leadership was united in support of engaging Japan and eliciting its assistance,[87] and the repression of anti-Japanese protests helped communicate China's determination to prevent popular sentiments from derailing bilateral engagement. Furthermore, anti-Japanese protests were unnecessary to communicate the fragility of a reform-oriented China; the upheaval of the 1980s and ensuing crackdown had volubly communicated that message. Given the uncertainty of a post-Tiananmen China and Deng Xiaoping's advanced age, the Japanese leadership sought to bolster China's moderates and encourage China to continue along the path of economic reform and openness.[88]

Anti-Japanese Protests Stifled during the 1996 Diaoyu/Senkaku Crisis

When a second controversy over the Diaoyu/Senkaku Islands erupted in 1996, China's international environment had changed dramatically. China's economic situation and international stature had improved, but a series of Chinese nuclear tests and provocative missile exercises across the Taiwan Strait had galvanized Japanese fears about Chinese intentions. After a right-wing Japanese group built a lighthouse on one of the smaller disputed islands in July, large protests took place in Hong Kong and Taiwan. But a high-level Chinese circular instructed local authorities to "properly channel young students' patriotism" and "inform the leading body at a higher level in a timely manner when students are likely to go on to the streets and demonstrate, hold campus rallies or deliver written protests to the Japanese embassy or consulates, so that the problem will be nipped in the bud."[89] Even after a Hong Kong activist drowned while trying to plant a flag on the islands, anti-Japanese protests were stifled in mainland China before they could emerge on the streets.

As the lighthouse controversy unfolded, China sought to avoid provoking closer security cooperation between Tokyo and Washington.[90] After China conducted two underground nuclear tests in 1995, Japan suspended $75 million in grant aid, backed by criticism from across the political spectrum. Japanese conservatives accused the government of subsidizing China's military buildup, and even the liberal *Asahi Shimbun* questioned the efficacy of Japan's aid to China.[91] During the same period, China launched a series of live ammunition missile exercises after Taiwan's president, Lee Teng-hui, was granted a visa to visit the United States. A second bout of firings took place on the eve of Taiwanese elections in March 1996. One missile landed close to the Okinawa island chain, leaving "a big psychic scar" on Japan and causing an "earthquake for the entire East Asia region," according to Japanese analysts.[92] During the crisis, the United States dispatched two aircraft carrier groups to the waters near the Taiwan Strait, including one battle group based in Japan.[93]

Chinese observers became increasingly concerned that the U.S.-Japan alliance was becoming a cloak for Japanese remilitarization and an impetus for a more active Japanese role in the Asia-Pacific region. In a worst-case scenario, Chinese analysts feared that Japanese and American intervention would prevent China from using force to halt Taiwan independence.[94] From Beijing's perspective, calls for Japan to share more of the defense burden meant that Washington was now encouraging rather than restraining a more assertive Japanese foreign policy.[95] In 1994, the Japanese government had issued a comprehensive security report stating that Japan must take responsibility for its defense in the "areas surrounding Japan," viewed in China as a sign that Japan planned to take a larger role in regional security.[96] In February 1995, a high-level U.S. strategic report led by Joseph Nye called for the strengthening of the security alliance and Japanese support for U.S. operations in East Asia. That fall, a Japanese defense strategy report reiterated that U.S.-Japan security cooperation "guaranteed the peace and stability of the areas surrounding Japan."[97]

In April 1996, President Bill Clinton and Prime Minister Ryutaro Hashimoto issued a joint declaration reaffirming the alliance as the "cornerstone for achieving common security objectives, and for maintaining a stable and prosperous environment for the Asia-Pacific region."[98] American concerns about Japanese support in a North Korean crisis were the primary impetus for revitalizing the alliance, but "the Hashimoto government would not exclude the possibility that Taiwan could be one of the situations that the guidelines would encompass," notes Richard Bush, former senior U.S. diplomat with responsibility for Taiwan.[99] The U.S.-Japan joint declaration came one month after the March 1996 missile exercises and included language referring to "situations that may arise in areas surrounding Japan," exacerbating Chinese fears that the U.S.-Japan alliance would be used in a Taiwan contingency.[100] According to Tsinghua professor Liu Jiangyong, the declaration was further evidence that the alliance had "become an instrument of joint intervention in regional conflict."[101]

Although senior Chinese officials expressed their concerns about the future direction of the alliance to their American and Japanese counterparts, China's response was otherwise fairly muted.[102] China's Foreign Ministry spokesman stated that Taiwan was an internal Chinese matter, warned that the alliance should not target a third party, and urged Japan to adopt a "prudent attitude" in handling its expanded defense role.[103] When China ratified the UN Convention on the Law of the Sea (UNCLOS) in May 1996, it refrained from drawing baselines around Taiwan in order "to avoid triggering a dispute with Japan over the Diaoyu Islands" that might further push Japan toward the United States, Downs and Saunders note.[104]

Chinese leaders worried that a more assertive stance on the East China Sea islands would risk the hardening of the U.S.-Japan alliance against China. Although Japanese officials had pressed China about its military modernization for a few years,[105] China's nuclear tests and missile exercises prompted a "sudden and unprecedented sense of insecurity about China" among the Japanese public, Green notes.[106] Japan's annual defense white paper, released a week after the lighthouse controversy erupted, named China's military modernization as Japan's major defense concern.[107] Conservative and nationalistic currents in Japanese politics had also been gaining strength, fed by the insecurity of Japan's "lost decade" of economic growth and reflected in the establishment of right-wing groups advocating alternative history textbooks.[108]

The influence of Japanese conservatives was prominently displayed in 1995, when Japan's Socialist prime minister, Tomiichi Murayama, introduced a Diet resolution apologizing for Japan's historical misdeeds to mark the fiftieth anniversary of the war's end. Domestic opposition led the Japanese government to replace the word "apology" with "deep remorse" and "aggression" with "aggressive acts." Still, nearly half the legislature abstained.[109] Chinese officials pointed to the fiftieth anniversary resolution as "irrefutable evidence that 'in Japan there are still, indisputably, recalcitrant elements who do all they can to distort history and glorify invasion.'"[110] As one Chinese scholar put it, "The bill the Diet finally adopted was ambiguous, and the wording empty and short of self-examination."[111]

Chinese concerns about provoking Japan on the eve of anticipated revisions to the U.S.-Japan defense guidelines created incentives to repress anti-Japanese protests during the islands row. On July 14, 1996, right-wing activists sailed from Japan and erected a makeshift lighthouse on one of the smaller islands. Days later, Japan claimed a 200-nautical mile exclusive economic zone around the islands under UNCLOS, which the Diet had ratified in June.[112] Chinese Foreign Ministry spokesman Cui Tiankai emphasized that the lighthouse issue should be resolved in "a restrained, friendly manner."[113]

Demonstrators surrounded Japanese diplomatic offices in Taiwan and Hong Kong, but no protests took place in mainland China.[114] Activists in Taipei and Hong Kong pressed the PRC and ROC governments to take a stronger stance. One Hong Kong legislator, Albert Ho Chun-yan, stated: "If the two governments put the event at the top of their agenda, I am sure Japan won't be so aggressive.... But it seems they only care about economic interests and turn a blind eye to Japanese aggression on our territory."[115] Taiwanese and Hong Kong activists began organizing a protest flotilla to demolish the lighthouse. Asked about these plans, Taiwan's Foreign Ministry spokesman stated that the government "cannot stop or prevent possible clashes between Taiwan fishermen and the Japanese authorities,"[116] showing greater lenience than their Chinese counterparts. Beijing-based activist Tong Zeng told reporters that his organization had not yet been able to register in mainland China but that he hoped to convince the authorities that his organization did not threaten social stability. Tong admitted that "it is understandable that the authorities are concerned about stability when so many people are involved," citing the millions of Chinese who suffered in the war with Japan, including an estimated 200,000 "comfort women" in China alone.[117]

The lighthouse controversy escalated when Japanese activists applied to have the lighthouse recognized as an official beacon and Prime Minister Ryutaro Hashimoto visited Yasukuni Shrine on his birthday, July 29. Though Hashimoto visited in a "private capacity," he was the first prime minister to do so since Nakasone's official visit eleven years earlier. The same day, China conducted its forty-fifth nuclear test.[118] Two weeks later, a second group of Japanese activists planted a flag on the main disputed island near the lighthouse that had prompted the 1990 controversy. On August 28, Foreign Minister Ikeda reaffirmed Japan's sovereignty over the islands during a visit to Hong Kong, where protesters burned his picture and the Japanese flag outside his hotel.[119] China's rhetoric toughened, with the Chinese Foreign Ministry spokesman Shen Guofang calling Ikeda's remarks "irresponsible" and criticizing the Japanese government for giving "the green light" to right-wing organizations.[120] Yet Shen emphasized that economic ties should not be affected by the dispute, noting that "loans from Japan and the issue of safeguarding China's territorial integrity and sovereignty are two completely different questions."[121]

In early September, the Chinese leadership met and reportedly decided upon a "gradualist approach so as to avoid expected incidents."[122] Restricting China's response to diplomatic steps, the leadership prevented Chinese fishing boats from approaching the islands and closely monitored grassroots anti-Japanese activities. On September 9, Japanese activists made another landing to repair the makeshift lighthouse, which had been damaged during a typhoon. When the Japanese Foreign Ministry asserted that the landing was legal because the islands were privately owned by a Japanese family, China's Foreign Ministry spokesman reminded Japan of its responsibility to take "effective measures," lest the activities of right-wing groups "cause serious damage to Sino-Japanese relations."[123] China's ambassador to Japan lodged a diplomatic protest in Tokyo.

Even as China's diplomatic warnings became more forceful, the government stepped up efforts to prevent anti-Japanese demonstrations. Fearing that "strong tactics might result in a closer Japan–United States alliance," the Chinese government instructed local authorities to keep protests "from getting out of hand," preventing protests if possible and otherwise directing protesters "away from the city center."[124] As posters denouncing Japanese actions began to appear on university campuses, Beijing public security officials rejected student applications for permission to protest.[125] An internal circular instructed university officials to prevent students from staging demonstrations.[126] In Shanghai, university administrators shut Internet sites and BBS used to air anti-Japanese views, citing "extreme comments" and the delicacy of the "security issue[s] involved."[127]

Chinese authorities also ordered Tong Zeng and several of his associates to leave Beijing for the approaching sixty-fifth anniversary of Japan's invasion of Manchuria on September 18, 1931, criticizing their activities for interfering with Sino-Japanese relations.[128] Tong Zeng had signed an open letter with 257 signatories, calling upon Jiang Zemin to send military troops to the islands to end Japanese "occupation."[129] Along with more than a dozen activists from around China, Tong Zeng announced the establishment of the civilian China Federation for Defending the Diaoyu Islands (CFDD) on September 8. The group made plans for a small demonstration to mark the September 18 anniversary and demanded that the Central Military Commission take "concrete steps" to stop Japanese right-wing activities.[130] Under pressure from his work unit, Tong Zeng announced that he would defer plans to hold a demonstration until after the "sensitive period" had passed.[131] Plans to make a protest voyage to the islands and join activists from Hong Kong, Taiwan, and Macao were also scuttled.[132] Heavy security thronged the Japanese embassy in Beijing on September 18. While thousands demonstrated in Hong Kong and Taiwan, the anniversary passed without protest in mainland China.

From a domestic perspective, the government faced a dilemma in deciding whether to repress or allow protests. Neither course of action was safe. On the one hand, Chinese leaders feared that protests against Japan might get out of hand. A Chinese military officer noted that "if the Party allowed the people to protest unhindered, the first day they would be protesting against Japan, the next day against the lack of response by the government, and on the third day against the government itself."[133] The internal circular banning anti-Japanese protests intimated that student feelings might escalate into "student strikes" and link up with off-campus activism.[134] As Tong Zeng noted, "As the 18th [of] September is approaching, the departments concerned have collected some information and they are aware that university and college students are looking for me. For the sake of the overall situation, these departments have advised me to hide myself for the time being."[135] Chinese authorities also expressed concern that democratic dissidents might use the opportunity afforded by anti-Japanese protest.[136] Two democratic activists, Liu Xiaobo and Wang Xizhe, issued an open letter supporting military action against Japan in the East China Sea, writing: "If the Chinese government can use force against Taiwan and the students in Tiananmen Square, why doesn't it dare use force against Japanese militarism?"[137]

On the other hand, Chinese authorities were concerned that the decision to repress protests would generate widespread resentment. The *People's Daily* and *People's Liberation Daily* received more than 37,000 letters and 150,000 signatures on petitions calling for the government to defend Chinese sovereignty more forcefully.[138] Tong Zeng's call to action had also garnered support among some Party elites. The planned demonstration for September 18 involved over a dozen cadres and Chinese People's Political Consultative Conference (CPPCC) representatives.[139] Fourteen graduates of the prestigious Whampoa Military Academy signed a petition circulated by Tong Zeng calling on the Chinese military to destroy Japanese markers on the islands and escort civilian boats to the islands.[140] Concerned about the potential backlash, the Chinese leadership initially indicated that local authorities should not "excessively suppress" displays of patriotic feelings.[141] The president of the Chinese Academy of Social Sciences stated that mismanagement of anti-Japanese sentiment "could well lead to nationwide unrest against both a corrupt and incompetent government and the privileged stratum. . . and may even bring about greater trouble than the political turbulence of 1989."[142] CPPCC standing committee member Xu Simin reportedly warned Jiang Zemin that stifling anti-Japanese protests would tarnish the government's legitimacy, writing: "If that news is true, you will lose people's hearts. That should immediately be put to a halt."[143]

Faced with a domestic dilemma between allowing and stifling protests, China's diplomatic incentives appear to have tipped the scales toward preemptive repression. Allowing protests would have made it even more difficult for the Chinese leadership to resist domestic demands to take a more aggressive stance against Japan. With protesters in the streets, the government would have been hard-pressed to maintain a restrained stance and resist calls to defend China's claim to the islands with force. Rather than risk pushing Japan closer to the United States on the eve of a major revision in the parameters guiding the U.S.-Japan alliance, Chinese leaders decided in favor of "restrained yet adequate" steps: addressing the issue through diplomatic channels and eschewing the pressure of nationalist protests.[144]

The Chinese leadership bore the domestic costs of repression, censoring Internet discussions, banning protests, and stationing a heavy police presence in front of the Japanese embassy. Tong Zeng and other activists were sent out of Beijing and told that their activities posed too great a risk to "the stability of China's entire environment."[145] To mitigate the cost of repression for the September 18 anniversary, mainland news media were instructed not to cover anti-Japanese protests in Hong Kong and Taiwan, lest the news embolden mainland students to take to the streets.[146] Even the National People's Congress was prevented "from issuing a letter of protest regarding the problem, for fear of provoking the nationalistic sentiments of the public at large."[147]

These efforts did not eliminate popular resentment, as international media were quick to point out. One Tsinghua University student told the *South China Morning Post*: "The police should let students hold parades according to law.... Why should we have to keep silent while people in Hong Kong and Taiwan are expressing their anger by going on marches?"[148] Efforts to stifle online commentary were also imperfect, as users found alternative venues to voice their discontent. One disgruntled message read: "Why has the Fudan bulletin board been closed? Could it be that criticizing Japan endangers the leadership position of our party?"[149]

Diplomatic Impact: Reshelving the East China Sea Issue

By repressing anti-Japanese demonstrations and taking a "restrained attitude," as Foreign Minister Qian Qichen explained to his Japanese counterpart, the Chinese government sent a costly signal of its commitment to insulating the bilateral relationship from nationalist pressure.[150] Given visible attempts by students and activists to organize demonstrations in mainland China as well as voluble protests in Hong Kong and Taiwan, there was little doubt about the credibility of Chinese efforts to stifle nationalist protests. Indeed, Downs and Saunders note that the domestic backlash against the government's decision to repress protests was even stronger in 1996 than during the 1990 lighthouse controversy,[151] given the growing popularity of the war reparations movement and books like *China Can Say No* and *Behind the Demonization of China*. Chinese officials emphasized that the government was trying to keep the dispute from harming the "overall view" of Sino-Japanese friendship despite the popular anger aroused by Japanese actions.[152] Distancing the PRC from protests in Hong Kong and Taiwan, Vice Premier Zhu Rongji told a visiting Japanese delegation that "China has never brought problems to Japan and I hope the Japanese government will consider the thoughts of the Chinese people."[153]

Although the Japanese government did not concede on the underlying sovereignty issue, it recommitted to restraining the activities of right-wing groups concerning the islands, restoring the status quo ante. As one Chinese scholar summed up, "Facing the continuously rising protests by the Chinese government and civilians, the Japanese government began to take a more cautious stance on whether the lighthouse would become a navigation marker.... Japanese efforts to forcibly seize the islands failed, and the two governments reaffirmed the principle of 'shelving disputes.'"[154] In light of popular anger in China, Japanese officials were concerned about the Chinese government's ability to maintain a policy of restraint without reciprocal measures on the Japanese side. Indeed, conservative Japanese media urged the Hashimoto administration to emulate China's strategy, stating that "The

Chinese government insists it is acting favorably towards Japan by saying that China has adopted a self-restrained stance—and the result would appear to be what the Chinese side has been seeking. The Japanese government should draw lessons from such cunningness."[155] Richard Bush describes the resolution of the controversy more kindly, noting the strategic benefit of two governments working together to prevent nationalist sentiments from disrupting the relationship. "In order to preserve the two countries' shared interests," Bush writes, "a cyclical ritual emerged in which nationalists acted to assert their country's claim but diplomats worked in concert both to accommodate these shows of patriotism and to maintain basic control."[156]

The resolution of the 1996 Diaoyu/Senkaku crisis illustrates that the specter of nationalist protests can be diplomatically advantageous even when stifled. Although Japan had taken a firmer stance at the outset of the 1996 lighthouse controversy than in the 1990 dispute, Japan became more accommodating as China took a tougher rhetorical stance and repressed nationalist demonstrations. Initially, the Japanese chief cabinet secretary acknowledged the possibility of a diplomatic incident arising from the new lighthouse but said that "I personally don't think we should say this and that about something being constructed legitimately with permission from the Japanese landlord."[157] By mid-September, according to Akihiko Tanaka, "the Japanese government, seeing the heated reactions in Taiwan and Hong Kong, and observing the situation in Beijing where protest movement might occur, set out to wrap up the situation."[158] On September 17, the Japanese Foreign Ministry spokesman stated that "We attach great importance to relations with China. We are worried about Chinese people's strong feelings on the matter."[159] A few days later, the U.S. State Department spokesman also tacitly referenced Chinese public anger, acknowledging the "great emotional content" that could escalate the dispute beyond a "war of words."[160]

On September 24, Foreign Minister Ikeda told his Chinese counterpart Qian Qichen that Japan would suspend its decision on the lighthouses as official navigation markers, the same concession that had ended the lighthouse controversy in 1990.[161] Although both sides were determined to shelve the issue, protest flotillas had already set sail from Hong Kong and Taiwan. When Japanese coastguard vessels blocked the protest boats from advancing further, Hong Kong activist David Chan drowned after jumping into the rough sea, hoping to swim ashore and plant the Chinese flag.

Following the drowning incident, both governments redoubled their efforts to prevent nationalist sentiment from derailing diplomatic progress toward reshelving the dispute and stabilizing bilateral relations. In October, Hong Kong activists managed to plant a flag on the islands. Protesters broke into the Japanese consulate in Hong Kong before being removed by police.[162] Yet China's response was largely limited to verbal statements.[163] In a major speech, Premier Li Peng urged Japan to safeguard the "overall interests" of relations between China and Japan, warning that "no action that hurts the feelings of the Chinese people will get anywhere."[164] In Beijing, Chinese students said they were too afraid to protest. While they applauded the Hong Kong protests and felt the Chinese government had been too weak in defending the national interest, they feared punishment.[165] Under close surveillance, Tong Zeng faxed a letter of protest to the Japanese embassy and organized a campaign via telephone to wear black armbands in memory of David Chan.[166] In November, authorities took away Tong Zeng's passport and prevented mainland activists from attending a Diaoyu conference in Macao.[167] The government also sought to rein in popular sentiments, making it difficult for nationalist authors to publish further works and instructing journalists not to cover the "say no" books because they promoted sentiments that conflicted with the government's strategy.[168]

The Japanese government also took steps to buttress its commitment to bilateral relations. Prime Minister Hashimoto voiced fears that popular anger over Chan's drowning would jeopardize efforts to calm the dispute, telling reporters: "I do not have the optimism to believe it will not have any diplomatic impact."[169] The Chief Cabinet Secretary expressed Japan's condolences, stating that the government was earnest about preventing the situation from worsening.[170] On October 3, Japanese police raided the headquarters of the right-wing organization that had built the lighthouse and charged one of its members with illegal possession of a handgun.[171] On October 4, the Japanese government formally suspended the lighthouse decision, noting that "recent developments should not be allowed to adversely affect Japan's relationship with the People's Republic of China and other neighbors including Taiwan and Hong Kong."[172]

At China's request, Prime Minister Hashimoto also called off his plans to visit Yasukuni Shrine on October 16, the anniversary of his cousin's death in the war.[173] Hashimoto told reporters that the decision reflected "mutual understanding that the issue should in no way damage the overall relations between Japan and China," saying: "As prime minister, I must act cautiously so as not to generate unnecessary suspicion about Japan or cause trouble to Japan."[174] In December, the Japanese government pledged to help China clean up 700,000 chemical weapons left behind by the Japanese army in northeastern China.[175] After Beijing signed an international agreement to halt nuclear testing, Japan resumed grant aid to China the following March. The two sides made plans for visits by Hashimoto and Li Peng to mark the twenty-fifth anniversary of normalization in 1997 and Jiang Zemin to mark the twentieth anniversary of the Treaty of Peace and Friendship in 1998.[176]

Further illustrating their commitment to shelving the East China Sea issue after the 1996 lighthouse controversy, both governments acted with restraint when a Japanese legislator planted a flag on the largest island in May 1997. The Japanese government promised to investigate the landing, stating that from an "external point of view" it was "not desirable to stir up controversy."[177] Although the legislator claimed that a member of parliament should be able to inspect Japanese lands, the Japanese government for the first time criticized the landing as "illegal," pointing out that the island's private owner had not given permission. The Chinese Foreign Ministry acknowledged that the legislator's actions "contravened the policy of the Japanese government," and nationalist activists in Beijing and Nanjing reported that Chinese authorities instructed them not to organize any activities. Tong Zeng indicated that he would refrain from any contact with other activists during the sensitive period surrounding the June 4 anniversary, stating: "I don't want the Government to discredit our activities and smear us as rioters."[178]

China's repeated efforts to stymie anti-Japanese protests gave credibility to the government's signal of restraint and reassurance in the diplomatic standoff over the islands—a signal that Japanese observers appear to have received, including conservatives that bemoaned the success of China's strategy.[179] China succeeded in restoring the status quo ante in the East China Sea, coaxing the Japanese government to reshelve the issue and discourage domestic nationalists from further provocations on the islands. The Hashimoto government referenced the reactions of the Chinese people in explaining its concessions, declining to approve the lighthouse as a navigation marker and refraining from subsequent visits to Yasukuni. It is noteworthy that Japanese observers understood the domestic pressures on the Chinese government in the absence of street demonstrations in mainland China, suggesting that grassroots mobilization was sufficiently visible to make the act of repression credible. China's restraint was apparent to other foreign governments as well. Singaporean deputy prime minister Lee Hsien Loong pointed out that anti-Japanese protests had occurred in Hong Kong and Taiwan but not mainland China, noting: "I see China taking a cautious attitude."[180]

As to China's broader diplomatic objectives, the revised U.S.-Japan defense guidelines were approved in September 1997 with language that was less provocative to China than the 1996 joint declaration. The revised guidelines dropped the controversial "Asia-Pacific" phrase and instead defined the alliance as covering "situations in areas surrounding Japan."[181] In short, the new language remained ambiguous on the issue of whether a Taiwan scenario fell under the purview of U.S.-Japan security cooperation. According to Premier Li Peng, Prime Minister Hashimoto "refused to state clearly whether the scope of the Japan-U.S. security defense cooperation guidelines included Taiwan" during his visit to China in September 1997.[182] Yet the revised guidelines were not as pointed as they might have been. Hook et al. conclude that the Japanese Foreign Ministry's concern for bilateral relations edged out the Ministry of Defense's desire to define the alliance geographically, noting that "Given the Chinese criticism and the anti-militarist norms still embedded in domestic society, the government has opted for a 'situational,' not 'geographic,' interpretation."[183]

Whether the moderated language can be attributed to China's restraint during the islands row depends on our assessment of the counterfactual. Had China decided to allow anti-Japanese protests, the increased costs of defying street demonstrators might have pressed the government to satisfy protest demands by taking

action, including the dispatch of patrol vessels. Chinese protests and other escalatory measures may have pushed Japan and the United States to adopt a more pointed
interpretation of the revised guidelines—as they would under President Bush and
Prime Minister Koizumi in February 2005, as we will see in the following chapter.
Even without protests, the Japanese public was already set against Japanese concessions on the islands and critical of the government's conciliatory stance. Following
China's nuclear tests, opinion polls revealed that 44 percent of the Japanese public
believed that the decision to freeze grant aid was too lenient.[184] Regarding the East
China Sea controversy, nearly half of Japanese respondents believed that their government had been too soft, a quarter believed the status quo was acceptable, and
only 7 percent believed the Japanese government should have made concessions.[185]
In the face of more provocative Chinese actions, the Japanese government might
have faced even higher costs of adopting a restrained stance.

American officials might also have been galvanized by Chinese protests to take
a stronger position during the crisis. Throughout the lighthouse controversy, U.S.
officials maintained a low-key stance. U.S. State Department spokesman Nicholas
Burns stated that "we do not support any individual country's claim to these islands"
and urged the "orderly and peaceful and stable" resolution of the dispute.[186] Asked
whether the United States would intervene in the event of a military clash over the
islands, Burns responded: "My policy is not to comment upon hypothetical situations unless it's in my self-interest to do so."[187] U.S. ambassador to Japan and former
vice president Walter Mondale had also told reporters that an attack on the Senkaku
(Diaoyu) Islands would not automatically trigger the U.S.-Japan security treaty and
American military intervention.[188] According to Michael Green, "The administration's extension of neutrality on the territorial issue to neutrality in the event of
Chinese use of force seemed safe, since military confrontation was so unlikely."[189]

Had China allowed protests, U.S. officials might have been quicker to clarify that
Article 5 of the U.S.-Japan security treaty covers the Senkaku Islands, as a report by
the Congressional Research Service later that year pointed out.[190] It was not until
after the resolution of the 1996 dispute that the Clinton administration clarified the
U.S. treaty commitment, having drawn criticism from hawks in Congress and Japan.
In November, Deputy Assistant Secretary of Defense for Asia and the Pacific Kurt
Campbell became "the first U.S. official to confirm that the security treaty applies
to the Senkaku Islands," according to the *Yomiuri Shimbun*. Campbell stated that
"The United States has a very strong commitment to Japan under Article V of the
security treaty. . . requiring the United States to support Japan and its territories."[191]
Although some Chinese analysts lamented that the "superficially 'neutral' U.S. posi-
tion on the Diaoyu Islands changed" to favor the Japanese side,[192] by 1997 U.S.-
China relations had improved to the point where President Clinton and President
Jiang jointly declared their intent to build a "strategic partnership."

China's efforts to restrain anti-Japanese unrest and signals of reassurance helped
persuade Japan to reshelve the territorial issue, exercise caution in subsequent

decisions over the islands and Yasukuni, and provide further bilateral assistance. But China's Taiwan missile exercises had done damage that restraining nationalist protests could not fully undo. As one Japanese scholar noted, "Those crises [in the Taiwan Strait] ironically had the effect of giving life to the redefinition of the security relationship."[193] Yet the outcome of the lighthouse controversy and the language of the revised guidelines could have been worse. Had the Chinese government not repressed protests and communicated its commitment to restraint over the islands, the U.S. and Japanese governments might have perceived a greater threat of Chinese military action concerning Taiwan and the nearby islands in the East China Sea.

Conclusion

The simultaneous repression of anti-Japanese protest and encouragement of patriotic propaganda suggests that a domestic legitimation strategy that relies on nationalism need not require antiforeign street protests, which carry additional domestic and diplomatic risks. Although "the rise in negative attitudes toward Japan was a foreseeable side effect"[194] of nationalist propaganda, China's diplomatic options were less constrained by popular anger than they would have been had anti-Japanese demonstrations been allowed. As Yinan He notes, "Public opinion also limited policy options toward Japan over the East China Sea dispute [but] this does not mean that the government could not take ad hoc measures to temporarily deescalate a dispute to avert a serious crisis."[195]

At the same time, the sincerity of popular sentiment and the difficulty of repressing anti-Japanese protests provided an important source of credibility in China's efforts to signal reassurance. Stifling protests enabled the government to show flexibility and demonstrate the value it placed on other strategic objectives, particularly economic engagement with Japan. In stifling anti-Japanese protests, the Chinese government also eschewed the opportunity to demonstrate solidarity with Taiwan and Hong Kong, including pro-democratic legislators in Hong Kong. As Yongnian Zheng notes, "It was a rare opportunity for the mainland to unify so many diverse political forces and form a national solidarity among different parts of China. However, for Chinese patriots things turned out quite badly. . . . the government clearly expressed its unwillingness to support these demonstrations by adopting hard measures to control rising anti-Japanese voices on the mainland."[196]

With popular anger threatening to spill over into the streets, the Japanese government expressed concern about Chinese feelings and took actions to relieve pressure on the Chinese government during the two lighthouse controversies. Indeed, Chinese control over domestic activists remained imperfect, as Japanese observers were reminded in 1997. Despite efforts to prevent protests during Prime Minister Hashimoto's visit to northeastern China, 40 war victims demonstrated in the city

of Harbin and demanded a formal apology for Japanese atrocities.[197] The following year, police detained several of Tong Zeng's supporters for signing a petition
to the National People's Congress calling for his election as the next president of
China.[198] The petition gathered almost 200 signatures from across three provinces, a
reminder that anti-Japanese activism, while nominally directed outward, also posed
a potential challenge to the regime itself.

It is also worth noting that insecurity and divisions among China's elite in the
1990s did not translate into permission for anti-Japanese protests. As Deng Xiaoping
grew ill, Jiang Zemin began to consolidate power in 1994 and 1995. As Susan Shirk
notes, Jiang was "worried about challenges from rival leaders and doubts from the
public—memories of the Tiananmen crisis were fresh—and as a result, was much
more attentive to nationalist public opinion."[199] Yet there is little evidence that Jiang's
insecurity tempted either him or his opponents to use anti-Japanese protests to gain
a tactical advantage in the mid-1990s. Jiang's weakness may better explain China's
confrontational approach during the Taiwan Strait crisis, where the U.S. decision to
allow Lee Teng-hui to visit the United States was said to strengthen the position of
Chinese military hawks.[200] Jiang's desire to demonstrate leadership may also have
prompted his tough remarks on history when he visited Japan in 1998.[201] Jiang's
personal insecurity and sensitivity to public feelings may have led him to "push for
more concessions on his trip to Japan than Tokyo was willing to give," as Fewsmith
and Rosen note, but these factors did not spell permission for anti-Japanese protests.[202] It was not until the 2000s that China took a more permissive attitude toward
anti-Japanese activism, as we see in the following chapter.

6

The 2005 Anti-Japan Protests and Sino-Japanese Relations in the 2000s

Policeman A: How many are coming? Thirty?

Policeman B: No, 20.

Policeman A: When do they arrive?

Policeman B: 10:00 a.m. is the official start time. They'll arrive around 9:45.

Policeman A: Has it been approved?

Policeman B: Definitely not approved, but the government has given tacit consent.[1] This group plays by the rules. Before coming, they call the government and say, "Tomorrow at 10:00?"

—Overheard while waiting for protesters to assemble outside the Japanese embassy, June 18, 2007

Large-scale anti-Japanese demonstrations broke out across China in April 2005, spearheaded by an online signature campaign against Japan's bid for a permanent seat on the UN Security Council. Why did the Chinese government allow anti-Japanese protests in the spring of 2005, and what impact did these protests have upon negotiations over the expansion of the UN Security Council (UNSC)? The protests and petitions coincided with a critical period of international deliberations, a time when there was rising confidence that the proposal by Japan, Germany, Brazil, and India—the so-called G4—might succeed if put to a vote in the UN General Assembly. As a Japanese Foreign Ministry official recalled, "For a long time, the possibility of permanent membership was like a dream. But at that moment, it was a reality."[2]

As the likelihood of a vote in the General Assembly increased, so did the Chinese government's determination to halt the G4 campaign before it progressed further.[3] If the G4 proposal were to pass with two-thirds support, an amendment to the UN Charter would have been raised for ratification. At such a juncture, China as a permanent member of the Security Council would have been faced with a painful decision: to veto an amendment supported by two-thirds of the General Assembly, or to accept Japan as a permanent member of the Security Council.

China regarded casting a solo veto as an option of last resort, creating uncertainty about whether China would ultimately exercise its veto power if the G4 proposal were to pass the General Assembly. As Samuel Kim notes, "Given its long-standing assault on the veto as an expression of hegemonic behavior, China tried hard—and successfully—not to allow itself to be cornered into having no choice but to cast its solo veto."[4] To veto an amendment to the UN Charter would mean opposing a reform package that a supermajority of the General Assembly had already approved, making China look doubly hypocritical for claiming to represent the developing world. For China, a better outcome would be to persuade another permanent Security Council member to block the G4 proposal with China, and the best outcome would be to mobilize enough opposition to prevent a General Assembly vote in the first place.

The anti-Japanese petitions and protests helped China get its preferred outcome without having to exercise a solo veto. By allowing grassroots petitions and protests, the Chinese government could more credibly claim that its hands were tied by public opinion, lessening uncertainty over whether China would ultimately acquiesce to reforms endorsed by the UN General Assembly. China could have prevented the anti-Japanese protests, but repression would have been costly and at odds with Chinese opposition to Japan's bid.

Diplomatic success also enabled the Chinese government to curtail anti-Japanese protests after three weeks with relative ease. Following the anti-Japanese protests, the United States and key regional actors reduced their public support for the G4 proposal. Japan offered an apology for Japan's misdeeds in World War II and declined to press China for an apology for damages during the anti-Japanese protests. While the United States continued to support Japan's bid, it also publicly opposed a General Assembly vote on the issue, siding with China in stressing the need for "consensus" before moving forward with UNSC reform. In the end, on the eve of a potential vote in the General Assembly, China and the United States agreed to block the G4 proposal.

Backdrop to the 2005 Protests: Bilateral Tensions and the Koizumi Administration

Sino-Japanese relations had already deteriorated when anti-Japanese protests broke out in 2005. Prime Minister Junichiro Koizumi hoped to maintain good relations with Beijing, but his annual visits to Yasukuni Shrine and revisions to Japanese history textbooks drew Chinese ire. Although Koizumi initially avoided visiting Yasukuni on the sensitive August 15 anniversary, Chinese officials declared that his visits "seriously hurt the feelings of the Chinese people" and "violated the Japanese government's serious expressions and promises on the historical issue."[5] In April 2002 and January 2003, Koizumi visited Yasukuni for the second and third time since taking office, an act that Chinese officials said "undermines the political foundation of China-Japan relations and runs counter to the Japanese government's commitment to face up to and review its history of aggression."[6]

After Japanese media revealed that the Japanese government had leased three of the Diaoyu/Senkaku Islands from their private owner in 2002, Chinese authorities began taking a more permissive stance toward grassroots "protect the Diaoyu Islands" (Bao Diao) activities. The Internet also provided new platforms for nationalist sentiment and anti-Japanese activism in China, including web forums, chat groups, and online signature campaigns.[7] One of the founders of the Patriots Alliance Network (*Aiguozhe Tongmeng Wang*) web forum recalled that 2003 was a kind of "test year" for mainland Chinese activism against Japan, including two Bao Diao voyages and two signature petitions, one against the use of Japanese high-speed rail technology and one demanding compensation for victims of chemical weapons left behind by the Japanese army in World War II.[8] In June 2003, Bao Diao activists were allowed to sail from mainland China for the first time before being turned back by Japanese patrol vessels. Patriots Alliance Network chief Lu Yunfei told reporters that "the government's attitude was made clear by the fact that this time, we were able to set sail, and our return was greeted a welcoming chorus of media reports."[9] Tong Zeng concurred, noting: "This is a civilian, patriotic action. The Chinese authorities have not opposed or stopped it."[10]

In August 2003, China criticized the landing of Japanese activists on the islands despite Tokyo's claim that leasing the islands would help prevent "the illegal landing of third parties."[11] When mainland activists again set sail for the islands in October 2003, the Chinese Foreign Ministry spokesperson asserted that "the determination of the Chinese government and people to safeguard national sovereignty and territorial integrity is unswerving."[12] State media featured photos of the second mainland Bao Diao voyage in what the *South China Morning Post* called "the first time state media has endorsed the protest, signaling an apparent change of official attitude."[13]

The landing of seven activists from mainland China prompted a potential crisis in March 2004. Japan arrested the Chinese activists for violating domestic immigration laws and indicated that the government would "refrain from actions taken out of consideration for China."[14] For three days, Chinese authorities allowed demonstrations of up to 90 participants outside the Japanese embassy in Beijing, while smaller protests took place in Guangzhou and Shanghai. As Japanese ambassador to China Koreshige Anami noted, "I cannot remember flag burning ever having happened in front of the embassy in the presence of Chinese police."[15] The year before, anti-Japanese protests over the islands and chemical weapons victims had been limited to no more than a dozen participants.

The crisis abated after Japan deported the Chinese activists on the third day. Koizumi said he had "instructed government officials to consider how to handle the issue from a comprehensive view so as not to hurt the bilateral relationship with China."[16] Afterward, Chinese authorities began to scrutinize the activities of nationalist organizations more closely, often taking preemptive action to shut down online petitions before they could trigger offline mobilization. Nationalist sentiment continued to simmer, however, and even escalated to violence when Chinese soccer fans in Beijing rioted over Japan's 3-1 win against China in the August 2004 Asia Cup final.[17] Later that month, the Chinese government suspended the Patriots Alliance Network website after an online signature campaign opposing the adoption of Japanese bullet train technology gathered nearly 70,000 signatures in under 24 hours.[18] "The government thinks we're going off to oppose Japan," said a Patriots Alliance Network member. "It's the social instability factor. So they closed the website."[19]

Meanwhile, both governments continued to take unilateral actions in the East China Sea, including surveys by Chinese and Japanese research vessels for natural gas. In November, Japan protested the appearance of a Chinese submarine in waters near Okinawa, an incident for which Chinese officials later expressed regret.[20] On February 9, 2005, Japan for the first time announced that it would officially recognize and put a lighthouse on the disputed islands under "state control," actions that China denounced as "illegal and invalid."[21] While preventing activists from continuing with plans for tourist cruises and sea voyages, Chinese authorities allowed a group of 50 Chinese activists to stage a two-hour protest in front of the Japanese embassy in Beijing on February 15.[22]

Political relations continued to cool even as economic ties deepened, with China becoming Japan's number one trading partner in January 2005. At the February 19 "two plus two" meeting between American and Japanese foreign and defense ministers, the issue of Taiwan was for the first time listed as a common strategic objective. The reference to Taiwan raised Chinese concerns "that the Japanese-U.S. security cooperation mechanism has breached a bilateral framework...interfering with China's internal affairs and setting an impediment to its great cause for reunification," according to Xinhua.[23] A senior analyst at the Shanghai Institute for International Studies noted that the statement was "taken very seriously" as a sign that "in a contingency, Japan would provide logistical military support."[24] According to Shi Yinhong, a prominent Japan expert at People's University in Beijing, the statement joined a growing list of Japanese actions that China deemed provocative, "includ[ing] not only Japan's tampering with the history of aggression against China and the long-standing issue over the Diaoyu Islands, but Japan's recent unilateral move to explore the oil and gas fields in the East China Sea as well."[25]

Negotiations over UN Security Council Expansion

Despite the strain in bilateral relations, it was not until Japan's bid for a permanent Security Council seat gained momentum that large-scale anti-Japanese protests erupted with the tacit consent of the Chinese government in April 2005. Anti-Japanese protests occurred over a period of three weeks, mainly on the weekends: April 2–3 in the cities of Chengdu and Shenzhen, April 9–10 in Beijing, Chengdu, Guangzhou, Shenzhen, and others, and April 16–17 in Shanghai, Shenyang, Shenzhen, and other cities across China. By my count, at least 38 cities held anti-Japanese demonstrations, including protest marches and street signature campaigns. An estimated 280 organizations, 107 universities, 41 technical schools, and 28,230,000 Internet users signed petitions against Japan's bid.[26]

The 2005 anti-Japanese protests took place during a crucial window in the international deliberations over UNSC expansion. When Secretary-General Kofi Annan endorsed Japan's candidacy and announced in March 2005 that he would like a decision by September, there was uncertainty over three issues: first, whether the G4 could win a two-thirds majority of the General Assembly to pass a framework resolution expanding the permanent membership of the Security Council; second, whether each of the G4 nations could win a two-thirds majority within their respective regions in the selection of new permanent members; and third, what positions the permanent UNSC members would take in the final ratification stage, particularly as Beijing and Washington both sought to avoid the reputational costs of opposing a reform agenda supported by two-thirds of the General Assembly. As one Italian newspaper noted, "it is by no means a foregone conclusion that the United States or China would veto it: On the contrary, the diplomatic tangle is so complex that, as on other occasions, they would probably decide to fall into line with the will of the majority."[27]

Since the opening of debate on UNSC reform in 1993, Japan had made multiple attempts to gain a permanent seat. Although four non-permanent seats were added in 1963, the composition of the permanent, veto-wielding seats had not changed since the establishment of the United Nations in 1945. The UNSC was still composed of five permanent members with veto power and 10 non-permanent seats without veto power. Although the need for reform had been almost universally acknowledged, disagreement over the appropriate formula had stymied previous rounds of debate. In the late 1990s, Japan and Germany's efforts to expand the Council's permanent membership met with opposition from a group of nations dubbed the "Coffee Club," led by Italy, Mexico, South Korea, and Pakistan. Moreover, U.S. opposition to expansion of the Council beyond 21 seats, which a majority of UN members believed was too small, had effectively halted progress on reform. As Yukio Satoh, Japan's ambassador to the United Nations at the time, noted: "it was pointless to discuss Security Council reform as long as the United States remained rigid on that position, which [most member states] considered a non-starter."[28]

In 2000, a shift in the U.S. position gave impetus to a new round of debate on Security Council reform. Richard Holbrooke, U.S. ambassador to the United Nations, declared that the United States was "prepared to consider proposals that would result in a slightly larger number of seats than twenty-one."[29] By the end of the year, Ambassador Satoh recalled, "well over two-thirds" of UN member states had expressed support for expansion of both permanent and non-permanent member-ship.[30] In 2001, President Bush and Japanese prime minister Yoshiro Mori issued a joint statement supporting Japan's bid for a permanent seat, a commitment reiter-ated by Bush to Mori's successor, Junichiro Koizumi.

In September 2004, Japan and the other members of the G4 began jointly cam-paigning to increase the number of permanent and non-permanent members, attracting support from about 120 member states. Discussion over UNSC reform gained momentum in December 2004, when the expert panel convened by UN secretary-general Kofi Annan released its findings and recommendations, outlin-ing two models (A and B) for expansion. Consistent with the G4 proposal, Model A would create six new permanent seats and three new non-permanent seats. Model B would create eight semi-permanent seats of four-year renewable terms and one new nonpermanent seat, a proposal closer to the position of the Coffee Club. Both models would expand the size of the Council from 15 to 24 members.

Within days, Model A gained the support of three of the five permanent mem-bers whose approval would be needed to expand the Council. France and Russia expressed support for adding permanent members with veto power, and Britain stated support for adding permanent members without veto power.[31] On December 14, a U.S. official for the first time expressed support for giving Japan a seat with veto power.[32] Over the next three months, both camps continued to mobilize support in preparation for the General Assembly debate on April 6 and 7. Opposing the G4 proposal was the newly formed "Uniting for Consensus" movement, a spin-off of the Coffee Club, which supported a decision by "consensus" rather than a vote in the General Assembly, which the G4 favored.

Three events in March appeared to tilt the board in favor of the G4 proposal, prompting fear among official and popular circles in China that the G4 proposal might succeed in getting a two-thirds majority if put to a vote in the General Assembly. First, the 53-member African Union reached a unanimous decision to seek two permanent seats with veto power, along the lines of Model A.[33] By announc-ing their preference for expanding the permanent membership of the Council, the African Union strengthened the G4's position.[34] Second, U.S. secretary of state Condoleezza Rice stated in Tokyo that the United States "unambiguously supports a permanent seat for Japan on the United Nations Security Council."[35] Third, UN secretary-general Annan endorsed Japan's candidacy by suggesting that "those who contribute most to the United Nations financially, militarily, and diplomatically" should be given increased "involvement in decision-making."[36] Furthermore, Annan sided with the G4 in stressing that he wanted a decision—by vote if necessary—in time for the sixtieth anniversary celebration of the United Nations in September. His remarks produced consternation in states that opposed the expansion of perma-nent membership but were warmly welcomed by Japan, which released a statement saying that "the report of the Secretary General gives momentum toward the realization of the reform in line with Japan's position."[37]

Although the Chinese Foreign Ministry reacted mildly, stressing the importance of "broad consensus" and "unanimity through consultation,"[38] other parts of the party-state apparatus began to highlight a grassroots campaign among mainland and overseas Chinese to oppose Japan's candidacy. The *People's Daily* website covered the Internet petition against Japan's bid that had been launched by overseas Chinese associations in San Francisco and New York in late February.[39] The website also listed the names of two participating mainland sponsors, nationalist websites based in Beijing and Shanghai whose servers were quickly overloaded. The webmaster of 9.18 Patriot Net, Wu Zukang, sought help from several commercial sites. The signature campaign quickly spread to more than 250 mainland websites and Internet portals, including Sohu and Netease.[40] According to a Sina.com news editor, seven additional servers had to be added to handle the traffic.[41]

Street petitions began to take place in cities across China, sponsored by the China Federation for Defending the Diaoyu Islands and the Patriots Alliance Network. The first street petition to turn violent occurred on Saturday, April 2 in Chengdu, the capital of Sichuan province in the southwest. Not far from where a dozen activists were collecting signatures, a large crowd smashed the windows of a Japanese supermarket, Ito Yokado, before police dispersed the protest. A raucous demonstration took place the next day in Shenzhen, one of China's youngest and wealthiest cities. Demonstrators gathered for a one-hour rally and signature drive followed by a four-hour march through the city. More than 200 police prevented several protesters from entering another Japanese supermarket, Jusco, prompting some demonstrators to throw garbage at the police and shout "Beat down the traitors!"[42] The same weekend, street petitions against Japan's candidacy took place in 13 other Chinese cities.

Meanwhile, Japan's UNSC bid continued to gain momentum. On March 31, 134 nations attended a meeting in support of the G4 proposal, well over the two-thirds necessary to pass a General Assembly vote. When Japanese education officials approved new history textbooks on April 5 that were viewed in China and Korea as glossing over Japan's wartime atrocities, "it was like pouring oil on fire," said a senior Patriots Alliance Network activist.[43] On April 4 and 6, China's UN ambassador, Wang Guangya, "took the unusual step of expressing his position" in support of "consensus," statements that were interpreted by Japan as "strongly suggesting that China has allied itself with the Uniting for Consensus Group."[44] Chinese media also featured photos of anti-Japanese demonstrations in Seoul, where Korean legislators were also considering a resolution against Japan's bid.[45]

Yet Chinese officials still had not explicitly stated whether they would oppose Japan's bid, leaving the issue open to speculation. In the Japanese press, one report stated that Wang had "indicated cautiousness about Japan's bid" and that China had "not made a decision on whether to support or oppose a specific country's bid for a permanent council seat."[46] Chinese media suggested that the success of the G4 proposal hinged on China's stance, while stressing the potential international repercussions of taking a negative stance. On April 6, a widely reposted article stated that the Chinese government's stance would "directly influence the outcome" of the G4 proposal, but that "to this day, the Chinese government has not declared where it stands...in order to avoid directly provoking Japan."[47] On April 7, the major Internet portals all reposted an article by Singapore's *Lianhe Zaobao*, which stated that the likelihood of two-thirds support for the G4 proposal was "quite large", but since all of the other permanent members had expressed support for Japan's bid, it would be "extremely difficult for China to exercise its veto power."[48]

The first indication that the G4 proposal was in trouble came on April 7, when U.S. ambassador Shirin Tahir-Kheli, senior adviser on UN reform to the secretary of state, stated that "the United States would like to move forward on the basis of broad consensus" and "without artificial deadlines."[49] Her statements prompted dismay in Japan and delighted speculation in the Chinese media. "Is the United States dumping (*paoqi*) Japan?" asked *China Newsweek*.[50] The next day, a member of Annan's High-Level Panel, former U.S. national security advisor Brent Scowcroft, stated that "the likelihood of Japan becoming a UNSC member is very small."[51] As Japanese deputy permanent representative Shinichi recalled, "Washington was clearly displeased with the fact that reform had picked up momentum with little U.S. involvement. In any case, the opposition of two permanent members of the Security Council to the secretary general's timetable could not but have a powerful impact."[52]

That weekend, tens of thousands of protestors attended demonstrations in Beijing, Guangzhou, Shenzhen, and Chengdu. In Beijing, what began on the morning of April 9 as a rally in the northwest university district became a march that ended several hours later outside the Japanese embassy and ambassador's residence in the eastern business district. Demonstrators shouted slogans against Japan's UNSC bid and claim to the Diaoyu Islands, urging a boycott of Japanese goods. According to estimates by the Beijing Public Security Bureau, over 10,000 protesters took part.[53] Riot police stationed at the embassy and ambassador's residence prevented demonstrators from entering but otherwise did not interfere with the protest. Demonstrators threw stones and empty water bottles. A few cars were overturned and smashed. As a Japanese official who snuck outside the embassy to observe the crowd recalled: "The demonstrators were smart, chanting 'Patriotism is not a crime!' and 'Never forget national humiliation!' They said to the police, 'You are our friends. We are demonstrating against Japan, so if you stop us that means you are supporting Japan.'"[54] Buses were provided to take students and protesters back to the university district, but many students refused offers of transportation. Other participants were local to the area, including migrant workers who threw bricks from nearby construction sites.

Following the April 9 protest in Beijing, Japan's foreign minister summoned the Chinese ambassador to Japan and demanded a formal apology and compensation for damages. The Chinese ambassador criticized the vandalism but did not apologize. As the diplomats met, tens of thousands of demonstrators protested again in Shenzhen, where anti-Japan protests had erupted the weekend before, as well as in Guangzhou, where protesters surrounded the Japanese consulate. At the United Nations, a reporter asked Kofi Annan whether he found it "reasonable" that "public opinion in Asian countries like China and Korea is demanding that Japan should redress its past atrocities before it can become a permanent member of the Security Council."[55] Annan said he "followed the developments you are talking about" and hoped that "when the Council takes up the issue of expansion, some of these issues would have been worked out within the countries so that the Representatives can come to the General Assembly ready to take decisions or with a clear position."[56] Chinese media quickly highlighted his remarks with the headline, "Whether Japan Joins the UNSC Should First Be Decided by Asian Countries."[57]

On April 11, statements by U.S. and Chinese officials indicated that Japan's bid was unlikely to succeed. U.S. ambassador to the United Nations John Bolton stated at his confirmation hearing that it would be "politically very difficult to make any change in the composition of the permanent membership" in light of the "things that were going on in China over the weekend, combined with public statements made by senior Chinese officials."[58] At a meeting of the Uniting for Consensus movement, China's ambassador declared China's opposition to a vote before reaching a consensus. More than 110 countries attended the Uniting for Consensus meeting, "raising doubts" about the G4's ability to achieve two-thirds support.[59] "Let us not kid ourselves," said Germany's UN ambassador. "Everyone knows that a consensus on this issue is impossible." Japanese prime minister Koizumi acknowledged the negative turn of events but expressed qualified optimism: "It is true that things are not going very smoothly, [but] the momentum for reforming the United Nations has never risen this high. It is a chance in that sense."[60]

On April 12, Chinese premier Wen Jiabao publicly opposed Japan's candidacy, telling reporters during his visit to India that "the strong responses from the Asian people should make the Japanese Government have deep and profound reflections. . . . Only a country that respects history, takes responsibility for its past, and wins over the trust of the people of Asia and the world at large can take greater responsibility in the international community."[61] Koizumi proposed a meeting with the Chinese president on the sidelines of the upcoming Asian-Africa summit in Bandung, Indonesia but otherwise held firm. On April 13, as working-level talks between China and Japan were held in Beijing, the Japanese Ministry of Economy, Trade and Industry announced that it would grant oil and gas test-drilling rights to companies in the East China Sea, a move that the Chinese Foreign Ministry spokesman called "a serious provocation of China's rights and international norms."[62] On April 14, Japanese foreign minister Nobutaka Machimura told a parliamentary committee that he would take a tough line during his visit to Beijing that weekend.[63]

Meanwhile, Japan took steps to retool its UNSC strategy. On the heels of the Chinese premier's remarks, Russia's foreign minister told Japan that "consensus is needed" and expressed reservation about putting the issue to a vote.[64] With three permanent UNSC members in support of "consensus" rather than a vote in the General Assembly, Japan's prospects looked grim. In the run-up to the Bandung summit, where Japan sought to rally support among the 100-odd nations attending, Japan's UN ambassador, Kenzo Oshima, stated that Japan would consider expanding the number of nonpermanent seats in the G4 proposal. Oshima said, "We will listen to many countries' views and adopt the views that we think are acceptable. By doing so, we will increase the number of nations supporting our resolution."[65]

In China, netizens began planning for a third round of protests over the weekend of April 16–17, timed to coincide with the visit of Japanese foreign minister Machimura.[66] One widely circulated flyer called for demonstrations in at least 12 cities, including one in Tiananmen Square.[67] In Beijing and Guangzhou, heavy police presence and paramilitary vehicles parked outside diplomatic compounds were effective at preventing protests. Despite the quiet in Beijing and Guangzhou, large protests broke out in Shanghai, Hangzhou, Tianjin, and other major cities. On April 16, more than 10,000 protestors gathered in Shanghai in a march that began on the riverfront and proceeded to the Japanese consulate. Demonstrators shouted anti-Japanese slogans and vandalized buildings and signs with Japanese characters on them. In Hangzhou, Xinhua reported that "The protesters marched in orderly files in downtown streets, singing the national anthem of China and chanted slogans…. Local policemen were seen guiding the public to ensure traffic is not disrupted."[68]

The day after the April 16 protests, visiting Japanese foreign minister Machimura demanded an apology and compensation, but Foreign Minister Li Zhaoxing only offered assurances that Japanese nationals would not be harmed. Indeed, a Chinese Foreign Ministry statement noted that Machimura had "expressed deep reflection and apologies."[69] Machimura later denied that he had apologized, saying that he had only expressed regret. Li reportedly told Machimura that "I do not want to see vandalism caused by the demonstrators. I want to take countermeasures,"[70] but street protests continued throughout the day. Thousands of protestors attended demonstrations in Shenzhen, Shenyang, Chengdu, Nanning, Guangzhou, Dongguan, and Zhuhai.[71]

The day after the ministerial meeting, Prime Minister Koizumi requested a meeting with Chinese president Hu Jintao on the sidelines of the Bandung conference on April 22–24. Agence France-Presse reported that Koizumi "held out an olive branch to China," suggesting that he would not repeat demands made by Foreign Minister Machimura for an apology, stating that "it is better not to make it an exchange of accusations."[72]

Following Koizumi's signal, the Chinese government began a concerted effort to bring an end to the wave of anti-Japanese protests. On April 19, PRC state-run television gave prominent coverage to a large meeting presided over by Foreign Minister Li, attended by officials from the Propaganda Department, People's Liberation Army, and the central government. Li emphasized that the "only correct option" was "friendly coexistence and win-win cooperation" with Japan, and that the Party and government were "completely capable" of upholding China's "fundamental interests" and "properly handling" problems with Japan.[73] On April 20, *People's Daily* reiterated the call for calm, this time mentioning Japan specifically. On April 21, Chinese president Hu Jintao stated that "we must always remember that nothing can be accomplished without social stability."[74] The Public Security Bureau and provincial security departments released a statement expressing understanding for the patriotic sentiment of the students and general public, while issuing a stern warning against the undesirable and illegal actions that took place during the protests.[75] Former diplomats were sent across the country to speak at universities and local government offices, including police units. Cell phone users in Beijing received a text message from the Public Security Bureau saying that in expressing patriotism, citizens should not participate in protests.[76] In fact, one Chinese journalist noted that cell phone users were unable to send text messages with phrases such as "Japan," "anti-Japan," or "protest" for over a week.[77]

On April 22, Koizumi stated his "deep remorse and heartfelt apology" for Japan's historical wrongdoings at the fiftieth anniversary of the Asian-African Summit in Bandung, the first time since 1991 that a Japanese prime minister had done so before a multilateral forum.[78] Simultaneously, Koizumi pressed forward with the G4 proposal on the sidelines of the meeting, which a senior Japanese diplomat called "a golden chance" to regain support for Japan's bid.[79] At the meeting between Koizumi and Hu, both leaders spoke in restrained generalities and made no pointed demands. Relations with China remained strained, however, and worsened again in June when PRC vice premier Wu Yi canceled her meeting with Koizumi in protest at his remarks about Yasukuni at a legislative committee meeting.

Negotiations over UN reform continued through the summer, but statements in July by China and the United States and a tacit U.S.-China agreement to oppose the addition of permanent members finally halted momentum for Security Council enlargement.[80] On July 1, Chinese ambassador Wang stated that China would veto the G4 plan if submitted. On July 14, U.S. ambassador Tahir-Kheli said, "Let me be as clear as possible: the U.S. does not think any proposal to expand the Security Council—including one based on our own ideas—should be voted upon at this stage."[81] The U.S. and Chinese ambassadors met on the eve of an emergency African Union summit to decide whether to drop demands for two veto-wielding seats or to support the G4 proposal (which had been modified to eliminate the veto power of new permanent members for 15 years). According to Wu Miaofa, former counselor to the Chinese UN mission, the American and Chinese representatives agreed to oppose the essentially "premature" G4 proposal and any attempts to set a time limit or force a vote.[82] In early August, the African Union voted to reject the G4 proposal, effectively putting an end to the possibility of a General Assembly vote before September. Wu Miaofa described the twin developments as a "fatal blow" to the G4 proposal, quoting a UN official: "Under this pincer attack, it can be said that the 'G-4' Security Council bid has basically been defeated, and the four nations should draw lessons at every level."[83]

Anti-Japanese Protests as a Diplomatic Asset

When discussion of Security Council enlargement gained momentum at the end of 2004, the Chinese government was concerned about openly opposing the emerging consensus for reform. Privately, China was loath to see Japan added as a permanent member of the Security Council. As a government-affiliated think tank researcher noted, "China is quite satisfied with the current situation in the United Nations Security Council. China doesn't want reform. It certainly doesn't want Japan to be a political power on the international stage without a correct attitude on historical issues. China wants to keep the status quo."[84]

Given the international costs of blocking reform, there was uncertainty about whether China would publicly oppose Japan's candidacy and veto the G4 proposal if it were to reach that stage. By allowing grassroots mobilization against Japan's bid, including a signature campaign and protest marches, Chinese officials could point to visible evidence that popular pressure required a tough stance, demonstrating the strength of Chinese resolve and effectively tying the government's hands. By contrast, when the same nationalist activists hosted an Internet petition in August 2004 against the use of Japanese bullet train technology, Chinese authorities shut down the petition after 22 hours. In 2005, the government made no effort to shut down the Internet petition even after protests erupted. Having opened the floodgates of public opinion, the Chinese government then found itself pressed to oppose Japan's candidacy more actively.

At the outset of renewed discussions of UNSC reform in September 2004, uncertainty over China's willingness to oppose the G4 proposal stemmed from the Chinese Foreign Ministry spokesman's mild reaction: "Regarding Japan, I can make clear this principled stance, that we understand Japan's aspiration to play a greater role in international affairs."[85] The statement, prominently reported on official and commercial news sites,[86] provoked a backlash among nationalist netizens. On September 18, the anniversary of Japan's invasion of Manchuria in 1931, 30 members of the Patriots Alliance Network gathered in front of the Japanese embassy to protest Japan's UNSC bid and the "Ministry of Foreign Affairs' vague expression of 'understanding.'"[87] According to a senior Japan expert at a government-affiliated institute, "Starting in October 2004, the Chinese government did not mention Japan's bid again, because there was such a large gap between the phrase 'we understand Japan's aspiration' and the public mindset at the time. We had to be cautious."[88] Liu Ning, a Japan expert and freelance writer, noted that

> The Chinese government is painstakingly avoiding a direct fight with Japan in the international arena and trying to keep the temperature of bilateral relations above the freezing point. But this earnest intention may not move Japan and could easily give the international community the impression that China is indecisive. . . . If China doesn't want Japan's "fond dream" to come true . . . then China should communicate this to the international community and loudly say 'no'. . . . This is Japan's biggest worry.[89]

In March 2005, statements by Kofi Annan and Condoleezza Rice had a galvanizing effect. The submission of Annan's report and accompanying statements "marked the beginning of a new round of comparatively deep, comprehensive reforms," noted Wu Miaofa, former advisor to the Chinese permanent mission to the United Nations.[90] With only two weeks remaining before the General Assembly debate on April 6–7 and the Uniting for Consensus meeting on April 11, Chinese concern began to grow. "If the four countries put the guidelines in place by June and then put the issue to a vote, China would be isolated," noted Liu Jiangyong.[91] For China, this represented a window of opportunity to kill Japan's bid and the G4 proposal at an early stage, before the G4 submitted its framework proposal to the UN General Assembly in mid-June.[92]

Rather than openly announce its opposition to Japan's bid, the Chinese government endorsed a grassroots campaign against Japan's candidacy for permanent membership, beginning with an online signature campaign. According to a Sina.com news editor, permission to host the Internet petition was verbally requested from and granted by the State Council Information Office, the agency charged with managing China's international image and monitoring the content of Internet news sites. "The government wanted this petition to happen among the public," said the news editor. "You have to understand the political context."[93] Official websites joined the fray, with even Xinhua.net creating a petition to "resolutely oppose Japan's bid for a permanent UNSC seat."[94] Two days after the quasi-official launch of the Internet campaign in mainland China, Foreign Ministry spokesman Liu Jianchao defended the online petition, stating: "I do not think that this is anti-Japanese feeling; on the contrary, it is a demand that Japan take a correct and responsible attitude toward historical problems."[95]

On March 29 and 31, the Chinese Foreign Ministry spokesman again defended the Internet petition and the boycott of Asahi beer that had begun in two provinces, stating: "We have noted that many Internet users have signed their names online to show their objection to Japan's wish to become a permanent member of the UN Security Council. This once again demonstrates that the Japanese side should adopt a responsible attitude toward historical issues, so as to win the trust of the people of

Asian countries, including China."[96] Even the Chinese embassy in the United States posted an article about the signature campaign on its website.[97]

The Foreign Ministry spokesman's remarks were taken as a green light to continue organizing street petitions. One student in Huizhou, Guangdong, posted a notice on the university BBS announcing a petition campaign on April 3, asserting that "this is precisely the view and attitude held by the Ministry of Foreign Affairs."[98] On the ground, the street petitions occurred with government consent if not active support. "Once the Internet petition took off, we organized a series of street petitions all over the country," said a leading activist in Beijing.[99] Typically, activists "negotiated" (*shangliang*) with the local Public Security Bureau over the timing, content, and location of the petition drive. For example, a few dozen Bao Diao activists held a signature drive in Beijing's Chaoyang Park on March 31.[100] According to one protest organizer, the police wanted the protest to be held in Chaoyang Park because the space was large and generally empty. "We could have held it in front of the Japanese embassy, but it would have had to be shorter, with fewer participants," the organizer noted.[101]

Although the Chinese government initially endorsed the grassroots campaign, anti-Japanese demonstrations quickly gained momentum and began to show signs of getting out of hand. "At the very beginning, the government wanted to use public opinion as a bargaining tool in their diplomacy with Japanese and to win sympathy from the international community," said an expert on Sino-Japanese relations at Beijing University. "But now they're finding some unintended consequences are showing up and this has begun to worry them. The protests turned out much bigger than they expected, and also much more complicated. Not everyone took to the street to voice their resentment of the Japanese."[102] A police officer who was on duty during all three anti-Japanese protests in Shenzhen described to me the difficulty of maintaining order during the protests:

> You don't know who is a good person and who is a bad person. The trouble-makers also carry "Boycott Japan" banners. In such a large protest march, there will inevitably be a small minority of people with different objectives, even some who are intent on destruction and inciting the masses to make trouble—and not against Japan.[103]

To some extent, Chinese authorities were able to steer protests by prenegotiating the content of banners and slogans with activists. But small-scale street petitions often escalated into protest marches or riots, including the April 2 protest in Chengdu. According to firsthand accounts by members of the Patriots Alliance Network, organizers of the street petition had telephoned the Public Security Bureau multiple times to discuss the location of the signature drive and the slogans to be used on the banners. However, according to Lu Yunfei, "Those who participated in the attack on Ito Yokado [a Japanese department store] were not gathering signatures but venting (*fa xie*). Our members had no way to stop them. Even if this were to happen in Beijing, we would have no way to stop them. Under such circumstances, we must immediately stop collecting signatures and draw a clear demarcation between us and them."[104]

The Chinese government continued to point to the protests as a legitimate reaction to Japanese behavior. Queried about the vandalism in Chengdu, Foreign Ministry spokesman Qin Gang blamed Japan's "wrong stand on history and other issues" for generating "strong resentment" among the public, while expressing hope that "the Chinese people will use rational methods to express their feelings and wishes."[105] Popular anger was directed not only at Japan but at the Chinese government for taking such a soft position. As state-run media lambasted Japan's approval of new textbooks on April 5,[106] Chinese netizens expressed their anger over the government's failure to take a harder stance against Japan's bid for a permanent seat on the UN Security Council. One netizen wrote directly to the public BBS of the Ministry of Foreign Affairs, saying that "the Chinese government should clearly take a stance opposing Japan's bid to become a permanent member on the UNSC."[107] Another netizen, posting to the Patriots Alliance Network, stated that

> To this day, the government has not taken a clear stance opposing Japan's permanent membership. If the Chinese government doesn't veto Japan's entry into the UNSC, this government will be no different than the Qing government. If the government doesn't veto Japan's permanent membership, we will know in our hearts that the government is weak and useless. How can the government continue to rule and hold its head up, losing face for the Chinese people! What ability can it have to reunify with Taiwan?[108]

Backed into a corner by popular outrage that it had allowed to mobilize, senior Chinese officials began to take a more public stance against Japan's bid. A Foreign Ministry official described the change in China's stance on the UNSC issue in this way:

> China had to make its stance clear because other countries were no longer being so active. The uncertainty over the outcome of the G4 proposal was too great. Domestically, the atmosphere was intense. There were signature campaigns and online petitions. The government had to respond (*dafu*), or it would be seen as too soft and weak. The people want the government to uphold certain principles. If the government didn't take a stand on the UNSC issue, it would lose public confidence.[109]

After the protests on April 2 and 3, China's representative to the United Nations, Wang Guangya, spoke in favor of "consensus" rather than a vote on UNSC reform. Following the protests on April 9 and 10, Premier Wen Jiabao publicly stated that

Japan was not a suitable candidate for permanent membership, citing the "strong responses from the Asian people." Asked if the nongovernmental activities (*minjian huodong*) in China and Japan had gotten out of control (*shikong*), Chinese Foreign Ministry spokesman Qin Gang again blamed the protests upon "Japan's erroneous attitude and actions on issues such as its history of aggression," this time adding: "As to how to prevent the situation from getting out of control, this too is something that the Japanese side must seriously reflect upon."[110]

Internet petitions and street protests visibly demonstrated the domestic costs to the Chinese government of staying mute, giving credibility and legitimacy to Chinese opposition and threats to veto the G4 proposal. As Shi Yinhong commented:

> As for the masses, the resolute opposition to Japan's bid for a UNSC permanent seat has already become a form of fixed mentality. In fact, China's attitude toward Japan's bid for a UNSC permanent seat already has not much leeway for concession. . . .. China has no alternative but to cast a veto under the grim situation [even though] this may have a negative impact on the prospect of Sino-Japanese ties and the security and stability of the Asia Pacific region. At the same time, China will also offend Germany, India, Brazil, and other countries bidding for a UNSC permanent seat. However, under the present circumstances and after weighing the pros and cons, China must use this way to block Japan.[111]

From Petitions to Protest Marches: The Escalation of Anti-Japanese Mobilization

The extent and intensity of anti-Japanese activity increased over the course of the month, illustrating the tendency for nationalist mobilization to escalate and gain momentum. "Without the online petition, there wouldn't have been street petitions, and without the street petitions there wouldn't have been protest marches and vandalism. This is the natural course of things," said a leading Bao Diao activist and web manager.[112] Figure 6.1 illustrates the pattern of escalation from the online signature campaign to street petitions to protest marches. As measured by coverage on Sina.com, one of the three most popular Internet portals in China, the online signature campaign against Japan's bid took off after the statements by secretary of state Condoleezza Rice and UN secretary-general Kofi Annan on March 19 and 21 generated momentum for Japan's candidacy and the G4 proposal. Following the domestic launch of the Internet signature campaign on March 23, street petitions were the first offline activities to take place, peaking on the weekend of April 2–3.

The street petitions were largely stationary events, held at a city square or park, with a core group of five to 50 activists collecting signatures and distributing

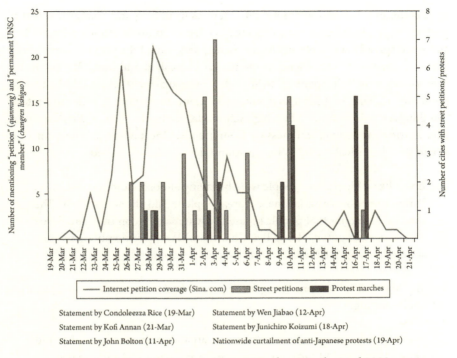

Figure 6.1 From Petitions to Protest Marches, March–April 2005

leaflets. Street petitions tended to be smaller in size than protest marches, which typically processed through the city center, growing in size as protesters called upon bystanders to join in, and often ended in a confrontation with the police over the vandalism of Japanese businesses or diplomatic buildings. Over the following two weeks, protest marches increasingly replaced street petitions as the modal form of anti-Japanese activity. Had the government not intervened, a fourth wave of protests would likely have taken place on May 1 and May 4, based on messages circulating on Internet forums at the time.

As the number of protests increased, so did popular determination to stage additional protests. By the third weekend, netizens in Shanghai said that Shanghai must hold a protest, just like Beijing and Guangzhou. Moreover, for some participants the experience of protest lent force to the belief that protest was a right. One Bao Diao activist was moved to anger when his application to hold a protest on May 4 was rejected. He said: "The people are exercising their legal rights to assemble and protest and this should not be suppressed because they serve to uphold the country's sovereign rights externally and Chinese people's human rights internally."[113] Such anecdotes illustrate the danger of allowing protests for even a short while, as the experience of protesting may embolden citizens and activists to demand domestic as well as foreign policy changes.

A common observation among interviewees in Beijing and Shanghai was that protests were much larger than expected, as demonstrations attracted bystanders and word spread via cell phone. Many participants joined the protest march along the way, often because a friend in the march had called and said, "It's not just a rumor—it's actually happening." In Shanghai, one participant said that he had heard the march moving past his apartment, so he went downstairs to join the protest, "thinking it would be fun."[114] Two high school classmates decided to join the protest after hearing about it via text message from friends. One student said he wanted to attend this "historical event." When he found the march, he recalled:

> It was like a big party—people were behaving almost without conscience. When someone saw a Japanese store, people would shout, smash it! The slogans were ones that people seemed to just make up on the spot. Some people even shouted, "Long live Chairman Mao!" I remember someone shouted, "Long live the CCP!" but no one chimed in.[115]

Another high school student thought the protest had been approved and went on an impulse, saying:

> I've changed a lot since then. If the same situation were to arise today, and I knew that it would turn out to be as extreme as it was, I wouldn't go. . . . Emotions were really running high. If the police had tried to stop the protesters, I think there might have been bloodshed.[116]

Yet the Chinese government also took a number of preventive measures to mitigate the risk that protests would get out of control, including restricting domestic media coverage of protest demonstrations and instructing leading Bao Diao activists to stay home on the day of planned protests. Tong Zeng, head of the China Federation for Defending the Diaoyu Islands, said that "we were told this was an entirely spontaneous event, so the people leading the movement must have no role."[117] An activist in Shanghai who had participated in previous anti-Japanese protests said that the Public Security Bureau sent a plainclothes policeman to accompany him all day. They were "worried that I would participate and inflame (*naoda*) the situation," he said.[118]

No mention of the protests in Chengdu or Shenzhen on April 2–3 appeared in local or national media. One netizen noted that two local commercial newspapers, *Huaxi Dushi Bao* and *Chengdu Shang Bao*, had been ordered on April 1 not to report on the protest in order "to give the government leeway" (*yudi*).[119] The petition campaign was widely reported, but any mention of a protest march or demonstration was conspicuously avoided, prompting criticism on nationalist websites. One netizen on the Patriots Alliance Network BBS stated, "I am extremely disappointed with the Chengdu media!"[120] According to a senior reporter at the *Global Times*, a commercial subsidiary of the *People's Daily*, "We reported on the Internet petitions against

Japan's UNSC bid—those were entirely different from the anti-Japanese [protest] activities."[121] According to a *Global Times* editor, they decided not to report on the anti-Japanese protests because "if we did report the demonstrations, people would do it again... there would be five million people in Tiananmen Square.... We didn't need the government to tell us that. We have our political responsibility."[122]

Figure 6.2 traces the fluctuation in online coverage of the anti-Japanese petitions on People.com.cn, the portal site of the official *People's Daily*, and Sina.com.cn, one of the three major commercial portals that hosted the Internet petition.[123] Despite the commercialization of the media and the proliferation of online news sites, the most prominent Internet portals are still closely monitored and given direction by the State Council Information Office. The anti-Japanese petition was covered more heavily on Sina.com.cn than on People.com.cn until the weekend of April 2–3, when street petitions in Chengdu and Shenzhen escalated into violent riots. That weekend marked a turning point. After the protests in Chengdu and Shenzhen, an internal circular reportedly restricted media coverage of anti-Japanese activities.[124] Indeed, coverage on People.com.cn was heavier than on Sina.com.cn, suggesting that a blackout order had been imposed on all but official reports, which the commercial sites could carry. Moreover, Sina.com.cn was completely silent on the anti-Japanese petition on the second and third weekends of protest (April 9–10 and April 16–17). Had the issue been widely reported while protests were in the streets, bystanders might have seen the media coverage as a signal from the government that it was safe

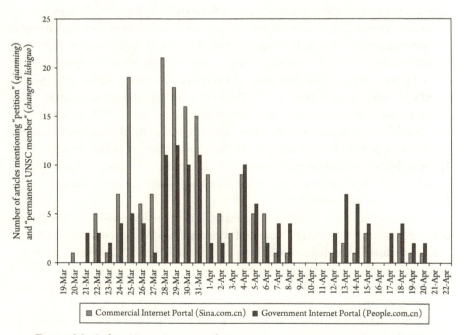

Figure 6.2 Online News Coverage of Anti-Japanese Petitions, March–April 2005

and even desirable to join the protests, inflaming the risk that protests would further escalate. The April 16 protests were not mentioned in the Chinese domestic press, which instead put a positive spin on the foreign ministers' meeting.

Difficulty of Curtailing Protests without Evidence of Diplomatic Success

The government was able to assuage popular pressure and facilitate the curtailment of protests by taking a tougher stance against Japan's UNSC bid and pointing to positive diplomatic developments. As a senior Chinese expert on Sino-Japanese relations noted, "Taking a stance greatly heartened the public," he said, adding that "if the government ignores the people, the people will rise up against the government. The government will be thrown out."[125] The Chinese government gradually toughened its stance against Japan, culminating in Premier Wen Jiabao's remarks on April 12, when he openly questioned Japan's suitability for permanent membership. But the government's efforts to curtail the protests were gradual, beginning with Beijing and Guangzhou after the April 9–10 protests and extending nationwide once Prime Minister Koizumi's stance softened following a third round of protests on April 16–17. Chinese officials recognized the difficulty of reining in anti-Japanese protests before the Japanese side offered symbolic concessions.

Without evidence of diplomatic progress, it would have been more costly for the Chinese government to prevent protests in Beijing during Japanese foreign minister Machimura's visit. Prominent nationalists expressed satisfaction with the change in the government's stance and international recognition of their concerns. According to a bestselling nationalist author, "The protests certainly brought pressure to bear on the government. . . . On the issue of Japan's entry into the UNSC, the government's position changed dramatically. Before the protests, the government was very vague (*mohu*). Afterward, they clearly opposed Japan's entry."[126] A senior Patriots Alliance Network organizer stated that the protest on "April 9 had an impact on government policy. Tens of millions of signatures reflected public sentiment and spurred the government to oppose Japan's UNSC bid. . . . Because of all these activities, Annan took a stance and asked Japan to adopt a correct understanding of history. We were quite satisfied."[127]

In the week after the April 9–10 protests, Chinese media headlined Japan's growing difficulties at the United Nations and criticism from Western nations.[128] Chinese netizens saluted Wen Jiabao for taking a stronger stance.[129] On Friday, April 15, authorities began detaining anti-Japanese activists to prevent protests that weekend. Additional police patrolled Tiananmen Square.[130] Tong Zeng attributed the quiet in Beijing to "effective publicity by the government. . . . The authorities have made sufficient publicity about protests which receive no approval by the government."[131]

Although China took pains to prevent repeat protests in Beijing and Guangzhou, nationwide curtailment did not begin in earnest until Prime Minister Koizumi indicated on April 18 that he would drop demands for a Chinese apology at a potential meeting with President Hu Jintao at the Asia-Africa Summit. Not all popular anger was directed at Japan's candidacy, and Chinese officials were concerned protests would be difficult to wind down despite the tough stance taken by Premier Wen Jiabao and favorable developments at the United Nations. Protesters also fumed over the Japanese government's perceived lack of remorse on historical issues, stoked by a new round of textbook revisions, as well as reports of Japanese activities in the East China Sea. One young man from Foshan, who circulated a call to protest in the nearby provincial capital of Guangzhou on April 10, recalled: "At the time we marched to show Japanese politicians that they [couldn't just] glorify Japan's invasion of China, distort history textbooks, and visit Yasukuni Shrine."[132] In Beijing, Chinese leaders expressed concern that student protesters might not obey instructions to desist. According to a senior professor at Tsinghua University, the university administration was afraid that students would not obey orders to stop further demonstrations:

> Party Secretary Liu called me at 11:00 p.m. to tell me that a certain number of Tsinghua students were involved in the anti-Japanese demonstrations—and that the central leaders have held a meeting and decided that there should be no more demonstrations. He asked me to tell my students not to participate in the demonstrations. I told him that really this should not be my responsibility, but the school administration's responsibility. He said that they already told the student leaders at a meeting not to participate in any more demonstrations, but he said, "We are afraid they will not listen to us, but they will listen to you."[133]

As Japan remained steadfast in demanding a Chinese apology and compensation for protest damages, on April 16 and 17 large-scale protests occurred in Shanghai, Shenzhen, Hangzhou, Shenyang, Tianjin, Zhuhai, Dongguan, and other cities, even though local police knew about protest plans days in advance. In Shenzhen, a junior officer with the People's Armed Police told me that the protests had been authorized. "The protest routes had all been examined and approved (*shenpi*) beforehand. The routes were set (*guiding*) by the government," he said as he showed me the video footage he had taken during the protest—with a Sony camcorder, no less. "Before going on duty, we received orders: 'Don't strike back, don't yell back' (*da bu huan shou, ma bu huan kou*)."[134] One protest organizer in Shenzhen was still dissatisfied despite the government's open opposition to Japan's bid. As he told Phoenix Television: "anti-Japanese demonstrations will not stop until Japan's UNSC bid is brought to an end."[135] Other demonstrators shouted slogans unrelated to Japan's

UNSC bid, including "Give us back the Diaoyu Islands" and "Oppose Japan's tampering with history."[136]

The Shanghai Public Security Bureau BBS received 30 posts in the three days prior to the protest, asking if the rumors were true and if permission to protest had been granted. Several of the posts mentioned the time, location, and route of the protest march. The response from the bulletin board monitors was nearly uniform:

> Saturday's protest is pure rumor. According to the PRC Law on Assemblies, Processions, and Demonstrations, it is illegal to hold a protest march without a permit from the Public Security Bureau. To obtain a permit, a written application must be submitted five days in advance. We fully understand your patriotic enthusiasm. Our government has already taken a clear stance through diplomatic and appropriate media channels. We hope that you will remain calm, rational, and reasonable, and uphold social stability as you set forth.[137]

Similar guidelines were sent out via text message to cell phone users in Shanghai and Guangzhou.[138] One young woman who designed several banners for the protest march told me that she had called the Public Security Bureau on the twelfth to ask if a protest had been approved for the sixteenth. When the police said that no one had applied, she decided to submit an application herself, but the police told her there would not be enough time to process her application.[139]

The Chinese government did not begin a concerted effort to stifle anti-Japanese protests until the day after Koizumi relented, indicating that he would not press Hu for an apology at the Bandung summit. On April 19, Foreign Minister Li Zhaoxing presided over a high-level meeting of 3,500 senior officials and emphasized the importance of "friendly coexistence and win-win cooperation" in Sino-Japanese relations, remarks that were widely broadcast by state media.[140]

Senior officials, diplomats, and foreign policy experts emphasized the adverse consequences of anti-Japanese activities in the Chinese media and in mass meetings in cities across the nation.[141] Commerce minister Bo Xilai acknowledged the "strong dissatisfaction and indignation among the Chinese people" caused by Japanese "activities on a series of important issues, repeatedly hurting the feelings of the Chinese people." Yet Bo also cautioned that a boycott of Japanese goods would harm the interests of both countries and vowed that "commodities from all nations will have a just treatment in the Chinese market."[142] As former Ambassador Wu Jianmin wrote in Renmin Ribao, "If 90 percent of Japanese-branded goods are made in China, isn't boycotting Japanese goods the same as boycotting ourselves?"[143] Tsinghua University's Liu Jiangyong told netizens on the Strong Nation Forum that boycotting Japanese goods was "a little blind (mangmu)" and that the likelihood of Japan becoming a permanent UNSC member was "extremely small."[144]

Applications to hold anti-Japanese protests over the weeklong May holiday were denied, and students in Beijing and Shanghai reported that security on university campuses were tightened through the May holiday, with campus guards denying entry to anyone without a school ID. As a Chinese scholar and Japan expert noted:

> After the large-scale anti-Japanese demonstrations all over the country, the Chinese government held several meetings in Beijing to report on the current situation and sent out senior diplomats in groups to give lectures on central policy toward Japan, calling on young students to have a clear understanding of the overall situation of Sino-Japanese relations and not to act emotionally.[145]

Although evidence of diplomatic victory made it easier for the Chinese government to suppress further protests without prompting a popular backlash, its heavy-handed tactics still generated quiet resentment. Some individuals who participated in the 2005 protests became disenchanted with the government after being brought in to "drink tea" with security officials and put under police surveillance. The Foshan protest organizer recalled befriending a middle-aged woman who professed to hate Japan during the Guangzhou protest march. As he later learned, she was also an undercover state security agent. For a year, state security required him to make weekly reports of his activities. Noting that the police vehicles maintaining order along the protest march were all Hondas, he remarked: "The regime uses the people, letting them protest then sending in the police at the end. They want you to make some noise, but not too great a noise."[146]

Leading nationalist activists were similarly cynical about their circumscribed role, preferring to focus on their achievements during moments of opportunity than the inevitable curtailment of their activities. As a Bao Diao activist in Shanghai remarked: "We can only push the government to take action in areas where the government has not taken a clear position. Afterward, we must retreat (*tuibu*)."[147] The Patriots Alliance Network itself was briefly suspended after the protests, but authorities found no evidence that its organizers had planned the large-scale protests. As a senior organizer explained, "There was no evidence. We evaded responsibility. The fact is, the protests were like a butterfly effect. Information about protests spreads quickly online. There's no point to investigating who started it; why it happened is more important."[148]

Other domestic observers, particularly liberal intellectuals, were more critical of what they saw as the regime's callous use of grassroots sentiment. Liu Ning asked rhetorically:

> Why did these protests start as "spontaneous mass patriotic actions against Japan's wrong attitude and actions regarding its historical aggression" (the Foreign Ministry spokesman's words) but then become a small number of

"criminals" with "ulterior motives," arrested for inciting illegal assemblies and demonstrations to beat and smash? They had the same goals, the same purpose, the same action, the same scale, the same target—the Japanese embassy and consulates and Japanese-invested enterprises—and the same large-scale police presence. Why was the Beijing protest march on April 9 "patriotic action," but a week later the April 16 Shanghai protest march was an "illegal crime"?[149]

Liu Xiaobo, who would be awarded the 2010 Nobel Peace Prize, was even more scornful of the government's Machiavellian tactics. "To tout the regime's diplomatic achievements, Koizumi's apology at the Asia summit meeting was treated as the victorious result of the anti-Japanese unrest and reported prominently," Liu noted.[150] He went on to criticize the government's Janus-faced treatment of popular opinion, including the arrest and trial of Tang Ye, a white-collar worker in Shanghai who circulated a protest flyer and was charged with crimes of "disturbing the social order." Liu Xiaobo wrote:

> The popular anti-Japanese wave in April was completely controlled by the government's political needs. Popular will is just a "plaything" in the hands of the authorities, used when needed and discarded when unneeded, like a pair of worn shoes. Under the system of Party supremacy, the regime used the judiciary to extinguish anti-Japanese flames, reducing it to a tool of suppressing popular will.[151]

In widely publicized remarks, the Ministry of Public Security warned on April 21 that "we must guard against people with ulterior motives from taking advantage."[152] Several other dissidents were detained for organizing anti-Japanese protests. One activist, Guo Feixiong, better known for his pro-democracy views, was arrested and held for 16 days after applying for permission to hold a 1,000-person protest on May 4, the anniversary of the 1919 protests that led to the sacking of three government officials who had signed the Treaty of Versailles.[153] Xu Wanping, an activist who had been imprisoned for several years after Tiananmen, was interrogated for organizing an anti-Japanese signature drive in March and later sentenced to 12 years in prison.[154]

Foreign Perceptions

Japanese and foreign officials recognized the Chinese government's complicity in allowing grassroots nationalism to mobilize, first with the signature campaign and then large-scale street demonstrations. At the same time, many foreign observers recognized the risks posed by nationalist mobilization to domestic and diplomatic stability. Japan's deputy permanent representative to United Nations, Shinichi Kitaoka, acknowledged the role that anti-Japanese petitions and protests played in China's campaign to undermine Japan's candidacy. The diplomatic impetus, Kitaoka wrote, was Kofi Annan's March 21 statement of support for putting Security Council reform to a vote if necessary and his implicit endorsement of Japan's candidacy:

> This was the outcome we had expected, and it seemed to be a major blow to the Uniting for Consensus Group. In all likelihood it also spurred China, which opposes Japan's inclusion as a permanent member, to make serious plans to derail Tokyo's bid and to begin implementing that strategy. This, then, [was] the background to the Internet petition and the anti-Japanese demonstrations that broke out in China.[155]

The government's tacit endorsement of the signature campaign and boycott were readily apparent to Japanese observers. As a Japanese political analyst at the embassy in Beijing recounted, "Xinhuanet reported on the boycott, and then many people copied and pasted this other places online. Even though it was only two or three stores that participated in the boycott, you wouldn't have known from the publicity it received. The government secretly supported this—it was pasted all over the Internet."[156] Before the April 9 protest in Beijing, the Public Security Bureau notified Japanese embassy personnel on Thursday that a protest would take place on Saturday. On the day of the protest, "The police told us that protesters were coming, and that we should move our cars if they were parked out front," a Japanese embassy employee recalled.[157]

During the April 16 protest in Shanghai, a Japanese consular official photographed Chinese police holding a sign telling protest marchers to "proceed this way" toward the Japanese consulate (figure 6.3). In video footage shown on Japanese television, a police officer told a female protestor, "Turn right at the street in front of you. It is easier to take that street to go there."[158] According to the *New York Times*, several thousand riot police surrounded the consulate but "looked on passively. Asked by a reporter whether anything could be done to rein in the violence, a Chinese officer answered, 'By whom?' and then walked away as if annoyed. In several hours, there appeared to be only one arrest."[159]

Japanese politicians across party lines criticized China's response—or lack thereof—to the protests. Opposition leader Ichiro Ozawa stated, "It's unforgivable that the Chinese government gave the demonstrators silent approval."[160] Shoichi Nakagawa, a conservative cabinet member, characterized the protests as led by "controlled mobs" carried out "under the control of the Chinese government."[161] Foreign Minister Nobutaka Machimura told a parliamentary committee that he would take a tough line during his visit to Beijing and publicly criticized the Chinese government's role in the protests: "The Chinese foreign ministry saying that it [the protest] is tolerable and natural means the government approved it," Machimura

Figure 6.3 "March This Way"
Photo courtesy of a Japanese consular official in Shanghai.

said.[162] The Japanese Foreign Ministry released a statement saying: "Even though information was available beforehand to infer that there would be a demonstration [in Shanghai], nothing was done to prevent it."[163] Other prominent leaders attributed the protests to state-led propaganda and unrelated domestic grievances. Shinzo Abe, acting LDP secretary-general, said that "Japan is an outlet to vent that anger. . . . Since the Tiananmen incident, these kinds of demonstrations were severely restricted, but the authorities tolerated these kinds of anti-Japanese gatherings, and the people themselves used these anti-Japanese marches. . . . Because of the anti-Japanese education there, it's easy to light the fire of these demonstrations and, because of the Internet, it's easy to assemble a lot of people."[164]

Chinese officials sought to combat the perception of government facilitation, emphasizing the spontaneity of the protests and the concerted police effort "to maintain order and prevent escalation of the situation, in order to ensure safety of the Japanese organizations and Japanese citizens in China, as well as safeguard the overall interests of Sino-Japanese relations," as State Councilor Tang Jiaxuan told the visiting president of Kyodo News Agency. Tang denied that anti-Japanese protests were ginned up by the government and emphasized the sincerity of popular opposition to Japan's UNSC bid:

Regrettably there is a formulation in Japan, which views these [demonstration] activities as being supported by the Chinese Government and as the outcome of the Chinese Government-sponsored patriotic education with "anti-Japan" as the theme. I must point out that such formulation is unfounded. It is distortion of facts and extremely harmful to the future Sino-Japanese relations. I believe that it is very normal for any country to conduct patriotic education among its own people. China's patriotic education is by no means anti-Japanese education. . . . Frankly, the latest demonstrations and protests by segments of the Chinese public stemmed specifically from the Japanese Government's approval of right-wing history textbooks, which distort and beautify the historical facts of aggression; and from the opposition to Japan's vying for the position of permanent member of the Security Council.[165]

Although many Japanese and international observers remained convinced of the government's role in facilitating the protests, the risk posed by anti-Japanese protests was also evident. According to a Japanese embassy official who was trapped inside the building until the morning after the April 9 protests in Beijing, "It was definitely tacitly approved, but many more showed up than expected. The organizers didn't know how large it would be. Neither did the police. It was organized over the Internet, after all."[166] A retired Japanese ambassador and prominent expert at the Japan Center for International Exchange remarked, "When protests occurred, the [Chinese] leadership was surprised—though some may have wanted them—by the magnitude and momentum of the protests."[167] The *Yomiuri Shimbun* noted the risk that protests could turn against the government: "What the Chinese government fears most now is that anti-Japanese protests could turn to criticism that its diplomacy is weak-kneed and develop into anti-government demonstrations. Add into the mix pent-up frustration among labor groups and farmers, and the Chinese government could be facing a shakeup."[168]

U.S. officials also acknowledged that the anti-Japanese protests showed signs of getting out of control. Commenting on the protests in Beijing, State Department spokesman Richard Boucher said that that it was "very regrettable that this one did turn violent and was not under control."[169] As a senior White House official recalled, "We believed at the time that the Chinese government was piggybacking on something that was indigenous and spontaneous concerning Japanese textbooks and the like. What we were worried about with this protest was that things started to get out of control."[170]

Despite widespread recognition of the Chinese government's role in fanning anti-Japanese sentiment through patriotic education, Japanese observers were also aware that these sentiments made it difficult for the government to repress nationalist protests. LDP politician and Japan-China Society chairman Takeshi Noda acknowledged the "difficulties the Chinese government faces in containing demonstrations held under the banner of patriotism."[171] A *Nikkei* editorial stated that "After years of constantly denouncing Japan's war of aggression against China, the party leadership probably finds it difficult to criticize demonstrations against Japan that clearly echo the party rhetoric."[172] Japanese observers also recognized that the sentiments fueling anti-Japanese protests were sincere, not merely a figment of state education. As former ambassador Kazuhiko Togo wrote,

> The education system has certainly played a role in instilling anti-Japanese sentiments, but narratives from the society were the root cause that Chinese youngsters have developed strong feelings against Japan.[173]

While partially state-led, popular anger against Japan still put visible pressure on Chinese officials to take a tough stance. Even the conservative *Sankei Shimbun* noted that "Hu's call for Japan's reflection on history does not run counter to his eagerness to rectify the aggravated relations because Hu's call was probably intended to calm down anti-Japanese feelings."[174] While undesirable, China's willingness to take a strong stance against Japan became more understandable in light of popular sentiment.

Diplomatic Impact

China's campaign bore fruit on the bilateral as well as multilateral front. After the third weekend of anti-Japanese protests, Koizumi offered his "deep remorse" and "heartfelt apology" for Japanese wartime atrocities in a speech at the Asia-Africa Summit. Chinese Foreign Ministry spokesperson Kong Quan commented positively on Koizumi's speech, saying: "For Koizumi to have made the comments he made in such a forum, to express such an apology, we welcome that."[175] Koizumi's speech was heralded by Singapore's *Straits Times* as "Japan's most public apology in a decade [and] clearly an attempt to ease growing tensions with Beijing over Tokyo's handling of its wartime past and its bid for a permanent seat in the United Nations Security Council."[176] To calm the situation, Koizumi did not demand an apology or compensation for damages incurred during the protests. Koizumi told reporters: "We were able to confirm at the meeting that, rather than criticizing each other's past shortcomings and aggravating antagonistic feelings, we should make efforts to develop the bilateral friendship."[177] At the meeting, Hu did not raise the Yasukuni issue, and Koizumi demurred when asked by reporters whether he would visit Yasukuni again that year, only indicating that he would "make an appropriate judgment."[178]

The detente over Yasukuni did not last long, but it would be resurrected under Koizumi's successor. The Yasukuni issue resurfaced in May when Koizumi told a Diet committee, "I don't understand why I should stop visiting the Yasukuni Shrine."[179] Chinese vice premier Wu Yi retaliated a week later by abruptly canceling a scheduled meeting with Koizumi. Koizumi paid two more visits to Yasukuni Shrine before leaving office, but his successor, the conservative Shinzo Abe, seized upon this face-saving compromise. By remaining ambiguous about visiting the shrine, Abe could claim that he had not made any promises while still enabling Chinese leaders to assert that the two sides had "reached a consensus on overcoming the political obstacle affecting the bilateral relationship and promoting a friendly and cooperative relationship."[180]

Although anti-Japanese protests had soured Japanese attitudes toward China, the Japanese public had also become weary of Koizumi's provocative behavior. Opinion split between criticizing China for using the anti-Japanese protests as a "political card" to pressure Japan[181] and faulting Koizumi's "complete failure in Japan's foreign policy."[182] The popularity of Koizumi and the ruling LDP declined. According to a survey by the *Mainichi Shimbun,* 76 percent of respondents felt that Koizumi had not made sufficient efforts to improve Japan's worsening relations with China and South Korea. Within a month, the LDP's approval rating had dropped eight points to 25 percent.[183]

Rising dissatisfaction with Koizumi's Asia diplomacy extended to the Yasukuni issue, with both conservative and liberal newspapers endorsing the construction of a new, nonreligious facility to commemorate Japan's war dead apart from Class A war criminals.[184] Retired ambassador Kazuhiko Togo called for a moratorium on Yasukuni visits, arguing that "China also needs breathing space to reflect on history. . . . And if this practical consideration necessitates either of the two countries to make the first concession, Japan should take the first step."[185] As two Chinese scholars noted, "All this created a favorable public opinion environment for change after Abe became prime minister and changed Koizumi's approach."[186] In succession, six prime ministers that followed Koizumi—Shinzo Abe, Yasuo Fukuda, Taro Aso, Yukio Hatoyama, Naoto Kan, and Yoshihiko Noda—all avoided visiting Yasukuni while in office.

Internationally, China's efforts also helped to undermine global support for Japan's UNSC candidacy and prevent the G4 proposal from being put to a vote in the General Assembly. Although it is difficult to isolate the influence of the anti-Japanese protests within China's broader diplomatic campaign, many international officials publicly voiced their concern about the prospects for Japan's candidacy in terms of domestic "developments" and "what was going on" in China.[187] The United States joined China in speaking out against the G4, although it continued to support Japan alone. Regional support for Japan and the G4 ebbed, particularly in Southeast Asia. The 10-member Association of Southeast Asian Nations (ASEAN) endorsed Japan but split over the G4 proposal. In addition, Singapore, Vietnam, Cambodia, and Laos—all recipients of Japanese aid and investment since World War II—surprised Japanese diplomats by refusing to cosponsor the G4 proposal.

Before the anti-Japanese protests, senior U.S. officials publicly supported Japan's candidacy but remained silent on the G4 proposal. Like China, the Bush administration privately opposed the G4 proposal but had been reluctant to take blame for publicly blocking reform. As a Japanese Foreign Ministry official who worked closely with Machimura on Security Council reform recalled: "Our policy toward the United States was just to ask the United States to keep silent, not be negative toward our initiative, just stay neutral—so that if we could get two-thirds support, we would then ask the United States to recognize reality."[188]

After the protests, the United States rejected Annan's calls for a swift decision on reform. According to the *Asahi Shukan*, "Japan knew that, deep down inside, the United States was against the G4's plan. But it was unexpected that the United States would announce its opposition stance so openly."[189] As James Traub laments, Ambassador Bolton went further than was necessary to "wave the banner of opposition," meeting with the Chinese ambassador and "agree[ing], as the latter immediately announced to the press, that the United States would be joining China in blocking Security Council expansion."[190]

The anti-Japanese protests also helped Chinese diplomats undermine support for Japan and the G4 proposal within Asia. As a National Security Council official with responsibility for East Asia recounted,

> I think the student protests and the rest of it was really designed to remind Southeast Asians and others that would be part of the voting at the United Nations of the danger involved—that these were serious issues to the Chinese people and that it certainly wasn't time for Japan to get on the Security Council.[191]

Although ASEAN supported Japan's candidacy as early as November 2004, the organization was ultimately unwilling to endorse the G4, and its most supportive members refused to cosponsor the proposal. According to the Japanese Foreign Ministry official who advised Machimura on UNSC reform,

> Many told us that because of China's opposition, they would not cosponsor the resolution. Take Cambodia, for example. Cambodia has always had very good relations with Japan, and Japan has given Cambodia a lot of aid. But when we visited Cambodia, they said, "Our king is in Beijing, and we cannot ignore his intentions. . ." Similarly, take Brunei: they said that Hu Jintao was scheduled to visit next year and they could not risk angering him.[192]

As one of Japan's representatives to the UN recalled:

> If China had kept silent, the difference would have been only 10 countries. What changed was that in Asia, especially among ASEAN nations, there were no cosponsors. Two countries stood up—Singapore and

Vietnam—and could have become cosponsors if China had not opposed. Two other countries were supportive but asked us not to refer to it because of Chinese pressure. Several other countries were also support- ive but didn't want their support known before a vote. Myanmar decided to abstain, and some among the Pacific Islands—Tonga—also decided to abstain.[193]

By allowing anti-Japanese protests and bringing up Japan's misdeeds during World War II, China gave ASEAN nations—who in November 2004 had signed a trade accord with China—grounds for resisting Japan's entreaties for support at the UN deliberations. Although Singapore endorsed Japan's candidacy, Prime Minister Lee Hsien Loong bracketed his support with criticisms of Koizumi's visits to Yasukuni Shrine and Japanese history textbooks.[194] Singaporean foreign minis- ter George Yeo opposed an early vote on the G4 proposal, noting that it was "not realistic" and might "polarize the global community of nations and cause serious damage to the U.N."[195] As Malloch Brown, chief of staff to Kofi Annan, summarized at the time: "Demonstrations against the Japanese embassy and consulates reminds one [that] there is a China-Japan dimension to which Germany's membership is hostage. . . . Germany and Japan and India really need to listen to their regions and give their regions assurance that they are not going to use their membership to settle scores within the region."[196]

Conclusion

This chapter has examined China's motives for allowing large-scale anti-Japanese protests to erupt in 2005 as well as their diplomatic consequences. This reading of events is consistent with scholarship that emphasizes the difficulty Chinese lead- ers face in defying nationalist anger,[197] but it also emphasizes the government's complicity in allowing this wave of popular sentiment and street protests to gain momentum in the first place, contrasted with previous episodes in which the gov- ernment had restrained anti-Japanese mobilization.

Seeking to repair the damage to Japan's Security Council bid, Prime Minister Koizumi made a historic apology and refrained from demanding that China apologize and provide compensation for the protest damages. Regional support for Japan's candidacy diminished and the United States joined China in block- ing a vote on the G4 proposal. Although most foreign observers suspected that Chinese government had allowed the protests against Japan to take place, they also recognized that protests could spin out of control and that popular pressure required the Chinese government to take a tough stance against Japan.

Although the government tolerated anti-Japanese protests, it is less clear that this decision was motivated by a desire to distract public attention from domestic grievances. Inculcating nationalism may bolster the regime's legitimacy, but nationalist protests per se are a relatively risky diversionary tactic. Textbooks, films, and school field trips to museums glorifying the Communist Party's defense of China are a much less dangerous means of encouraging nationalism and rallying the public around the flag than street protests. As Yukio Okamoto, special advisor to Japanese prime minister Koizumi on foreign affairs, observed: "The government is losing its ability to control events. Taking the lid off to release pent-up pressure is one thing, but the authorities are finding that they can't get the lid back on."[198] At the individual level, participants joined anti-Japanese protest activities for various reasons, including curiosity and thrill-seeking. But there is little evidence to suggest that a desire to distract citizens guided the timing of the government's lenience toward anti-Japanese protests. Moreover, the government remained concerned that anti-government elements might utilize anti-Japanese protests as an opportunity to "instigate trouble," underscoring the risks of street protests as a diversionary tactic.

Diversionary or "venting" perspectives are also silent on the costs of suppressing demonstrations after they have begun and gained momentum, namely, the disenchantment of protest participants and activists with the government for cracking down. In 2005, these costs were not very large, because the government had already taken a tougher stance against Japan and could claim victory in blocking momentum for a vote on UNSC reform. Nevertheless, the evidence suggests that *without* a diplomatic victory and a tougher foreign policy stance, suppression would have been very costly, as momentum built for a fourth round of protests over the May holiday, including the anniversary of the May Fourth movement. The government was able to curtail further protests, as others have noted,[199] but it is important to recognize that the government's ability and willingness to repress popular sentiment was contingent on being able to show domestic audiences a positive diplomatic outcome.

Relaxing the assumption that the government is a unitary, rational actor, some observers have speculated that the Hu Jintao–Wen Jiabao leadership sought to strengthen its populist credentials against the Jiang Zemin clique by giving nationalist groups more space to organize activities.[200] Others have pointed to the uneven curtailment of protests, particularly the eruption of a large-scale anti-Japanese protest in Shanghai following national-level meetings to calm the situation, as an indication that anti-Japanese protests were stoked by supporters of the former leader, Jiang Zemin, to discredit the Hu-Wen administration.[201] These competing interpretations are indicative of the difficulty in marshalling evidence for intra-elite or bureaucratic divisions. Although some have interpreted the uneven curtailment of protests as a sign of internal power struggle,[202] many other cities witnessed protests the same weekend as Shanghai, and it was only in Guangzhou and Beijing, which Foreign Minister Machimura was visiting, where the streets were conspicuously quiet after large-scale protests the previous weekend. In the absence of more concrete evidence, rumors of elite schisms are likely to remain rumors. Yet such rumors also serve as important reminders of the latent risk that protests may widen fissures in the regime. By appearing to intensify elite conflict, nationalist protests add to the risk of broader instability, emboldening potential opponents and creating perceived windows of opportunity.

Protests Restrained

Repairing Sino-Japanese Relations (2006–2010) and
the 2010 Trawler Collision

> When the leaders express condemnation, it means that you're allowed to express condemnation. When the leaders express regret, it means your time for expressing condemnation is over. The leaders want to condemn, but you want to take action. There lies the limit of the leaders' tolerance. If you really take action, the leaders will have to punish you. This is because they've played a big chess piece and it would be inappropriate for you, a little chess piece, to jump off the board.
> —Han Han, racecar driver and blogger, September 13, 2010[1]

By the late 2000s, the explosive growth of the Internet and social media in China—including Weibo, China's homegrown version of Twitter—provided greater space for views that diverged from the party line. As a senior Chinese diplomat confided, "I'm worried. Public opinion is more and more influential. There are many irrational voices."[2] The government also put greater emphasis on online social media as means of guiding and gauging public opinion. Zou Jianhua, former press counselor to the Foreign Ministry, wrote:

> The Internet has raised the bar for us. We must be timely in responding to sudden incidents, reacting with more speed and agility in order to grasp the initiative with public opinion. . . with QQ, BBS, Weibo and the rise and universal usage of online technologies, the speed with which the government should publish information has increased from 24 hours to four hours.[3]

As technology has accelerated the spread of information, to what extent can the strategic logic of nationalist protest account for China's evolving management of anti-Japanese protest? Has the government still been able to moderate the degree to which nationalist pressure constrains foreign policy, allowing or repressing antiforeign demonstrations when necessary for its diplomatic objectives?

China's management of anti-Japanese protest from 2006 to 2012 provides an opportunity to evaluate the strategic framework in light of new events.[4] The pattern is largely consistent with expectations. When the Chinese government sought to reassure Japan of its commitment to improving bilateral relations between 2006 and 2010, it took pains to restrain anti-Japanese protests despite the costs of repression. When China sought to show resolve during the escalation of a maritime incident in 2010 and Japan's purchase of three disputed islands in 2012, the government allowed anti-Japanese protests despite the risk that demonstrators would use the opportunity to air domestic grievances. During this period China witnessed hundreds of thousands of "mass incidents" and inter-ethnic riots in Tibet and Xinjiang, yet paranoia about "stability maintenance" did not uniformly counsel repression of antiforeign protests. China also hosted the 2008 Olympics and successfully weathered the most severe global economic crisis in decades, yet this confidence did not necessarily translate into a greater willingness to allow nationalist protest. Domestic factors were not unimportant, but the domestic trade-off between the risk of allowing and the cost of repressing nationalist protest was sufficiently indeterminate to allow diplomatic goals to play a key role.

This chapter traces China's management of anti-Japanese protest from 2006 to 2010 in three parts. The first describes how China kept anti-Japanese demonstrations to a minimum between 2006 and 2010 as both governments sought to repair bilateral ties. The second part analyzes China's reaction to the 2010 collision of a Chinese fishing trawler and Japanese Coast Guard patrols. As the Chinese government sought to prompt an early resolution to the maritime collision, it prevented large-scale anti-Japanese protests on the anniversary of September 18. It was not until China accused Japan of escalating the crisis— extending the trawler captain's detention and publicly asserting that no territorial dispute existed—that China showcased nationalist anger and permitted larger anti-Japanese protests.

The last part of the chapter considers Japanese perceptions of Chinese signals during the 2010 trawler crisis. Japanese officials recognized China's efforts to restrain protests at the outset of the trawler collision. But the sporadic character of the 2010 anti-Japanese protests, combined with the appearance of unrelated protest slogans, raised doubts over whether China needed to take a tough stance against Japan in order to appease domestic pressures. As China's most prominent cities remained quiet, the uneven outbreak of anti-Japanese protests in interior cities reduced the visible risk and cost of curtailment. As we will see in the next chapter, the conclusions drawn from the 2010 crisis may have contributed to Japanese miscalculations in 2012. Even after large-scale protests took place against Japan's planned "nationalization" of three islands in August 2012, Japanese decision-makers downplayed the protests as evidence of Chinese resolve or a constraint on Chinese policy toward Japan.

Mending Fences with Japan:
Containing Anti-Japanese Protests, 2006–2010

As China and Japan sought to improve relations and forge a "mutually beneficial strategic relationship," Chinese authorities took pains to restrain anti-Japanese sentiment and nationalist activities between 2006 and 2010.[5] Chinese authorities censored Internet forums and kept activists under surveillance during important diplomatic visits, restricted the size and duration of token protests on war anniversaries, and discouraged mainland and Hong Kong activists from making protest voyages to the disputed islands. Following the curtailment of the 2005 protests, senior diplomats and policy analysts were dispatched to university campuses to explain government policy toward Japan, "calling on young students to have a clear understanding of the overall situation of the Sino-Japanese relationship and not to act emotionally."[6] An online petition to declare a "Diaoyudao" national holiday was forced to close in June 2006.[7] In advance of Prime Minister Koizumi's final visit to Yasukuni Shrine on the sensitive August 15 anniversary in 2006, the Patriots Alliance Network web forum was shut for "server maintenance" and the cleanup of provocative posts.[8]

During state visits by Prime Minister Shinzo Abe in October 2006 and Prime Minister Yasuo Fukuda in 2007, Chinese authorities kept anti-Japanese activists under strict surveillance and censored discussions on nationalist forums.[9] Protests outside the Japanese embassy in Beijing were confined to small demonstrations on war anniversaries[10] and occasional incidents, such as the detention of a Chinese man at the Tokyo airport for throwing a water bottle at former Taiwan president Lee Teng-hui.[11] In October 2007, mainland activists set sail for the islands from Fujian province but were repelled by the Japanese Coast Guard. On their return, Chinese security authorities interrogated the activists and required them to sign papers promising not to try again.[12]

When China and Japan reached a consensus on joint development in the East China Sea in June 2008, activists with the China Federation for Defending the Diaoyu Islands (CFDD) called for demonstrations in Beijing and Changsha.[13] The gas agreement reflected a softening in the Chinese position by allowing Japanese participation in the Chunxiao gas field (which China had unilaterally developed since 2004) and joint development of a new field, Longjing (which straddles the Japanese-claimed median line between China and Japan). In previous talks, China had refused to include the Chunxiao field, which lies to the west of the Japanese-claimed median line, or to discuss joint development of fields straddling the line, since doing so might undermine China's refusal to recognize the median line and weaken China's claims to an exclusive economic zone extending to the Okinawa trough.[14]

In an open letter to the Central Military Commission and National People's Congress, Chinese activists accused the government of sacrificing the fundamental interests of Chinese on both sides of the Taiwan Strait. CFDD founder Tong

Zeng warned that the agreement would arouse strong reactions among the Chinese public, claiming that Deng Xiaoping's principle of "shelving disputes" only applied to the islands themselves, not the East China Sea.[15] Anti-Japanese activists were instructed to take down their open letter or the website would be shut down.[16] A protest in front of the Japanese embassy on June 18 was restricted to less than two dozen activists, "with police stopping traffic in front of the embassy at the designated time to make room for the activists."[17]

Visible evidence of nationalist opposition, while kept in check, served as a reminder that the Chinese government was willing to spend political capital to reciprocate Japanese overtures to improve bilateral relations. As Japanese vice minister for Foreign Affairs Yabunaka noted, Hu Jintao had high expectations for further improvement in Sino-Japanese relations under Prime Minister Fukuda.[18] Two weeks before the June 2008 agreement, Fukuda gave a speech emphasizing that "for the sake of Asia's future, Japan should cooperate with China, and ensure China's stability and development," according to a Chinese Foreign Ministry–affiliated institute.[19] Fukuda had visited China in December 2007 and welcomed Hu to Japan in May 2008, the first time that a Chinese head of state had visited in a decade. Hu's visit was "hailed as the arrival of a warm spring in bilateral ties" that "crowned a year-long political rapprochement starting from ice-breaking to ice-thawing," according to Yang Bojiang.[20] A month later, Chinese negotiators compromised on the terms of the agreement with Japan on gas resources in the East China Sea.

Chinese officials repeatedly reassured the public that Japanese participation in Chunxiao and joint development did not undermine Chinese sovereignty,[21] including Foreign Minister Yang Jiechi, Vice Foreign Minister Wu Dawei, and China National Offshore Oil Corporation vice president Zhou Shouwei.[22] Hu Jintao made a rare appearance on an online chat forum, telling netizens that the "Internet is an important [tool] through which we [can] understand what people think and appreciate their wisdom."[23] After his appearance, observers noted that Internet comments became less critical of the gas agreement, prompting speculation about the role of Chinese censors and paid commentators.[24]

As implementation of the gas accord stalled, many foreign analysts cited nationalist opposition to explain China's unwillingness to continue negotiations toward a formal agreement, despite the absence of large-scale protests against the agreement.[25] As the *Nikkei Weekly* China bureau chief noted, "the reaction in China on June 18 when the agreement was officially announced turned out to be worse than expected, and the Internet was flooded with criticisms of the government. . . . The working-level discussions where the details of the joint development agreement will get hammered out cannot ignore the public opinion of China's wired masses."[26] Diminished confidence in the Japanese leadership may have also contributed to Chinese reluctance to continue the negotiations. Three months after the joint agreement, Prime Minister Fukuda announced his surprise resignation amid domestic mismanagement scandals and sliding approval ratings. Given the LDP's dismal popularity, few observers expected Fukuda's successor, Taro Aso, to last long; even Fukuda had lasted less than a year in office. Knowing that Aso would have to call for general elections within a year, Chinese officials reportedly deemed it wise not to take up sensitive negotiations under Aso.[27]

Starting in late 2008, Chinese activity in the East China Sea began to increase. Combined with China's success in weathering the global financial crisis,[28] many Japanese and American observers began to express concerns about China's "post-2008 hubris" and growing "assertiveness."[29] In December 2008, Japan protested the entry of two Chinese Marine Surveillance ships into the territorial waters surrounding the Diaoyu/Senkaku Islands, the first time that Chinese government vessels had breached the 12-nautical mile limit around the islands.[30] In January 2009, Japan condemned unilateral Chinese drilling activities at a second gas field, Tianwaitian, which China maintained had not been covered by the 2008 agreement.[31]

At the same time, China continued to restrain nationalist activities during the new Aso administration, which turned out to be less hawkish on China than Aso's reputation and past statements might have indicated. Aso had humorously referred to himself as "a candidate deemed a probable enemy of China" in an LDP election debate, but as prime minister he "clearly expressed his readiness to continue furthering Fukuda's efforts in consolidating relations with Beijing."[32] During Aso's visit to China in October 2008, he reaffirmed his desire for "strategic and mutually beneficial relations," stating that China and Japan were "perpetual neighbors." According to the *CIIS Blue Book*, "We have reasons to believe that the joint statement and other cooperation projects signed by President Hu Jintao and the former Japanese Prime Minister will not be changed by Aso's cabinet."[33]

Both governments continued to emphasize diplomatic progress and high-level exchanges.[34] In January 2009, security authorities detained Chinese activists for organizing a "defend the Diaoyus" conference in Changsha.[35] After China expressed "strong dissatisfaction" over Aso's remarks to Japanese legislators that the U.S.-Japan security alliance covered the islands in the event of an attack, the two foreign ministers agreed that the issue should not harm bilateral ties.[36] A month after Aso's visit to Beijing in March 2009, the Japanese government refused to permit the Ishigaki mayor to land on the islands and conduct a property tax investigation.[37] Chinese authorities curtailed attempts to organize protest voyages to the islands in May, even reportedly pressuring Hong Kong activists to desist through the central government's liaison office in Hong Kong. When Hong Kong activists refused to heed the warning, their boats were turned back by the Marine Department on safety grounds—the first time Hong Kong authorities had blocked such a protest voyage.[38]

Anti-Japanese Protests and the 2010 Fishing Trawler Incident

On September 7, 2010, a Chinese fishing trawler collided with two Japanese Coast Guard vessels near the Diaoyu/Senkaku Islands. The ensuing dispute can be broken into two phases, beginning with the September 7 collision. During the first phase, Japanese officials arrested the Chinese trawler captain on charges of obstructing official duties, accusing him of reckless and aggressive behavior and indicating that the case would be handled in accordance with domestic law. During the captain's initial detention, effective through September 19, only small-scale anti-Japanese demonstrations were permitted. The Chinese government took pains to prevent large-scale protests on September 18, the anniversary of Japan's invasion of Manchuria in 1931.[39] The web forum of the China Federation for Defending the Diaoyu Islands, where multiple threads had been started for protests in various cities, including Beijing, Nanjing, Xiamen, Shenzhen, Shenyang, and Zhengzhou, was shuttered during the anniversary.[40] Activists were invited to "drink tea" with police officers and reported that many of their QQ chat groups had been shut down.[41] Local authorities also prevented mainland activists who had gathered in Xiamen from setting sail for the islands.[42]

The dispute escalated on September 19 when Japan extended the captain's detention and continued to insist on handling the case through domestic legal procedures, marking the second phase of the crisis. China responded with a much tougher series of countermeasures: halting bilateral exchanges, arresting four Japanese employees for allegedly filming Chinese military sites, and allegedly restricting the export of rare earth metals to Japan.[43] Although new street demonstrations did not arise, state-run media showcased the small anti-Japanese protests that had taken place. The crisis began to abate after Japan released the captain without charge on September 24. China took reciprocal measures to defuse the situation, releasing the Japanese employees and refuting allegations that it had halted rare earth exports to Japan. The larger territorial issue remained rancorous, however, as China denounced Japanese officials for denying the existence of a territorial dispute and "internationalizing" the incident by publicizing American treaty assurances. The harassment of Chinese tourists in Japan and anti-Chinese demonstrations in Tokyo sparked reciprocal protests in second- and third-tier Chinese cities, marking the first large-scale demonstrations that had taken place over the disputed islands in mainland China.[44]

Why did China prevent large-scale anti-Japanese protests on September 18, and why did protests break out in October after the Chinese captain's release? As in the rest of this book, my analysis focuses on Chinese perceptions and motivations in order to explain the government's management of anti-Japanese protests before turning to Japanese perceptions to assess the impact of China's actions.[45] The Chinese government faced a difficult domestic dilemma: repressing protests would

exacerbate popular disenchantment and nationalist resentment, but allowing protests would be risky at a time when grievances over land seizures and forced demolitions might turn anti-Japanese protests against the regime.

During the initial phase of the trawler incident, China hoped that Japan would
adhere to past precedent and release the captain, expecting that diplomatic rebukes
would be sufficient to dissuade Japan from prosecuting the case through domestic
channels. As Japan continued to stand firm, China gradually escalated its diplomatic
countermeasures, perhaps judging that the longer the Japanese held the captain, the
greater the domestic costs to the Chinese government of keeping anti-Japanese
demonstrations in check. As Johnston notes, "They were likely worried that if the
captain were not released before September 18, China would look diplomatically
weak, thus making it even harder to control anti-Japanese demonstrations on or
around that special day in nationalist history."[46] Yet China also refrained from taking the sort of escalatory countermeasures it employed during the second phase,
after Japan extended the captain's detention on September 19. Had China wanted
to send a stronger signal of resolve from the outset, it could have done so by taking a more lenient attitude toward nationalist activists and anti-Japanese protests.
Instead, the government squelched attempts to mobilize large-scale demonstrations
on September 18, 2010.

During the second phase of the trawler crisis, the dispute remained acrimonious
even after China's forceful measures prompted the captain's release. From China's
perspective, Japanese actions and statements indicated that Japan was no longer
willing to abide by an implicit agreement to set aside the sovereignty issue. As
Japanese officials continued to refute the existence of a territorial dispute or a tacit
consensus to shelve the issue, China sought ways to show resolve while partially
restoring exchanges that had been frozen. During this period, Chinese authorities
made no concerted effort to prevent anti-Japanese protests. Small-scale protests
quickly gained steam in two dozen second- and third-tier cities in October 2010,
with the appearance of unrelated domestic grievances illustrating the risks that
nationalist protests could turn against the regime.

The Diplomatic Context: Initial Restraint and Gradual Escalation

The trawler incident occurred at a sensitive time in Sino-Japanese relations. With
the change of Japanese party control in 2009, China welcomed the Democratic
Party of Japan (DPJ)'s intent to rebalance Japanese foreign policy toward China and
East Asia. But with the resignation of the DPJ's first prime minister, China feared
that his successor, Naoto Kan, might revert to more a hawkish stance on China and
reinvigorate the U.S.-Japan alliance. In the weeks before the trawler collision, China
took steps to engage the Kan administration, inviting him to visit China and beginning talks to implement the 2008 gas accord.

Until Japan extended the captain's detention and announced that the United States had confirmed that the Diaoyu/Senkaku Islands were covered by the U.S.-Japan alliance, China was cautiously optimistic that the incident could be resolved without damaging progress in Sino-Japanese relations. After the Liberal Democratic Party (LDP)'s defeat in September 2009, the new DPJ prime minister Yukio Hatoyama had pledged to seek greater autonomy from Washington and emphasized the importance of building an "East Asia Community" that appeared to exclude the United States.[47] Hatoyama aggravated the Obama administration by taking up his campaign pledge to relocate the Futenma Marine Corps Air Station outside of Okinawa and renegotiate an arrangement that had been painfully hammered out with the LDP. The strain on the U.S.-Japan alliance was not lost on Chinese observers. As the Foreign Ministry–affiliated *CIIS Blue Book* notes, "decisions by the Hatoyama administration, including moving the bases in Okinawa, impacted America's trust in Japan and confidence in bilateral cooperation."[48] Chinese analysts welcomed the DPJ's new focus on Asia and China, seeing Hatoyama's initiatives as reflecting "a new direction in [the] DPJ's as well as Japan's foreign policy."[49] State media commended Hatoyama's pledge to not visit Yasukuni Shrine, quoting experts on the DPJ's "intelligent and forward-looking approach" to China-Japan relations, particularly compared to the LDP.[50]

Under Hatoyama, Japan and China continued to strengthen bilateral ties and high-level exchanges. Within two months after taking office, Hatoyama met with Hu Jintao four times.[51] During Chinese Defense Minister Liang Guanglie's visit to Japan, the two sides issued a nine-point joint communiqué, agreeing to continue military exchanges and to undertake joint training for maritime search-and-rescue missions.[52] In December 2009, China welcomed a delegation of more than 150 Japanese legislators and businessmen, led by DPJ heavyweight Ozawa. In May 2010, after two years of stalled progress on implementing the gas field agreement, Premier Wen Jiabao offered to begin formal talks on joint exploration during his visit to Tokyo. The two prime ministers also agreed to set up a hotline between the two leaderships.[53]

At the same time, many Chinese analysts wondered whether the inexperienced DPJ would follow through with its diplomatic rebalancing toward Asia, noting the pressure from public opinion, the LDP, and the United States.[54] Hatoyama's popularity plummeted after he backtracked on his promise to find an alternative base location for Futenma. After Hatoyama resigned in June 2010, his successor, Naoto Kan, vowed to restore relations with the United States, pledging to honor the Futenma agreement and calling the U.S.-Japan alliance the "cornerstone" of Japanese diplomacy.[55] With Kan signaling an interest in distancing his foreign policy from the Hatoyama administration's, China took early steps to stabilize bilateral relations. Noting the DPJ's failure to meet public expectations thus far, Chinese scholars characterized the situation facing Hatoyama's successor as "very fragile."[56]

Days after Kan took office in June 2010, the Chinese leadership took steps to shore up the progress in bilateral relations achieved under Hatoyama. Wen Jiabao activated the prime ministerial hotline, congratulating Kan and extending an invitation to visit China, which Kan accepted.[57] At the end of June, Hu Jintao met Kan on the sidelines of the G20 summit in Toronto and reaffirmed his desire to strengthen bilateral ties.[58] Hu repeated the invitation to visit China, and Kan expressed his desire to visit at a convenient time.[59] Talks to implement the 2008 gas agreement began in late July.

Yet China was also sensitive to indications that Kan was more of a China hawk than his predecessor. Chinese Foreign Ministry spokesman Qin Gang warned that the U.S.-Japan alliance should not target a third country after Kan remarked that the U.S. military presence in Japan was an important "deterrent" against China. Xinhua quoted Kan as saying that he was "paying great attention to China's burgeoning military power and thinking that we must watch out for it."[60] A Phoenix editorial described Kan's remarks as careless and untimely due to China's uncertainty regarding the trajectory of bilateral relations under the new Kan administration.[61] A month before the trawler incident, a Japanese expert panel also reaffirmed that the LDP-DPJ transition had not affected the centrality of the U.S.-Japan alliance to Japanese security.[62]

First Phase: Restraining Protests to Defuse a Potential Crisis

When news of the trawler collision reached China, Beijing hoped to nip the crisis in the bud. Given past precedent, China was hopeful that the incident would be resolved quickly. In 2004, the Koizumi administration quickly deported the Chinese activists who had landed on the Diaoyu/Senkaku Islands.[63] In 2008, after a Taiwan fishing boat sank after colliding with a Japanese patrol vessel, Japan rescued the Taiwanese crew and deported them, later apologizing and offering compensation.[64] As Johnston notes, "The Chinese claim that there has been an unwritten norm to release fishermen who violate the twelve mile limit around the islands, and that past Japanese practice had led China to believe the captain would be released quickly and without publicity."[65]

Given the tentative rapport with Kan and uncertainty about the direction of the U.S.-Japan alliance, China responded firmly but with restraint at the outset of the incident, eschewing the stronger measures that it employed after Japan extended the captain's detention. China's initial response to the trawler incident was moderate, gradually escalating as the Japanese side took steps to prosecute the Chinese captain in accordance with domestic law. China feared that Japan's use of domestic law to try the trawler captain would set a negative precedent and undermine China's sovereignty claim. According to the *CIIS Blue Book*, the incident "arose from an ordinary maritime clash, but the Japanese side painstakingly used domestic legal procedures to detain the Chinese fishing boat and fishermen and publicly denied that a territorial dispute exists between China and Japan."[66]

On September 7, Xinhua reported that a Japanese patrol vessel had collided with a Chinese fishing trawler that morning near the islands.[67] That afternoon, Vice Foreign Minister Song Tao summoned Japanese ambassador Uichiro Niwa and urged Japan to halt the "illegal interception" of Chinese fishing vessels.[68] Asked about the incident at a regular press briefing, Chinese Foreign Ministry spokeswoman Jiang Yu asserted China's sovereignty over the islands but indicated only that "we will closely follow the situation and reserve our right to take further actions."[69] That evening, Japanese Foreign Ministry director-general Akitaka Saiki told Chinese ambassador Cheng Yonghua that the case would be handled calmly and in strict accordance with Japanese laws, noting that the issue should not damage bilateral relations. Cheng responded that the islands were not Japanese territory, so it was not illegal fishing.[70]

On September 8, Japanese authorities formally arrested the Chinese captain on charges of obstructing official duties, accusing him of ramming Japanese patrol vessels while attempting to flee. Chief Cabinet Secretary Yoshito Sengoku reiterated that the case would be handled strictly based on the nation's laws, stating that "Japan's position is that there's no territorial problem concerning the Senkaku Islands."[71] In response, Assistant Foreign Minister Hu Zhengyue summoned Ambassador Niwa a second time, using stronger language and a higher-ranked official to demand the immediate release of the ship and its crew.[72]

On September 8, Chinese authorities allowed small demonstrations to take place outside the Japanese embassy in Beijing and consulate in Chongqing. The *People's Daily* website reported that more than 40 protesters from the "unofficial China Federation for Defending the Diaoyu Islands" (CFDD) had "organized the half-hour protest on Wednesday noon" outside the Japanese embassy.[73] In Chongqing, 11 CFDD activists delivered a protest letter to a Japanese consular officer before dispersing.[74] Netizens commended their efforts and called for demonstrations outside Japan's other diplomatic offices in China.[75] A *Global Times* editorial noted China's restraint and urged Japan to respond in kind, implying that to do otherwise would inflame popular anger: "China did not encourage or instigate its people to cruise into the Diaoyu waters. Japan should also refrain from overreacting to civilian boats occasionally entering this area. . . . [Japan's] actions send a strong signal to the Chinese public, and will definitely draw condemnation and protest."[76]

As Japan proceeded with the captain's case and publicly refuted Chinese media reports that the Japanese side was to blame for the collision, the Chinese government increased the strength of its diplomatic rebukes.[77] On September 10, a local Okinawa court granted a request by Japanese prosecutors to extend the Chinese captain's detention by 10 days, effective through September 19.[78] Foreign Ministry spokesperson Jiang Yu stated that Japan had "obstinately decided to put the Chinese captain under the so-called judiciary procedures," describing Japan's handling of the case as "ridiculous, illegal and invalid."[79]

China also took its first diplomatic countermeasure, postponing bilateral talks on joint development of gas resources that had been scheduled for mid-September.[80] China's response was "relatively mild," according to a Beijing analyst, "showing that China still had a lot of room to maneuver, hoping that Japan would quickly release the fishermen and boat."[81] Japan did not relent, lodging a protest over China's decision to suspend talks. Seiji Maehara, who was then minister of land, infrastructure, transportation and tourism, criticized China's postponement, saying: "it is very regrettable if China linked the two issues. The Chinese government should deal with the situation calmly."[82] In the early hours on Sunday, September 12, Ambassador Niwa was summoned by State Councilor Dai Bingguo, the highest-ranking Chinese official yet to do so. Dai urged the Japanese side to make a "wise political resolution" and immediately release the fishermen and fishing boat.[83]

Even as China took more stern diplomatic measures, domestic authorities took measures to restrain nationalist mobilization. On September 10, CFDD organizers were instructed to delete their open letter of protest to the Japanese government.[84] Mainland activists who had gathered in Xiamen to set sail for the islands were stopped on September 11, the day before their planned voyage.[85] Hong Kong's *Apple Daily* reported that police had disrupted anti-Japanese protest attempts in Beijing, Nanjing, and Changsha.[86] As netizens called for protests the following Saturday to mark the anniversary of the Mukden Incident on September 18, Chinese censors restricted online comments that included the word "Diaoyu." The irony of censoring this term was not lost on the popular blogger and racecar driver Han Han, who was able to post using the term "Senkaku," the Japanese name for the islands.[87]

Like Han Han, other netizens skirted Chinese censors and web editors. On another site, seven netizens announced the formation of a new group, the Chinese Civilian Alliance Against Japan, using the term "resist Japan" (*kangri*) and "anti-Japan" (*fanri*) rather than mentioning the islands by name.[88] One Beijing netizen reported that he had gone alone to the Japanese "shit house" (屎馆, a homophone for 使馆, or "embassy"). When he showed up, police stationed outside the embassy took away his protest sign.[89]

On September 13, Japan released the 14-member fishing crew and boat but continued to detain the captain. With the crew's release, China claimed a measure of success. Foreign Ministry spokeswoman Jiang Yu stated that "the entire Chinese people and compatriots both at home and abroad have condemned Japan's illegal acts with one voice, which fully embodies the firm will and resolve of the Chinese Government and people to defend their territory and sovereignty."[90] But China also kept up its diplomatic pressure on Japan to release the captain, summoning Ambassador Niwa again, postponing NPC Standing Committee Vice Chairman Li Jianguo's visit to Japan, and warning that "Japan will reap as it has sown, if it continues to act recklessly" in detaining the captain.[91] The Chinese Foreign Ministry spokeswoman also defended Chinese activities in the East China Sea as "completely under both reason and law," including reports that Chinese equipment "resembling an excavator" had been spotted at the Chunxiao gas field.[92]

As September 18 drew nearer, Chinese authorities stepped up efforts to prevent anti-Japanese protests, holding campus "stability maintenance meetings" on university campuses,[93] interrogating activists, and shutting down Internet chat groups and threads calling for protests. Major news portals headlined the Chinese Foreign Ministry's statement of "confidence that the Chinese people will rationally, lawfully express their thoughts towards Japan." In Shanghai, security officials brought in activists to "drink tea" and "harmonized" online calls for protests outside the Japanese consulate on September 18.[94] In Xiamen, activists who had remained on the beach in protest over their foiled voyage were told by local government authorities to disperse or be taken away.[95] One expatriate blog likened an anti-Japanese protest in Chengdu to "more of a cancelled pop show than a violent, torrid outpouring of anger and nationalism. . . . After the crowd was dispersed and sent north toward the city center, the police jumped into buses and headed downtown, where they closed off Tianfu Square, shut down the Tianfu Square metro station and kicked protesters out of Chunxi Lu."[96] On the CFDD bulletin board, netizens complained that their QQ chat groups had been shut down, all receiving the same notice that their group had "violated relevant national laws."[97]

The Risk of Instability and Cost of Repression

Grassroots efforts to mobilize large-scale anti-Japanese protests as the September 18 anniversary presented the Chinese government with a difficult choice between repression and tolerance. Anti-Japanese protests might be used as a cover for other purposes, yet censorship and repression would also be detrimental to the government's legitimacy and patriotic credentials. Given these countervailing concerns, China's diplomatic objectives appear to have tipped the scales. China hoped Japan would follow precedent and sought to prevent the dispute from escalating at a moment when China was trying to stabilize ties with the new Japanese leadership.

On the one hand, the Chinese government had reason to fear that nationalist demonstrations might escalate beyond criticisms of Japan. As the trawler controversy unfolded, high-profile Chinese bloggers—including Ai Weiwei, Han Han, Ran Yunfei, and Michael Anti—ridiculed the idea that Chinese citizens would be concerned about the nation's territorial claims when they had no right to defend their own homes.[98] On September 10, three Yihuang county residents had self-immolated after being forcibly evicted from their homes, drawing widespread attention on Weibo. Three days before the September 18 anniversary, Ai Weiwei retweeted a call to use the anti-Japanese protests to criticize the government on land use and forced evictions: "Can we turn the anti-Japanese protest into anti-forced demolition protests? That would be more meaningful." An hour later, Ai Weiwei tweeted: "If it's a protest, I'll be there."[99] On September 17, in a blog post that was quickly deleted by government censors, Han Han wrote:

> If I could freely come forward, I would first demand the government do its job. Only then would I denounce the invaders. . . . In this country, the people don't own an inch of land. It's all rented from the government. . . . Why should a tenant with no dignity defend his landlord's dignity?. . . Anti-foreign protests by a nation of people that cannot peacefully protest at home are completely worthless. They are nothing but a group dance.[100]

Fears that nationalist protests might be used for insidious purposes were reflected in a *Global Times* editorial, which warned:

> The minority who try to kidnap patriotism and undermine social order will always exist. How to restrain such "patriotic thieves" and facilitate the normal expression of social thoughts is also a part of China's political enlightenment. . . . What the Chinese government needs to do is to facilitate orderly and effective delivery of ordinary people's voices to the outside world, whereas making sure that overly impulsive voices and actions will not bring about internal friction.[101]

One CFDD member in Beijing was told after being brought in to "drink tea" that the government didn't mean to repress (*da ya*) their activities, but unsavory organizations and external forces might try to take advantage.[102] A Hong Kong–based activist told the *South China Morning Post*, "We received an SMS from the rally groups in the mainland saying that all weekend protests there have been cancelled. I think the Chinese authorities were concerned that they will cause trouble."[103]

Nationalist activists had also become more willing to challenge the government. Whereas anti-Japanese organizers had described their activities as supporting the government's diplomatic struggle against Japan between 2001 and 2005, by 2010 they had become increasingly disenchanted with the government's willingness to improve relations with Japan at the expense of China's sovereignty in the East China Sea.[104] The week before the trawler incident, four CFDD protesters showed up outside the Chinese Foreign Ministry to mark the September 3 anniversary of Japan's formal surrender in World War II aboard the USS *Missouri*.[105] The protesters held a banner denouncing the resumption of East China Sea gas talks to implement the "treasonous accord," calling it a "surrender of sovereignty and national humiliation" (*sang quan ru guo*).[106] One of the protesters, Li Wenjia, reportedly accused Foreign Ministry officials of taking "bribes from foreign governments" to explain why "no effective measures" had been taken against Japanese "encroachment" in the East China Sea.[107] The location of the protest outside the Foreign Ministry was as inflammatory as the content. In 2008, small-scale protests over the gas accord had also taken place, but outside the Japanese embassy. And CFDD activists had reserved their most direct criticisms of the government, including accusations of treason, for online letters they were then told to remove.[108] On September 3, 2010, activists took this confrontational tone to the street.

In another sign that nationalist activists were becoming less circumspect, the Xiamen-based CFDD activist Li Yiqiang had been detained by authorities on June 3, 2007, after participating in protests against a proposed paraxylene (PX) chemical plant.[109] The participation of a nationalist activist in a domestic protest underscores one of the government's greatest fears: linkage across aggrieved groups, mobilized via social media.[110] Li had fallen out with the Beijing-based CFDD leadership and participated in the PX march on his own. During the protests, Li was photographed at the front of the crowd wearing a gas mask and "Japan, get out of the Diaoyu Islands" T-shirt, waving the national flag.[111] In 2009, the conference he tried to organize in Changsha was shut down, and it was his group that Xiamen authorities prevented from setting sail on September 11, 2010.[112]

On the other hand, efforts to prevent large-scale protests on September 18 were also costly to the government's patriotic and populist credentials, drawing a variety of cynical and derisive comments from nationalists and liberals alike. One netizen wrote: "Can a country that attacks patriotic action still be democratic? Can it still have space for the common people?"[113] After hearing that a fellow netizen on the CFDD forum had been asked to "drink tea" with the authorities and call off protest plans, one netizen wrote: "Our attitude toward the government should be the same as the government's attitude toward Japan: struggle but don't smash. Against the government's might, we must bow our heads. But if you believe what the government says, then you're an idiot."[114] Another netizen punned that Chinese state security (国保 *guobao*) was also Japan's "national treasure" (国宝 *guobao*).[115] Other activists fumed at local authorities in Xiamen for preventing the protest voyage to the islands, calling the government soft and soulless.[116]

Anger at the government's high-handed ban on protests was not limited to nationalist netizens. Liberal blogger Wen Yunchao criticized Xiamen authorities for banning the protest voyage, saying that "in the absence of the freedom to defend the Diaoyu Islands, so-called public opinion is nothing more than a bargaining chip of the authorities held in the face of foreigners."[117] Wen tweeted: "At first the authorities thought they could incite and use public opinion, like in the 1999 embassy bombing. But then they became worried that popular demands would change course and get out of control, so they used the emergency brakes."[118]

A dedicated issue of *Phoenix Weekly* featured an essay by the late Duke political scientist Tianjian Shi, who rebuked the government for suppressing nationalist sentiment:

> This policy [of shelving disputes] does not have public support and indeed gave rise to the civilian *baodiao* movement, which began in the United

States in the 1970s and quickly spread to Hong Kong, Taiwan, and mainland China. . . . Under these circumstances, we must throw off our delu-
sions and prepare to fight, no longer believing Japanese proposals to move
toward strategic reciprocity. . . . As far as Japan is concerned, so-called strategic reciprocity means "I illegally occupy your territory, but you should
welcome me with a smile and help me suppress popular anti-Japanese sentiments in China.". . . Some so-called strategic experts say at this moment
we must carefully consider the larger context of Sino-Japanese relations.
The Japanese will certainly interpret this kind of speech to mean we are
chicken, that we lack the resolve and courage to struggle against Japan. [119]

Despite widespread disgust, China's efforts to prevent large-scale anti-Japanese
demonstrations were successful. As the September 18 anniversary approached, a
CFDD activist denied having applied for permission to protest in Beijing, emphasizing that this was a "sensitive time for Sino-Japanese relations" in his remarks on
Phoenix Television:

> There are no plans for protests [in Beijing] this weekend. *Asahi Shimbun*—
> which is one of the most important media outlets in Japan—must have
> some deep-seated political motives for fabricating this report and publish-
> ing it on its website at such a sensitive time for Sino-Japanese relations
> following the ongoing detention of the Chinese trawler captain whose
> boat was commandeered in waters near the Diaoyu Islands. In fact, *Asahi
> Shimbun* never contacted us on this matter—and we have not applied to
> any government department to initiate a so-called large-scale demonstra-
> tion in Beijing. [120]

A CFDD organizer told *Ming Pao* that security officials had instructed him to stay
home or leave Beijing to avoid arousing suspicion on the 18: "We've all been controlled (*bei kongzhi*). Going out is problematic. Protecting the Diaoyu Islands,
alas—it's complicated!" [121]

On September 18, the day before the captain's detention was set to expire,
anti-Japanese protests were much smaller than media reports had anticipated. In
Beijing, several dozen protesters were outnumbered by the heavy security presence
stationed outside the Japanese embassy. [122] At least three protesters were detained
during the half-hour demonstration, including one who tried to stage a sit-in in
front of the embassy. According to the *South China Morning Post*, he "was soon taken
away when he claimed he had been persecuted by authorities for being a patriot and
vented his anger at the government's diplomatic weakness in dealing with Japan." [123]
Police blocked off the street for the rest of the day, allowing two more demonstrations of 15 minutes and 30 minutes later that day, according to Japanese reports. [124]
Demonstrations in other cities, including Shanghai, Shenzhen, and Shenyang, were

also small. In Shenzhen, police appeared to outnumber the dozen or so protesters "15 to 1" and dispersed the crowd after a half hour.[125]

Until records of internal deliberations become available, it is difficult to know the balance of China's domestic and diplomatic motivations in restraining protests on the eve of the September 18 anniversary. What we can discern is that repressing protests was costly, illustrated by the frustration of nationalists whose chat groups were shut down and posts removed. At the same time, allowing protests would have been risky, given overt signs that anti-Japanese demonstrations might be hijacked by other grievances, including forced evictions and demolitions. Against the backdrop of this domestic dilemma, China's desire to preserve the progress in bilateral relations and resolve the incident in accordance with past practice appears to have tipped the scales toward restraint during the initial phase of the crisis.

Second Phase: Demonstrating Resolve

Despite China's efforts to restrain protests on the September 18 anniversary, Japanese authorities extended the captain's detention on September 19, 2010. As Japanese media reported that "the indictment of the captain had become a certainty,"[126] the Chinese Foreign Ministry toughened its stance, stating that Japan's refusal to release the captain had "severely damaged" relations between the two countries. Vice Foreign Minister Wang Guangya told Ambassador Niwa that "Japan shall suffer all the consequences that arise" if the captain were not immediately and unconditionally released.[127] A Foreign Ministry statement announced that all provincial and central government exchanges with Japan had been suspended.[128] The All-China Youth Federation postponed the visit of 1,000 Japanese students to the Shanghai World Expo, citing the "inappropriate" atmosphere.[129]

Chinese state media now emphasized popular anger rather than downplaying the previous day's protests. According to Xinhua, "hundreds of Chinese gathered outside Japanese diplomatic residences across the country on Saturday to protest Japan's seizure of the captain as sirens wailed to mark the 79th anniversary of Japan's invasion."[130] Xinhua reported that a Chinese health food company had decided to cancel the visit of 10,000 employees to Japan the following month, quoting the company's vice manager: "Japan's illegal detention of the Chinese boat captain has severely hurt Chinese people's feelings."[131] According to the *People's Daily*, "millions of Chinese people vented their anger online on Monday after Japan extended its detention of a Chinese fishing trawler captain, calling for a boycott of Japanese goods and asking the Chinese government to take stronger measures."[132] The article quoted one post from bbs.163.com: "I hope the Chinese government adopts an even tougher attitude in tackling this issue. Don't let the public lose confidence."[133]

On September 21, Premier Wen Jiabao became the highest-ranking Chinese official to comment on the incident. Calling the islands part of China's "sacred territory," Wen demanded the immediate and unconditional release of the Chinese captain and warned of "further steps" if Japan did not comply.[134] Wen declined to meet with Kan on the sidelines of the UN General Assembly, with the Chinese Foreign Ministry spokeswoman stating that "obviously the atmosphere is not suitable for such a meeting."[135] Xinhua quoted a senior analyst at the Chinese Academy of Social Sciences: "Wen's criticism on Japan's mistake reflects the indignation of the Chinese people, and his words show that China will never give in on sovereignty issues."[136]

On September 23, Japanese foreign minister Seiji Maehara stated that Secretary of State Hillary Clinton had assured him that the U.S.-Japan alliance covered the islands.[137] Maehara remarked that it was a big step for the United States, saying that "this time they've clearly stated that the Senkakus are under Japanese jurisdiction and are part of the territory covered by the security treaty."[138] Some analysts speculated that Maehara made Clinton's assurances more public than she had intended.[139] But in briefings later that day, U.S. officials confirmed that the Japanese reports referred to "a longstanding U.S. policy," whereby "because the Senkaku Islands are under Japanese jurisdiction, [they are] covered by the U.S.-Japan security treaty."[140]

The same day, news media reported that China had effectively halted the export of rare earths to Japan, minerals that are vital to the production of high-tech products. Chinese officials claimed that the reduction in export quotas had been announced months prior and declared that "China will not use rare earths as a bargaining tool."[141] On September 24, China arrested four Japanese Fujita employees on charges of illegally entering and photographing military sites. Two Chinese fisheries enforcement vessels also appeared near the disputed islands, accompanied by a *Global Times* journalist who was allowed to report on its patrols for a Chinese readership.[142]

Japan released the captain without charge on September 24. Although the Kan administration denied political involvement in the decision, the local prosecutor's office cited the impact on China-Japan relations in its public remarks: "Considering the effect on the people of our nation and on China-Japan relations, we decided that it was not appropriate to continue the investigation."[143] Along with Chinese pressure, U.S. concern over the risk of escalation and the "strong nationalist fervor that had been generated both on the Chinese side and the Japanese side" may have also helped persuade Japan to release the captain, although publicly U.S. officials affirmed that "this was a Japanese decision to make."[144] On returning to China, the captain expressed his deep thanks for the Chinese government's assistance and the nation's concern in bringing him safely home.[145]

Shortly after the captain's return, China demanded an apology and compensation. The Chinese Foreign Ministry released a statement saying that his arrest "seriously infringed upon China's territorial sovereignty and the human rights of Chinese citizens" and demanded that Japan apologize and provide compensation for his "illegal detention."[146] However, China did not press the issue after the Japanese Foreign Ministry called such demands "groundless" and "totally unacceptable."[147]

Furthermore, Japan demanded that China pay for damages to the two Japanese Coast Guard vessels involved in the collision.[148]

As Japan refused to make further concessions, China appeared to take a softer tone. At a September 29 press conference, Foreign Ministry spokesperson Jiang Yu stated that "China highly values China-Japan relations," but noted that "safeguarding bilateral relations requires that the two sides meet halfway and requires Japan to take candid and practical actions."[149] The next day, Japanese media reported that China had begun clearing shipments of rare earths to Japan, according to the *Nikkei Weekly*. China also released three of the Japanese employees it had arrested, releasing the fourth on October 9.[150]

China's punitive measures during the second phase of the crisis—arresting Japanese nationals, demanding an apology after the captain's release, and allegedly restricting rare earth exports—were a response not only to the captain's extended detention but also what China regarded as Japan's willingness to breach a tacit understanding to shelve the sovereignty dispute by invoking domestic law and "internationalizing" the issue. As Feng Zhaokui noted: "I don't think the freeing of the Chinese captain will be a turning point for the Sino-Japanese relationship. It will take some time to heal. . . . The Chinese government will have a tough policy as a response."[151] In China's view, the stakes had escalated beyond a simple maritime incident. As the *CIIS Blue Book* concluded,

> The boat collision incident was just an opportunity and an excuse [for Japan] to shift policy. . . . After the Diaoyu boat collision incident, Japan linked the territorial dispute to the security issue, exaggerating the "China threat theory," seizing the opportunity to adjust its security policy, and strengthening the U.S.-Japan alliance. . . . There was nothing left of the DPJ desire under Hatoyama for a foreign policy more independent from the United States.[152]

Some Chinese experts saw a worrisome trend in Washington's willingness to get involved in China's maritime disputes. According to the Foreign Ministry-affiliated China Institute of International Studies Blue Book, "The United States seized the opportunity to warm relations with Japan and openly supported Japan on the Diaoyu Islands issue."[153] Two months before the collision, Hillary Clinton had told Southeast Asian nations, "The United States has a national interest in freedom of navigation, open access to Asia's maritime commons and respect for international law in the South China Sea."[154] Now, the United States had weighed in publicly on the East China Sea. In addition to Secretary Clinton's assurances, Vice President Biden had also told a U.S.-Japan Council meeting on September 20 that "frankly, I don't know how the [U.S.-China] relationship can be made right other than going through Tokyo."[155]

Other Chinese observers faulted Japan for dragging in the United States, taking advantage of the U.S. "pivot" to Asia to bolster Japan's military strength and solidify the U.S.-Japan alliance.[156] As a Foreign Ministry–affiliated think tank analyst noted, "Japan internationalized the incident of Japanese patrolling ships bumping against a Chinese fishing vessel and detaining Chinese fishermen with the obvious purpose of involving the United States. Japan asked the United States repeatedly whether the Japan-US Security Treaty was applicable to the Diaoyu Islands."[157] Shanghai analyst Lian Degui noted that Maehara might have read too much into Clinton's comments, which reflected a consistent refusal to take a stance on the islands' sovereignty and a habit of "forgetting" to mention whether the U.S.-Japan security treaty covered the islands. Yet he also concluded that Washington's "ambiguous stance" had spurred Tokyo to take a strong position, ultimately forcing the United States to reiterate its endorsement of Japanese control over the islands.[158] As Liu Jiangyong later put it, "Japan, once again, leads the U.S. by the nose."[159] Whether it was Washington pushing or Tokyo pulling, the outcome was the same: a public statement of U.S. support for Japan's de facto control.

Continued Tension and Protests in China and Japan

Despite the trawler captain's release, tensions continued to simmer through October. Under heavy domestic political pressure, Prime Minister Kan apologized to the Japanese public, criticized China's behavior, and reaffirmed Japanese sovereignty over the islands. In a key policy address on October 1, Kan expressed concerns about China's maritime activities and urged China to adopt "appropriate roles and actions befitting its position as a responsible member of international society."[160] The ruling DPJ paid a high domestic price for appearing to capitulate to Chinese demands, made worse by the trawler captain signing "V" for victory.[161] Opposition leaders called it "our nation's biggest foreign policy blunder since the end of World War II."[162] Amid a growing chorus to release the Japanese Coast Guard footage of the collision, Foreign Minister Maehara stated that the video clearly demonstrated that the Chinese trawler had been at fault.

Bilateral ties remained strained despite cautious outreach efforts. On October 4, the two prime ministers met informally in Brussels and agreed to "return to the starting point of improving our strategic mutually beneficial relations."[163] Both sides refrained from referring to demands for an apology or compensation and agreed to hold a high-level meeting "at an appropriate time."[164] Although many Chinese netizens were satisfied that Wen "refused to budge an inch," others called for a boycott of Japanese goods.[165] On October 12, China approved the postponed Japanese youth visit to the Shanghai Expo but also called off a scheduled port visit by a Japanese Maritime Self-Defense Force training fleet, citing ill feelings caused by the collision incident.[166]

China remained wary of Japanese intentions in light of remarks by conservative leaders and domestic pressure on the increasingly unpopular Kan administration. In early October, four Japanese Diet members, including a former cabinet member, surveyed the islands by charter plane.[167] Asked for comment, the Chinese Foreign Ministry spokesman called it an "illegal 'inspection from the air' in an attempt to infringe upon China's territorial sovereignty and undermine China-Japan relations, which will arrive nowhere."[168] The same day, several Japanese municipalities adopted resolutions demanding that the central government firmly defend the islands and ensure the safety of Japanese fishermen in the surrounding waters.[169] On October 13, the Japanese Lower House Budget Committee unanimously requested that the collision video be released to demonstrate that the Chinese captain had been at fault. On October 14, Foreign Minister Maehara told a Diet committee that his ministry had asked Google maps to remove the Chinese names for the islands since there was no territorial dispute in the East China Sea.[170]

China also gave prominent media coverage to right-wing protests in Japan, which sparked renewed calls for anti-Japanese protests and boycotts in China. China issued a travel advisory for Japan after Japanese right-wing trucks fitted with loudspeakers surrounded a Chinese tourist bus in the southern Japanese city of Fukuoka on September 29.[171] Posts by Chinese netizens looking to join anti-Japanese activities and QQ groups began to appear, including calls for protests in Guangzhou on October 1 and Zhengzhou on October 5.[172] On October 2 and 3, thousands of Japanese activists gathered at major shopping districts in Tokyo to protest against China and the Japanese government's decision to release the captain. The Chinese embassy in Tokyo reported receiving an anonymous note with a bullet and a warning, "Don't come near the Senkaku islands."[173] On October 3, a dozen Chinese activists in Changsha urged shoppers to boycott Japanese goods.[174] Although their activities were not reported by mainland media, photos of the anti-China protests in Japan were given prominent coverage. *Global Times* reported that right-wing Japanese groups held anti-China protests in 18 cities, a story that was widely reposted.[175]

Between October 16 and 26, anti-Japanese protests broke out in two dozen second- and third-tier Chinese cities. On Saturday, October 16, anti-Japanese protests broke out in several Chinese cities, including Chengdu, Xi'an, Hangzhou, and Zhengzhou.[176] No protests were reported in Beijing, where Chinese leaders gathered for an annual plenum of the CCP Central Committee and a cordon of riot police blocked off the Japanese embassy. The same day, 2,500 Japanese demonstrators gathered outside the Chinese embassy in Tokyo to denounce Chinese claims to the islands.[177]

In Chengdu, demonstrators distributed fliers opposing Japan's "invasion" of the Diaoyu Islands. Local media reported that a protest of 200 college students swelled to a crowd of 2,000, prompting city authorities to dispatch emergency forces to maintain order and route traffic.[178] The windows of two Japanese department stores were broken during the protest.[179] Smaller demonstrations took place in Luoyang and Ningbo, where protesters shouted "Get out of the Diaoyu Islands" and "Die, little Japan!"[180] In Ningbo, protesters demonstrated for three hours before police reinforcements arrived and dispersed the march. In a post that was later deleted, one Ningbo participant expressed frustration with the police and censors, writing: "if this post is 'harmonized,' I'd like to say, '*cao ni ma!*'" [a homonym for "fuck your mother"].[181]

Chinese Foreign Ministry spokesperson Ma Zhaoxu sympathized with the demonstrations that evening but urged calm, saying: "It is understandable that some people expressed their outrage against the recent erroneous words and deeds on the Japanese side. . . . We maintain that patriotism should be expressed rationally and in line with law. We don't agree with irrational actions that violate laws and regulations."[182] Protests spread to other cities on Sunday and Monday.[183] A protest in Wuhan grew from a hundred to a thousand participants as the march moved through the city, vandalizing a Japanese store before riot police dispersed the crowd. City authorities told protesters that "bad elements" had infiltrated the demonstration, and Wuhan universities reportedly imposed a curfew to prevent students from participating.[184]

Whether local authorities were caught by surprise or chose to allow small-scale protests that got out of control, it is evident that the Chinese government did not undertake the same repressive efforts to prevent and shut down calls for protest that it had before the September 18 anniversary. Some retired diplomats had counseled Chinese citizens to "express patriotism rationally" and avoid boycotting Japanese products, since most Japanese-branded goods were manufactured in China.[185] But no nationwide effort was made to forbid protests, detain activists, or censor calls for anti-Japanese protests as they appeared. As Renmin University's Shi Yinhong pointed out: "If the government very consciously opposed or didn't want these demonstrations, if they resolutely didn't want them, then there would be nothing."[186]

Although China had succeeded in securing the captain's release, the government remained determined to refute Japan's public assertions that no territorial disputed existed and show resolve in the face of Japanese efforts to "internationalize" the issue. According to Shi Yinhong, the "protests also had the advantage of attracting attention," noting that Japan had sent a "high official" to "earnestly handle the situation."[187] After three consecutive days of anti-Japanese protests, a close associate of Prime Minister Kan, Satsuki Eda, met with Foreign Minister Yang Jiechi in Beijing. Eda told reporters that he had relayed Prime Minister Kan's message of developing positive relations and that the two sides had agreed on the importance of mutual restraint.[188]

Speaking before parliament, Prime Minister Kan stated that the "regrettable" protests in China were unlikely to affect "a very important bilateral relationship."[189] Foreign Minister Maehara, who had described China's actions as "extremely hysterical,"[190] struck a milder tone. "I am not aware that the recent series of protests in China are interfering with our mutual goals of holding Japan-China foreign ministers' talks or a summit meeting," Maehara said.[191] Asked whether the government would lodge a protest over the anti-Japanese demonstrations, Maehara replied:

The recent anti-Japanese demonstrations that have led to destructive actions by a portion of the demonstrators are extremely regrettable. On the other hand, I think that it is vital for the Government of Japan that both countries' governments and peoples react rationally, taking a broad perspective of Japan-China relations.[192]

As the two governments renewed their commitments to repairing bilateral ties, the Chinese government began to calm anti-Japanese sentiment. Chinese propaganda authorities issued a five-point advisory on October 20 prohibiting local media from reporting independently on the anti-Japan protests.[193] The restrictions forbade local media from publishing front-page coverage of the protests and required them to use only Xinhua articles for relevant items, including the right-wing protests in Japan. When the Guangzhou magazine *Southern People Weekly* published a 14-page feature on the nationalist Tokyo governor, Shintaro Ishihara, censors deleted online versions of the story.[194] On October 20, heavy security prevented demonstrations in Shenzhen.[195] Yet calls for anti-Japanese protest remained visible, prompting the Japanese embassy to issue a warning that demonstrations could arise anywhere in China. Japanese media reported plans for anti-Japanese protests in Deyang, Kaifeng, Huangshi, and Wuxi on Saturday, Nanjing, Lanzhou, and Baoji on Sunday, and Chongqing the following Tuesday.[196]

New statements by Foreign Minister Maehara provoked Chinese ire as the weekend approached. On Thursday, October 21, Maehara told the House of Representatives that Japanese officials had never agreed to the proposal that Deng Xiaoping had "one-sidedly" put forth in 1978 to "shelve" the territorial issue, adding that such a proposal would be unacceptable were the Chinese side to propose it again.[197] Assistant Foreign Minister Hu Zhengyue condemned Maehara's remarks, stating that "Every day, Japan is using words to attack China, even using extreme words that should not come out of the mouth of a foreign diplomat."[198]

As anti-China protests took place again in Japan, anti-Japanese protests broke out for a second weekend in relatively minor Chinese cities, including Deyang and Lanzhou, where several hundred protesters demonstrated for an hour before police dispersed them.[199] Bao Diao activist Liu Feng noted that the protests "seem to be organized by ordinary people," adding: "They're being held in smaller, more remote cities to avoid too much attention and pressure from the central government."[200] In Baoji, a small city west of Xi'an, hundreds of anti-Japanese demonstrators also carried banners that said, "We oppose corruption in the bureaucracy" and "Curb high housing prices."[201] Japanese media showed images of Baoji protesters holding banners calling for a multiparty political system.[202]

In other cities, particularly those that had already witnessed large-scale protests, authorities stepped up efforts to prevent further demonstrations. In Xi'an, where anti-Japanese protests had turned violent the weekend before, university students were required to show permission slips from school authorities in order to leave campus, whereas students in Beijing and Xiamen reported no such policies.[203] In Changsha and Deyang, school authorities required students to attend extra classes over the weekend.[204] Police also interrogated and tailed several Bao Diao activists who had planned activities in Changsha that weekend.[205] A *People's Daily* editorial called the protests "understandable" but emphasized that the "government's stance has always been clear" on China's sovereignty over the Diaoyu Islands. The editorial stressed that "we must focus on the overall context and express our patriotic feelings in a calm, rational, lawful, and orderly manner, taking it upon ourselves to safeguard social order and turn patriotic passions into concrete work and study."[206] On Monday, China's top official in charge of security and law enforcement, Zhou Yongkang, told a meeting of senior officials: "We must strengthen propaganda and opinion work to guide the public to voice its patriotic aspirations in a rational and orderly way according to the law, protecting social and political stability."[207]

The final anti-Japanese protest to take place in 2010 occurred in Chongqing on Tuesday, October 26. According to Xinhua, a march of several hundred students swelled to "thousands of college students" before police convinced protesters to disperse after two hours.[208] It is unlikely that the protests caught local authorities by surprise, since calls for a Tuesday protest in Chongqing had circulated days in advance and drawn international media coverage. The day before the protest, a CFDD web manager posted the following message to a thread announcing the Chongqing protest location:

> Remember: it is OK to take a small-scale "anti-Japan stroll," but the timing, participants, slogans, and routes must be carefully considered, with actions self-disciplined. Absolutely no beating, smashing, or looting!!! Secret measures must also be taken. Large-scale protest marches must be approved beforehand by the relevant authorities.[209]

Li Yiqiang, a leading Xiamen-based Bao Diao activist, denied that the protests had been preapproved or organized by government authorities, saying: "If I apply, will you grant permission, or is it easier for me just to go ahead and do it without permission? [The authorities] are scrambling to stay in control of these protests. They haven't got time to be trying to instigate them as well."[210]

That the Chongqing protest took place after the Chinese government had urged the public to turn patriotism away from protests and into productive efforts underscored the government's dilemma in curtailing protests. Although the captain had been released, subsequent Japanese remarks and actions indicated little willingness to accommodate Chinese concerns over the larger territorial issue. Japanese officials publicly denied that the two sides had ever reached an unofficial consensus to "shelve the dispute," the tacit agreement that had facilitated the 1978 peace treaty. According to Liu Jiangyong, Japan's actions in the aftermath of the trawler collision had brought Sino-Japanese relations to their lowest point since the normalization of relations:

> The Japanese government repeatedly denied the objective fact that a territorial dispute exists between China and Japan, denied that a mutual consensus to "shelve the dispute" had already resolved the sovereignty issue, and tried to strengthen control over the surrounding islands and waters through a new national defense plan. The Chinese side absolutely could not accept this and firmly opposed it.[211]

Diplomatically, the Chinese government was caught between two objectives: repairing bilateral ties while countering Japanese attempts to "internationalize" the territorial dispute. As Shi Yinhong told Phoenix Television,

> Strategy requires using different methods to alternate between tension and relaxation. We must proactively respond to Japan's efforts to internationalize (*guojihua*) the issue and gain the sympathy of foreign publics and governments. Whether to hold immediate high-level talks must be carefully considered. When we were working to oppose the Koizumi government in 2005, we still had talks beneath the highest level.[212]

At a 90-minute meeting with Japanese foreign minister Maehara in Hanoi, Chinese foreign minister Yang Jiechi reiterated Chinese sovereignty over the islands but agreed that "it is in the fundamental interest of the two countries as well as the two peoples to maintain and promote the bilateral relations."[213] But after Maehara was quoted saying that China had agreed to resume talks on joint exploration in the East China Sea, China abruptly canceled the scheduled meeting between the Chinese and Japanese prime ministers, only allowing the two prime ministers to meet informally before the start of the summit.[214] Xinhua accused Japan of having "inflamed" the dispute and "disseminated information violating China's territorial claims."[215]

The Chinese government also publicized its steps to defend Chinese sovereignty over the islands. Two Chinese fisheries patrol vessels appeared near the islands, prompting the Japanese government to lodge a protest.[216] The State Oceanic Administration announced the expansion of its surveillance fleet to "safeguard sea rights" in the South and East China Seas.[217] After U.S. secretary of state Hillary Clinton reiterated that the U.S.-Japan security treaty covered the islands at a joint press conference with Foreign Minister Maehara, Chinese media headlined Foreign Minister Yang Jiechi's warning that the United States should not use "wrong words" in order to create a positive environment for President Hu Jintao's visit to the United States.[218]

Repressing grassroots sentiment remained costly, although not as costly as curtailment would have been without the government's well-publicized countermeasures

and claims that Japanese provocations were doomed to fail. Nationalist netizens
vented their anger at tightened censorship online. One Bao Diao member complained that all his QQ chat groups had been shut down, even the new ones he had
set up. "To protect the Diaoyus we must first exterminate Tengxun!" he declared,
blasting QQ's parent company.[219] The domestic risks associated with anti-Japanese
street protests had also become apparent. In Baoji, protests had strayed to demands
for domestic reform. Liberal bloggers continued to ridicule the protests. After the
October 16 protests in Chengdu, Ran Yunfei tweeted: "The 'valiant' university students of Chengdu dare with tacit consent to support the government against Japan.
Through painstaking efforts, the government has found others to let off steam, a
mass stampede unworthy of a great power."[220] The next day, a Weibo user retweeted
an apparently ironic call for protesters to escalate their tactics, adding the words
"Angry youth, charge!" to the original post: "Anti-Japanese demonstrations, smashing Japanese products, that was all done years ago. . . . If you really wanted to kick it
up a notch, you'd immediately fly to Shanghai to smash the Japanese Expo pavilion."
According to Amnesty International, she was sentenced to one year of re-education
through labor by a local Henan court for having "disturbed social order."[221]

Diplomatic Impact: Japanese Perceptions

The timing, content, and uneven curtailment of anti-Japanese protests made it difficult for foreign officials and observers to draw clear conclusions about China's
motivations, feeding skepticism about the degree to which public opinion constrained China's policy options. During the first phase of the crisis, China's efforts
to contain anti-Japanese protests in advance of the September 18 anniversary were
widely reported by Japanese media, which described the protests as "minor" and
"much smaller" than the 2005 anti-Japanese protests.[222] Foreign Minister Maehara
stated that protests were "sporadic" as a result of Chinese efforts to restrain them,
with security forces on high alert around Japanese diplomatic compounds.[223] At the
same time, Japanese officials accused China of having misled the Chinese public
about the facts of the collision, creating the domestic pressure to which it then had
to respond. Japanese foreign minister Katsuya Okada stated that it was "extremely
regrettable" that Chinese media had blamed the Japanese Coast Guard vessels for
ramming the Chinese trawler, saying it "contradicts the facts."[224] Japanese officials
emphasized that the video made clear that the Chinese trawler was at fault, even if
the prime minister's office refused to release the footage for fear of provoking China
and compromising its use as evidence in court.[225] As Maehara stated, "It is very clear
which side started colliding under what circumstance. I believe the Chinese public
would recognize the Chinese fishing boat's malicious behavior."[226]

Other foreign officials took a more cautious tone, urging both governments
to restrain nationalism rather than singling China out for fanning popular sentiment. Jeff Bader, senior director for East Asia at the National Security Council, told

reporters: "There are nationalist sentiments in both countries that can be stirred up should the problem stagnate."[227] Japanese chief cabinet secretary Yoshito Sengoku also emphasized the importance of mutual restraint, telling reporters: "Both Japan and China should be careful not to provoke narrow-minded, extreme nationalism."[228]

Despite China's perceived complicity in stoking popular anger, foreign media pointed out that the Chinese government's tough stance was meant to assuage domestic pressure, particularly after Japan extended the captain's detention. A *Yomiuri* editorial asserted that China had taken "a strikingly hard line" over the captain's detention and Japanese concessions "to earn brownie points with the public,"[229] calling on Beijing to take a "level-headed approach" and "avoid a recurrence of the massive anti-Japan protests that took place five years ago in China, with public opinion on the Internet keeping the pot boiling."[230] When Wen Jiabao publicly demanded the captain's release and warned of further countermeasures, the *Yomiuri* reported that while Wen's comments were clearly directed at Japan, "it also was an apparent attempt to show the Chinese people that Beijing would not give in to Japan on the matter."[231]

Other commentary portrayed the Chinese leadership as more vulnerable and constrained by popular sentiments. *Kyodo* published an article on Chinese nationalism, quoting a Chinese professor of international relations: "The Chinese government has no room to back down.... It cannot be ignored that Chinese public opinion is a strong influencing factor in China's foreign policy."[232] A prominent Japanese expert, Ryosei Kokubun, argued that Japan should have released the trawler captain "much sooner and thereby minimized its impact," noting that "The current row must have put Chinese leaders advocating a conciliatory relationship with Japan in a difficult position. They faced domestic criticism for 'weak-kneed diplomacy.'"[233] The *Sydney Morning Herald* reported that the Chinese government's warning of "strong countermeasures" against Japan was featured on the front pages of Chinese newspapers and on net forums, noting that if official countermeasures were seen as insufficient, "Beijing can find itself accused of being weak."[234] The article quoted Bao Diao activist Li Nan: "If the Chinese government continues to simply declare the Diaoyu Islands are Chinese territory while avoiding substantive action then I feel the islands are drifting further and further away from us."[235]

After protests broke out in October, Japanese officials publicly credited China's efforts to restrain anti-Japanese demonstrations but remained suspicious of their origins. Foreign Minister Maehara told a regular press conference that the protests were "spontaneous gatherings convened by appeals through the Internet"[236] but later conveyed his doubts about their spontaneity. Asked why the Chinese protests had erupted when the diplomatic situation "finally seemed to be calming down," Maehara stated:

Reports said that most of the protestors were young people responding to calls on the Internet to take part in the demonstrations, but I can't really see how that could be the case. I should note that Japan received credible assurances through diplomatic channels that the Chinese government was working to cool off these protests as soon as they began cropping up.[237]

Japanese media speculated that the protests reflected domestic grievances more than sincere anger at Japan. Some commentators cited the appearance of unrelated slogans against corruption and housing prices as evidence that the protests were a cover for anti-government dissent. Others saw the protests as a safe outlet for recent graduates without strong employment prospects to vent their anger.[238] Criticizing China's sympathetic stance toward the protests, a *Daily Yomiuri* editorial concluded:

> Leaders of the Chinese Communist Party are apparently most afraid that young people's frustrations, which are now taking the form of anti-Japan protests, could transform into anti-government movements demanding democracy. That is why some observers suspect Chinese security authorities are maneuvering anti-Japan demonstrations to alleviate young people's discontent. [239]

The timing of the protests also led some Japanese commentators to speculate that conservative elements fomented the protests to force the central leadership to take a more assertive stance against Japan at a delicate time in China's political succession. The October 16 protests coincided with a key CCP Central Committee plenum, at which Xi Jinping was promoted to vice chairman of the Central Military Commission, confirming his status as Hu Jintao's designated successor. The *Yomiuri* quoted unnamed experts as saying "it is difficult to rule out the possibility that the military and the conservative wing of the party, which are profoundly wary of Japan, have staged the demonstrations to pressure party leaders so they will not readily make concessions to Tokyo over the Senkaku incident."[240] Even without evidence of elite backing for the protests, others suspected that China's leadership needed to take a tough line vis-à-vis Japan to ensure a smooth handover to the "moderate" Xi Jinping.[241]

Other Japanese officials and commentators were more skeptical that the Chinese government was constrained by popular and elite pressure. Some Japanese commentators dismissed domestic explanations for China's escalatory behavior as "too convenient," seeing in Beijing's actions an attempt to "unilaterally impose its own territorial agenda on all of its neighbors in the South China Sea and East China Sea."[242] Others were convinced that the Chinese government would ultimately rein in the demonstrations, even if popular sentiments were real and useful in pressuring Japan. A high-ranking Japanese Foreign Ministry official told the *Yomiuri* that the captain's arrest "could aggravate anti-Japanese feelings among Chinese, especially young people, for a long time."[243] But the article concluded: "Beijing will likely take advantage of the surge in anti-Japanese feeling among its people to intensify pressure on Japan, while at the same time paying attention to the need to control anti-Japanese demonstrations calling for the captain's release."[244]

Whether sincere or not, peaceful anti-Japanese protests were sometimes described by Japanese officials as relatively harmless. During the October 26 Chongqing protest, for example, the Japanese consul general stated: "It was just the burning of the Japanese flag. . . . We are not overly concerned. Today's protest was pretty orderly. There was no smashing of shops or stores by the roadside, or any Japanese-made cars. It was pretty calm and reasonable compared with some other places [in China]."[245]

China's ability to curtail anti-Japanese protests in October may have indicated that the government would rein in popular sentiment once protests began to spill over into domestic concerns. Foreign media noted the effectiveness of state repression despite popular disgruntlement. One student complained that the extra weekend classes were ridiculous, asking: "were the authorities worried about anti-Japan protests or afraid that the public might seize the opportunity to air social grievances?"[246] The impression that China had "oversold the story on the streets" during the trawler dispute, as the *Economist* put it,[247] may have played a role in undercutting the signal sent by anti-Japanese protests two years later, when a new controversy erupted over Japan's nationalization of the islands.

Conclusion

Despite the rapid growth of the Internet and social media, China's management of anti-Japanese protests between 2006 and 2010 illustrates the continued role of diplomatic factors in shaping the government's response to nationalist mobilization. China's efforts to restrain nationalist opposition were evident to foreign observers, who noted the domestic price the government was willing to pay in order to improve relations with Japan, including a 2008 agreement on joint development of resources in the East China Sea. The initial phase of the 2010 trawler collision illustrates that when the Chinese government anticipated a swift resolution to a potential crisis, it remained able and willing to shut down widespread calls for anti-Japanese protest. During second phase of the trawler incident, when Japan extended the Chinese fishing captain's detention and continued to deny the existence of a territorial dispute, China responded with much a firmer stance, accompanied by a spate of anti-Japanese protests. Well-publicized measures to assert Chinese sovereignty, including the announcement of patrols in the East China Sea, facilitated the ultimate curtailment of protests in late October.

Yet the appearance of unrelated grievances that surfaced in anti-Japanese protests in second- and third-tier cities made it difficult for foreign observers to interpret the protests. According to the theory, the more that nationalist protests appear insincere or a cover for domestic grievances, the more likely foreign governments are to discount them as signals of resolve or a constraint on foreign policy. In 2010, Japanese observers were both unimpressed by "sporadic" protests that turned to domestic concerns and alarmed by the "hysterical" nature of China's countermeasures. In short, China's actions in 2010 communicated resolve but primarily through other means, including increased patrols, the arrest of Japanese employees, and the alleged embargo on rare earths. Japan effectively capitulated to international pressure by releasing the captain, but the domestic backlash in Japan set the stage for the crisis that was to erupt two years later. As former prime minister Shinzo Abe put it, China's maritime ambitions were akin to Hitler's demand for "living space."[248] In communicating resolve, Chinese actions also exacerbated fears in Japan, reducing the political space for compromise in 2012.

8

The 2012 Anti-Japan Protests and the Diaoyu/Senkaku Islands Crisis

In 2012, more than 200 Chinese cities witnessed protests against Japan's decision to purchase three of the Diaoyu/Senkaku Islands in the East China Sea. Although the Japanese government had leased the islands from their private Japanese owner since 2002, China regarded Japan's "nationalization" of the islands as a change in the legal status quo and a threat to Chinese sovereignty claims. By contrast, Japan reasoned that state ownership would be less provocative to China than letting the right-wing Tokyo governor Shintaro Ishihara buy the islands. As China sought to dissuade Japan from proceeding with the purchase while preserving plans to commemorate the fortieth anniversary of normalized relations, the Chinese government showcased the landing of Hong Kong activists on the islands and allowed anti-Japanese street protests in dozens of cities. As protests gained momentum and became violent in some cities, high-level "stability maintenance" directives sought to stage-manage and mitigate the risk that protests would get out of control as the September 18 anniversary of Japan's invasion of Manchuria approached.

Consistent with signaling resolve, the Chinese government was complicit in tolerating widespread anti-Japanese demonstrations and fanning popular anger through blanket media coverage. At the same time, Chinese restraint vis-à-vis Japan would have been difficult once protests against Japan were allowed to erupt and domestic attention was focused on the territorial issue, consistent with the commitment mechanism. After Japan purchased the islands, the Chinese government escalated with a series of unprecedented countermeasures in the East China Sea, satisfying domestic pressures to take a tougher stance and banking the fires it had helped light. As China's tough foreign policy measures assuaged nationalist demands and the risk of instability grew as protests spilled over into domestic concerns, it became safer and easier for Chinese authorities to stage-manage and ultimately curtail the protests in late September, after the September 18 anniversary had passed.

Despite widespread anti-Japanese protests in the month before Japan's purchase of the islands, the Japanese leadership discounted Chinese resolve. That Japan was undeterred is not problematic for the theory, since escalation may be met with counterescalation. Chinese actions during the 2010 trawler crisis and growing maritime activity had created a sense of "desperation" in Japan.[1] Nonetheless, the Japanese leadership did not revise its beliefs about the likely severity of China's response to the planned purchase. Less than two weeks after buying the islands, Prime Minister Yoshihiko Noda admitted to underestimating China's resolve: "I understand [that] the nationalization would bring reactions and tensions to some extent, but the scale is broader than expected."[2] Although many factors may have contributed to excessive optimism on both sides,[3] I focus here on explaining why Japanese observers discounted the protests as indicators of resolve and popular pressure on Chinese policy toward Japan.

Japanese officials acknowledged the anti-Japanese protests but also expected China to curtail them at an early stage, particularly on the eve of events to celebrate the fortieth anniversary of normalization and the Eighteenth Party Congress, which would anoint Xi Jinping as the next CCP general secretary. As in 2010, the appearance of unrelated slogans muddied perceptions of protesters' true grievances. Some observers understood these digressions as evidence that the protests were getting out of hand, but more saw the protests as a cover for unrelated concerns and a convenient outlet for societal discontent. As suggested by the logic depicted in table 2.1, nationalist protests that appear manufactured or insincere are likely to be met with foreign skepticism. Because manufactured protests are relatively easy to curtail and insincere protests are less likely to require foreign policy measures to satisfy their demands, foreign observers are more likely to discount such protests as a costly signal of resolve or a credible diplomatic constraint.

The 2012 crisis illustrates one of the greatest dangers of nationalist protest. When nationalist protests are perceived as a diversionary or venting strategy, foreign observers may misjudge the extent to which the government intends to stand firm. Diverting domestic grievances toward foreign policy issues may work if the government can also claim diplomatic success and deliver on its diversionary gambit. But outside observers may not be able to accurately gauge whether domestic concerns have been channeled outward, demanding diplomatic victory in lieu of domestic progress. As a result, foreigners may underestimate the degree to which nationalist protests reveal grassroots sentiment and restrict the government's foreign policy options. Both sides may be galvanized into taking increasingly escalatory actions to force the other side to acknowledge their resolve and back down.

Consistent with the research design used throughout the book, this chapter seeks to explain two outcomes of interest: China's management of nationalist protest—whether grassroots mobilization was initially tolerated or restrained—and the diplomatic consequences of this decision. To illuminate China's motivations in allowing the 2012 anti-Japanese protests, the first part of the chapter analyzes

Chinese perceptions of the diplomatic context and Japanese actions, tracing China's evolving objectives and lenience toward anti-Japanese activism.[4] The second part of the chapter examines Japan's perceptions of the protests and decision to proceed with the purchase.

The Diplomatic Context: Bilateral Cooperation amid Escalation in the East China Sea

Bilateral relations had not fully recovered from the 2010 trawler collision when the controversy over the islands purchase began. Even as high-level meetings aimed at improving bilateral cooperation and maritime crisis management, both sides continued to engage in a tit-for-tat process of escalation in the East China Sea. In August 2011, a new Japanese defense white paper described China's behavior as "assertive" for the first time, expressing concern about China's "overbearing ways to address its clashing interests with neighboring countries including Japan."[5] Later that month, two Chinese fisheries patrols entered the territorial waters extending 12 nautical miles around the islands, prompting the Japanese ambassador to lodge a protest.[6]

After Finance Minister Yoshihiko Noda was elected prime minister on August 29, 2011, both governments sought to foster pragmatic cooperation in the first several months of his tenure. As a candidate, Noda had called China's growing maritime presence, military capabilities, and "high-handed foreign posture" a "cause of great concern for not only Japan but the entire region."[7] On the sensitive August 15 anniversary of Japan's surrender in World War II, Noda had also defended an earlier statement that the class-A war criminals enshrined at Yasukuni were not war criminals under Japanese law. Tsinghua University's Liu Jiangyong stated that Noda's comments were "tantamount to having the viewpoint that Hitler wasn't a war criminal."[8]

Despite these concerns, China sought to patch up relations with Noda once he took office. As Feng Zhaokui, a Japan expert at the Chinese Academy of Social Sciences, wrote: "Noda is considered a hardliner toward China, but as prime minister he will have to make economic recovery his priority, so he might be more moderate in diplomacy."[9] Premier Wen Jiabao congratulated Noda and invited him to visit Beijing at a convenient time,[10] emphasizing the importance of developing a "good-neighborly and friendly relationship of long-term stability."[11] At the same time, a Xinhua editorial urged Japan to "respect China's core interests" and "show enough respect for China's national sovereignty and territorial integrity, especially when it comes to matters concerning Diaoyu islands, which are an integral part of China's territory."[12]

In September, Noda pledged not to visit Yasukuni while in office and to visit China at a convenient time.[13] China welcomed Noda's remarks and began to lay the groundwork for a series of high-level summits. According to the *China Daily*, "Though voicing his concern about China's military development, [Noda] also said

Japan wants to deepen relations with China in the run-up to next year's 40th anniversary of the restoration of diplomatic ties."[14] Meeting with Noda on the sidelines of the G-20 and APEC summits, President Hu Jintao expressed his "readiness to deepen the China-Japan mutually beneficial relationship of strategic significance in a sustained way and jointly celebrate the 40th anniversary of the normalization of bilateral ties with Japan next year."[15] During the meeting, Noda also raised the issue of joint development in the East China Sea, talks that had stalled after the 2010 fishing boat collision. Hu reportedly replied that China "wants to continue communications and prepare for an early resumption of negotiations."[16]

On December 19, in a "sign of resuming China-Japan military exchanges," a Japanese Self-Defense Force destroyer embarked on a five-day visit to the naval base in Qingdao. The visit sought to "pave the way for Noda's visit" later that month, according to government-affiliated think tank analyst Yang Bojiang, renewing the naval exchanges that had been halted after the September 2010 trawler incident.[17] New maritime incidents did not disrupt plans for Noda's visit and preparations for the fortieth anniversary celebrations. China downplayed the arrests of two fishing captains off the coast of Nagasaki, describing the cases as "ordinary" and "no cause for a diplomatic flare-up."[18]

Noda arrived in Beijing on December 25, becoming the first Japanese head of state from the DPJ to visit China. Noda described himself as a "son of Japan-China exchanges," referring to his experience as part of a youth exchange program to China in 1984.[19] Liu Jiangyong described the visit as a "Christmas present" for bilateral relations, saying that it "sets the tone for the 40th anniversary."[20] Noda and Wen agreed to create a bilateral mechanism to discuss maritime security and crisis management, and China followed up by proposing joint research on marine environmental protection in the East China Sea.[21]

Despite the flurry of cooperative exchanges and high-level meetings in 2011 to lay the groundwork for the fortieth anniversary celebrations and a "Friendship Year of People-to-People Exchanges," a series of unilateral actions and reactions in the first half of 2012 set the stage for the crisis that was to erupt in August and September. Nine days after Noda's visit to Beijing, four Japanese citizens landed on the Diaoyu/Senkaku Islands, including two local Japanese politicians. The Japanese Coast Guard warned the men that it was illegal to land but said it could not stop them from fishing. The same day, Hong Kong marine police prevented 12 activists from setting sail from Hong Kong, citing "grounds to believe that the vessel would not be used for fishing."[22]

In mid-January, Japanese media reported the intrusion of a Chinese fisheries patrol vessel in the waters surrounding the islands. Days later, Chief Cabinet Secretary Fujimura announced that Japan would assign names to 39 small islands, including four of the Diaoyu/Senkaku Islands. The *People's Daily* called Japan's move a "flagrant attempt to harm China's core interests" and cautioned against "testing China's resolve to protect its sovereignty,"[23] the first time that China had used the phrase "core interest" to refer to the islands.[24] In late January, Japan protested new reports of Chinese seabed exploration at the Chunxiao gas field, on grounds that unilateral activity violated the stalled accord on joint development. China rejected Japan's accusation, asserting that the activities were within Chinese waters and thus "completely normal."[25]

In February, Nagoya mayor Takashi Kawamura expressed his doubts about the "so-called Nanjing Incident" to a visiting delegation of Chinese officials from Nanjing, Nagoya's sister city. Kawamura, whose father had served in the Japanese army, refused to retract or apologize for his denial, which Tokyo governor Ishihara defended as "correct."[26] In early March, Japan completed the island-naming process as the basis for Japan's 200-nautical mile exclusive economic zone. China retaliated by announcing Chinese names and locations for 71 islets in the East China Sea, including separate names for four of the Diaoyu/Senkaku Islands that Japan had named the day before.[27]

In a largely symbolic gesture, a citizens' judicial panel in Japan indicted the Chinese trawler captain involved in the 2010 collision, prompting Chinese condemnations.[28] Days later, Chinese naval vessels conducted an exercise near gas fields in the East China Sea. After a Chinese patrol ship again briefly entered the territorial waters around the islands, China's State Oceanic Administration website posted a statement saying that its actions "showed our nation's sovereign rights and jurisdiction."[29] In an interview with the *People's Daily*, a State Oceanic Administration official stated that China "will break [Japan's] intent to acquire a so-called 'statute of limitation' and eventually steal the Diaoyu Island."[30]

Amidst this escalating tit-for-tat, Chinese officials emphasized the growing pressure of popular sentiment in discussions with their Japanese counterparts. On March 6, Foreign Minister Yang Jiechi urged Japan to "properly handle sensitive issues" concerning history and the East China Sea and called for more people-to-people exchanges to improve "national sentiment toward the other side."[31] On March 23, CCP Central Committee Organization Department chief Li Yuanchao stressed the growth of online anti-Japanese sentiment to DPJ secretary-general Azuma Koshiishi. The two sides agreed to establish a crisis "hotline" between the Central Committee International Department and the DPJ Secretariat in order to facilitate accurate communication "over the disputed Senkaku Islands and possible launch of a missile by North Korea," Koshiishi said.[32]

Despite these positive gestures, both sides continued to pursue unilateral efforts to shore up the legal and physical basis of their territorial claims. Days after the memorandum to improve bilateral communications, the Japanese government announced that it had registered one of the five islands as a national asset,[33] a move that the Chinese Foreign Ministry condemned as "unlawful and invalid."[34] Liu Jiangyong called it "a probing activity to test Beijing's reaction, as Japan might try the same trick to register other islands."[35] On April 5, two Chinese fisheries patrol vessels sailed near the islands, claiming that they were conducting an "ordinary patrol" when warned by Japanese Coast Guard vessels "not to enter Japanese waters."[36] Nevertheless, efforts to bolster bilateral ties continued with the April 7 meeting of Chinese and Japanese foreign ministers.

Chinese Views of Ishihara's Gambit and Japan's Plan to Purchase the Islands

It was against this backdrop of mutual escalation in the East China Sea and attempts to shore up bilateral relations through high-level diplomatic engagement that Tokyo governor Shintaro Ishihara announced his plan to purchase three of the Diaoyu/Senkaku Islands from their private owner. With the government's lease set to expire in March 2013, Ishihara announced on April 16 at the Heritage Foundation in Washington that he had been in negotiations with the owner since December and intended to purchase them by the end of the year. Ishihara launched a public donation campaign to fund the purchase, criticizing the Japanese Foreign Ministry and the DPJ-led government for failing to block China's "radical movements" to "knock down Japan's effective control."[37] Ishihara challenged Japan's policy of forbidding citizens from landing on the islands and pledged to develop facilities on the islands.[38] A well-known nationalist and China hawk, Ishihara argued that the Japanese government had taken insufficient measures to protect Japanese territory against growing Chinese assertiveness.

China's initial response was mild. Three days after Ishihara's remarks, the Chinese Foreign Ministry spokesperson responded to a question about Ishihara's bid, calling it "illegal and invalid."[39] State-run media did not immediately cover Ishihara's remarks, although *Asahi* pointed out that Chinese citizens "were quick to flood the Internet with protests."[40] Official functions to celebrate the fortieth anniversary of normalization proceeded as planned, including a tree-planting event attended by nearly a thousand Chinese and Japanese citizens as well as Japanese ambassador Uichiro Niwa and former state councilor Tang Jiaxuan.[41] When Prime Minister Noda and Premier Wen Jiabao met at the trilateral summit in Beijing on May 13, both sides agreed that the islands should not adversely impact bilateral ties and welcomed the first round of high-level maritime talks.[42]

Although early reactions to Ishihara's announcement in Japan were mixed, Chinese media paid close attention to the growing popularity of Ishihara's campaign. A Japanese cabinet official had criticized "Ishihara's shtick" as "only good for gaining momentary popularity,"[43] but Chinese media reported that 92 percent of Japanese respondents to a Yahoo! Internet poll supported the Tokyo government's bid to purchase the islands.[44] Gao Hong, deputy director of the Japan Institute at the Chinese Academy of Social Sciences, warned on CCTV that while Ishihara might fail to raise sufficient funds, his plan was very dangerous because it could galvanize anti-China sentiment in Japan and change the direction of Japan's future policy.[45] State television reported that the Noda cabinet's approval rating had dropped 10 percent since Ishihara's announcement.

With a general election on the horizon, the Noda administration grew more reluctant to criticize Ishihara's plan. Many local opposition politicians had voiced support for Ishihara's campaign, and the Japanese public had become increasingly agitated about Chinese moves in the East China Sea.[46] Noda himself referred to popular pressure in Japan, telling Premier Wen Jiabao that "China's stepped-up activities in areas including those around the Senkaku islands are inflaming Japanese public opinion."[47] When Japanese ambassador Uichiro Niwa told the *Financial Times* that Ishihara's plans would "result in an extremely grave crisis" and destroy "decades of past effort," the Japanese government distanced itself from Niwa's "personal opinions."[48] Facing calls for Niwa's resignation, Chief Cabinet Secretary Osamu Fujimura revealed that the central government was considering buying the islands as one means to "continue administering the Senkaku islands in a calm and stable manner."[49]

By early July, Chinese analysts concluded that the Noda government was struggling to govern, hemmed in by pressure from the LDP and public opinion. According to CICIR Japan expert Yang Bojiang, Ambassador Niwa had "fallen victim to domestic politics" for his truthful and rational statements.[50] In June, more than a hundred Japanese citizens, including six Diet members, surveyed the islands by ship and participated in a "fishing competition" near the islands. According to Xinhua, the Japanese Coast Guard had escorted the entourage.[51] On July 5, Chinese media reported that two Japanese activists had landed on one of the smaller Diaoyu/Senkaku Islands, the site of the controversial lighthouse built in 1996.[52] The same day, Japanese Coast Guard vessels intercepted a Taiwan protest boat near the islands and instructed it to "leave Japanese territorial waters."[53] A Chinese scholar in Okinawa stated that the situation had reached a critical point since the DPJ was no longer able to restrain right-wing groups as the LDP had before.[54]

Two days later, on the July 7 anniversary of Japan's full-scale invasion of China, Prime Minister Noda confirmed the government's plan to buy the three islands.[55] A high-ranking Japanese official stated that "relations between China and Japan will further worsen" if Ishihara were allowed to proceed, claiming that the central government could "better manage" the situation by purchasing the islands.[56] The idea had been mooted internally as early as 2004 and raised with the private owner since 2006. But it was not until Ishihara's campaign had raised one billion yen that the Japanese administration realized that his purchase plan "was becoming a reality," a Noda aide recalled.[57]

The timing of the announcement was widely condemned in Chinese state media. A CCTV news host accused Noda for breaking a "tacit consensus" (*moqi*) on a sensitive issue on a sensitive date.[58] A Xinhua editorial criticized Noda for "playing with fire" at this sensitive time, reflecting the rising influence of right-wing forces as well as the DPJ government's attempt to divert attention from domestic problems and salvage its shrinking popularity.[59] Chinese activists gathered to commemorate the anniversary at the Marco Polo Bridge on the outskirts of Beijing. Chinese authorities reportedly capped the number of participants at 15 and prevented four others from taking part.[60] Police reminded the activists from time to time to "watch the scale of their activities" (*zhuyi huodong chidu*) and "prevent a crowd from gathering or becoming chaotic."[61] When some passers-by criticized the government's foreign policy after viewing the protest posters, the activists quickly put away their materials. As soon as the event ended, state security vehicles sent the organizers back to Beijing.[62]

Senior Chinese diplomats remained circumspect in voicing their opposition. At the July 11 meeting of Chinese and Japanese foreign ministers in Cambodia, both sides sought to reassure the other that their intentions were benign and agreed to "set up a council as soon as possible to promote exchanges as a way to improve public sentiment toward each nation."[63] Regarding the proposed purchase as simply a transfer of title within Japan, Japanese diplomats refrained from using the phrase "national ownership."[64] Although Chinese foreign minister Yang Jiechi insisted that the islands were Chinese territory, his tone was "not belligerent," according to a Japanese diplomat, who concluded that "There is also the feeling within the Chinese Foreign Ministry that national ownership would allow for better control of the situation as opposed to having the anti-Chinese Ishihara gain the upper hand in the issue."[65] Chinese media also noted that while the two sides had failed to reach a consensus, the conversation was not acrimonious.[66]

Despite the restrained tone of China's initial objections, many Chinese analysts regarded the proposed "nationalization" of the islands as a threat to Chinese sovereignty and a breach of what China regarded as a mutual understanding to set aside the territorial dispute. "From the viewpoint of the Chinese government," Michael Swaine writes, "the Japanese purchase involved the exercise of 'sovereign rights,' and not a mere transfer of 'property rights' (as Tokyo insisted), thus constituting an adverse change in the status quo and hence a violation of the agreement to shelve the sovereignty issue."[67] Qu Xing, director of the Foreign Ministry–affiliated China Institute of International Studies, told CCTV that Noda's plan reflected dual intentions: preventing Ishihara from taking further action but also strengthening Japan's effective control and reinforcing Japanese sovereignty by legalizing ownership of the islands.[68] Legal scholar Luo Guoqiang argued that Japan intentionally sought to strengthen its sovereignty claim under international law by completing the private transfer of property rights under domestic law.[69] Hu Lingyuan, deputy director of the Japan Research Institute at Fudan University, likewise stressed the negative repercussions for China's sovereignty claims, writing that Japan sought to "launder" (*xibai*) its illegal occupation of the islands in the eyes of the international community by purchasing them.[70]

Further developments eroded Chinese confidence in Japan's claim that buying the islands would enable the central government to administer the islands more peacefully and stably. Controlling access to the islands was central to the Japanese government's justification for buying the islands. According to a Japanese position statement,

The Government of Japan will continue to maintain the policy of refusing entry to the islands, in principle, to all except certain Japanese government officials. This policy is aimed to ensure the peaceful and stable maintenance and management of the Senkaku Islands which are now a government property, as landing by Japanese nationals could prompt people from neighboring countries and region to enter the territorial waters and land on the islands.[71]

But Chinese observers grew more skeptical amid signs that the Japanese government had softened its stance toward right-wing activism and was no longer willing or able to prevent Japanese activists from landing on the islands. The day after the foreign ministers' July 11 meeting in Cambodia, Chinese official media reported that the Noda government "might allow" a group of Japanese activists to land for a commemorative ceremony, discerning a "change of attitude" in Japan toward the principle of forbidding ordinary Japanese citizens from landing.[72] In early August, Xinhua reported that Japan had "basically agreed" to permit a multipartisan coalition of Japanese lawmakers to land on the largest island in two weeks' time.[73]

In light of the DPJ government's unpopularity and rising public antipathy toward China, many Chinese observers discounted the Japanese government's assertion that the purchase would stabilize the status quo. Moreover, with the LDP likely to return to power by the end of the year, most Chinese analysts doubted the credibility of Japan's commitment to prevent landings, whether in the present or in the future. As Zhai noted,

"Nationalization" has no clear aim. It is outcome of a political process in which various political forces fought for advantage. Therefore, as the situation changes, the content of this policy will also change, expanding or moving in unknown directions. The policy itself thus contains elements that contradict the original intention of "stable administration." . . . No matter how many domestic and diplomatic reasons the Japanese government gives for "nationalization," for China this move is nothing but a stark provocation and confrontation.[74]

In China, the Noda administration was increasingly regarded as passive at best and complicit at worst in revising the status quo. Many Chinese analysts accused Noda of taking advantage of the situation, claiming to desire stability but actually seeking to strengthen Japanese control over the islands and international support for Japan's position. According to the blue book of the Foreign Ministry's research institute:

Instead of stopping Ishihara's move, the Japanese central government, taking advantage of its opportunity, tried to use the so-called pressure from

Ishihara as an excuse to strengthen Japan's claim over the Diaoyu Islands through the so-called "nationalization" of the islands, an act that was in contravention of the understanding and consensus on shelving the Diaoyu Islands dispute reached at the time of the establishment of Sino-Japanese diplomatic relations.[75]

Another Chinese analyst concluded that "the Noda administration, though seemingly passive, actually skillfully took advantage of the current chaos, and accomplished a policy outcome that the LDP had long dreamed about but never dared to try."[76] Wu Jinan, a scholar at the Shanghai Institute for International Studies, wrote that the Japanese justification of "peacefully and stably managing" the islands was "totally without a leg to stand on" (*wanquan shi zhan bu zhu jiao de*).[77] According to Wu, Noda shared Ishihara's desire to strengthen Japanese control of the islands, pointing out that Noda had proposed a bill declaring Japan's sovereignty over the disputed islands in 2004 when he was head of the DPJ's Policy Research Committee.

For many Chinese analysts, the so-called "islands-buying farce" provided further confirmation of Japan's eagerness to challenge China with the assurance of U.S. support.[78] On July 24, Foreign Minister Gemba announced that Secretary of State Hillary Clinton had confirmed that the U.S.-Japan security treaty covers the Senkaku Islands.[79] Two days later, Noda stated that Japan would respond with Self-Defense Forces if necessary "in case a neighboring country engages in illegal acts on our territorial soil and in our territorial waters, including the Senkaku Islands" and told the Diet that U.S. Osprey aircraft would "enhance the Japan-US alliance's deterrence in the Asia-Pacific region."[80] China's Foreign Ministry spokesperson called Noda's remarks "extremely irresponsible" and called on Japan to make "concrete efforts" for the sake of "uphold[ing] the larger interests of bilateral relations."[81]

From Reassurance to Resolve: Showcasing Anti-Japanese Sentiment

As Chinese concerns about the proposed purchase mounted, the Chinese government sought to persuade Prime Minister Noda to find an acceptable alternative to Ishihara's plan, whether by preventing the sale altogether or providing credible reassurances not to develop the islands or allow further landings, thus abiding by China's cherished principle of "shelving" the issue. Believing that Noda could still kill Ishihara's bid, the Chinese government sought to pressure Noda to put off the proposed purchase. Although it remains unclear exactly what alternatives the Chinese government envisioned, senior Chinese officials believed that there were other courses of action available, a view shared by some Western analysts.[82] In mid-August, Chinese authorities allowed widespread anti-Japanese protests and gave blanket media coverage to the landing of Hong Kong activists—the first time Chinese activists had landed since 2004.

At the same time, China's desire to show resolve was also tempered by the desire to preserve bilateral cooperation. Chinese officials continued to emphasize the "big picture" of Sino-Japanese relations, urging Japan to abide by past understandings and remove obstacles to celebrating the achievements of 40 years of diplomatic relations. As CASS scholar Jiang Lifeng noted, "China adjusted its routine diplomatic emphasis on the 'big picture' to prevent the islands dispute from further escalating. . . combining idealism with realism."[83] This blend of resolve and reassurance confused Japanese observers, who emphasized Chinese understanding and discounted the harder side of China's response.

In hindsight, signals from both sides were misinterpreted. Japanese officials have admitted to underestimating Chinese opposition, while some Chinese scholars have privately complained that China should have sent more unambiguous signals to deter Japan, including threats of more severe consequences. More conspiratorial theories have accused China of planning to make Japan look like the aggressor, thereby enabling China to challenge Japan's control in an apparently "reactive" fashion and drive a wedge between the United States and Japan. Before analyzing Japanese perceptions and decision-making, let us first trace China's efforts to dissuade Japan from purchasing the islands.

On August 12, a protest boat set off from Hong Kong, with five of the activists successfully landing on the largest Diaoyu/Senkaku island on August 15, the anniversary of Japan's defeat in World War II. Although the Chinese government continued to prevent activists from setting sail from the mainland, its attitude toward the Hong Kong voyage reflected a marked change from past practice. Since 2009, attempts by Hong Kong activists had been halted several times by local authorities, rumored to be acting on instructions from Beijing. In May 2009, an official with the Chinese government liaison office in Hong Kong warned the activists not to set sail, according to an activist involved in the failed attempt.[84] The local Marine Department then used a variety of administrative measures to scupper the voyage, leading a *Ming Pao* editorial to conclude that pressure from Beijing could only be responsible.[85] Despite the outcry among activists and pro-democratic legislators over Beijing's alleged interference, the Marine Department halted further Bao Diao attempts and dismissed the boat owner's request for a judicial review.[86]

When Hong Kong activists set sail for the islands at the height of the 2010 trawler crisis, they were tailed for two days and their boat towed back by marine police. Local authorities refused to allow the boat to leave Hong Kong waters on grounds that the boat could only be used for fishing, not carrying activists.[87] After four Japanese landed on the islands in January 2012, the Hong Kong marine police again halted a Bao Diao voyage, saying it was "illegal to fish near the Diaoyu Islands," according to Chinese reports.[88] The abortive attempt had been organized by a new Bao Diao alliance founded by activists from Taiwan, Hong Kong, and mainland China.[89] In July 2012, the Bao Diao alliance was more successful, this time sailing from Taiwan with the escort of Taiwan patrol vessels around the islands. Images of the voyage were widely posted on official and commercial Chinese news sites. Hu Lingyuan, deputy director of the Japan Studies Center at Fudan University, stated that the protest voyage should serve as a warning to Japanese politicians from the Chinese public.[90] The activists brandished the PRC flag even though the boat had sailed from Taiwan, fueling speculation about the organization's mistake in "forgetting" to bring the Taiwan (ROC) flag.[91]

In August 2012, activists and observers noted a further warming in the Chinese government's attitude toward grassroots Bao Diao efforts. When the Bao Diao vessel sailed out on August 12, 2012, this time Hong Kong marine police did not haul it back with tugboats. Chen Miaode, Hong Kong Bao Diao association chairman, commented that the authorities seemed to have "let them off the hook."[92] Legislative Council member Leung "Longhair" Kwok-hung noted that the Chinese government has the final say in whether local authorities let Bao Diao activists sail out, noting that "the Hong Kong government has no decision-making power" in such matters.[93] According to Leung, the Chinese side wanted to escalate the situation with Japan to show its toughness on sovereignty issues, accommodate public opinion, and counter U.S. moves to increase its security presence in Asia. The Chinese government preferred to let Hong Kong activists take the lead because the situation would be less likely to get out of control, Leung said. If China sent boats, he said, "it wouldn't just be Fujian—Shanghai, Shandong, other places would all send vessels to protect the Diaoyu Islands. The situation would be unmanageable (wu fa shoushi)."[94]

Although 13 mainland activists were prevented from sailing from Fujian, one mainland activist, Fang Xiaosong, managed to participate in the voyage from Hong Kong. Fang expressed his surprise that Chinese authorities had not prevented him from traveling to Hong Kong, as they had in 2009. Although internal security had asked him not to participate, perhaps the government simply let him go this time, Fang said.[95] According to mainland activist and Bao Diao alliance deputy president Li Yiqiang:

> We have witnessed some changing attitudes by the authorities. Letting the Hong Kong ship sail to the islands this time marks a great change. We hope the government can give us more room in safeguarding the islands, given that there have been more conflicts in the dispute.[96]

With the voyage underway, Chinese state television began showcasing the Bao Diao effort, a change that Hong Kong media called a "deviation from normal behavior" and a shift from "cold to hot."[97] Five of the 14 activists swam ashore, carrying two PRC flags and one Taiwan (ROC) flag. CCTV provided live coverage of the landing, with correspondents reporting from Hong Kong, Japan, and Korea. Liang Yunxiang, a Japan expert at Beijing University, said that the official media coverage represented the Chinese government's changed stance: "The Chinese government did not quite support the grassroots Bao Diao movement, but at least it is more active and tolerant than before."[98] According to Professor Zhou Yongsheng of the Foreign Ministry–affiliated China Foreign Affairs University,

> Given that the previous plans by Hong Kong activists to sail to the Diaoyu Islands were blocked by the authorities, it is fair to say that their recent successful attempt has been approved by Beijing. . . . Beijing is subtly telling Tokyo that China does not want confrontation, but Tokyo should not mistake Beijing's attitude as weakness.[99]

In Beijing, two dozen activists staged a half-hour demonstration in front of the Japanese embassy while many more police looked on. The activists delivered a protest letter and knife to express their hope that the Japanese prime minister would kill himself by committing *harakiri*.[100] The next day, official and commercial Chinese media featured blanket coverage of the landings, with front-page photos highlighting the PRC flags carried ashore.[101] Tong Zeng, head of the China Federation for Defending the Diaoyu Islands (CFDD), called the successful landing "a forceful counterattack on Japanese prime minister Noda's plan to nationalize the Diaoyu Islands."[102] Tong also called on the Chinese government to increase the frequency of maritime patrols and prevent Japan from using domestic law to try the Hong Kong activists. Calls for anti-Japanese demonstrations that weekend began to circulate online, including venue, time, and routes.[103] Many calls for protest remained on Weibo and BBS forums such as *Tianya*, while others were quickly deleted.[104]

The Japanese government complied with Chinese demands to release the Hong Kong activists immediately and unconditionally, deporting them on August 17 amid criticism from both DPJ and LDP politicians.[105] A flotilla of 150 Japanese activists, parliamentarians, and local assembly members set sail for the islands "to solidly reaffirm our own territory," according to conservative parliamentarian Koichi Mukoyama.[106] On August 19, ten Japanese activists, including five local assembly members, swam ashore and planted Japanese flags.

The same day, anti-Japanese demonstrations took place in three dozen cities, including Beijing, Shanghai, Chengdu, Hangzhou, Guangzhou, Shenzhen, Jinan, Changchun, and Wuhan.[107] Most of the demonstrations remained peaceful, with lines of police flanking the marchers. In Shenzhen, protesters overturned Japanese-brand cars, including a police sedan, and began vandalizing Japanese-themed restaurants and Japanese department stores before police corralled marchers into a stadium.[108] In Henan, one Weibo user scorned police for seizing protest banners, accusing the government of "weakness" and paranoia toward even self-organized (*zifa*) protests against Japan.[109] In Beijing, authorities kept a careful watch over anti-Japanese activities, suggesting greater concern for stability in the capital in the run-up to the Eighteenth Party Congress.[110]

Following the Hong Kong activists' release, Beijing authorities took measures to contain further activities outside the Japanese embassy, pressuring activists to call off demonstrations on August 17 and detaining several protesters.[111] Bao Diao alliance member Li Nan speculated that the Chinese government was afraid that further protests could inflame the situation and trigger widespread unrest, particularly "if the government does not respond to popular dissatisfaction with its weak stance" against Japan.[112] The Chinese government's desire to manage the risk posed by anti-Japanese protests was also apparent in mainstream media coverage of the August protests. A front-page article in the *China Youth Daily* called the acts of violence during some anti-Japanese protests "stupid" (*yuchun*) for harming China's image and stability, "paining friends and pleasing enemies."[113] *Ming Pao* noted that commercial newspapers were also forbidden from printing photos of the protest damage and instructed to use Xinhua copy in covering the protests.[114] Vice Foreign Minister Fu Ying reassured Ambassador Niwa that the authorities would protect Japanese businesses and citizens in accordance with law.[115]

Tensions continued to rise the following week as voices in both Japan and China condemned the landings and called for further action. The Japanese lower house passed a resolution affirming Japanese sovereignty over the islands. The Tokyo Metropolitan Government requested permission to land on the islands to conduct a prepurchase survey. Although Chief Cabinet Secretary Fujimura called the landing of Japanese activists "regretful" in light of the government's long-standing policy against civilian landings, he also reiterated that "there exists no issue of territorial sovereignty to be resolved."[116] On television, Noda's foreign policy advisor Akihisa Nagashima urged consideration of "a policing force, including the SDF, to respond to the escalation of the situation."[117] Noda himself stated that the government would exert "every effort to strengthen information gathering and be fully prepared through surveillance and guarding activities" in order to "prevent the repetition of illegal landings on the islands."[118] Noda urged the Diet to enact "at any cost" a bill that would "enable the JCG to swiftly respond to criminal activities occurring on remote islands."[119]

The Chinese media blasted military exercises between American and Japanese forces as "a clear signal that the U.S. was throwing its military weight behind Japan over the Diaoyu Islands issue," citing a Japanese defense official who described the exercises as a drill to "seize back" islands occupied by enemy forces.[120] Major net portals gave prominent coverage to the military exercises, with the *People's Daily* website, *Renmin Wang*, featuring a special interview with Tong Zeng, who criticized Japan for pulling in the United States. Tong congratulated his comrades for successfully landing on the islands and invited others to join the Bao Diao effort, advertising the CFDD website.[121] A *Global Times* editorial emphasized the diplomatic value of public pressure in pressing Japan to back down, writing that

> The Diaoyu issue is facing a possible escalation. More than a few Chinese cities saw anti-Japan protests. . . . With the public's deepening interest and

influence, official efforts will also increase, making it more difficult for Japan to withstand the pressure. China has no intention of engaging in a military clash with Japan over Diaoyu. But China can suppress Japan's control gradually until the trend reverses.[122]

The weekend of August 25–26, anti-Japanese demonstrations were reported in several cities. Over a thousand protesters gathered in Zhuji (Zhejiang), and Rizhao (Shandong), where protesters smashed the windows of a local Japanese restaurant.[123] In Dongguan (Guangdong), police detained several protesters for trying to break into a local government office. Smaller protests occurred in Haikou (Hainan), Yangquan (Shanxi), and Huaibei (Anhui).[124]

Based on further communications and signals from Japan, Chinese officials appeared to believe that they had succeeded in softening Noda's stance. On August 27, the Japanese government turned down Tokyo's request for landing permission, reported by *Cankao Xiaoxi* as a sign of consideration for Chinese concerns.[125] On August 28, Japanese vice foreign minister Tsuyoshi Yamaguchi carried a personal letter from Noda to Hu.[126] Because Noda's letter did not mention the nationalization plan, the Chinese leadership believed that "there was still room for Japan to re-examine the purchase plan," according to later reports.[127] On August 29, Tang Jiaxuan, former state councilor and president of the China-Japan Friendship Association, emphasized "sustaining the big picture, managing and controlling the crisis" at a high-level conference attended by the Japanese ambassador. During the meeting, Tang stated that both sides should acknowledge rather than deny the territorial dispute and stabilize the situation rather than take unilateral actions to complicate and escalate the crisis.[128] Although no specific reassurances were mentioned, Phoenix reported that Chinese officials had asked Japan to abide by "three no's"—no landings, no surveys, and no construction on the islands.[129] Vice Foreign Minister Fu Ying told her visiting counterpart that Japan should proceed with caution and prevent damage to the overall relationship.[130] No anti-Japanese protests occurred that weekend, although nationalist sentiment remained agitated online.[131] Mainstream Internet portals featured Tang's criticism of "irrational patriotism" during an incident two days earlier, when the Japanese ambassador's car was stopped and its flag snatched by two Chinese citizens.[132]

Less than a week later, in early September Japanese media reported that the Noda administration had reached an agreement with the private owner to buy the islands. Xinhua blasted the announcement, writing:

> Japan has ignobly engaged in double dealing with China on the islands. Last week. . . in the letter [from Noda to Hu], the Japanese side vowed to strengthen dialogue and communication with China to properly handle the disputes over the islands. Within days, the Japanese government suddenly changed course and chose to seek a purchasing deal on the islands.

What the Japanese side did was a breach of commitment and calculated violation of mutual trust between China and Japan.[133]

Angered by the announcement, the Chinese leadership refused Japanese requests for a formal meeting between Noda and Hu at the APEC summit in Vladivostok but agreed to a informal meeting on the sidelines on September 9. [134] During the 15-minute meeting, at which both leaders remained standing, Hu warned Noda that "any action by Japan to 'buy' the Diaoyu Islands is illegal and invalid and China is firmly against it."[135] Hu stated that Japan ought to "fully recognize the gravity of the situation and should not make wrong decisions."[136]

Despite Noda's domestic difficulties, Chinese leaders believed that the central government could still prevent the sale, particularly after Ishihara indicated his support. Chinese observers recognized that Noda was "in deep trouble"[137] by August, especially after the LDP-dominated upper house passed a nonbinding censure motion and called for elections.[138] In early September, however, Ishihara publicly indicated that he was willing to go along with the central government's plan, despite complaints from donors who asked for their money back.[139] According to Japanese media reports, Ishihara had softened his stance after meetings with Noda and his foreign policy advisor, Nagashima, even though Nagashima had rejected Ishihara's demand that the government develop facilities on the islands. On September 5, Ishihara relented, telling reporters: "Since the government has struck a deal, we shouldn't intervene."[140]

According to a Chinese academic who has frequently advised the Chinese leadership on Sino-Japanese relations, Ishihara's support may have confused the Chinese leadership.[141] In hindsight, he said, the Chinese government should have done more to deter Japan from buying the islands. Together, the combination of Noda's personal letter and Ishihara's acquiescence gave Chinese leaders the impression that Noda was still willing to reconsider or indefinitely delay the purchase, an assessment that was in hindsight overly optimistic. The day after the Hu-Noda meeting in Vladivostok, Japanese chief cabinet secretary Fujimura announced that the government was moving forward with the sale. On September 11, the Japanese government signed the contract for 2.05 billion yen.

According to Japanese postmortems, the Noda government believed that buying the islands was necessary to prevent Governor Ishihara from doing greater damage to bilateral relations. "Having observed Governor Ishihara's words and deeds," Noda later wrote, "I am convinced that there was no other alternative but to let the national government purchase the Senkaku Islands."[142] Of the several options that had been considered, including building facilities and stationing SDF forces on the islands, Noda himself favored repairing a lighthouse on the main island but was persuaded not to by Foreign Minister Koichiro Gemba and Deputy Prime Minister Katsuya Okada, who warned of China's response.[143] As Chief Cabinet Secretary Fujimura told reporters on September 11, "We do not want anything that would affect the general bilateral relations between Japan and China."[144] Japanese analysts rejected the idea of a conspiracy between Noda and Ishihara to strengthen Japan's effective control over the islands. "Anyone with even minimal knowledge about Japanese politics recognizes that Prime Minister Noda made a good-faith effort to maintain the status quo and stymie the Tokyo governor's unilateral and hazardous actions," wrote former ambassador Kazuhiko Togo.[145]

China's Counterescalation: Challenging Japanese Control over the Islands

The timing of the purchase was seen as a major blow and a loss of face for China's leaders.[146] Since Hu Jintao's warning the day before had been widely publicized in the Chinese media, the insult was hard to miss.[147] "We never imagined that Japan would nationalize the Senkakus right after President Hu and Prime Minister Noda met on the sidelines of the APEC summit," Tang Jiaxuan stated, indicating that the slight had aroused popular anger and incited demonstrations against Japan.[148] "At the very least, it [the Noda administration] should have been able to delay the decision," a Chinese Foreign Ministry official said.[149]

The timing of Japan's announcement exacerbated suspicions that Noda had taken advantage of domestic pressure to strengthen Japanese control over the islands. According to a statement by the Chinese Foreign Ministry:

> The Japanese government has repeatedly stirred up troubles in recent years on the issue of the Diaoyu Island. Particularly since the start of the year, the Japanese government has endorsed rightwing forces to clamor for the "purchase" of the Diaoyu Island and some of its affiliated islands in an attempt to pave the way for a government "purchase" of the islands. People have reason to believe that what Japan did regarding the Diaoyu Island was nothing accidental. The political tendency these actions point to may well put people on the alert. We cannot but ask: where is Japan heading to? Can anyone rest assured of Japan's future course of development?[150]

Some dissenting voices acknowledged Noda's move as an effort to "help contain the situation," as *Caixin* managing editor Wang Shuo noted.[151] But state media commentary accused Japanese politicians of deliberately trying to undermine China's sovereignty. "Any Japanese conspiracy is doomed to fail," concluded an article in the *People's Daily*.[152]

Chinese observers viewed the purchase as a deliberate change in the status quo and a particularly pointed abrogation of the tacit agreement to shelve the dispute. A Zhong Sheng column in the *People's Daily* stated that "The Japanese government staged a farce of 'purchasing' the Diaoyu Islands in the vain hope of breaking the consensus on shelving the Diaoyu Islands issue."[153] Asked why China had reacted so harshly, Vice Foreign Minister Fu Ying said that Japan had effectively broken past promises. "Should such common understanding [reached years ago] be denied or reneged on, what basis would there be for China to continue exercising restraint?" Fu asked rhetorically.[154] The Chinese leadership was also apparently concerned that a restrained response would set a bad precedent. As maritime disputes had also grown acrimonious in the South China Sea, China feared that a weak response to Japanese provocations might invite other territorial disputants, such as Vietnam and the Philippines, to press their claims. As Fu Ying later noted, China chose to respond "decisively" to territorial provocations in order to send an "important signal" to the region.[155]

In the days following Japan's announcement, the Chinese government unleashed a series of actions to assert its sovereignty, undermine Japan's de facto control over the islands, and pressure Japan to acknowledge and abide by a tacit agreement to shelve the territorial dispute. On September 12, Chief Cabinet Secretary Fujimura called the intrusion of six Chinese marine surveillance ships into the territorial waters around the islands "unprecedented."[156] In addition to increasing the frequency of its maritime patrols, China announced territorial base points and baselines around the islands in accordance with the UN Convention on the Law of the Sea. Li Guoqiang, deputy director of the CASS Center for China's Borderland History and Geography Studies, stated that "the reason China didn't announce the territorial baseline before was that the territory is disputed and the Chinese government restrained itself. . . . But now there has been a change to the worse and China had to react."[157] According to the Foreign Ministry–affiliated *CIIS Blue Book*, "China threw a 'combination of punches' against Japan on various fronts. . . thus terminating the so-called exclusive actual control of the islands by the Japanese side."[158]

China's public rhetoric also escalated. Within three days of Japan's announcement, Premier Wen Jiabao and two other Politburo Standing Committee members publicly denounced Japan's actions as "illegal and invalid."[159] In a tone that *Asahi* described as "unprecedentedly tough," Wen stated that China would make "absolutely no concession on issues concerning its sovereignty and territorial integrity."[160] Several state organs released statements, including the Ministry of Defense, CPPCC, NPC, and All-China Youth Federation.

An important strand of the government's rhetoric emphasized Japan's past wrongdoings and China's determination to resist further humiliation. The Foreign Ministry's statement asserted that Japan's nationalization of the islands

> does not change, not even in the slightest way, the historical fact of Japan's occupation of Chinese territory, nor will it alter China's territorial sovereignty over the Diaoyu Island and its affiliated islands. Long gone are the days when the Chinese nation was subject to bullying and humiliation from others.

As Vice Premier Li Keqiang sought support from visiting Papuan prime minister Peter O'Neill, Li referenced their nations' common experience under Japan's "fascist invasion" in World War II.[161]

With nationalist sentiment running high, fanned by official rhetoric and blanket media coverage, the Chinese government made little attempt to prevent anti-Japanese demonstrations. On the contrary, the pressure of nationalist sentiment was real but not unwelcome, enabling the Chinese government to present its actions as a legitimate response to popular demands and conveying the government's willingness to stay the course until Japan was forced to "correct its mistakes," despite the economic costs of a prolonged standoff. As Vice Foreign Minister Fu Ying stated,

> It's hardly surprising that [the purchase] should have stirred strong emotions among the Chinese people, who expect and trust that today's China is better able to protect its national interests. Official statements from China about Japan's "purchase" of the islands are reflections of the views and feelings of the Chinese nation. These statements are highly principled and send clear signals.[162]

In the same vein, a Zhong Sheng column in the *People's Daily* asserted that "the Chinese government has followed the popular will, and resolutely taken a series of strong measures to safeguard China's sovereignty over the Diaoyu Islands. It is reasonable for China to take lawful measures to hit back at Japanese provocations."[163]

As Chinese officials called upon Japan to acknowledge the territorial dispute and "come back to the very understanding and common ground reached between the two sides" in the 1970s,[164] the Chinese government could then present itself as the "good cop" in comparison with the extreme demands of protesters in the streets. As Fu Ying noted, the Chinese public has little patience for compromise when faced with foreign insults—and instead "hopes that China will be even more assertive."[165]

On September 11, anti-Japanese demonstrations continued in several cities, including Beijing and Guangzhou.[166] By the weekend of September 15–16, nearly 100 Chinese cities witnessed anti-Japanese protests. The wave of protests culminated on September 18, the anniversary of Japan's occupation of Manchuria, with anti-Japanese demonstrations taking place as many as 180 cities across mainland China. As it had the month before, the Chinese government allowed anti-Japanese street demonstrations to take place but sought to mitigate the risk that they would get out of control. On September 11, Foreign Ministry spokesman Hong Lei told reporters that Japan's "wrong actions have aroused the indignation of the Chinese people at home and abroad" but maintained that the public should "express their patriotic passion in a rational and lawful manner."[167] In Beijing, a thick cordon of police kept protesters away from the Japanese embassy gates, with rarely seen helicopters hovering nearby.[168]

Protesters came from a variety of classes and occupations, including veterans, construction workers, auto club members, and white-collar employees.[169] Although students were successful in organizing and joining demonstrations in other cities, including Hefei, Wuhu, and Suizhou,[170] authorities tried to prevent university students from organizing anti-Japanese demonstrations in Beijing,[171] perhaps reflecting the capital's history of student protest at the vanguard of revolution and social "turmoil." One student also accused university officials in Qiqihar of repressing a spontaneous campus protest on September 16, "demonizing" their "righteous response to the government's call to resist the foreign enemy" even though the city government had "organized" a demonstration the day before.[172]

Although most demonstrations remained peaceful, those that turned violent were more destructive than previous waves of anti-Japanese protest. In Qingdao, several Japanese factories and one Japanese car dealership were set on fire.[173] Despite heavy security in front of the Japanese consulate in Guangzhou, which is located inside an upscale hotel, protesters broke in and smashed the windows of a Japanese restaurant on the second floor before being detained.[174] Although police only allowed protesters to approach the Shanghai consulate in small groups, the consulate reported that several Japanese nationals were harassed in the street.[175] Protests became more violent in Changsha, where the Japanese department store Heiwado was vandalized, and in Shenzhen, where police beat back protesters with water cannons and tear gas.[176] In Xi'an, protesters nearly beat to death the owner of a Toyota car.[177]

Many Chinese netizens were quick to condemn the violence. "Apologies, Xi'an. Today, the virtuous soul of 13 dynasties has been tarnished, your beautiful old lanes and alleys trampled by thugs," read one Weibo post that was retweeted more than 10,000 times before being deleted.[178] In another widely retweeted post, Han Han argued that vandalism has "nothing to do with patriotism," saying: "The protestors have wasted their time in a wrong battle. They have gone too far, even though what they are doing might have been officially approved."[179]

As the September 18 anniversary approached, Chinese authorities stepped up efforts to guard against further violence. However, the government did not try to prevent protests altogether, which would have been at odds with its escalatory campaign and would have exposed the government to charges of hypocrisy and weakness during a symbolic national anniversary. State media emphasized that citizens should express their patriotism "rationally" and "say no" to "beating, smashing, and looting."[180]

On September 17, a high-level circular instructed all government units to "properly manage issues arising from some mass marches against Japan's illegal 'islands purchase'" and convene emergency meetings to uphold social stability during the "critical moment" of September 18 until after the conclusion of the Eighteenth Party Congress.[181] One provincial agency sent out a text message: "Patriotic passion, rationally expressed, makes a civilized and law-abiding citizen."[182] In one Liaoning city,

Party officials warned that protests against Japan's "island-buying farce" had begun to spread and expand in size and momentum, in some cases becoming mixed up with "idle persons" who "used patriotic passions to create a disturbance." In accordance with central instructions, relevant authorities were to "actively guide, plan, and carry out stability maintenance work on '9.18' and thereafter."[183]

On September 18, the government succeeded at ensuring that protests remained largely peaceful on the Tuesday anniversary, even as two Japanese citizens landed on the islands, marking the fourth Japanese landing that year.[184] More than 180 cities witnessed "basically lawful and peaceful" anti-Japanese demonstrations, according to the *Global Times*.[185] Even the *New York Times* reported that the protests "appeared much better controlled than those over the weekend, which included extensive rioting and vandalism."[186] But the contrast also highlighted the government's failure to prevent the out-of-control behavior that occurred beforehand. Images of burned-out Japanese factories and vandalized shops were widely broadcast in Japan. Angered by the developments in China, Prime Minister Noda asked his aides: "Is the Chinese government going to tacitly approve 'yakiuchi' [a form of arson used in battle]?"[187]

Following instructions to implement "stability maintenance" measures between the September 18 anniversary and the Eighteenth Party Congress, Chinese authorities moved to curtail further demonstrations. State media featured stories of rioters who had been punished for out-of-control behavior during anti-Japanese protests.[188] But the government also continued to take a tough stance against Japan, placating popular pressure with further countermeasures and harsh rhetoric. Chinese leaders vowed "zero tolerance" for Japan's provocations and repeatedly raised the issue in international forums and meetings.[189] Government vessels continued to patrol the islands on a near daily basis, with the State Oceanic Administration announcing for the first time that its fleet had "expelled a number of Japanese vessels illegally sailing in waters around the Diaoyu Islands."[190] Fortieth-anniversary celebrations were canceled, and Japanese novels were reportedly removed from state-run bookstores.[191] The State Council Information Office published materials detailing China's claims to the islands.[192] Top Chinese officials refused to attend the annual IMF and World Bank meetings in Tokyo, further signaling that Beijing was willing to allow political tensions to affect economic ties.[193]

Underestimating China's Opposition: Japanese Perceptions

The strength of China's response surprised Japanese officials, who had discounted evidence of Chinese opposition and given greater weight to China's reassuring signals. When the Japanese government first announced its plan to purchase the islands in July, China's relatively restrained opposition gave Japan the impression that buying the islands "would not antagonize China as much" as letting Governor Ishihara purchase and develop them.[194] But as anti-Japanese protests erupted in mid-August and official Chinese rhetoric grew more strident in early September, why did Japanese officials not revise their beliefs about Chinese resolve?

On the one hand, Japanese observers noted the growing pressure of Chinese public opinion and the state's willingness to showcase grassroots activism, amplified by media outlets eager to attract attention. In May, amid speculation over whether Premier Wen Jiabao had referred to the islands as one of China's "core interests," the *Yomiuri* concluded that "the Chinese state media apparently attempted to portray the Senkaku Islands as part of China's core interests because expressions of public discontent over the issue on the Internet and through other means are growing in China."[195]

In August, Japanese observers recognized that China's "tacit approval" of the Hong Kong protest voyage and anti-Japanese protests indicated Beijing's opposition to the proposed purchase. Foreign policy advisor Makoto Iokibe noted that China had "tacitly allowed"—but not encouraged—the Hong Kong activists to set sail.[196] According to a *Yomiuri* editorial, "Hong Kong authorities could have prevented the departure of the anti-Japan organization's boat, but instead gave it tacit approval. We sense the Chinese government's intention to pressure Japan over the Senkaku issue."[197]

On the other hand, Japanese observers were confident that China would be willing and able to rein street protests, particularly on the eve of a once-in-a-decade leadership transition. Despite indications that Chinese media coverage had begun to harden its tone, many Japanese interpreted China's overall restraint and emphasis on the "big picture" as evidence that the Chinese government retained the upper hand vis-à-vis popular sentiment. With the elite scandal surrounding Chongqing Party boss Bo Xilai still unfolding, China's top leadership was expected to be particularly vigilant against popular protest in the run up to the Eighteenth Party Congress. As former national security advisor and senior LDP parliamentarian Yuriko Koike noted in May:

> So far, China has not unleashed the sort of mass demonstrations against Japan and others that it has used in the past to convey its displeasure. But that probably reflects the jittery state of China's leaders in the wake of the Bo purge: they cannot guarantee that an anti-Japan demonstration would not turn into an anti-government protest.[198]

After anti-Japanese protests took place in August, Japanese media reported that Chinese authorities had taken strict measures to prevent demonstrations from turning against the government, limiting their size in key cities while allowing them in others. As *Nikkei* reported:

> With the National Party Congress that will determine the next leadership transition approaching, authorities are keeping close surveillance, so the anti-Japanese protests in Beijing and Shanghai have been extremely small.

In Shenzhen, Changsha, and Chengdu, among others, there has been a succession of large-scale anti-Japanese protests. In China, perhaps the only protests to be allowed are patriotic anti-Japanese protests.[199]

Japanese media also portrayed the protests as a conveniently engineered opportunity for citizens to vent domestic grievances rather than sincere anger at Japan. A *Yomiuri* editorial read:

> The Chinese government has a weighty responsibility for causing turmoil by tacitly approving the demonstrations. . . . The Chinese government obviously is trying to counter Japan's moves over the islands, but at the same time it apparently wants Chinese people to vent their frustrations over economic disparities and other domestic issues through the demonstrations.[200]

A front-page story in *Sankei Shimbun* stated that Japan was just an excuse to protest for Chinese youth angered by growing economic disparities. "It's Japan's misfortune to be China's neighbor," joked one Japanese scholar.[201]

Japanese commentators were not alone in characterizing the protests as a tactic to divert attention or a cover for other concerns. Some Chinese liberals voiced similar skepticism. Mo Zhixu, a prominent writer, tweeted that some liberals had tried to use nationalist sentiment to mobilize, such as Guo Feixiong during the 2005 anti-Japanese demonstrations. While the attempt to combine nationalism and liberalism may work in the short run, Mo wrote, in the long run such opportunism does not deserve serious treatment.[202] Peng Dingding, a pro-democracy activist in Beijing, argued that the protests were a classic example of diverting a domestic crisis into external confrontation. Peng concluded that the protests would be short-lived (*tanhuayixian*) because the government would shut them down if they grew to a scale that could destabilize society.[203]

On balance, the appearance of widespread anti-Japanese protests in August did not dispel the Noda administration's beliefs that "China has shown its understanding of nationalization. Its opposition will only be temporary."[204] In late August, Noda dismissed suggestions from some Japanese Foreign Ministry officials that given the "growth of anti-Japan movements in China" it might be better to "keep the Japanese state out of the equation" and let Ishihara buy the islands.[205] Japanese officials believed that China was aware of the timing of Japan's plans to proceed, considering Hu's willingness to meet with Noda at APEC a "good sign."[206] Even if "strong criticisms from Chinese people" prevented Hu from meeting formally with Noda, the "unofficial talks allowed [Hu] to show to Japan his willingness to prevent bilateral ties from deteriorating further," Japanese officials concluded.[207]

Expectations that the outgoing Chinese leadership in China would be willing and able to shut down protests at an early stage contributed to Noda's willingness to discount the protests as a sign of serious opposition. As one of Noda's aides noted, "If we finalize the Senkaku issue during Hu Jintao's era, we can then repair relations after the new leadership is established. The worse timing would be to purchase the islands after the new leadership takes power."[208] According to a Japanese Foreign Ministry analyst, "As we saw what happened throughout China [after] the announcement of the purchase, we knew something of this sort was going to occur. Maybe not this violent, but similar to what happened in 2010. We also forecasted that the Chinese would start taking control" once the damage to China's international image and domestic stability became apparent.[209] The Japanese leadership also expected that Hu Jintao's leadership would not retaliate as strongly as it had during the 2010 trawler crisis, given the international backlash that ensued.[210] A WTO body concluded in January 2012 that China's rare earth restrictions violated WTO rules. Two months later, the United States, Japan, and the European Union jointly filed a WTO complaint against China's export restrictions on rare earth metals.[211]

Japanese observers correctly anticipated that the Chinese government would rein in anti-Japanese demonstrations—but not before anti-Japanese protests continued to gain momentum, taking place in over 200 cities by September 18. More problematic, from Japan's perspective, was that the Chinese government did not quell the protests until after it had satisfied domestic demands with an array of countermeasures that made its actions during the 2010 trawler crisis look moderate in comparison.

The anti-Japanese demonstrations in September made a larger impression than those in August. On September 19, Prime Minister Noda admitted on television, "I expected a certain degree of negative ramifications, but the scale of anti-Japanese street demonstrations is bigger than I expected."[212] Some Japanese commentary recognized the danger that popular nationalism posed to the Chinese government. Nobuyoshi Sakajiri, *Asahi Shimbun*'s China bureau chief, noted that many netizens were critical of Hu Jintao for being too friendly toward Japan, concluding: "China's leaders have reason for discomfort, as this public anger could turn on the corrupt Chinese government. Flaring patriotism will become not only a strength but a point of vulnerability for the Communist Party, which governs 1.3 billion people."[213]

Yet China's efforts to minimize the risk of violence and instability as the September 18 anniversary approached also meant that protests often appeared stage-managed. As an American diplomat noted,

> They [the Chinese authorities] can turn them on and off. When posts on Weibo say there will be protests, they can take those down, and they didn't have to provide buses. The protests here were well-timed groups. For 20 minutes, they changed the march route so it went by the Japanese consulate. Conveniently, there were construction materials and water bottles. After the consulate had been defaced, then they changed the protest route. Days ahead of time, the owners of Japanese restaurants took down their

signs. They were told to express their patriotism by changing the name of their businesses.[214]

Many Japanese observers also voiced skepticism about the sincerity and spontaneity of the protests. Katsuji Nakazawa, editor-in-chief of *Nikkei*'s China headquarters, accused the Chinese government of instigating the protests:

> Security closely aligned with the Youth League sent farmers and police academy students in plain clothes as protest agitators. The demonstrations became a mix of ordinary citizens, dissidents and hard-liners carrying portraits of Mao Zedong. The country's leadership, in expressing anti-Japan sentiment, conveyed to protesters that these actions would be protected by the aegis of the government.[215]

Other analysts remained skeptical that protesters were motivated by anger against Japan, viewing the protests as a safety valve for domestic grievances. An article published by the Foreign Ministry–affiliated Japan Institute of International Affairs highlighted the government's efforts to maximize the domestic benefits and minimize the domestic risks of allowing ostensibly anti-Japanese protests. Examining several protests in major cities between September 15 and 18, the article concluded that the protests enabled participants to let out frustration about the economy and social disparity, especially among youth who learned that "anti-Japan = patriotism = justice" in their patriotic education. On the other hand, the article argued that protests were repressed on September 18 in Tianjin because President Hu Jintao was visiting the city, and Dalian was quiet in part because of sensitivities surrounding Bo Xilai, who had been mayor there for several years.[216]

Many protesters carried Mao portraits, fueling speculation that leftists were using the anti-Japanese demonstrations as an opportunity to show their support for Bo Xilai, who had encouraged Cultural Revolution–style "red songs" and other Maoist paraphernalia. Although the *New York Times* coverage of the protests on September 18 emphasized that "many people came on their own and appeared to be genuinely angered at what they saw as Japan's failure to address its past behavior,"[217] the accompanying photo depicted dozens of protesters carrying Mao's portrait. Japanese media also speculated about a possible connection to Bo Xilai and his populist tendencies. Picturing Shanghai protesters carrying Mao's portrait on September 16, an *Asahi* article read: "Chinese authorities are now apparently concerned about whether the anti-Japanese sentiment among protesters will spill over into criticism of a government that has not adequately dealt with the growing economic inequality in the nation."[218]

In depicting anti-Japanese protests as a cover or opportunity to mobilize on other issues, these accounts pushed against the conclusion that protests were fueled by genuine grievances against Japan. Rather than putting pressure on the government to take tough action to counter Japan's actions, protests were seen as mostly a domestic problem, unrelated to the government's foreign policy performance. Whether the government was afraid of domestic grievances mixing in or appreciative that citizens were letting off steam, both beliefs reflected incredulity about protesters' motivations and the constraint on Chinese foreign policy. In the first, protesters appeared to be taking advantage of the opportunity to protest for reasons unrelated to Japan, and in the second, the government could easily close this carefully calibrated opening for popular mobilization.

Statements by Chinese observers supported foreign skepticism of the September protests. As Ai Weiwei told Reuters, "Chinese citizens need to thank the Japanese government because for the first time, they can mount a large protest on their own land. In China, there are no protests organized by the people."[219] Liu Junning, a former CASS researcher, told the *Washington Post* that "The party is skilled at manipulating such public opinion. . . and the signs that these demonstrations were organized by the government is very high. The protests come when the leaders need one to come, and the protests will stop when they want them to stop."[220] An article by *Caixin* exposed the limits of government tolerance in this exchange outside the Japanese embassy in Beijing:

> A nearby street was filled with police, most of them relaxed. When I photographed the protest, he smiled and said: "You can join the protest."
>
> "Can I? Won't I be pulled out?" I asked.
>
> "Since it is me who let you in, who dares pull you out!" he said.
>
> "But I haven't applied for permission," I said.
>
> "It is OK. The organizer has applied," he said.
>
> A middle-aged policeman also encouraged me to join the parade.
>
> "Can I shout 'Punish corruptions'?" I inquired.
>
> "No, you can't!" the middle-aged officer said, suddenly seriously.
>
> "Only slogans concerned with Diaoyu Islands are allowed," a young policeman chimed in.[221]

Not all Chinese commentary was so cynical. Several leading experts stressed the sincerity and grassroots nature of anti-Japanese protests. "Japan's provocation gave rise to the Chinese public's spontaneous boycott, and public opinion deserves respect," said CASS expert Gao Hong.[222] Tsinghua University's Liu Jiangyong rejected arguments by Shinzo Abe, among others, that anti-Japan protests were an expression of social discontent toward widening inequality or manipulated by the Chinese Communist Party to preserve its diminished legitimacy. "The Chinese government only directed and guided the protests when necessary out of concern for maintaining the stability of China-Japan relations as well as the stability of Chinese society," Liu wrote.[223]

Conclusion

As Governor Ishihara's campaign to purchase the Diaoyu/Senkaku Islands gained popularity, China hoped that the Noda administration would find a way to prevent the sale. Instead, the Japanese government announced its own intention to purchase the islands, arguing that doing so was necessary to prevent Ishihara from taking more provocative steps.[224] As Noda appeared less willing and able to restrain right-wing forces, China became increasingly incredulous that Japan's purchase of the islands would help stably administer the islands and ensure that the territorial issue remained "shelved." The landing of Hong Kong activists and unprecedentedly widespread anti-Japanese street demonstrations in China all sought to signal that the Chinese government would not quietly accept what it considered a unilateral change to the status quo and a challenge to Chinese sovereignty.

The latter part of this chapter has sought to explain why the Japanese leadership discounted signals of Chinese resolve in the run-up to the September purchase. The 2012 anti-Japanese protests gave rise to a variety of competing interpretations, underscoring one of the greatest dangers associated with nationalist protest. Not only may antiforeign demonstrations get out of control, but foreign observers may underestimate or disagree about the extent to which protests reveal resolve or constrain a government's diplomatic stance, particularly if the government was complicit in stoking popular sentiment in the first place. Had Japanese officials anticipated the extent of China's reaction, the Noda administration might not have pressed ahead with the purchase in the manner that it did.

In December 2012, an LDP victory brought Shinzo Abe back to the prime minister's office. Although Abe had been responsible for repairing ties with China in 2006–7, during his 2012 election campaign he called his prior restraint "extremely regrettable."[225] In an article published a week before the general election, Abe held the Chinese government fully responsible for the anti-Japanese demonstrations, writing that "what China is doing right now is damaging our economic ties by destroying Japanese companies and boycotting our products in order to achieve its political objective over the Senkaku Islands." Abe argued that "now is the time to demonstrate our resolve," saying that "simply put, what we need in the waters near the Senkaku Islands are not negotiations, but physical forces."[226]

After the election, Abe continued to emphasize Beijing's freedom of action, omitting any reference to the role of grassroots sentiment in driving Chinese nationalism alongside state-led patriotic education. Abe told the *Washington Post* that "it is fully possible to have China to change their policy" once Beijing recognizes the economic harm that the standoff is having on Japanese investment and employment in China, downplaying the steep legitimacy costs that China's leaders would pay for making unilateral concessions.[227] Rather than seeing nationalism as a source of vulnerability and pressure on the Chinese government, Abe emphasized the domestic benefits of nationalism for the CCP's continued rule, noting that China's tough measures against Japan are "resulting in strong support from the people of China, who have been brought up through this educational system that attaches emphasis on patriotism."[228] Only displays of resolve and a strengthened U.S.-Japan alliance would show China the error of her ways, Abe argued.

With both sides refusing to compromise, tensions remained high in the months after Abe's election. The risk of military conflict became clear when Japanese officials accused Chinese naval vessels of locking weapons-targeting radar on a Japanese destroyer and military helicopter in January. After initial denials, Chinese officials indicated that the incidents had taken place without authorization from senior military commanders.[229] In 2013, China's announcement of an air defense identification zone (ADIZ) over much of the East China Sea provoked new concerns about the risks of escalation.

Several Japanese opposition leaders, former officials, and experts called on Japan to moderate its stance on the territorial issue, recognizing that the Chinese side was unlikely to relent without reciprocal gestures.[230] Three-time foreign minister Yohei Kono argued that Japan had not provided China with credible reassurances in justifying the purchase, acknowledging that China's real concern had been not knowing "what kind of government would come into power next."[231] Former ambassador Kazuhiko Togo urged the Japanese government to acknowledge the territorial dispute in order to "help Beijing step back from hegemonism," giving China a symbolic concession in exchange for physical patrols that "chang[e] the status quo by force."[232] Although the Japanese government repeatedly denied that an understanding over the islands had been reached in the 1970s, Takakazu Kuriyama, who participated in talks with China as director of the Japanese Foreign Ministry's Treaties Division, testified that "top officials of the two countries had reached a tacit agreement" to shelve the island dispute.[233]

Despite these suggestions, the shadow of Japan's capitulation to Chinese pressure during the 2010 trawler incident continued to linger. Hitoshi Tanaka, former deputy minister for foreign affairs, stated that "if Japan were to bend to Chinese pressure again, it would set a highly negative precedent and embolden China to continue to use such coercive methods of diplomacy."[234] Shigeru Ishiba, who became LDP secretary-general after losing narrowly to Abe in a runoff vote for the party leadership, wrote that the government's capitulation in 2010 had made Japan the "laughingstock of East Asia."[235] Like Abe, Ishiba called for a more forceful posture vis-à-vis China, arguing that "the fundamental problem of the dispute is that the successive administrations, including those under the LDP, have been ambiguous. We should sincerely regret that our politics has maintained such a principle of ceding anything to avoid trouble."[236]

The lessons of the 2010 incident thus contributed to the 2012 crisis in several ways. First, the trawler crisis strengthened Japan's determination not to bow to Chinese pressure again. Second, the international backlash against China's rare earth policies led Japanese officials to believe that China would not risk similar measures. Finally, China's demonstrated ability and willingness to restrain anti-Japanese protests in 2010 also reduced their credibility two years later. Since the government had managed to curtail protests after signs of domestic dissent emerged in 2010, many Japanese observers reasoned that the Chinese government would be even more vigilant before the leadership transition in 2012.

China has sometimes benefited when new developments are viewed through the lens of prior events, as when U.S. analysts appreciated China's efforts to restrain anti-American demonstrations during the 2001 spy plane incident in light of the 1999 embassy bombing protests. But decision-makers do not always draw appropriate analogies from past events. Although Chinese authorities did step up efforts to manage the risk that anti-Japanese demonstrations got out of control before the Eighteenth Party Congress in 2012, the government did not curtail the protests before taking a series of unprecedentedly assertive measures to undermine Japan's control over the islands, thereby assuaging domestic anger at the government's previously "weak-kneed" policies.

In addition, Chinese measures to manage the risk posed by anti-Japanese protests were ironically both insufficient to prevent rioting in some cities and too heavy-handed in others, further undermining the perceived spontaneity, sincerity, and credibility of the demonstrations. Local variation in China's management of nationalist demonstrations made it difficult for observers to discern China's motives through an increasingly noisy set of signals, even as the appearance of unrelated slogans underscored the risk that patriotic demonstrations might exacerbate social instability by providing an opportunity for aggrieved citizens to mobilize.

Nonetheless, the broader pattern of China's management of anti-Japanese demonstrations between 2006 and 2012 is consistent with the strategic framework. When China's diplomatic objectives have counseled flexibility and reassurance, as they did when China believed that Japan would release the trawler captain during the first phase of the 2010 crisis, the government has been able and willing to prevent large-scale nationalist protests. Despite the increased domestic visibility and legitimacy costs of repressing protests in the Web 2.0 era, the Chinese government has demonstrated its ability to anticipate and prevent large-scale nationalist protests. At other times, China has continued to tolerate and even encourage protests when it seeks to demonstrate resolve to foreign audiences, as the escalation of anti-Japanese protests in August and September 2012 illustrates.

Nationalist protests are not the only way for China to signal resolve, of course. China has also employed other coercive measures, including the threat of diplomatic and economic retaliation, both explicit (cutting off talks) and implicit (reported slowdowns or stoppages of foreign exports or imports). Yet China has little diplomatic incentive to repress nationalist sentiment when it is prepared to take escalatory measures. Stifling popular sentiment when the government wants to force the other side to back down risks sending the wrong diplomatic signal—reassurance rather than resolve—while also undermining the government's nationalist credentials.

As an early step in the ladder of potential escalation, nationalist protests may strengthen the credibility of tough diplomatic demands while allowing the government to earn domestic plaudits for appearing responsive to public opinion. The government may not satisfy the most extreme of nationalist demands, including war to defend China's territorial claims. But once the government has taken assertive measures to defuse hawkish pressures, further protests become easier to curtail and less desirable as a means of demonstrating resolve, particularly as the risks to social stability continue to mount.

Although nationalist protests continue to be seen as opportune moments for citizens to vent and a convenient distraction from domestic injustices, diverting domestic grievances toward foreign policy issues does not strengthen the government's legitimacy if it cannot claim diplomatic victory or point to tough countermeasures that the government has taken to protect the nation's interest. One of the greatest difficulties with demonstrations that appear diversionary is discerning whether foreign policy accomplishments or concessions will actually assuage the madding crowd. If it appears that diplomatic countermeasures or foreign concessions will assuage street protests, then demonstrations give credibility to the government's foreign policy demands. But if popular grievances appear unrelated to the international dispute, street protests risk being dismissed by foreign decision-makers as a problem that the government must handle on its own. The concluding chapter reflects on the battle for credibility.

9

Conclusion

What role has nationalist protest played in China's foreign relations? Many a Chinese Foreign Ministry spokesperson has claimed that foreign actions or demands have "hurt the feelings of the Chinese people." Chinese diplomats increasingly point to public opinion when they state that a proposed compromise would be domestically impossible. Are such statements genuine, and more importantly, how can foreigners tell the difference? The argument of this book is that without visible evidence of popular anger, unelected leaders have greater difficulty convincing foreign observers that public opinion credibly constrains their diplomatic options. Antiforeign, nationalist protests enable authoritarian leaders to invoke the threat of a popular backlash if they make too many diplomatic concessions. Conversely, visible efforts to repress nationalist sentiment enable the government to play "good cop" relative to extreme voices in the street.

Repressing nationalist sentiment and antiforeign demonstrations is costly for the Chinese government, which has often been accused of being both unpatriotic and undemocratic in suppressing nationalist sentiment. Nationalist sentiments put pressure on the government to adopt a tougher foreign policy stance, but the government can choose the degree to which it invokes this pressure: allowing nationalist protests or nipping them in the bud. Confronted with an upsurge of antiforeign sentiment, the government must weigh the potential benefits of tolerating street demonstrations against the risk to stability and the cost of preemptive repression.

Popular nationalism is both a liability and a potential advantage in Chinese diplomacy. Just as the president can point to Congress and say his hands are tied in diplomatic negotiations, so can Chinese leaders point to nationalist sentiment and popular protests. For the Chinese leadership, nationalism is both a vulnerability and a source of strength: undermining the government's legitimacy if seen as weak against foreign insults and provocations, and strengthening its legitimacy if the public sees the government staunchly defending the nation's interests.

Nationalism helps prop up the Chinese regime but may also become its downfall. In today's porous and pluralistic information environment, including access to overseas websites and news media, the government cannot erase domestic criticism by "brainwashing" citizens with positive propaganda. Citizens and activists may restrain their actions, understanding that the window of opportunity for protest has closed. But their criticism cannot be completely silenced. Popular nationalism is partially the product of state-led patriotic propaganda but is also deeply rooted in society. The government does not have perfect control over antiforeign street protests, which can easily stray off message. Given limited channels for political mobilization, citizens may also seize the opportunity to advance other objectives.

From an authoritarian government's perspective, it is often unclear which is the lesser hazard: the danger to stability of allowing protest or the legitimacy cost of stifling patriotic protests. There are few easy cases in which the choice for repression or consent is obvious. Even when the size of a potential protest appears small—perhaps no more than two dozen activists—the government faces a dilemma, knowing that repression could alienate nationalists and drive mobilization underground, but also recognizing that "a single spark can start a prairie fire." Because this domestic trade-off is often indeterminate, international factors often play a decisive role in breaking the tie between consent and repression.

Popular nationalism, particularly in the form of antiforeign street protests, can constrain China's foreign policy options. Yet demonstrations of popular anger can also be helpful when the leadership seeks to signal resolve and demonstrate its commitment to defending China's sovereignty and national interests. After U.S. planes mistakenly bombed the Chinese embassy in Kosovo during NATO airstrikes in 1999, anti-American demonstrations across China conveyed domestic outrage and the government's determination to stand up to the United States. Although the government stepped in to control the demonstrations on the second day, on the first night the American embassy was nearly overrun and the consul general's residence in Chengdu set afire.

Domestic constraints make international cooperation more difficult but can also lend credibility and legitimacy to a tough negotiating stance, improving bargaining leverage. When Japan's bid for a permanent seat on the UN Security Council gained momentum in 2005, anti-Japanese demonstrations showcased popular anger over Prime Minister Koizumi's repeated visits to Yasukuni Shrine, which commemorates 14 A-class war criminals among Japanese war dead, helping China make a stronger case against Japan's candidacy.

Yet popular nationalism has not always forced the Chinese leadership to adopt a hawkish foreign policy stance. China has repeatedly stifled popular nationalism when street protests would have jeopardized the government's efforts to improve diplomatic relations and defuse a potential crisis. After the 2001 EP-3 incident, when a Chinese fighter jet and American reconnaissance plane collided over the South China Sea, China prevented anti-American street demonstrations. Seeking to preserve a fragile rapport with the new Bush administration, Chinese authorities instructed students to stay on campus and told the media to tone down its coverage of the crisis.

China has shown a similar willingness to restrain anti-Japanese demonstrations. After Japan arrested a Chinese trawler captain near the Diaoyu/Senkaku Islands in 2010, Chinese authorities prevented large-scale anti-Japanese demonstrations from taking place on the anniversary of September 18. Expecting Japan to follow precedent and release the captain, China shut down online calls for protest and brought in activists to "drink tea" in hopes of insulating bilateral relations from the collision. Consistent with a tacit agreement to shelve the territorial dispute in the East China Sea, China also repressed anti-Japanese demonstrations during two controversies over the islands in the 1990s. Even though China launched a patriotic education campaign to bolster the regime's diminished legitimacy, nationalist propaganda did not translate into permission for anti-Japanese protests. Determined to court Japanese assistance in breaking out of China's post-Tiananmen isolation, the government prevented anti-Japanese protests when Japanese activists constructed a lighthouse on the disputed islands in 1990. During a second lighthouse controversy in 1996, China again repressed protests, seeking to assuage Japanese concerns and mitigate the fallout of the 1995–96 Taiwan Strait crisis on the eve of revised U.S.-Japan defense guidelines. It was not until China perceived Japan as reneging on the tacit agreement to shelve the territorial dispute that it allowed anti-Japanese protests to take place, both in the latter phase of the 2010 trawler incident and during the 2012 controversy over Japan's purchase of the islands.

Allowing or repressing nationalist protests has helped the Chinese government to signal its diplomatic intentions and reveal the degree to which its hands are tied by domestic sentiments. The repression of anti-American demonstrations helped China send a signal of reassurance to the Bush administration as both sides negotiated a face-saving compromise over the release of the EP-3 crew. As John Keefe, special assistant to Ambassador Prueher, later recounted: "University students wanted to hold demonstrations to vent their anger. The government forbade them from taking such action [and] repeatedly stressed. . . that this event should not be seen as a major affair in U.S.-China relations."[1]

But it is vital to note that the theory does not imply a perfect correspondence between protests and diplomatic victory or repressed protests and mutual compromise. The diplomatic benefits of signaling resolve or restraint are probabilistic, not absolute, since other considerations may affect the foreign government's willingness to escalate or settle the dispute. For example, even if foreign decision-makers credit the authoritarian government's efforts to keep protests in check, the government's restraint may not be reciprocated. During the trawler collision incident, Japanese observers acknowledged China's efforts to prevent large-scale demonstrations on September 18, 2010. But without reciprocal gestures to justify and placate domestic sentiment, the Chinese government became less willing to contain nationalist protests. After the Japanese government insisted on using domestic law to try the

Chinese captain and denied the existence of a territorial dispute, China sought to combat Japan's perceived escalation with tough countermeasures and further protests.

The Search for Credibility

In the presence of nationalist protests, foreign governments are more likely to believe that the authoritarian leadership is constrained than when the issue or dispute has attracted little visible attention by citizens online and offline. But antiforeign protests are not a panacea for the information problems that impede negotiated settlements. Foreign observers often disagree about how "real" and how "induced" the apparent pressure of nationalist sentiment is, producing divergent estimates of the risk to stability and the effort required to curtail protests. As Assistant Secretary of State for East Asian and Pacific Affairs Stanley Roth asked rhetorically during a Senate hearing: "The nationalist card is being played. . . the hard question is how much and how permanent is it?"[2]

At one end of the spectrum, some foreign observers argue that China's fragile leadership is hypersensitive to nationalist sentiment, requiring a forceful response to any foreign slight since no Chinese leader can risk being seen as soft against foreign aggression.[3] As Tokyo University's Akio Takahara put it, "When nationalism is growing stronger, a powerful government may be able to have the public understand the situation, but China's current weak government in a period of power transition cannot persuade the public. Watching the series of actions China has taken, I really feel the fragility of the current Chinese government."[4] As Douglas Paal, former director of the American Institute in Taiwan and National Security Council staff member, similarly noted after the 2010 protests:

> Historically, these kinds of protests have taken down Chinese regimes in
> the past and so the government doesn't want to stir them up—these pro-
> tests are coming more from the people.[5]

The vulnerability of China's leaders and the threat of instability give foreign governments an incentive to behave prudently. Given China's historical "sense of humiliation," said Jeff Bader, senior director for East Asian affairs on the National Security Council under President Obama, it is vital to show respect for Chinese leaders.[6]

At the other end of the spectrum, many skeptical observers argue that Chinese leaders can turn nationalist demonstrations on and off. Proponents of this view maintain that China's leaders have considerable autonomy in setting foreign policy, concluding that the apparent constraints imposed by nationalist sentiment are often exaggerated. As Alastair Iain Johnston writes: "In a political system where there are no electoral costs to ignoring public opinion, it is unclear why China's authoritarian leaders would care much about public views."[7] Because China's leaders are domestically vulnerable, they tolerate protests only when doing so provides a convenient outlet and distraction—"an element of bread and circuses"—for domestic discontent.[8] China's leaders may choose a more adventurous foreign policy, but public opinion—which is subject to the government's "psychological engineering"—does not necessarily require it.[9]

This book stakes out a middle ground between these views. Authoritarian leaders care most about public opinion when protesters are in the streets and when nationalist sentiments are raging online. Large-scale protests are a stronger signal of resolve than small-scale demonstrations, which in turn communicate more than online comments. If we only look at episodes in which nationalist demonstrations are allowed, my argument concurs with those who view the Chinese government as sensitive to popular nationalism. Nationalist protests constrain the government's foreign policy options and require tough diplomatic actions to satisfy protest demands, lest street mobs turn against the government for being too soft.

But the government in China and many other authoritarian states is not feeble. When the government chooses to mount the effort, it can restrain both online and offline mobilization through censorship and repression.[10] It is critical to examine the full variation in how China has managed nationalist pressures in order to draw a more balanced portrait of popular influence on Chinese foreign policy. Protests are often kept in check, activists are often prevented from organizing conferences and voyages, and state-run and commercial media are often instructed to downplay foreign provocations. On these occasions, the influence of popular nationalism is more circumscribed, insulating foreign policy from popular scrutiny.

However, it is critical to note that government efforts to ensure that protests remain "under control" reduce the credibility of protests as a signal of resolve and a constraint on foreign policy. The more that nationalist protests appear manufactured, the more likely foreign observers are to accuse the government of "crying wolf" about the difficulty of defying nationalist sentiment. Although Chinese authorities maintain that they are trying to maintain law and order, police cordons and designated protest routes are often regarded as further evidence of state sponsorship.[11] On the one hand, the dangers associated with protest are cumulative, since past participation gives protesters experience with political action, a network that can be mobilized in the future, and firsthand experience that often produces disenchantment with government orchestration and eventual repression.

On the other hand, antiforeign protests may lose credibility over time as the regime demonstrates its ability to rein in demonstrations even when disparate voices seize the opportunity to air domestic grievances. Foreign observers may conclude that the government has bluffed about the dangers of popular nationalism when protests reoccur and the regime remains stable.[12] Larger and riskier protests may be required to overcome foreign skepticism and entrenched beliefs that China can easily "dial up" or "dial down" nationalist protests without evidence of diplomatic victory or escalation. Moreover, as each potential protest arises under a new set of circumstances, reputational effects may be weakened by perceived differences in China's domestic and diplomatic situation.[13] The shadow of the past may be eclipsed by new signals and circumstances, providing updated information about China's resolve that may trump past conclusions.

Local variation in the management of nationalist protest has also increased the difficulty of discerning China's intentions. As Evan Osnos has noted, "the national narrative, once an ensemble performance, is splintering into a billion stories."[14] The explosion of Weibo, QQ, and other social media platforms has facilitated more viral forms of mobilization, with calls for protest less and less centered on long-standing activists based in Beijing, Shanghai, and other first-tier cities. In theory, the diffusion of protest mobilization could strengthen the government's claim to imperfect control over grassroots nationalism. But the government's efforts to contain and manage nationalist activities in China's most prominent cities has reinforced perceptions that Chinese authorities retain sufficient strength to counteract the dangers implied by social media and increasingly viral forms of mobilization. During the 2010 and 2012 demonstrations, Chinese authorities more visibly stage-managed nationalist activities in first-tier cities than in second- and third-tier cities, consistent with China's broader emphasis on maintaining stability in the capital and other focal points for regime-destabilizing unrest.[15]

Efforts to "guide public opinion" by paying anonymous Internet commentators also undermine the apparent sincerity of nationalist sentiments.[16] The more capable the government appears of shaping popular sentiment at will, the less the government can credibly claim to be constrained by public opinion. As Susan Shirk, former deputy assistant secretary for East Asia under President Clinton, notes, "When they [China's leaders] read these extreme nationalist views on the internet, they have no way to know how broad or deep those views are."[17] Although Shirk argues that "they're so jittery that they feel they have to react by taking a tough stand to demonstrate what strong leaders they are," others remain unconvinced that the Chinese leadership is constrained by sentiments that it cultivates and retains the power to dial back. Not only do "highly unusual" outbursts of "assiduously reported" nationalist sentiment appear suspiciously convenient,[18] but efforts to restrain popular mobilization will be given less credit as signals of reassurance, since quashing popular sentiment requires less effort on the government's part.

Indeed, the grassroots content of Chinese nationalism is often eclipsed by foreign accusations that the Chinese government has "brainwashed" citizens through patriotic education. By discouraging and censoring alternatives to the official narrative of China's "national humiliation," the government has fueled suspicions that the apparent chorus of nationalist outrage is more orchestrated than genuine. In 2006, a popular weekly news magazine was closed after publishing a controversial article by Yuan Weishi, a noted historian at Zhongshan University who criticized Chinese high school textbooks for glorifying the Boxer Rebellion. "Our children are still being fed wolves' milk!" wrote Yuan, arguing that a one-sided view of history would only fan nationalist anger among Chinese teenagers.[19] Although the marketplace for ideas in China has become more pluralistic and commercialized, censorship and self-censorship remain prevalent.[20] The more the government appears responsible for seeding nationalist sentiment, the less believably it can play "good cop" vis-à-vis popular opinion.

Fostering a range of views rather than patrolling the domestic boundaries of the permissible would increase the transparency of Chinese intentions and give greater credibility to the hawkish views that are expressed. A more open airing of views would help balance nationalist opinions with moderate voices, tempering domestic debates but also giving greater credibility to the sentiments that are expressed. When citizens, netizens, and intellectuals feel safe in expressing their opinions without fear of reprisal from censors or vigilante-style "human flesh search engines," external audiences are more likely to believe that these sentiments are genuine rather than an instinctual deference to the party line or what is deemed "appropriate." Moving toward a more competitive marketplace of ideas may require government intervention to regulate discussion and protect unpopular opinions, particularly on the conciliatory or dovish end of the foreign policy spectrum. Encouraging the publication of both sides of a foreign policy debate, as the Chinese media has begun to do on certain issues, gives the government more diplomatic room to maneuver. Yet creating an atmosphere in which diverse voices are heard need not reduce the government's ability to leverage public opinion in diplomatic negotiations. On the contrary, when typically liberal and conservative voices agree on issues such as the defense of Chinese sovereignty over disputed islands, this unanimity of public opinion will send a more convincing signal of resolve.

Efforts to protect and showcase a wider array of domestic views will also increase the transparency of China's intentions. Whether China appears to be a "dissatisfied" power—whose interests can be reasonably accommodated—or an "insatiable" power—whose demands must not be appeased lest its appetite grow larger—turns on whether foreign observers can identify the limits to China's ambitions to revise the status quo.[21] As a former Japanese Finance Ministry official observed:

> [China] is the sort of country with which we must maintain friendly ties. This does not mean, however, that we are happy to welcome China as Asia's leader or the leading country of the world. We do not know today's China well enough to accept it as a leader.[22]

Allowing domestic voices to speak freely will help reveal China's preferences more credibly, enabling foreigners to understand the issues on which China is likely to be resolute as well as the issues on which China is likely to accept compromise. Along with people-to-people exchanges, a more vibrant and public debate about China's foreign affairs and national interests would help dispel fears of China as an inscrutable "alien presence," as Keio University professor Yoshihide Soeya termed it.[23] Whatever the scope of China's desires and the limits to which other powers in the international system are willing to accommodate China's rise, reducing the likelihood of missed signals and foreign incredulity can only improve the prospects for a peaceful adjustment.

Nationalism and Domestic (In)stability

With the fading of communism as an ideological basis for their rule, Chinese leaders have turned to what Samuel Huntington termed "performance" legitimacy to validate their position and stave off demands for political reform. In addition to economic growth, nationalism remains an integral part of China's authoritarian resilience. The Communist Party has used nationalist propaganda to amplify external threats, rallying the public around the flag and highlighting its success in defending the nation's interest. Wang Jisi, an influential scholar and advisor to the Chinese government, quotes the Chinese philosopher Mencius: "A state without an enemy or external peril is absolutely doomed."[24] Long-run propaganda policies and inflammatory news coverage "prime the pump" for street protests, magnifying the cost of repressing nationalist mobilization.

Although nationalist propaganda and antiforeign street protests are often said to benefit authoritarian legitimacy, the decision to inculcate national loyalty through the content of school textbooks, films, and field trips is not the same as the decision to allow or repress nationalist protests during an international dispute. Nationalist protests can get out of hand in many ways, whether by causing harm to foreign citizens and diplomatic property, turning against the government for its weak foreign policy performance, or facilitating broader opposition to the regime.

Chinese officials and activists in China recognize that nationalist activities, even small gatherings, pose a risk. As a Bao Diao activist in Shanghai put it, "There's no 100 percent guarantee that something will happen that the authorities can't control. If they say yes [and allow an event], they have to be on guard in case something arises. But if they say no, they can rest easy."[25] As security authorities said to Bao Diao activist Feng Jinhua on the eve of September 18, 2003: "The international and domestic situation is very complex right now. Can you guarantee that the [protest] activity won't be used by others?"[26]

Internal police publications attest to the regime's awareness that protests have a tendency to spiral out of control. According to one such study:

> During mass incidents, emotions spread from person to person via suggestion and mimicry. Mutually infecting one another with emotion, the element of irrationality among participants gradually increases, even to the point of fanaticism. Once emotions have passed a critical level, they must

find an outlet. In the context of certain social and environmental stimuli, people's emotions will spill over, leading to out-of-control behavior.[27]

Unless given orders from above, local officials have little incentive to allow patriotic protest. "We don't even know how high these things get approval," said a leading Bao Diao activist in Beijing. "Low levels will reject it, of course, because they don't want you to cause trouble."[28] Likewise, after police revoked permission for Bao Diao activists to hold a conference in Changsha in January 2009,[29] one of the organizers grumbled:

> For the bureaucracy, if nothing happens, if there's no conference, if the people have no voice, it's no skin off their back. But if there are a lot of people and something happens at the conference, then it's big trouble for them. So they'd rather that nothing happen. Someone at the higher levels must have said that we wanted to expand (*kuoda*), establish an organization (*chengli zuzhi*), and set sail.[30]

The analogy of protests to "pressure valves" understates the danger to regime stability, even from protests that it may initially allow or encourage. Even diverting domestic grievances toward foreign policy does not strengthen the government's legitimacy if it cannot claim diplomatic victory or point to tough countermeasures that the government has taken to protect the nation's interest. The use of the phrase "pressure valve" is misleading unless one also acknowledges that valves can break, with potentially disastrous consequences.

From Anti-Japan to Pro-Democracy: The Lessons of Tiananmen

For the Chinese government, the danger that nationalist demonstrations could lead to broader opposition is not hypothetical. Indeed, the past two Chinese governments fell to nationalist movements that accused them of failing to defend the country from foreign encroachments: the Nationalists under Chiang Kai-shek and the Manchu leaders of the Qing dynasty. In the post-Mao era, connections between the anti-Japanese protests of 1985 and the pro-democracy protests of 1986 and 1989 served to remind China's Communist leaders that antiforeign demonstrations can easily change direction and target the government itself. Although the Communist Party survived the tumult, two general secretaries were purged for mishandling the protests.

All three waves of protest—1985, 1986, and 1989—were rooted in concerns that government elites were selling out the nation's interests. To be sure, there were major differences in orientation. The 1985 protests criticized the open-door economic reforms for having let in "Japanese wolves"; by contrast, the 1986–89 protests looked to Western symbols of democratic freedom. But while the protests advocated different solutions, the underlying diagnosis of China's illness was the same: corrupt, unaccountable officials who had failed to protect China's interests from foreign depredations. As Geremie Barmé writes:

> Although it has been common for people to talk of the mass national protests of the spring of 1989 which led to the bloody repression of 4 June, as a "democracy movement"... there was also a powerful undercurrent that was pointedly anti-corruption, anti-privilege, and critical of a government that was perceived as having given in to major foreign nations on trade deals and issues of national pride. In particular, Japan.[31]

This bitterness toward Japan was evident in *River Elegy*, a television series that captivated public attention in 1988 and was later denounced by the Party as having contributed to the 1989 demonstrations:

> Over the past century we have continually been losers. First we lost to England, then to the Eight Powers during the Boxer Rebellion, then to the Japanese. Having finally gotten rid of the Japanese, New China enjoyed a short period of pride and achievement. Who was to guess that when we finally woke up from the thirty-odd years of internal turmoil we had created, we would find ourselves in the company of nations like Tanzania and Zambia? Even South Korea and Singapore were ahead of us. And as for the Japanese, they were the ones laughing, now that they were back with their Toshibas, Hitachis, Toyotas, Crowns, Yamahas, and Casios.[32]

In the last line, *River Elegy* references Japan's "second invasion" of China, the same complaint voiced during the 1985 anti-Japanese protests. As Suisheng Zhao writes, "in spite of its enthusiastic call for learning from the West, the series actually portrayed it as an aggressive, hostile power that had attacked, exploited and humiliated China. The challenge for China was to revitalize itself to compete with the West."[33]

Western and Chinese scholars have often overlooked the strong current of nationalism in the 1986 and 1989 protests, tending to focus on the pro-West, pro-democracy features of the two movements. Students seeking international sympathy played to this perception, erecting a "Goddess of Democracy" statue in Tiananmen Square that looked very much like the Statue of Liberty. But the students at Tiananmen sought democracy "because it would help strengthen the nation," Wasserstrom notes, writing that "within the general history of student activism during the Reform era, the downplaying of the role of patriotism... helps obscure the connection between events such as the anti-Japanese protests of 1985 and the demonstrations of 1989."[34]

The government's ambivalent attitude toward anti-Japanese protests in the fall of 1985 both emboldened and disillusioned students, setting a precedent for those who would take to the streets in 1986 and 1989.[35] The government's initially lenient treatment of anti-Japanese protests created the impression that it was safe for students to protest. After several hundred students defied campus authorities and marched to Tiananmen Square on September 18, 1985, Politburo member Hu Qili described the anti-Japanese demonstrations as "understandable," saying that in his youth he too had participated in such activities.[36] None of the students were initially arrested, and similar protests began to arise in other cities in the fall of 1985, denouncing corruption at the highest levels of government and urging the celebration of "Democracy '85." It was not until December that the government reined in the student protests, fueling resentment at the government's high-handed treatment and "unconstitutional" ban on demonstrations, according to one Beijing University student who helped organize the 1989 demonstrations.[37] When pro-democracy protests erupted in December 1986, one of the wall posters at Wuhan University explicitly referred to "the shame of having failed to [celebrate] the fiftieth anniversary" of December 9 in 1985.[38]

Risks of Nationalist Spillover after Tiananmen

The danger of "linkage" between antiforeign and domestic dissent is still pertinent. Nationalist protest remains a form of what Kevin O'Brien has called "rightful resistance," challenging the state to live up to its own rhetoric and ideals.[39] While nationalists may help the government demonstrate resolve and gain diplomatic leverage, they are not reflexively pro-government, often criticizing the Communist Party for failing to defend the nation's sovereignty from foreign encroachments and insults.

Nationalism is often characterized as a source of legitimacy for China's authoritarian rulers, but nationalist activists and intellectuals have also espoused democracy as a means to defending the national interest. In the early 1990s, a Shanghai activist who had participated in the 1989 democracy movement called upon the National People's Congress to hold a referendum on war reparations, stating that a referendum would "open the way to a constitutional democracy" in China.[40] In 1998, a petition urged the National People's Congress to elect the anti-Japanese activist Tong Zeng as president (see chapter 4). Nationalist authors like Wang Xiaodong have proclaimed their support for democracy, if only to prevent the current elite from "selling out the country for its own self-interest."[41] Two authors of the 1996 bestseller *China Can Say No* also participated in the 1989 pro-democracy movement.[42] One of them, Song Qiang, later qualified his position: "Liberalism is always attractive, but I am skeptical of whether it can help China at this point in time. . . . but if you simply equate nationalism with darkness, autocracy, and backwardness, I think you're being absurd."[43]

In addition, nationalists have often grown cynical and resentful of government manipulation. As one netizen noted on the Patriots Alliance Network discussion forum, "Can a country where patriotism is attacked ever be democratic? Can there

be space for common people?"[44] Partial tolerance and sporadic repression may create more cynicism and anger than a no-tolerance policy. A young organizer from
Foshan became disenchanted with the government after he was singled out for surveillance after participating in the 2005 anti-Japanese protests. Three years later, he
warned his friends not to participate in the protests against CNN and Carrefour, a
French supermarket chain rumored to have supported Tibetan independence:

> I told everyone not to be so childish, that we've all been brainwashed and
> schooled. They criticized me for having no patriotic feeling [but] I know
> that what you see in China is always fake. At the time, I wrote on my MSN
> status: "Even if CNN was wrong this once, you shouldn't be so harsh.
> China's media has been reporting fake news for decades and no one scolds
> them."[45]

For many participants, the experience of political participation may whet their
appetite for greater freedom of expression, leading to greater resentment with the
return of repression.

One of the government's greatest fears is that disparate groups of aggrieved citizens will link up and challenge the regime. The involvement of Bao Diao activist Li
Yiqiang in the 2007 Xiamen PX protests, noted in chapter 7, suggests that spillover
from nationalism to domestic dissent is already taking place. Some nationalists have
also adopted the rights-centric language more commonly associated with liberals.
According to one lawyer who has helped Chinese citizens prepare compensation
claims against Japan:

> I am not an extreme nationalist (jiduan de minzu zhuyi zhe). Rather, I am
> a human rights activist (renquan zhuyi zhe). I don't help sue just Japan but
> also the Chinese government. Right now I am still an assistant professor,
> but when I become full professor I will spend more of my time writing
> articles pointing out ways in which local city officials have violated the law.
> I won't direct my arguments against the central government—that's dan-
> gerous. But local officials aren't a problem.[46]

Indeed, many nationalists view their activities as helping the Chinese people rather
than the Chinese government. One of the founders of anti-CNN.com, a website
dedicated to exposing Western media bias against China, said that he was no more
inclined to trust the Chinese news media than the Western media, so he decided
that his next project would be a website dedicated to citizen journalism.[47] Two
founding members of the Chinese Civilian Alliance Against Japan, which formed
during the 2010 trawler crisis, identified themselves as having led a volunteer team
during the 2008 Sichuan earthquake relief effort.[48] Movement between nationalist
and domestic activism may run in both directions.

Just as nationalists have voiced support for democracy and individual rights, some of China's most prominent liberals have also supported a strident stance against Japan. Fang Lizhi, an intellectual who was active in mobilizing the 1986 and 1989 student demonstrations with his democratic rhetoric, criticized the CCP for giving up claims to war reparations from Japan. In the early 1980s, Fang wrote: "Japan ought to pay China war reparation in hundreds of billions of dollars, but with the consent of Premier Zhou [the debt] was canceled by one single stroke of writing."[49] During the 1996 lighthouse controversy, the future Nobel laureate and dissident Liu Xiaobo slammed the government's repression of Bao Diao activities and called for a tougher stance against Japan in an article with democracy activist Wang Xizhe:

> What is even more erroneous is that the CCP government has gone so far as to repeatedly suppress nongovernmental activities in China in protest against Japan. It bans demonstrations and forces Tong Zeng to leave, which dampens the morale of the compatriots and boosts the spirit of the Japanese. ... Has the common ailing of Chinese governments in modern times, which is characterized by being "adept at waging a civil war but poor at resisting foreign aggression," infected the CCP government which was so staunch yesterday? The CCP can use force against Taiwan and against students but it cannot use force against Japan. What is the reason behind this policy?[50]

Even as many liberals grew cynical about the government's manipulation of nationalist protest, they continued to defend the right of nationalists to mobilize and protest. "A healthy society where democratic values predominate shouldn't censor or repress waves of 'unorthodox' ideas, including nationalism," writes Liu Ning.[51] Many liberal dissidents joined and were later detained for participating in the 2005 anti-Japanese protests, including AIDS activist Hu Jia and 1989 activist Xu Wanping.[52]

Although these anecdotes underscore the potential spillover between nationalist activism and domestic dissent, in practice a relatively small number of voices regularly cross this divide. In part, the separation of domestic and foreign policy activism may reflect self-censorship by activists concerned about the risk of linking nationalist concerns to domestic demands. Many nationalists are quick to proclaim their support for the central government. "We want to assist the government," said Li Yiqiang.[53] When the Patriots Alliance Network organized an Internet signature campaign in 2003 to demand compensation for victims of Japanese poison gas bombs left in northeastern China, they announced: "We firmly support the Ministry of Foreign Affairs' stern negotiations with Japan [and] hope that this campaign will help the government put pressure on Japan."[54] Privately, however, activists were more willing to criticize the government. As a leading Bao Diao activist acknowledged,

In Sino-Japanese relations, the Chinese government overemphasizes government-to-government relations and neglects the interests of individuals (*geti liyi*). The government doesn't want the stories of the victims to come out, because the government would look bad for having done nothing so far. I'd like the government to adopt a more open-minded policy. The public security bureau did not agree (*meiyou tongyi*) to the Internet signature campaign, but we did it anyway.[55]

Self-censorship makes it difficult to know the latent potential for crossover between activism on foreign policy and domestic issues. As one QQ group, "Patriots," stated in its tag line: "Sensitive topics that concern national politics or reactionary statements against the motherland are forbidden. Violators will be removed from the group without exception."[56] Patriotic hackers likewise self-police their activities, explicitly warning their members against attacking domestic websites. At least part of their restraint appears to be tactical, not ideological. As James Mulvenon notes, "They are tolerated [as] 'useful idiots' for the regime, but they are also careful not to pursue domestic hacking activities that might threaten 'internal stability' and thereby activate the repression apparatus."[57]

Although repression and self-censorship have winnowed out the population that vocally mobilizes on both sides of the domestic-foreign policy divide, the gulf has also widened as liberals have grown more cynical about the use of nationalist mobilization as a protective cloak. Some liberals have suggested turning nationalist demonstrations toward other purposes, as Ai Weiwei's tweet indicated in September 2010. As a professor of communication studies in Beijing noted: "Many of my friends have said, 'There is no way to protest more important things, so we can only oppose Japan.'"[58] Yet the manner in which the government has curtailed nationalist protests after using them to support its policy objectives has disheartened many liberals. In 2005, Liu Xiaobo lamented that "when university students participate in anti-Japanese protests, there are nearly a thousand ways they voice their anger at Japan. But when it comes to calming public opinion, all is reduced to uniformity."[59] Yu Jie, another dissident, argued that liberal attempts to utilize nationalism were doomed to fail:

> Anti-Japan, anti-America, and anti-Taiwan are "puppet plays" directed by the Chinese Communist government and performed by some citizens. . . . Even self-proclaimed pursuers of democracy and liberty" also take anti-Japan thought as useful resources. Self-professed human rights activists Fan Yafeng, Guo Feixiong[60] and Chen Yongpu all participated in and planned anti-Japan activities. They tried to establish a democratic and constitutional government through nationalistic movements. This kind of thinking will not lead anywhere, but will push China into further misery.[61]

The thoughtless violence and destruction of private property has also fueled liberal disgust with nationalism. In "Confessions of a Traitor," liberal commentator Li Chengpeng denounced the 2012 anti-Japanese protests, asking: "What kind of brainwashing has made people think that buying a Japanese car is an act of treason?. . . . China wants to be fucking awesome, but some Chinese people always use fucking awful methods to try to achieve it."[62] Despite his 2010 tweet, Ai Weiwei also scorned the 2012 protests against Japan, saying:

> We all know in China that the last real organised demonstration was crushed by tanks and others. . . . Anybody watching the groups involved [in 2012 can see that] there are no leaders, no intellectuals. It is the kind of people that no-one can identify with. It is not students. It is not workers. It is not anybody.[63]

By delegitimizing the radical and thuggish behavior of China's "brainwashed" angry youth, antiforeign protests may also help prevent nationalism from becoming a unifying force against the regime.

Liberal cynicism toward "narrow nationalism" may give foreign observers hope that a more democratic China would also be more dovish in its foreign policy. But it is unclear whether these voices represent more than a narrow segment of society. Indeed, based on the frequency of anti-Japanese protests in Hong Kong, we might see a dramatic increase in nationalist protest if mainland China were to allow greater freedoms of speech and assembly. Although Hong Kong reverted to Chinese rule in 1997, individual liberties and the freedom to protest in the former British colony have remained robust. By my count, Hong Kong witnessed at least 85 instances of anti-Japanese protest between 1978 and 2005, almost twice the number in mainland China, where authorities have repressed more than a dozen anti-Japanese protests (see appendix).[64]

On the other hand, the relaxation of press and information controls might create a more balanced public discourse, with moderate voices less underrepresented in print and online discussions. Still, we would be naive to hold government censorship solely responsible for the risks of expressing views that appear dovish or pro-foreign. In 2003, prominent Chinese intellectuals who defended a more conciliatory approach toward Japan were excoriated in online forums and academic debates. The author of the proposed "New Thinking" toward Japan, Ma Licheng, received death threats, and his home address was posted online.[65] Five years later, netizens gave the same treatment to a Chinese undergraduate at Duke University, Grace Wang. For mediating between pro-Tibet and pro-China groups during the 2008 controversy over the Lhasa riots, she was denounced in online forums as a "race traitor." Chinese netizens posted her identification number, contact information, and directions to her parents' home in mainland China.[66] In light of these virulent sentiments, it may be some time before Chinese citizens feel safe voicing contrarian views, even if government censorship becomes more relaxed.

Survey data provide grounds for optimism as Chinese citizens become richer, more educated, and more widely traveled. Johnston and Stockmann find that higher levels of education, wealth, and international exposure are associated with lower levels of anti-American attitudes among Beijing residents.[67] However, these trends may be diluted by the massive rural-to-urban migration of roughly 200 million Chinese workers, who face discrimination in China's cities and whose attitudes may not match their urban neighbors.

The effect of overseas experience may also change as China becomes more powerful on the world stage. In surveys of Chinese who returned to China between 1990 and 2005, two researchers found that respondents were less "assertively nationalistic" than a comparison group of middle-class Chinese.[68] As China becomes a more hotly contested topic of debate and concern on foreign campuses, however, Chinese who spend time abroad may become more rather than less nationalistic. The frictions surrounding the 2008 Olympic torch relay in particular prompted an outpouring of support for China among overseas Chinese. For several weeks in the spring of 2008, it became politically correct for users of the popular MSN instant messaging service to post "Love China" next to their screen name. Reflecting back on the period, two Chinese undergraduates at the London School of Economics remarked that they felt more patriotic after studying abroad than they had back home.[69]

Other Targets of Nationalist Anger in China

Although state media have accused many countries of "hurting the feelings" of the Chinese people,[70] popular mobilization against foreign countries in the post-Mao era has primarily targeted Japan and the United States. Despite rising tensions over the South China Sea, for example, nationalist anger in China at Vietnam and the Philippines has been largely limited to online sentiments. Even the relatively nationalist *Global Times* rebuffed calls to "teach Vietnam a lesson" in 2011, cautioning that "indulging anger and fantasizing confrontation" is not the right way to manage disputes in the South China Sea.[71] In May 2012, an online petition gathered more than 12 million Chinese signatures against the Philippines' claim to Scarborough Shoal,[72] but police quickly intervened when several demonstrators unfurled banners in front of the Philippines embassy.[73] Although nationalist sentiment may make it difficult for Chinese officials to deny that the South China Sea is one of China's "core interests," bureaucratic and strategic calculations have probably contributed more to China's muscular actions in the South China Sea.[74]

Although scholars have documented the rise of public antipathy and online sentiment against many of China's neighbors,[75] anger at these countries is not rooted in the same historical memories that drive anti-Japanese sentiment in China. As Gries notes, for many Chinese "the Japanese are the paradigmatic 'devils' (*guizi*)—not just because of the brutality of the Japanese invasion of China and the sheer numbers of Chinese killed by Japanese troops, but also because of an ethical anger with earlier origins," beginning with China's defeat in the 1895 Sino-Japanese War.[76]

In contrast, Chinese grievances against the United States are more tied to contemporary concerns about American "hegemony" and intervention in China's sovereign affairs, particularly Taiwan, rather than historical misdeeds or competing territorial claims. As Johnston and Stockmann note: "Whatever level of anti-Americanism the Chinese express, they reserve their harshest, most essentializing view for Japan and the Japanese."[77] According to one nationalist activist: "Compared [with] anti-American and anti-French feelings, to ignite Chinese people's anti-Japan sentiments, only a tenth of the provocation is needed."[78]

Yet new events and perceived provocations may spark nationalist protest against other foreign targets. In March 2014, the disappearance of Malaysia Airlines flight 370 led hundreds of grieving Chinese relatives to march on the Malaysian embassy in Beijing, where they condemned the Malaysian government for mishandling the case and withholding information that might have saved passengers onboard. During the East China Sea crisis in 2012, demonstrators burned American flags along with Japanese flags. In 2008, protesters denounced France and Western media outlets for criticizing Chinese actions in Tibet and hinting at a boycott of the Beijing Olympics. And even apparently unrelated grievances may be linked by conspiracy theories to American influence. During the outbreak of avian flu in the spring of 2013, for example, one netizen accused the United States and Japan of disseminating the virus in order to bring about China's collapse.[79]

Other than Japan, foreign "interference" in China's "internal affairs," namely Taiwan and Tibet, has sparked the most nationalist mobilization. Despite—and perhaps because of—the centrality of Taiwan and Tibet to the CCP's nationalist claims, the government has been chary of allowing street protests over these issues. Nationalist sentiments over these issues are particularly risky because they could easily escalate to accusations that the CCP has failed to preserve the nation's unity and territorial integrity, leading to demands for regime change.[80] Chinese authorities have never allowed large-scale protests against Taiwan independence, using other means to demonstrate resolve. Protests over Tibet have been largely channeled toward external targets. By allowing limited protests against Western targets—targets that would concede in the face of Chinese pressure—the government was able to harness popular anger to fend off international pressure and mitigate the risk of further interethnic conflict.

Taiwan

Pro-independence politicians have sought greater international recognition for Taiwan as a separate political entity since democratization began on the island in the late 1980s. Rather than allow protests against Taiwan independence, the Chinese government has used other tactics, including military exercises, to signal resolve and assuage domestic concern over Taiwan. When I asked a senior professor at Tsinghua University if he was surprised that there had never been street demonstrations over Taiwan, he replied: "The public knows that the government is very firm on Taiwan. When Lee Teng-hui visited the United States, we sent missiles. I think the government has been tough enough that people are satisfied."[81] A government-affiliated expert on U.S.-China relations concurred: "People are satisfied with the government's response—the government is hard enough."[82]

In 1995, the United States granted Taiwan's president, Lee Teng-hui, a visa to give a speech at his alma mater, Cornell University. As Robert Ross notes, "The United States had long banned visits by Taiwan's leaders in deference to Beijing's insistence that Taiwan is a Chinese province. By suddenly allowing Lee to visit, Washington seemed to Beijing to be encouraging independence."[83] In response to Lee Teng-hui's provocative speech, the Chinese government began a series of missile exercises and mobilized troops along the coast facing Taiwan.[84] Although Chinese students applied for permission to protest in front of the U.S. embassy in Beijing, only small campus gatherings were allowed in mainland China, while groups of Chinese students gathered in New York City and at Cornell University to denounce Lee's visit.[85]

The series of missile exercises, which took place in the months leading up to Taiwan's first nationwide election in March 1996, led the United States to dispatch two aircraft carrier battle groups to waters near the Taiwan Strait. The escalation of tensions produced economic tremors on the island but did not reduce popular support for Lee Teng-hui. Swaine suggests that "Beijing's actions actually drove Taiwan voters to back Lee in unexpectedly high numbers. . . . [As] an embattled leader and symbol of Taiwanese nationalism," Lee and his party won the election with 54 percent of the vote.[86] The episode taught Chinese leaders that saber rattling to intimidate Taiwan voters was counterproductive, but it also underscored to foreign observers China's resolve to prevent Taiwan from declaring independence.

The Chinese government has continued to prevent popular demonstrations over Taiwan despite the election of pro-independence candidate Chen Shui-bian as Taiwan's president in March 2000 and his re-election and referendum on independence in March 2004. On the eve of the 2000 elections, Chinese authorities convened special meetings to guard against "unforeseen incidents" and protect Taiwanese investments in the event that Chen Shui-bian won. After his victory, police rejected protest applications in Beijing and Shanghai and broke up spontaneous demonstrations that arose in Chongqing and Wuhan.[87] Before the 2004 election, Chinese authorities initially allowed more than 10 nationalist websites, including the Patriots Alliance Network, to launch an online signature campaign against Taiwan independence. The launch of the petition in November 2003 gathered nearly 20,000 signatures in the first week after being picked up by major media outlets, including Xinhua.[88] The State Council Taiwan Affairs Office warned that

"Any person who attempts to make Taiwan secede from China is bound to be slapped in the face by 1.3 billion Chinese people, Taiwan compatriots included."[89]

As the 2004 election drew near, Chinese authorities took pains to calm popular sentiment and issued an internal circular directing university authorities to prevent radical student actions.[90] A senior expert at the Chinese Academy of Social Sciences was invited to give a series of lectures in Xi'an in order to discourage university students from staging protests if pro-independence leader Chen Shui-bian was re-elected, particularly since Xi'an students had been involved in a fracas with Japanese students a few months before. As he recalled:

> The Chinese government wants to keep public opinion from hurting or interfering with Chinese foreign policy, as well as Taiwan policy. . . . At the time, most of the students asked the question, "When shall we fight?" I said it is better not to fight, because it is not a critical moment to prevent Taiwan independence. We still have time, room to do other things.[91]

The special lectures and preventive efforts were reportedly successful. According to a university bulletin, "In order to prevent radical student activities after the election results came out, our school counselors and class supervisors embedded themselves among students, prepared to give students work to do, but students were abnormally quiet and online discussion more rational than usual."[92]

Rather than risk belligerent protests that might further alienate Taiwan voters and become difficult to control when Chen Shui-bian was reelected, China tried a softer campaign. On March 2, the Patriots Alliance Network spearheaded a new campaign to emphasize the close ties between Taiwan and the Mainland with a song and online petition, "Taiwan: my brother."[93] Guo Zhenyuan, a researcher at the government-affiliated China Institute of International Studies, stated that such activities could provide critical guidance for public emotions, since there was no shortage of "extreme emotions" concerning Taiwan.[94] When activists in Hefei tried to take the petition to the streets on March 7, they were taken to the police station as soon as they showed up. According to one of the organizers, the police persuaded him that the street petition might even help Chen Shui-bian, just as the People's Liberation Army exercises had helped Lee Teng-hui win the 1996 elections. "Our government learned from the experience and has since maintained restraint before Taiwan elections, so we shouldn't do anything different!!!" the organizer wrote online.[95] Another netizen remarked in response: "The Ministry of State Security is worried that our patriotism will be used by bad people and cause the situation to get out of hand (*bu ke shoushi de jumian*)."[96]

Although large-scale street protests over Taiwan independence have never occurred, the government may not always choose restraint. International support for Taiwan may spark protests against actors like the United States and Japan, who might be accused of helping split Taiwan from China. In December 2004, when

Japan granted a visa to former Taiwan president Lee Teng-hui, nationalist activists held a small demonstration outside the Japanese embassy in protest.[97] In January 2010, several prominent Internet portals hosted a signature campaign to condemn a proposed U.S. arms sale to Taiwan.[98] But the signature campaign only remained a front-page item for a few days before disappearing into the archives. When a few netizens on nationalistic forums called for "peaceful assemblies" to protest the U.S. arms sale, these posts were also censored by forum moderators, leading one netizen to plead: "Don't delete this post again! *Global Times* has already organized an Internet signature campaign; why shouldn't we be allowed to organize a protest?"[99] Perhaps the Chinese government deemed the issue too explosive, since a high-profile signature campaign could give the impression that offline protests were also acceptable.

So far, the Chinese government appears to have determined that tolerating street protests over Taiwan independence is not worth the risk, particularly since political developments in Taiwan since 2008 have given China more confidence that diplomatic and economic trends across the Taiwan Strait are favorable. Moreover, most foreign analysts already believe that the CCP leadership is constrained on the Taiwan issue by public opinion. As Kokubun and Liu note: "Those who favor taking a hard line on the Taiwan issue make up a majority in China. . . as high as 80 or 90 percent."[100] Swaine concurs, writing: "many think the loss of Taiwan could result in the collapse of the Chinese government."[101] Whether or not this conjecture is accurate, protests are unnecessary to increase perceptions of Chinese resolve if foreign policymakers already believe that the CCP would do anything to avoid such a fate—even launching a war that would end at best in a Pyrrhic victory. Rather, protests might put the Chinese government in the position of having to take actions it would have preferred to avoid, even war. As a former American intelligence official put it:

> There's a very calculated decision in Beijing—they only let protest happen on something they can do something about. Were they to allow protest over Taiwan, the government might come under pressure to take action. But on Taiwan they would run themselves into such deep water that it isn't worth it. So it's one thing to protest France—the Chinese are not going to have to fight the French. It's quite another thing to take on an issue like Taiwan where the only solution is a military one.[102]

Tibet

Nationalist mobilization among Han Chinese over the issue of Tibet has been comparatively rare but also poses large risks. With Tibet, the government's fear is that nationalist demonstrations by Han Chinese might exacerbate interethnic tensions and trigger further violence. In March 2008, riots in Lhasa killed more than a dozen civilians and injured hundreds more, including many Han Chinese. In the wake of the Lhasa riots, many Western leaders demanded that the Chinese government halt its repressive policies in Tibet and reopen talks with the Dalai Lama. A potential boycott of the Beijing Olympics was also raised at the European Union foreign ministers' meeting, with French president Nicolas Sarkozy, who would assume the EU presidency in July 2008, declaring that he would keep all options on the table and hinting that a possible boycott would "get results."[103] Eager to rebuff international criticism over its human rights policies on the eve of the 2008 Beijing Olympics, the Chinese government supported an online campaign to oppose "splittism" and channel the brunt of nationalist Han anger toward Western news media and foreign leaders accused of supporting Tibetan independence.

Beijing's bid to host the Olympics had from the beginning been beset by criticism of human rights in China, including Tibet. Before the July 2001 vote that awarded the Games to Beijing, U.S. congressional leaders asked the International Olympic Committee to disqualify Beijing unless China released political prisoners and ratified the International Covenant on Civil and Political Rights. Eight years before, the House of Representatives had passed a similar resolution, and Beijing lost the 2000 Summer Games to Sydney, Australia. Concerned that political issues would again torpedo Beijing's bid, Liu Jingmin, vice president of the 2008 Olympic bid committee, argued that "by allowing Beijing to host the Games you will help the development of human rights."[104] At the 2001 vote, many who opposed Beijing did so over concerns about Tibet, and even those who supported Beijing's victory commented on the link to political rights.

By 2007 it seemed to many foreign observers that Olympic-related pressure was working to change China's policies toward Sudan and the crisis in Darfur. In 2006, President Hu Jintao urged Sudan to accept a multinational peacekeeping force. In March 2007, Hollywood actress and UNICEF activist Mia Farrow criticized the Chinese government's inaction on the genocide in Darfur. Singled out for serving as artistic consultant to the Olympic ceremonies, director Steven Spielberg called upon China to take a more active role in stopping the genocide in Darfur. Within a month, China had removed Sudan from its list of preferred trading nations and sent an envoy to coax Khartoum into accepting a peacekeeping operation, which was accepted in July and put into place in December 2007.[105] The *New York Times* called it "a turnaround that served as a classic study of how a pressure campaign, aimed to strike Beijing in a vulnerable spot at a vulnerable time, could accomplish what years of diplomacy could not."[106]

On human rights, China also made modest concessions to defuse the growing campaign against the "Genocide Olympics," the label Mia Farrow had used. Shortly after Spielberg resigned as artistic advisor, protesting what he viewed as China's unwillingness to lean more heavily on the Sudanese government, the Chinese Foreign Ministry in late February agreed to reopen human rights talks with the United States, which had been suspended since 2004. "I think China was surprised at how much international pressure there was in the lead-up to the Olympics," said a senior Bush administration official.[107]

With the outbreak of riots in Lhasa on March 14, 2008, and China's subsequent crackdown on "troublemakers" in Tibet, as China's UN ambassador Wang Guangya put it, foreign leaders publicly contemplated a boycott of the Beijing Olympics and demanded China halt its repressive actions.[108] French foreign minister Bernard Kouchner put the issue of Tibet on the agenda of the EU foreign ministerial meeting on March 28 and 29.[109] EU Parliament president Hans-Gert Poettering demanded that China immediately open talks with the Dalai Lama and suggested that threatening a boycott would be the best way of "bringing our influence to bear in favor of the Tibetans."[110] Demands for dialogue between the Chinese government and the Dalai Lama were echoed by other EU leaders and heads of state around the world, even by those who did not favor a boycott.[111]

On March 25, French president Nicolas Sarkozy told reporters that "all options are open," refusing to rule out a possible boycott of the Olympic opening ceremony if the Chinese government continued its crackdown in Tibet.[112] "The strategy I'm proposing is firm on human rights and it can lead to results," Sarkozy said. "It's very important to express our strong concern and at the same time to step up our response."[113] On March 27, Sarkozy reiterated that he "reserved the right" not to attend the Opening Ceremony in August, "according to how the situation is looking at the time."[114] By then, Sarkozy would have assumed the six-month rotating EU presidency.

As pro-Tibetan demonstrations took place outside Chinese diplomatic compounds and along the Olympic torch route, the Chinese government sought to showcase grassroots efforts to support the Beijing Olympics and criticize Western media for portraying China's actions in Tibet as a brutal crackdown. On March 18, a young Chinese college graduate and IT entrepreneur had founded the website Anti-CNN.com, where volunteers submitted evidence of "anti-China bias" in CNN and other Western news media.[115] The website provided examples of errors and misleading materials, such as photos of Nepalese police beating protesters, mistakenly identified as Chinese police.[116]

The Chinese government endorsed these grassroots efforts by encouraging online signature campaigns against "splittism" and bias in the Western media and instructing major commercial web portals to give prominence to articles ridiculing CNN and other foreign news outlets. On March 27, Chinese Foreign Ministry spokesman Qin Gang acknowledged the anti-CNN website as "purely spontaneous condemnation and criticism by the Chinese people toward some Western media's irresponsible reports."[117] On March 30, Sina.com and other portals launched an Internet signature campaign against the Western media's "distorted coverage" of the Lhasa riots, whose banner headline read "Oppose Splittism, Protect the Torch" a few days later.[118] According to a news editor at Sohu.com, the signature campaign "was led by the government, but they told us to make it look like the voice of the people (*minjian de shengyin*)."[119] As a Chinese freelance writer and liberal commentator noted, "The government had to respond to France's talk about boycotting the Olympics. But the government couldn't directly oppose France because it has to host the Olympics, after all. So the government wanted the public to be angry."[120]

On April 7, the Olympic torch relay was disrupted by pro-Tibetan protestors in Paris, who at one stage tried to wrest the torch away from Chinese Paralympic fencer Jin Jing. The athlete was lauded as a hero in China, and her remarks about the "relatively light" security during the Paris leg of the torch relay sparked further anger at France.[121] CNN's Jack Cafferty also added fuel to the fire, saying that the Chinese were "the same bunch of goons and thugs they've been for the last 50 years."[122]

On April 13, a college graduate in Beijing staged a brief protest outside the supermarket Carrefour, whose major shareholder was rumored to have donated money to the Dalai Lama. "The French appear to be friendly," she told the crowd that gathered around,

> but their true nature has been revealed. They fear a strong China, so they hope our country will be divided and fall into chaos, thereby eliminating the "China threat.". . . I personally don't think it's realistic or necessary to boycott Carrefour completely, perhaps just on May 1. But so long as we make the French government see our attitude, we'll have fully achieved our goal.[123]

Several minutes after she began, a policeman commended her patriotism but told her that she was creating an obstruction. After she pointed out that moving her protest elsewhere would defeat the purpose of drawing attention to Carrefour, the policeman allowed her to continue for 20 minutes. Asked about the Carrefour boycott, the Chinese Foreign Ministry spokeswoman demanded that Cafferty apologize and stated that netizens had "good reason" for concern and that the French should "think hard and reflect" upon the situation.[124] The next day, CNN released a statement of apology, saying: "It was not Mr. Cafferty's nor CNN's intent to cause offence to the Chinese people, and we would apologize to anyone who has interpreted the comments in this way."[125]

Anti-French street demonstrations broke out in several Chinese cities between April 17 and 20, including Changsha, Fuzhou, Qingdao, Kunming, Xi'an, Chongqing, Nanjing, and Xiamen.[126] The protestors called for a boycott of French products and picketed various Carrefour branches. According to a senior foreign policy expert in Beijing,

> The Chinese government did not mobilize, but did allow the anti-French protests. If you look at the Foreign Ministry statements, the government was actually quite positive, even encouraging. The government wanted to send a signal to France that the Chinese people were angry, with France

and with the government, and that the Chinese government would have to toughen its position to respond to public pressure. . . . There were no instructions given by university administrators to prevent anti-French protests. There was anti-CNN online and a boycott of Carrefour and French products. But what the Chinese government worries about is demonstrations at Tiananmen and foreign embassies. The demonstrations outside French shops—this is a social and economic problem, not political—so the Chinese government felt more relaxed.[127]

Indeed, there were only two brief incidents outside the French embassy in Beijing and no protests outside French consulates, even when anti-Carrefour demonstrations took place in Chengdu and Wuhan, where France has consulates. Pro-China rallies continued to take place along the torch relay, with overseas Chinese and expatriates turning out to support the Olympic torch alongside pro-Tibetan protests.

Endorsing the grassroots campaign against Western media outlets and a French supermarket chain served China's domestic and diplomatic objectives. Domestically, the government sought to minimize the risk of interethnic retribution and give domestic anger a relatively safe target to attack. As a senior international relations expert at Fudan University noted:

> The students were very angry, both at the Dalai Lama and the government for not stopping the riots from destroying Han businesses. The students really wanted to take to the streets, but the university officials persuaded them not to. They were worried that the protests against the Dalai Lama might turn against the government. Protests against Carrefour were unlikely to turn against the government.[128]

A senior policy advisor in Beijing concurred, stating that "The government successfully persuaded students not to demonstrate over Tibet. The government is more nervous about anger against Tibetan people than about anger against France. The government is worried about ethnic tensions. There are 55 minorities in China!"[129]

Diplomatically, the display of Chinese nationalism both inside and outside the country enabled the government to demonstrate the depth of public anger and willingness to stand firm against international pressure regarding Tibet. President Sarkozy referred to Chinese nationalist sentiment on multiple occasions, acknowledging that "Our aim is not to have China freezing on a nationalistic position. We have to understand this whilst upholding religious and community rights."[130] On April 18, Sarkozy met with Hu Jintao's special envoy in Paris, and the following week three high-level French officials flew to China in what was heralded as "a diplomatic charm offensive aimed at limiting the political and economic fallout from the controversy. . . [as well as] to reassure the Chinese leadership that France has no intention to strain relations."[131] French Senate president Christian Poncelet carried a letter of sympathy to the Paralympic athlete, Jin Jing, who had been jostled while carrying the torch in Paris. The letter read: "I understand that the Chinese people's feelings were hurt by what went on that day, and especially by the intolerable attack you suffered and which I condemn with the utmost force."[132]

By publicizing France's goodwill overtures and statements of regret by Western media, the Chinese government minimized the cost of curtailing further protests. Police told university students to cancel demonstrations planned for the May 1 holiday and contacted those who posted calls for protest to dissuade them from demonstrating.[133] Propaganda authorities issued stern instructions to censor sensitive keywords, stating that "Internet users are in a most intense mood toward Western countries. . . . Such information has shown a tendency to spread and, if not checked in time, could even lead to events getting out of control as they did with the April 9 incident against Japan."[134] The following notice appeared on anti-CNN.com:

> Posts regarding certain topics will be politely refused: domestic politics, Taiwan, religious and ethnic tensions, Han-Tibetan conflict etc. Without exception, we will delete posts that attempt to announce and stir up (*shandong*) domestic protest marches, personal attacks, group or individual announcements, or other posts that may affect social stability.[135]

When small protests broke out in several cities over the holiday, police quickly broke up the demonstrations and detained several protesters.[136]

In June, President Sarkozy publicly indicated that he would attend the Olympic opening ceremony, so long as talks between China and the Dalai Lama continued to make progress. In justifying his decision to attend the Olympics, Sarkozy stated that "we absolutely must not push a population of 1.3 billion people into wounded nationalism."[137] American officials likewise noted the sincerity of Chinese nationalist sentiment, even if the government had taken advantage of it to rebuff international pressure. As a senior Bush administration official recalled: "On the torch relay, there was genuine nationalist backlash against what happened, particularly when the paraplegic athlete was jostled in France. That really set off a legitimate, spontaneous reaction. And I think the Chinese piggybacked on that."[138] Another senior administration official acknowledged that President Bush had taken a lot of heat for attending the Opening Ceremony after the Lhasa riots, but stated that boycotting the Olympics would only have alienated a large portion of the Chinese public.[139]

The government's willingness to tolerate and then curtail anti-French and anti-CNN sentiment in 2008 reflects many of the same considerations that motivate China's management of nationalist protest more generally—calibrating the domestic risk while maximizing the diplomatic benefit of grassroots anger. Although the government's actions helped steer the public face of nationalist anger toward Western targets, it is important to note that the anti-CNN and anti-Carrefour campaigns also had grassroots origins. At least two of the "early risers" who founded anti-CNN. com and staged the first anti-Carrefour protest had no prior history of activism or communication with the government. And although the protests against Carrefour were smaller and less violent than those against Japan in 2005, the eager participation of many young Chinese born after the 1980s gave rise to a new moniker, "April youth."[140] The emergence of a younger generation of activists and participants worried the Chinese authorities, who feared they might link up with more experienced organizers. As a freelance writer and Japan expert in Beijing noted:

> There was a Bao Diao activity planned but they decided to postpone it under pressure from Beijing until after the Olympics. The government is very concerned that with the anti-Carrefour protests, Tong Zeng and the others might link up with the post-1980s generation. The post-1980s generation has huge numbers but no organization. Tong Zeng and his group have an organization. The government is worried that the two combined would be even scarier.[141]

Nationalist Protest in Other Authoritarian States

The bargaining logic of antiforeign protest is not restricted to China, but in many ways China provides an ideal illustration. China is a relatively strong authoritarian state, both in its geostrategic position and its capacity relative to society. Yet China is not so strong that it cannot be shaken by protests. After the fall of longstanding dictators in Tunisia and Egypt in 2011, we may wonder if any authoritarian regime is truly invulnerable to the power of street protest.

If the logic of antiforeign protest as a bargaining instrument is not unique to China, what scope conditions limit its applicability to other states? First, we should expect nationalist protests to be an effective commitment tactic on issues where foreign observers understand that public opinion is more hawkish than the status quo ante. From Saudi Arabia to Pakistan, many of the world's remaining authoritarian regimes receive aid from the West in exchange for foreign policy concessions that are deeply out of sync with popular opinion, including basing rights, cooperation on terrorism, and favorable access to oil and other natural resources. Despite the relative opacity of these regimes, foreign observers are often able to infer how moderate the incumbent autocrats are relative to the "street." The more that street protests appear representative of prevailing public attitudes, the more legitimacy the government stands to lose by making diplomatic concessions. As a result, the government can more credibly claim that its hands are tied at the bargaining table.

Nationalist protests are most effective at inducing foreign concessions where the specter of instability is a shared risk, where foreign governments prefer the incumbent autocrat to the chaos or unknown outcome of a political transition. This holds regardless of the underlying distribution of public preferences. Even if foreign observers believe that regime change could bring a friendlier government to power, the risk of a failed state—particularly one with nuclear arms or other weapons of mass destruction—may be prohibitively high. Even the potential disruption of trade, investment, and supply of natural resources may be sufficient incentive to maintain stability.

Because autocracies are not equally capable of anticipating and responding to popular mobilization, we should also expect variation in the information revealed by nationalist protests and their foreign policy consequences. Where the government is relatively weak, the signal sent by protests is less clear, because observers cannot detect whether the protest occurred without the government's knowledge. When protests occur in weak autocracies, however, foreigners are more likely to believe that the government has no choice but to placate demonstrators with a tough diplomatic stance, so the commitment effect is stronger.

The 1991 Gulf War is a case in point. While street protests restricted which Arab governments joined the American-led coalition to drive Saddam's forces out of Kuwait, such as Jordan, Yemen, and Algeria,[142] other Arab states, such as Egypt, joined the American-led coalition and did not face popular resistance to the war until it after it began.[143] A number of Arab governments—Egypt, Saudi Arabia, Syria, Bahrain, Oman, Qatar, and the United Arab Emirates—were willing to join the coalition to push Saddam Hussein out of Kuwait. But as public support for Iraq began to materialize on the "Arab street," these governments drew the line at supporting Saddam's ouster. As Marc Lynch notes:

> Arab public opinion. . . . serves as a real constraint on Arab cooperation in schemes for the violent removal of Saddam Hussein. . . . Though these leaders allegedly want Saddam gone, they see public support for his removal as a threshold likely to trigger the street and therefore forego this policy. Regardless of the reality of such a threshold, it becomes politically real when Arab leaders adjust their behavior based on their anticipation of such a reaction.[144]

Another coalition member, Morocco, retracted its support after the regime proved too weak to prevent opposition parties from organizing a nationwide general strike. A month after the Fez riots, the king allowed a pro-Iraq, anti–United States rally, estimated at 300,000 participants to have been the largest protest in Morocco to date. Afterward, the *New York Times* reported that "The Moroccan Government has made the region's biggest shift on the war. After Iraq invaded Kuwait Aug. 2, King Hassan II of Morocco sent 1,500 troops to Saudi Arabia to show his solidarity with the rich gulf monarchies and the West. But the King changed after Morocco's opposition called for a troop withdrawal and after pro-Iraq demonstrators rallied in many cities."[145]

Just as importantly, U.S. leaders *believed* that the Arab coalition members were constrained at home and would not support Saddam's removal. In his memoir, President George H. W. Bush writes: "Trying to eliminate Saddam, extending the ground war into an occupation of Iraq, would have violated our guideline about not changing objectives in midstream. . . . The coalition would have instantly collapsed, the Arabs deserting it in anger and other allies pulling out as well."[146] Whether or not the Arab street actually would have erupted, the conviction that it would was instrumental in shaping the consensus to end the war without toppling Saddam.

As these anecdotes suggest, the logic of nationalist protest as part of a two-level game is not unique to the Chinese case. There appear to be parallel dynamics at work in other autocracies, ranging from Vietnam to Egypt to Jordan. Given the risks that antiforeign protests pose to regime stability, authoritarian governments often choose to prevent them. But when authoritarian governments allow such protests, or when they are unable or unwilling to stop them, their foreign policy must accommodate popular demands or else face popular wrath. When tolerated, antiforeign protests can strengthen the government's bargaining position by signaling resolve. Either way, such protests—unless seen as rent-a-mobs—demonstrate reduced room for maneuver at the international level.

Although the focus here has been on autocracies, antiforeign protests may also help democratic states achieve a more favorable outcome in diplomatic negotiations. The mechanism is different, however. Because the cost of repressing protest is much higher in democracies than in autocracies, democratic leaders cannot choose which protests to allow and which to prevent, undermining the role of protests as a signal of the government's willingness to go to the brink. In this regard, democracies are like weak autocracies. Hawkish protests affect diplomatic negotiations not by signaling resolve but by communicating information about the electorate's preferences and tying the government's hands. The degree to which democratic protests lock in a hawkish diplomatic stance depends upon factors such as the democratic incumbent's vulnerability to electoral challenge and whether protesters are partisans of the ruling or opposition party. These and other factors will affect whether antiforeign protests are more powerful diplomatic instruments for democracies or autocracies in international negotiations, a question that merits further investigation. However, if both types of regimes can utilize public opinion to reveal information and communicate credibly, other factors must account for the observation that democracies tend to settle disputes without the use of force. Moreover, a common critique of audience costs is that decision-makers may prioritize the need to maintain flexibility over the desire to tie their own hands in international disputes.[147] The strategic logic of nationalist protest recognizes that when decision-makers seek to preserve room for maneuver and compromise, they are more likely to repress nationalist protests.

From Tactical Asset to Strategic Liability?

It may be cynical to conclude that Chinese and other authoritarian governments are strategic about tolerating and repressing antiforeign protests. But this logic also illuminates why and when Chinese leaders will resist domestic demands to take a tougher stance, despite the domestic costs of defying nationalist pressure. Each time that nationalist, antiforeign demonstrations have erupted, as after the accidental U.S. bombing of the Chinese embassy in 1999 and Japan's purchase of uninhabited islands in the East China Sea in 2012, scholars and commentators have debated the role of domestic grievances and elite machinations in fomenting nationalist protests. Yet focusing only on cases where nationalist protests have erupted tends to bias our conclusions about the impact of public opinion on Chinese foreign policy. Rather than select on the dependent variable, it is critical to look at the full range of how the Chinese government has responded to nationalist sentiment and managed antiforeign demonstrations, including repression as well as acceptance. More often than not, the Chinese government has circumscribed the influence of popular opinion by restraining and even preventing public displays of nationalist anger.

One might ask why authoritarian governments preoccupied with maintaining "stability above all else" would choose to tolerate nationalist protests, if doing so increases the risk that demonstrations will trigger wider instability. Given the costs of suppression, tolerating protests may represent a risky but beneficial gamble, and even a united leadership may rationally choose to allow protests. By taking a tough line on foreign policy, authoritarian governments can address popular demands and strengthen their patriotic credentials.[148] At the same time, when their diplomatic objectives have counseled prudence and restraint, authoritarian governments have often sheathed this "double-edged sword," restraining nationalist protests despite the costs of appearing unpatriotic and repressive.

Yet government efforts to manage nationalist sentiment may also become a liability over time. Not only might the selective, Machiavellian tolerance of nationalist protest disillusion domestic liberals and nationalists alike, but heavy-handed tactics to mitigate risk may also harden foreign perceptions, requiring larger and more widespread protests to combat accusations that China has "cried wolf" about the pressures of popular nationalism. Nevertheless, the real specter of extreme nationalism and instability is a shared risk that outside actors have an incentive to mitigate—perhaps by offering a hand to help the Chinese government climb down from the tiger it is riding. As such, foreign governments may benefit by tempering their demands. As Henry Kissinger notes: "A prudent American leadership should balance the risks of stoking Chinese nationalism against the gains from short-term pressures."[149]

Whether foreign leaders will be able to resist their own domestic pressures is another matter. Particularly if Chinese protests fuel anti-China sentiment, stiffening foreign resolve, the immediate benefits of nationalist protest may be negated by second-order consequences. As in the classic security dilemma, actions that the government takes to strengthen its position may trigger a foreign response that leaves the government no better off than before. Protesters in Vietnam and the Philippines have already sought to push back against Chinese actions in the South China Sea, prompting some Chinese scholars to remark that anti-China nationalism is also a "double-edged sword" for Vietnam and the Philippines.[150]

But China also risks underestimating the domestic constraints imposed by rising anti-China sentiment. In 2011, Xinhua blamed anti-China protests in Manila on a handful of "pro-American" organizations that had obtained U.S. assistance.[151] Xinhua similarly dismissed anti-China protests in Vietnam as easily quashed, writing: "The Vietnamese government claimed the coordinated protests had been spontaneous, though this is highly unlikely in tightly controlled Vietnam; in fact, Hanoi had taken a leaf out of China's playbook and used the demonstrations to register its indignation with Beijing."[152]

Despite temptations to downplay the domestic constraints facing its counterparts, Beijing would be wise to look for opportunities to demonstrate restraint as well as resolve. If China's leadership wants to prevent a counterbalancing coalition of states from forming against China's rise, it will need to temper demonstrations of resolve with credible reassurances. A prudent Chinese leadership should also balance the long-term risks of stoking Chinese nationalism against the short-term gains of diplomatic pressure.

APPENDIX

Table A.1 **Antiforeign mobilization in China, 1985–2012**

Month	Year	Activity	Type
September–November	1985	Protests in Beijing, Xi'an, Wuhan, Chengdu against Japanese Prime Minister Nakasone's visit to Yasukuni Shrine and Japan's "economic invasion" of China	Protest
December	1985	*Official campus commemorations held in lieu of anti-Japanese protests in Beijing on December 9, 1935, anniversary*	Protest
December	1988	Anti-African riots in Nanjing against foreign "privileges" and alleged fraternization with Chinese women	Protest
November	1990	*Protests prevented over Japanese plans to recognize Diaoyu/Senkaku island lighthouse as official navigation mark*	Protest
October	1992	*Protests banned during Japanese emperor Akihito's visit; activists sent from Beijing or placed under house arrest[1]*	Protest
September	1993	*Anti-U.S. protests prevented after Beijing lost bid for 2000 Olympic Games[2]*	Protest
March	1994	*Protest in Beijing broken up and activists detained in Beijing and Shanghai during Japanese prime minister Hosokawa's visit[3]*	Protest

Note: Italics indicate activities that were prevented or swiftly repressed.

(Continued)

Table A.1 **Continued**

Month	*Year*	*Activity*	*Type*
June	*1995*	*Protests against Taiwan independence and President Lee Teng-hui's visit to the United States prevented*	*Protest*
August	*1995*	*Anti-Japanese activist Tong Zeng barred from international conference in Beijing; police broke up foreign press conference, denied activists permission to testify in Tokyo trial on comfort women*[4]	*Protest*
September	*1995*	*Tong Zeng sent out of Beijing for anniversary of September 18, 1931*[5]	*Protest*
September	*1996*	*Anti-Japanese protests in Beijing and Shanghai repressed during second lighthouse controversy; activists sent away from Beijing for anniversary of September 18, 1931*[6]	*Protest*
		China Federation for Defending the Diaoyu Islands established; open letter circulated; 3,500 signatures for Bao Diao cause collected in Shenzhen	Petition
		Hong Kong Bao Diao activist David Chan drowned trying to swim ashore	Hong Kong Voyage
October	1996	Successful landing by Bao Diao activists from Hong Kong, Macau, and Taiwan.[7]	Hong Kong Voyage
		Nearly 100 activists gathered in Shenzhen to support the Bao Diao cause[8]	Protest
May	1997	Hong Kong Bao Diao activists intercepted by Japanese patrols near the islands[9]	Hong Kong Voyage
September	1997	Small anti-Japanese demonstration in Harbin during Prime Minister Hashimoto's visit to Beijing, demanding formal apology and compensation for Japanese Unit 731 germ warfare experiments[10]	Protest

Table A.1 **Continued**

Month	Year	Activity	Type
December	*1997*	*Demonstration in Nanjing by Hong Kong activists prevented on sixtieth anniversary of Nanjing massacre*[11]	*Protest*
May	1998	Police rejected student application to protest violence against ethnic Chinese in Indonesia; one hundred students successfully demonstrated in front of Indonesian embassy but later required to write self-criticisms[12]	Protest
June	1998	Hong Kong Bao Diao voyage included one mainland participant for the first time; protest boat severely damaged in standoff with Japanese authorities[13]	Hong Kong Voyage
May	1999	Anti-U.S. and anti-NATO protests in Beijing, Shanghai, Chengdu, Guangzhou, Xian, Hangzhou, Shenyang, Guilin, et al. after NATO bombing of Chinese embassy in Belgrade	Protest
March	*2000*	*Police rejected applications to protest Taiwan independence and Chen Shui-bian's victory in Beijing and Shanghai, broke up demonstrations in Chongqing and Wuhan*	*Protest*
April	*2001*	*Anti-U.S. protests prevented after EP-3 collision; Internet forums censored*	*Protest*
August	2001	Small protests in Beijing and Nanjing and larger protests in Shenzhen against Japanese prime minister Koizumi's visit to Yasukuni Shrine[14]	Protest
January	2003	Small demonstration at Marco Polo Bridge near Beijing to protest Japan's leasing of Diaoyu/Senkaku Islands[15]	Protest
March	*2003*	*Authorities restricted anti-U.S. protests over Iraq war*[16]	*Protest*
June	2003	First Bao Diao voyage from mainland China turned back by Japanese patrols[17]	Mainland Voyage

(Continued)

Table A.1 **Continued**

Month	Year	Activity	Type
July	2003	Internet signature campaign opposing Japan's railway construction bid collected more than 80,000 signatures in 10 days	Petition
August– September	2003	Internet petition demanding compensation from Japan for chemical weapons victims; police rejected applications to hold anti-Japanese demonstrations in Beijing and Shanghai but allowed several activists to deliver the collected signatures[18]	Protest; Petition
October	2003	Second mainland Bao Diao voyage intercepted by Japanese patrol vessels[19]	Mainland Voyage
		Small demonstration in Beijing over Japanese interception of Chinese protest boat[20]	Protest
November	2003	Anti-Japanese riot in Xi'an over ribald skit performed by three Japanese students	Protest
November	2003	Internet signature campaign by 10 nationalist websites opposing Taiwan independence, including Patriots Alliance Network, China 9.18 Patriot Net, et al.[21]	Petition
December	2003	Small gatherings in Beijing and Shenyang to commemorate Nanjing Massacre[22]	Protest
January	2004	Mainland Bao Diao boat intercepted by Japanese patrols	Mainland Voyage
		Small demonstrations in Beijing and Shanghai against Japanese prime minister Koizumi's visit to Yasukuni[23]	Protest
March	*2004*	*University students instructed not to protest if Chen Shui-bian re-elected; police prevented street petition campaign opposing Taiwan independence in Hefei*	*Protest*
		"Taiwan, my brother" online petition launched	Petition

Table A.1 **Continued**

Month	Year	Activity	Type
March	2004	Landing of seven mainland Chinese activists on the Diaoyu/Senkaku Islands	Mainland Voyage
		Small protests in Shenyang, Shanghai, Guangzhou, and Beijing to demand Japan release of detained activists[24]	Protest
April	2004	Small demonstrations in Beijing, Shanghai, Chongqing, and Guangzhou to protest attack by right-wing Japanese activist on Chinese consulate in Osaka[25]	Protest
July	2004	Small anti-Japanese demonstrations in Beijing outside the Japanese embassy and Marco Polo Bridge to celebrate landing of Chinese activists, commemorate war anniversary, and protest Japanese exploration in the East China Sea	Protest
July	*2004*	*Mainland Chinese activists prevented from setting sail for the Diaoyu/Senkaku Islands by Chinese authorities*	*Mainland Voyage*
August	2004	Anti-Japanese soccer riot following Japanese win at Asia Cup final in Beijing	Protest
August	2004	Small anti-Japanese demonstration at Marco Polo Bridge to commemorate anniversary of Japan's surrender in World War II	Protest
August	*2004*	*Second Internet signature campaign opposing Japan's railway construction bid shut down by authorities after 22 hours, having gathered almost 70,000 signatures*	*Petition*
September	2004	Small demonstration at the Japanese embassy to protest Japan's bid for a permanent UN Security Council seat and commemorate the anniversary of September 18[26]	Protest
December	2004	Small demonstration at the Japanese embassy to protest Japan's decision to grant a visa to former Taiwan president Lee Teng-hui[27]	Protest

(Continued)

Table A.1 **Continued**

Month	Year	Activity	Type
February	2005	Small demonstration outside Japanese embassy and consulates to protest Japanese government recognition and control of Diaoyu/Senkaku lighthouse[28]	Protest
March	2005	Internet petition and street signature campaigns against Japan's UNSC bid in Shenyang, Changchun, Guangzhou, Shenzhen, et al.	Protest; Petition
April	2005	Protests against Japan's UNSC bid in Beijing, Shanghai, Chengdu, Guangzhou, Xian, Shenzhen, Shenyang, et al.	Protest
May	*2005*	*Protests against Japan's UNSC bid prevented in Shenzhen, Beijing, Zhuhai, Shanghai, et al.*	*Protest*
July	2005	Small demonstration at the Japanese consulate in Guangzhou against attack on Chinese consulate in Osaka[29]	Protest
August	*2005*	*Anti-Japanese protests prevented on the anniversary of Japan's surrender in World War II[30]*	*Protest*
October	2005	Small demonstration at the Japanese embassy to protest Prime Minister Koizumi's visit to Yasukuni Shrine[31]	Protest
June	2005	Taiwan legislators aboard a military frigate protested Japan's harassment of Taiwan fishing boats near the Diaoyu/Senkaku Islands[32]	Taiwan Voyage
December	2005	Gatherings and vigils to commemorate the Nanjing Massacre in Nanjing, Chengdu, Xi'an, Wuhan, Changsha, et al.	Protest
June	*2006*	*Authorities shut down petition to establish "Diaoyudao Day"[33]*	*Petition*
July	2006	Gathering of anti-Japanese activists at Marco Polo Bridge outside Beijing to commemorate anniversary of July 7, 1937[34]	Protest

Table A.1 **Continued**

Month	Year	Activity	Type
August	2006	Small demonstrations outside Japanese embassy in Beijing and Japanese consulate in Chongqing to protest Prime Minister Koizumi's visit to Yasukuni Shrine;[35] hundreds of taxi drivers demonstrated outside Japanese consulate in Shenyang after altercation between taxi driver and Japanese passenger[36]	Protest
		Patriots Alliance Network BBS closed for "maintenance" on eve of anniversary of Japan's surrender in World War II; activists urged not to organize large demonstrations; authorities ban protests in Shenzhen and Guangzhou[37]	
September	2006	Small demonstration urging boycott of Japanese goods outside Ito Yokado department store in Chengdu on anniversary of September 18[38]	Protest
October	2006	*Beijing activist Feng Jinhua confined at home during Prime Minister Shinzo Abe's visit; topic of Abe's visit censored on Patriots Alliance Network BBS*[39]	Protest
May	2007	Small demonstration outside Japanese embassy to protest Japanese court ruling against five compensation claims for forced labor during World War II[40]	Protest
June	2007	Small demonstration outside Japanese embassy to demand release of Chinese citizen Xue Yi, detained by Japanese authorities for throwing a bottle at former Taiwan president Lee Teng-hui at Narita Airport[41]	Protest
July	2007	Small gathering of Changsha activists to commemorate seventieth anniversary of Marco Polo incident on July 7[42]	Protest
September	2007	Small demonstration and street petition to boycott Japanese goods outside Ito Yokado department store in Chengdu;[43] large demonstration in Changsha to commemorate September 18 and protest opening of Heiwado department store[44]	Protest

(Continued)

Table A.1 **Continued**

Month	Year	Activity	Type
October	2007	Small gathering of anti-Japanese activists in Zhejiang Province to commemorate National Day[45]	Protest
December	2007	Gatherings to commemorate the seventieth anniversary of Nanjing Massacre in Chongqing, Nanjing, Hunan, et al.[46]	Protest
March-April	2008	Anti-CNN.com website launched; online signature campaigns against Tibetan "splittism," Western media bias, and to support Olympic torch relay; street protests in several cities against France and Carrefour	Petition; Protest
May	*2008*	*Authorities broke up anti-Carrefour protests over May 1 holiday*	*Protest*
June	2008	Small demonstration in Beijing over Japanese detention of Taiwan fishing boat captain after collision near disputed islands[47]	Protest
		Taiwan Bao Diao activists sailed around islands, escorted by Taiwan Coast Guard vessels[48]	Taiwan Voyage
December	2008	Internet petition to boycott French goods after President Nicolas Sarkozy met with the Dalai Lama, gathering 70,000 signatures in two days[49]	Petition
February	2009	Internet petition against South Korea UNESCO application	Petition
February	2009	Internet petition to boycott Christie's auction of Yuanmingyuan relics	Petition
May	*2009*	*Hong Kong Marine Department prevented Bao Diao activists from setting sail for Diaoyu/Senkaku Islands*[50]	*Hong Kong Voyage*
January	2010	Internet petition against U.S. arms sales to Taiwan gathered 40,000 signatures in two days[4]	Petition

Table A.1 **Continued**

Month	Year	Activity	Type
September	2010	Small anti-Japanese demonstrations in Beijing, Tianjin, Shanghai, Shenyang, Chongqing, Shenzhen, Changsha, et al. to protest detention of Chinese trawler captain and to commemorate September 18 anniversary; *large-scale protests prevented*	Protest
		Bao Diao activists not allowed to set sail from Xiamen[51]	*Mainland Voyage*
		Hong Kong Bao Diao activists not allowed to set sail[52]	*Hong Kong Voyage*
		Taiwan Bao Diao vessel escorted near islands by Taiwan Coast Guard with activists from Taiwan, Hong Kong and Macau onboard[53]	Taiwan Voyage
October	2010	Larger anti-Japanese demonstrations in second- and third-tier cities	Protest
June	2011	First voyage of World Chinese Bao Diao Alliance from Taiwan intercepted by Japanese patrols[54]	Taiwan Voyage
July	2011	Authorities prevented internet petition opposing Guidelines to Implement the Declaration of Conduct in the South China Sea[55]	Petition
September	*2011*	*Authorities prevented September 18 commemorations Shenyang; activist detained*[56]	*Protest*
January	*2012*	*Hong Kong authorities stopped Bao Diao activists (including four mainland citizens) from sailing for the islands*[57]	*Hong Kong Voyage*
May	2012	Internet petition condemning Philippine actions around Scarborough Shoal[58]	Petition
		Small protests outside Philippine embassy in Beijing before police intervened[59]	Protest
June	2012	Bao Diao boat from Taiwan sailed around Diaoyu/Senkaku islands with Taiwan Coast Guard escort; activists threw PRC flag onto one of the islands[60]	Taiwan Voyage

(Continued)

Table A.1 **Continued**

Month	Year	Activity	Type
July	2012	Small demonstration to commemorate seventy-fifth anniversary of Marco Polo Bridge Incident under tight surveillance[61]	Protest
August	2012	Anti-Japanese protests in Beijing, Shanghai, Ningbo, Qingdao, Jinan, Hangzhou, Chengdu, Wenzhou, Xi'an, Shenzhen, et al. to condemn Japanese plans to nationalize islands and landing of Japanese activists[62]	Protest
		Successful landing by Bao Diao activists sailing from Hong Kong, including one mainland citizen	Hong Kong Voyage
September	2012	Anti-Japanese protests in nearly 200 cities culminated on September 18 anniversary; *further anti-Japanese protests curtailed*	Protest

Note: This list excludes official assemblies or indoor gatherings that did not seek to attract public attention, such as this official commemoration of the September 18 anniversary ("我国各地举行活动纪念九一八事变76周年," Xinhua, September 18, 2007, http://news.sina.com.cn/c/2007-09-18/223213919345.shtml) or this January 30, 2000, gathering of scholars at the official memorial hall next to the Marco Polo Bridge site: "首都抗日战争史专家集会," 人民日报, January 31, 2000, accessed at http://www.people.com.cn/item/njdts/24/13101.html. Missing events may have occurred but were not reported by activists or the media, or not found by the author.

NOTES

Chapter 1

1. *Cankao Xiaoxi,* June 30, 1987, cited in Whiting 1989, 164.
2. Willy Lam, "China Bans Antiwar Protests," CNN.com, March 12, 2003; "Antiwar Demonstrations Approved by Beijing Police," Wen Wei Po, March 29, 2003.
3. Katherine Zepf, "Syrian Government Mobilizes a Vast Rally to Support Assad," *New York Times,* October 25, 2005.
4. Iranian Students News Agency, *FBIS* IAP20050928011044, September 28, 2005.
5. By implication, nationalist protests will not be effective at eliciting international concessions when foreigners actively seek to destabilize the regime.
6. Banks 2010.
7. Although the theory expects patriotic, antiforeign protests to be more costly to repress than pro-democratic protests.
8. Pickering and Kisangani 2010.
9. Zhao 2004, 44–46.
10. Spence 1999, 310; Mitter 2004.
11. Harris 1991.
12. Callahan 2010, 16.
13. Liao 1990, 142.
14. In doing so, the PRC followed the precedent set by Chiang Kai-shek. See He 2009, 152.
15. Reilly 2006, 192.
16. Haas 1986, 727–28.
17. On different strands of Chinese nationalism, see Oksenberg 1986; Zhao 1998; Fewsmith 2001; Callahan 2010.
18. Regarding antiforeign protests in the 1950s, for example, Masuda notes that "all these campaigns resulted from officially designed, top-down programs that were often coercive and brutal." Masuda 2012, 23. On antiforeign protests during the Cultural Revolution, see Liao 1976.
19. There may also be cases in which an official rally is substituted for protest in an attempt to appease citizens. If opposition groups succeed in taking over the rally, then the rally has marginally decreased the costs of collective action against the government. But this presumes a failure of state capacity to control even its own activities, which is a special circumstance and not the general case.

Chapter 2

1. FTS19961005000057, Hong Kong *Ming Pao*, October 5, 1996.
2. Interview with anti-Japanese activist and website manager, no. 81, Shanghai, China, April 16, 2007.
3. This chapter develops in greater detail the ideas presented in Weiss 2013.
4. Weeks 2008; Weeks 2012.
5. Putnam 1988.
6. Shirk 1993; Roeder 1993; Bueno de Mesquita et al. 1999.
7. Mayhew 1974.
8. An exception may be "tin-pot" or "bandit" leaders, whose strategy is to steal resources, flee the country, and enjoy the illicit gains during retirement.
9. See Geddes 1991, 374.
10. Goemans 2000b.
11. Acemoglu and Robinson 2006.
12. Schelling 1960.
13. Fearon 1995.
14. Powell 1990; Schelling 1960; Fearon 1997.
15. E.g., Martin 1993; Fearon 1994a; Smith 1998; Schultz 2001a; Baum 2004; Leventoglu and Tarar 2005.
16. E.g., Schultz 2001b; Smith 1998; Sartori 2002; Slantchev 2006; Snyder and Borghard 2011; Downes and Sechser 2012; Debs and Weiss forthcoming.
17. Fearon 1994a.
18. Smith 1998, 623.
19. Schultz 1999, 237.
20. Guisinger and Smith 2002.
21. Tomz 2007. More recent survey experiments have found that audience costs are sensitive to both new information and partisan affiliations. See Trager and Vavreck 2011; Levendusky and Horowitz 2012.
22. Snyder and Borghard 2011; Debs and Weiss forthcoming.
23. Leeds 1999; Partell and Palmer 1999; Eyerman and Hart 1996; Mansfield et al. 2002; Lohmann 2003; Pevehouse 2002.
24. Fearon 1994a; Schultz 2001a.
25. Weeks 2008.
26. The original use of this phrase referred to the risk of nuclear war. Schelling 1960.
27. The risk that nationalist protests destabilize the regime depends on many factors, including the level of societal discontent, intra-elite fissures, and organization among opposition groups.
28. Schelling 1978; Kuran 1991; Lohmann 1994; Laitin 1998.
29. Tarrow 1998.
30. O'Donnell and Schmitter 1986.
31. Pool 1973.
32. Snyder 1991; van Evera 1994.
33. Breuilly 1994, 19.
34. Haas 1986, 727–28.
35. Snyder 1993, 16; see also Shirk 2007, 256.
36. Goemans et al. 2009.
37. On protests and authoritarian turnover, see Wallace 2013.
38. Telhami 2002, 73.
39. I thus assume that the "mobilization" effect of protest dominates the "venting" effect, particularly during the initial "rapid diffusion" phase of the protest cycle (Tarrow 1998, 141). That is, the government cannot wait out the protests and assume that crowds will disperse or fizzle out in the absence of satisfaction or suppression.
40. Insincere protests, if recognized as such by foreign observers, are less likely to induce foreign concessions, as I explain further below.
41. Johnston and Stockmann 2007, 194. On the concession-repression dilemma more generally, see Cai 2008.

42. "Vietnam Hands Lengthy Jail Sentences to Two Patriotic, Anti-Chinese Activists," *South China Morning Post*, May 16, 2013.
43. Tarrow 1998, 84.
44. Jane Cai, "Crackdown Infuriates Dog Owners," *South China Morning Post*, November 12, 2006.
45. Schelling 1966, 94.
46. Schelling 1960, 1966.
47. Schelling 1960; Powell 1990; Fearon 1992.
48. Willingness to take risks is only one method of demonstrating resolve. See Morrow 1989, 942.
49. Schelling 1966, 94.
50. Domestic costs make these signals of reassurance credible. Other costly signals of reassurance include measures that leave one side vulnerable to defection and benefit the other side. See Kydd 2005, 187.
51. Interview with senior expert at the Chinese Academy of Social Sciences, no. 34, Beijing, China, July 18, 2006.
52. Interview with best-selling nationalist author, no. 42, Beijing, China, July 26, 2006.
53. As a *Global Times* op-ed lamented: "In present-day China, where public opinion is increasingly powerful in influencing national decision-making, short-term interests become more prominent, especially when dealing with foreign policy. . . . strategies need patience, which the public often lacks. Ordinary people attach more attention to instant results." "China's Strategy Requires More Public Patience," May 31, 2013.
54. It is important to be clear that the terms "dovish" and "hawkish" are used in a particular sense that differs slightly from its causal usage. Here, "hawkish" denotes a hard-line position in reference to a particular dyadic negotiation. For instance, if State B is trying to convince State A to join a coalition to fight a war against State C, the theory predicts that State A should only allow protests against joining the coalition, as this represents the "hard-line" view in the negotiation between State A and State B. These protests are in fact against the war, and so in some sense are dovish and pro-foreign, where "foreign" indicates State C. In the context of the primary negotiations, however, such protests are opposed to cooperation with State B, and would therefore be considered "hawkish" or "hard-line."
55. Lynch 2006, 95, 114.
56. On private versus public rhetoric, see Sartori 2002; Baum 2004; Leventoglu and Tarar 2005; and Kurizaki 2007. At a higher level of escalation, economic sanctions and military mobilization are alternative methods of signaling resolve, e.g., Slantchev 2005.
57. On selection effects and crises, see Fearon 1994b.
58. Lynch 2006, 112.
59. If the government disperses protests after placating demonstrators with a tough foreign policy stance and/or foreign concessions, the costs of curtailment are reduced. In such cases, curtailment does not demonstrate that the government's prior claims were bluffs.
60. Perry 2002, xiv.
61. Gries 2004, 131.
62. Ijiri 1990; Reilly 2012; Fewsmith and Rosen 2001.
63. Rubin 2002.
64. Chang 2006; see also Waldron 1999; He 2007b; Coser 1956; Mueller 1973.
65. See Gourevitch 1978. On the importance of the international environment in circumscribing the influence of domestic politics in Chinese foreign policy, see Ross 1986.
66. See, for example, He 2009, 46.
67. Waltz 1979.
68. Putnam 1988.
69. A slew of recent work has suggested that attempts to systematically test models of strategic interaction will inevitably run into problems of selection effects. Selection effects arise when the process of selection into the sample is nonrandom. Schultz (1999) demonstrates that if a leader is able to generate very high audience costs, then the other side is likely to back down

and the leader will not be punished. Alternatively, if the other side does *not* back down (perhaps having generated its own audience costs), then escalation is more likely and we will still not observe audience costs. See Smith 1996; Fearon 1994a, 2002; Morrow 1989b; Signorino 1999.

70. Telhami 2002, 72–74; see also Brand 1991.
71. Shirk 2007; Gries 2004; Ross 2011.
72. Christensen et al. 2006, 405.
73. Wu 2007b, 185.
74. See, e.g., Zheng 1999; Zhao 2004.
75. He 2009, 32–33.
76. Fewsmith and Rosen 2001, 174.
77. Reilly 2012.
78. As Susan Shirk notes: "Large protests increase the risk of a split by showing leaders that a following is already in place,. . . The danger is not a matter of the particular personalities in the Party oligarchy at any one time, but is built into the structure of communist systems" (2007, 48).
79. "China's True Colors," May 11, 1999.
80. Shen 2004.
81. See, for example, Goemans 2000a; Peceny et al. 2002; Horowitz et al. 2005; Weeks 2008, 2012.
82. Fearon 1994a; Schultz 2001; Goemans 2000a.
83. Snyder and Borghard 2011; see also Snyder and Diesing 1977, 215.

Chapter 3

1. Associated Press, September 5, 2012.
2. Qian 2005, 322; Zhang 2009, 27.
3. Xinhua News Agency, May 8, 1999; *Renmin Wang*, "Waijiaobu Fayanren Zhu Bangzao Tan Meiguo Junyong Zhenchaji Zhuanghui Zhongguo Junyong Feiji Shijian Zhenxiang He Zhongfang Youguan Lichang" [Foreign Ministry spokesman speaks the truth relating to the US military reconnaissance plane collision with the Chinese fighter jet and China's position], April 3, 2001.
4. According to the U.S. side, the EP-3 was flying over international waters.
5. Wang 2002, 6, who nonetheless notes that "the initial threat [was] limited, but if poorly controlled [could] escalate to threats of war and even the outbreak of war." See also Ding 2004, 55.
6. Wilkenfeld 2006, 111.
7. Wang and Xu 2006, 137.
8. To the extent that decision-makers see subsequent situations as similar. See Mercer 1996; Jervis 1976.
9. Jiang 2006, vol. 2, 321.
10. Tang 2010, 42.
11. Tang 2011, 328.
12. Victor Mair, "How a Misunderstanding about Chinese Characters Has Led Many Astray," http://www.pinyin.info/chinese/crisis.html.
13. Ibid.; see also Swaine and Zhang 2006, 2–3.
14. Xia 2006, 63, quoting *Current International Crisis* (Academy of Military Science Publishing House, China, 1988), 258.
15. Xia 2006, 63.
16. George 1991, 23.
17. Qian 2005, 322.
18. Indeed, effective threats require a modicum of reassurance that the threat will not be carried out if the opponent complies. If foreign actors believe that they will be punished or the crisis will escalate regardless of their actions, they have little incentive to cooperate or offer concessions.

19. "Zhide fansi de biaojue" [A vote deserving reflection], *Renmin Ribao*, March 30, 1999.
20. Swaine and Zhang 2006, 7, 26.
21. Swaine and Zhang 2006, 29.
22. Wang 2002, 14.
23. ***Anti-U.S. protests under Mao targeted U.S. involvement in the Korean War (1950–51), the U.S.-Japan Security Treaty (1960), U.S. activities in Taiwan, Cuba, and Vietnam (1960–62), and the United States and other foreign targets during the height of the Cultural Revolution, including the Soviet Union, India, Indonesia, Burma, and Japan (1967–69). See Liao 1990, 138.
24. Although we cannot rule out unobserved mobilization, protest attempts that are not reported by international sources or uncovered in domestic sources are likely to have had little to negligible diplomatic impact.
25. "Zhonghua Renmin Gongheguo Waijiaobu Guanyu 'Yinhe hao' Shijian de Shengming," *Renmin Ribao*, September 5, 1993. Protesters demonstrated outside the U.S. consulate in Hong Kong. "Group in Freighter Protest," *South China Morning Post*, September 12, 1993, accessed at http://www.scmp.com/article/43782/group-freighter-protest.
26. Fewsmith 2001, 106–7.
27. H.Res 188, "To express the sense of the House of Representatives that the Olympics in the year 2000 should not be held in Beijing or elsewhere in the People's Republic in China," accessed at http://thomas.loc.gov/cgi-bin/query/z?c103:H.RES.188.
28. Patrick E. Tyler, "Olympics; There's No Joy in Beijing as Sydney Gets Olympics," *New York Times*, September 24, 1993.
29. Wasserstrom 1999, 67.
30. Liao Ya-meng, "Antiwar Demonstrations Approved by Beijing Police, to Take Place 30 Mar," *Wen Wei Po*, March 29, 2003, translated by FBIS; Willy Wo-Lap Lam, "Beijing Curbs Anti-war Protests," CNN.com, March 20, 2003; Lam 2006, 214–15.
31. E.g., Gries 2004; Shirk 2007; Zhao 2003; Wu 2006a; Wilkenfeld 2006; Campbell and Weitz 2006; Blair and Bonfili 2006; Zhang 2006; Swaine and Zhang 2006; Wu 2008b.
32. According to various accounts, permission was granted by the Public Security Bureau and university authorities. See Zhao 2003, 15; Wu 2006a, 362; Wong and Zheng 2000, 333.
33. "Chinese Vice-Foreign Minister Lodges Strongest Protest," *Beijing Zhoubao* [Beijing review], May 24, 1999, 13.
34. Suettinger 2003, 370.
35. "PRC Issues 'Text' of Statement on Embassy Bombing," FBIS translation, FTS19990508000044, May 8, 1999.
36. Joint Statement by Secretary of Defense William S. Cohen and CIA Director George J. Tenet, available at https://www.cia.gov/news-information/press-releases-statements/press-release-archive-1999/pr050899.html.
37. "Letter to Minister of Foreign Affairs of the People's Republic of China," available at http://secretary.state.gov/www/statements/1999/990508.html.
38. Suettinger 2003, 372.
39. Full text available at http://www.pbs.org/newshour/bb/europe/jan-june99/china_statement_5-9.html; see also "Hu Jintao fabiao zhongyao dianshi jianghua" [Hu Jintao gives important speech on television], *Wen Hui Bao*, May 10, 1999.
40. According to Tang Jiaxuan, a decision in favor of "postponing or canceling exchanges and dialogues with the United States" was made at the May 8 meeting of the Central Authorities. Tang 2011, 216.
41. *South China Morning Post*, May 12, 1999.
42. Associated Press, May 10, 1999.
43. Associated Press, May 10, 1999.
44. *Renmin Ribao*, May 11, 1999.
45. Xinhua News Service, May 11, 1999, quoted in Zhao 2004b, 81; see also "New WTO Hopes Despite Crisis," *Hong Kong Standard*, May 12, 1999.

46. "Students Turn Indignation into Motivation," Xinhua Domestic Service in Chinese, FBIS, FTS19990512000854, May 11, 1999.

47. *South China Morning Post,* May 12, 1999.

48. Associated Press, May 11, 1999.

49. Associated Press, May 11, 1999.

50. "Chinese and U.S. Presidents Held Phone Conference," PRC Ministry of Foreign Affairs, http://test.fmprc.gov.cn/eng/wjdt/2649/t15797.htm.

51. "U.S. President's Personal Envoy in China to Present the U.S. Government's Report on Its Investigation into the Bombing of the Chinese Embassy in the Federal Republic of Yugoslavia—the Chinese Government Emphasizes that the U.S. Side Must Give Satisfactory Account and Explanation of the Incident," Ministry of Foreign Affairs of the People's Republic of China, June 16, 1999, available at http://www.international.ucla.edu/eas/NewsFile/bombing05-99/9906-cmfa1.htm.

52. Edward Chen and Mark Magnier, "U.S.-China Relations 'Back on Track' after Clinton, Jiang Mend Fences," *Los Angeles Times,* September 12, 1999.

53. Campbell and Weitz 2006, 342.

54. Sang Ye, "Zayiza Meishiguan You Shenme Liaobuqi?" *Mingpao Monthly,* August 1999, 46.

55. Perry 2001, 170.

56. Tong 2002b.

57. Jiang 2006, vol. 2, 319–20.

58. One government-affiliated think tank came to this conclusion in its report. See Wang 2012, 174.

59. See, e.g., Nicholas Kristof, "Is There a Reformer In China's Future?" *New York Times,* June 17, 1990; "Yao Minzhu, Zhao Ziyang!" [If you want democracy, find Zhao Ziyang], May 20, 2009, accessed at http://kristof.blogs.nytimes.com/2009/05/20/yao-minzhu-zhao-ziyang/.

60. Zong Hairen, "The Bombing of China's Embassy in Yugoslavia," *Zhu Rongji in 1999,* translated in *Chinese Law and Government* 35 (1) (January–February 2002): 79.

61. Perry 2002, xiv.

62. Gries 2004, 131.

63. Wang and Xu 2006, 145.

64. *Nanfang Zhoumo,* May 11, 1999, quoted in Shirk 2007, 218.

65. "Behind the Bombing of the Chinese Embassy," *Beijing Review,* May 24, 1999, 5.

66. Wang 2012, 175.

67. Sang Ye, "Zayiza Meishiguan You Shenme Liaobuqi?" *Mingpao Monthly,* August 1999, 47.

68. Ruan 2004, 16.

69. Zhao 2003, 14; see also *Washington Post,* May 10, 1999.

70. Zhao 2003, 9.

71. Jiang 2006, vol. 2, 322.

72. Jiang 2006, vol. 2, 322.

73. Wu 2005a, 4; and Wu 2006a, 362.

74. Wu 2005a, 4; and Wu 2006a, 362.

75. Yu and Zhao 2006, 1772.

76. Zhao 2003, 16.

77. Tang 2011, 214–15.

78. Tang 2011, 207.

79. Li 2008, 652–53.

80. Eric Schmitt, "Leading Senators Demand U.S. Limit Help for Beijing," *New York Times,* March 16, 1999.

81. Pearson 2001, 35.

82. According to Barshefsky, their intent was "to arrest any Chinese backsliding, but also not to do an agreement under the press of a deadline because of the visit." Hearings before the Senate Committee on Finance, "China's Application for Accession to the World Trade Organization," April 13, 1999, 27.

83. Joseph Fewsmith, "China and the WTO: The Politics behind the Agreement," NBR Analysis, November 1999; Zong Hairen, "Visit to the United States," *Zhu Rongji in 1999*, translated in *Chinese Law and Government* 35 (1) (January–February 2002): 36–52.
84. Xiong 2006, 397–406.
85. Many Chinese analysts suspected that the Pentagon and CIA had sought to punish China for providing Milosevic with intelligence and logistical support. A government-affiliated analyst at the time recalled that "several people doubted that the Clinton administration would be part of the conspiracy, [but] the majority of researchers agreed that the bombing was an intentional action approved by top US leaders." Wang 2012, 174.
86. Jiang 2006, vol. 2, 321–23.
87. "The Bombing of China's Embassy in Yugoslavia," in Zong 2002, translated in *Chinese Law and Government* 35 (1) (January–February 2002): 76–89.
88. Ibid., 77.
89. Ibid., 76–77, 81.
90. Ibid., 80. Zong suggests that Zhu Rongji was unfairly constrained by Jiang's bidding, preventing him from postponing his Washington visit and from taking a stronger public stance after the Embassy bombing. See "Bombing of China's Embassy in Yugoslavia," 98.
91. Tang 2011, 237–38.
92. Xiao 2001.
93. Nathan 2002, 12.
94. Jiang 2006, vol. 2, 323.
95. Wu 2006a, 363.
96. "Chinese in Belgrade, Beijing Protest NATO Embassy bombing," CNN, May 9, 1999, transcript available at http://www.cnn.com/WORLD/asiapcf/9905/09/china.protest.03/.
97. Interview with senior U.S. diplomat, no. 131, Washington, D.C., March 11, 2009.
98. Interview with a former National Security Council official, no. 109, Ann Arbor, Mich., November 19, 2007.
99. Tang 2011, 215.
100. Li 2008, 654.
101. Joint Statement by Secretary of Defense William S. Cohen and CIA Director George J. Tenet, available at https://www.cia.gov/news-information/press-releases-statements/press-release-archive-1999/pr050899.html.
102. "Remarks on Departure from Tinker Air Force Base, Oklahoma," available at http://frwebgate1.access.gpo.gov/cgi-bin/waisgate.cgi?WAISdocID=623040148392+6+0+0&WAISaction=retrieve.
103. Yan 2000, 42.
104. Xiong 2006, 399.
105. Wu 2008a, 12–13.
106. Wu 2008a, 12–13.
107. Fong 2007.
108. Interview with male protest participant and class leader, no. 47, Beijing, China, January 26, 2007. See also Zhao 2003, 16.
109. http://www.pbs.org/newshour/bb/europe/jan-june99/intelligence_5-10.html.
110. Ibid.
111. Campbell and Weitz 2006, 337.
112. Campbell and Weitz 2006, 335–36.
113. Campbell and Weitz 2006, 335–37.
114. Stanley Roth, Testimony before the Senate Committee on Foreign Relations Subcommittee on East Asian and Pacific Affairs, May 27, 1999, available at http://www.usembassy-china.org.cn/press/release/1999/roth.html.
115. Tang 2011, 229.
116. Tang 2011, 229.
117. Wu 2008a, 12.

118. Sang Ye, "Zayiza Meishiguan You Shenme Liaobuqi" [What's the big deal about destroying the US embassy], *Mingpao Monthly*, August 1999, 48.
119. Wu 2005a.
120. Jiang 2006, vol. 2, 324.
121. Tang 2011, 229.
122. Wu Xinbo notes that "the Chinese leadership, while turning on a green light for public demonstrations, did not fully anticipate the scale and intensity of the protests, so the safety measures taken to protect U.S. diplomatic facilities were inadequate. Although the Chinese government rushed to redress the situation on the second day of the protests by calling for restraint and strengthening security measures around NATO missions, there was a real danger that demonstrations might get out of control." See Wu 2008a, 14.
123. Li 208, 653.
124. Jiang 2006, vol. 2, 324–26.
125. Jiang 2006, vol. 2, 324–25.
126. Available at http://www.pbs.org/newshour/bb/europe/jan-june99/china_statement_5-9.html.
127. Suettinger 2003, 372.
128. "Press Briefing by Joe Lockhart," May 10, 1999, 3:43 p.m. EDT, accessed at http://www.presidency.ucsb.edu/ws/index.php?pid=47736; Associated Press, May 10, 1999.
129. Associated Press, May 11, 1999.
130. Accessed at http://www.pbs.org/newshour/bb/europe/jan-june99/bombing_5-10.html.
131. Associated Press, May 10, 1999.
132. Brian Knowlton, "Hit on Chinese Embassy Laid to Bad Intelligence: NATO 'Regrets' Accident but Presses Air Campaign," *International Herald Tribune*, May 10, 1999.
133. "China's True Colors," *Washington Post*, May 11, 1999, A20.
134. PBS NewsHour Transcript, May 10, 1999, accessed at http://www.pbs.org/newshour/bb/europe/jan-june99/li_5-10.html.
135. Quoted in Tang 2011, 230.
136. Jiang 2006, vol. 2, 327.
137. Tang 2011, 236.
138. Sang Ye, "Zayiza Meishiguan You Shenme Liaobuqi" [What's the big deal About destroying the US embassy], *Mingpao Monthly*, August 1999, 49.
139. Interview with Chinese Academy of Social Sciences senior analyst, no. 99, June 25, 2007, Beijing, China.
140. Zhao 2003, 24–25.
141. Agence France-Presse, May 12, 1999.
142. E. J. Dionne Jr., "China Pall; a Revealing Reaction to Embassy Bombing," *Washington Post*, May 14, 1999.
143. Suettinger 2003, 380. For an expert critique, see "The Cox Committee Report: An Assessment," available at http://iis-db.stanford.edu/pubs/10331/cox.pdf.
144. Robert A. Manning, "The Makings of a Cold War," *Japan Times*, June 13, 1999.
145. John Pomfret, "The Reaction in Beijing; China Says Bombing Halt Is Condition of U.N. Settlement," *Washington Post*, May 11, 1999.
146. Brian Knowlton, "Hit on Chinese Embassy Laid to Bad Intelligence: NATO 'Regrets' Accident but Presses Air Campaign," *International Herald Tribune*, May 10, 1999.
147. Associated Press, May 10, 1999.
148. Wu 2006a, 357.
149. Li 2008, 655.
150. Xiao Gongqin, "Zhongguo Zhece Touqipiao Shi Gaozhao" [China's abstention was a wise move], *Lianhe Zaobao*, June 15, 1999. According to Xiao, since Russia had led the resolution negotiations and had urged China not to veto the resolution, casting a solo veto would have implied that China was ignoring the larger situation to retaliate against Macedonia. Following

Macedonia's decision to recognize Taiwan, China had vetoed a February resolution to extend a peacekeeping mission in Macedonia.

151. Michel Oksenberg, "Reviving the Grand Bargain," *Newsweek*, June 14, 1999.

152. Hsueh 2011, 73.

153. As released by USTR website on April 8: "Under present circumstances, China allows no foreign investment in telecommunications services. With this agreement, China will allow 49% foreign investment in all services, and will allow 51% foreign ownership for value added and paging services in 4 years." U.S. Trade Representative, "Market Access and Protocol Commitments" (released April 8, 1999), accessed at https://www.uschina.org/public/wto/ch-memo.html.Lardy 2002, 67–68; see also U.S. General Accounting Office, "World Trade Organization: Status of China's Trade Commitments to the United States and Other Members," May 2000, appendix 1, table 6: China's Service Sector Commitments in November 1999 U.S.-China Bilateral Agreement, 25.

154. Shirk 2007, 46.

155. Joseph Fewsmith, "China and the WTO: The Politics behind the Agreement," NBR Analysis, November 1999, 3.

156. Suettinger 2003, 367.

157. Interview with Barshefsky, February 23, 2009, Washington, D.C.

158. Interview with Barshefsky, February 23, 2009, Washington, D.C.

159. Pearson 2001, 367.

160. Zong Hairen, "Visit to the United States," *Zhu Rongji in 1999*, translated in *Chinese Law and Government* 35 (1) (January–February 2002): 46–47.

161. Hearings before the Senate Committee on Finance, "China's Application for Accession to the World Trade Organization," April 13, 1999, 5.

162. Senator Chafee (Rhode Island) noted: "You read the various statements that the Chinese leaders were angry after the summit. That is not good news. They certainly gave a lot.... There are some concerns here that the Chinese might back off. You [Barshefsky] have said here, 'the U.S. does not give up anything in this.' Well, I suppose the Chinese follow that, the Chinese public." Senator Murkowsi said: "The Chinese side could see this... going back with the Premier having nothing tangible, taking a hard line and saying, all right, they did not take it. We are concerned about the imagine [*sic*] in China." Hearings before the Senate Committee on Finance, April 13, 1999, 4, 22, 26.

163. Jiang 2010, vol. 2, 317.

164. "Stand Toughens on US Demands after NATO Missile Strike Destroys Belgrade Embassy; Beijing Rejects WTO Wish List," *South China Morning Post*, May 10, 1999.

165. "China Seeks U.S. Concessions: Beijing Says Washington Must Act to Bring Relations Back on Track after Embassy Attack," *Financial Times*, May 12, 1999.

166. Willy Wo-Lap Lam, "Politburo Says Crisis Must Not Be Allowed to Damage Trade Ties," *South China Morning Post*, May 11, 1999.

167. Associated Press, May 11, 1999.

168. Knight Ridder, May 12, 1999; "WTO Ru Hui Tanpan, Zhong Gong Zhuan Qiangying, Mei Jinggao Wu Cun Feifen Zhi Xiang" [On entering WTO negotiations, China becomes tougher, United States warns that China should not have presumptuous thoughts], *Zhongguo Shibao*, May 13, 1999.

169. "U.S. Expects Talks Soon with China; WTO Accession; Timing of Negotiations Dependent on Diplomatic Maneuvers after Embassy Bombing," *Financial Times*, May 20, 1999; see also Agence France-Presse, May 20, 1999.

170. Stanley Roth, Testimony before the Senate Committee on Foreign Relations Subcommittee on East Asian and Pacific Affairs, May 27, 1999, available at http://www.usembassy-china.org.cn/press/release/1999/roth.html.

171. Interview with Wu Baiyi, senior analyst and institute director at the Chinese Academy of Social Sciences, June 26, 2007, Beijing, China.

172. Wu 2006a, 368.

173. Guy de Jonquières, "China to Shun Further Trade Talks with U.S.: Beijing Takes Harder Line," *Financial Times*, May 27, 1999.

174. *Dagongbao*, May 27, 1999, quoted in Fewsmith, "China and the WTO: The Politics behind the Agreement," NBR Analysis, November 1999, 10.

175. Pearson 2001, 366.

176. Joseph Fewsmith, "China and the WTO: The Politics behind the Agreement," NBR Analysis, November 1999, 35.

177. Zhu 2011, 357–58.

178. Interview with Barshefsky, February 23, 2009, Washington, D.C.

179. Shirk 2007, 230–31.

180. Interview with Barshefsky, February 23, 2009, Washington, D.C.

181. PBS NewsHour transcript, May 10, 1999, accessed at http://www.pbs.org/newshour/bb/europe/jan-june99/intelligence_5-10.html.

182. Blair and Bonfili 2006, 380.

183. Keefe 2001, 6.

184. Keefe 2001, 5.

185. "Xinhua Cites PRC FM Spokesman's Remarks on Military Aircraft Incident," Xinhua Domestic Service in Chinese, FBIS, CPP20010401000069, April 1, 2001.

186. United States Pacific Command, Transcript, Camp H. M. Smith, April 1, 2001, available at http://www.pacom.mil/speeches/sst2001/010401blairplane.htm.

187. Agence France-Presse, April 2, 2001.

188. Zhang 2006, 396.

189. "President Bush on March 31 U.S.-China Aircraft Accident," Office of International Information Programs, U.S. Department of State, accessed at http://usinfo.org/wf-archive/2001/010402/epf104.htm.

190. Wu 2007a, 326.

191. "Statement by the President," Office of the Press Secretary, April 3, 2001, available at http://www.whitehouse.gov/news/releases/2001/04/20010403-3.html; Kan et al. 2001, 3.

192. U.S. Department of State, "Briefing for the Press Aboard Aircraft En Route to Andrews Air Force Base," April 3, 2001, available at http://www.state.gov/secretary/former/powell/remarks/2001/1932.htm.

193. Tang Jiaxuan, "Huiyi 2001 nian Zhong Mei Nan Hai 'zhuang ji shi jian'" [Remembering the 2001 South China Sea US-China plane collision], *Wanxia*, 2010, no. 6.

194. Elisabeth Rosenthal, *New York Times*, April 5, 2001.

195. U.S. Department of State, "Remarks Following Meeting with King Abdullah of Jordan," April 4, 2001, available at http://www.state.gov/secretary/former/powell/remarks/2001/2006.htm.

196. Keefe 2001, 7.

197. "U.S. Secures Fourth Visit with Spy Plane Crew," CNN, April 9, 2001, quoting an interview by *Fox News Sunday*.

198. Dali L. Yang, "Economic Liberalization and Its Political Discontents," *Asian Survey* 42 (1) (January–February 2002): 21. See also Tong 2002a.

199. Xiao Xingguo, "2001 nian Beijingshi Chaoyangqu Xingshi Anjian Fenxi" [Analysis of Beijing City Chaoyang District criminal cases], *Gongan Yanjiu*, 2002, no. 6, 21, 25.

200. Tanner 2005. Although the term "mass incident" has not been clearly defined and the numbers are not considered particularly reliable (including the absence of data for 2001), the reported trend appears to reflect at least the government's belief in rising unrest. See also Tanner 2004; Roland Soong, "Statistics of Mass Incidents," November 15, 2006, accessed at http://www.zonaeuropa.com/20061115_1.htm.

201. "Zhongguo Wangmin Nu Hou Hu Zhengfu Kou Ji Liu Ren" [Chinese Internet users are angry and call on the government to detain the plane and crew], *Lianhe Zaobao*, April 3, 2001.

202. Zhang 2006, 393; Wang and Xu 2006, 143, 145.

203. Johnston and Stockmann 2007, 163, 166.
204. Tang 2010, 43.
205. For details of China-U.S. cyberattacks after the EP-3 incident, see Wu 2007b.
206. Interview with journalist at China Radio International, no. 30, June 3, 2006, Beijing.
207. "Jiu Meiguo zhenchaji zhuanghui Zhongguo junyong feiji shijian: Waijiaobu fayan ren fabiao tanhua," *Renmin Ribao*, April 2, 2001, 4.
208. Zhang 2006, 396–97.
209. John Pomfret, "New Nationalism Drives Beijing; Hard Line Reflects Public Mood," *Washington Post*, April 4, 2001.
210. *Renmin Ribao*, April 4, 2001, 4.
211. Gonganju 2002, 18.
212. Zhu Jianling, "Zhuangji Shijian Jiang Chi Bu Xia, Dalu Fan Mei Qingxu Shenggao, Zhonggong Jinzhi Youxing" [Deadlock in collision incident, anti-US sentiment rises, CCP prohibits marches], *Zhongguo Shibao*, April 5, 2001.
213. Tang 2010, 42.
214. Wu 2007a, 324.
215. Agence France-Presse, March 23, 2001.
216. Liu Jianfei, "Create Conditions for the Development of Sino-US relations," *Liaowang*, FBIS, CPP20010402000107, April 2, 2001. Ironically, Liu's article was published the day after the plane collision, in a weekly magazine that presumably went to press before the incident occurred.
217. Interview with a senior analyst at the Shanghai Institute of International Studies, no. 71, April 10, 2007, Shanghai, China.
218. Shirk 2007, 236.
219. Interview with an assistant professor at the Institute of American Studies, China Institutes of Contemporary International Relations, who was a PhD candidate in Beijing at the time, no. 93, May 24, 2007, Beijing.
220. Quoted in Shirk 2007, 236.
221. Mulvenon 2002, 4.
222. Wu 2008a, 21.
223. Wu 2006a, 364.
224. Interview with a senior analyst at the Shanghai Institute of International Studies, no. 71, April 10, 2007, Shanghai; interview with a senior analyst at the Chinese Academy of Social Sciences, no. 99, June 25, 2007, Beijing.
225. As Tang Jiaxuan noted: "Although it may seem like an accidental (*oufa*) incident, it was actually inevitable. . . . From the second half of 2000, U.S. military reconnaissance activities had become more frequent and increasingly close to our territorial waters." Tang 2010, 41.
226. Wu 2008a, 16.
227. Agence France-Presse, April 2, 2001.
228. "Statement by the President," Office of the Press Secretary, April 3, 2001, available at http://www.whitehouse.gov/news/releases/2001/04/20010403-3.html.
229. H.R. 1467, http://thomas.loc.gov/cgi-bin/query/z?c107:H.R.1467.IH:.
230. Zhang 2006, 401.
231. Xia 2006, 168.
232. Li 2005, 12–13.
233. Li 2005, 12.
234. Tang Jiaxuan, "Huiyi 2001 nian Zhong Mei Nan Hai 'zhuang ji shi jian'" [Remembering the 2001 South China Sea US-China plane collision], *Wanxia*, 2010, no. 6, 43, 45.
235. Wu 2008a, 21.
236. Wu 2007a, 326.
237. Wu 2007a, 334.
238. Tang 2011, 343.
239. Keefe 2001, 9, 11.

240. Keefe 2001, 6.
241. U.S. Department of State, "Interview of the Deputy Secretary of State on China, The News Hour with Jim Lehrer," April 13, 2001, available at http://www.state.gov/s/d/former/armitage/remarks/2001/2297.htm.
242. "Zhongguo Jujue Rang Mei Zhenchaji Cong Hainan Fei Hui Guo, Baigong Ze Xiwang Kandao Zhenchaji Fei Huiqu" [China refuses to let the US reconnaissance plane fly back to the United States, while the United States hopes to see the plane fly back], Lianhe Zaobao, May 9, 2001; Ding Xiaowen, "Zhongmei chuli liangguo waijiao weiji de tedian bijiao" [Comparing the characteristics of US-China diplomatic crisis management], Guoji Wenti Yanjiu, 2004, no. 6, 57.
243. Wu 2007a, 333.
244. Zhang 2006, 407; Kan et al. 2001, 7.
245. Kan et al. 2001, 3; Yee 2004, 65. The demand that the United States halt its surveillance flights was first made public on April 3 by Jiang Zemin and reiterated by Tang Jiaxuan to Ambassador Prueher on April 4 as one of China's four demands. "Jiang Zemin: Mei Ying Tingzhi Zai Zhongguo Yanhai Kong Yu Zhencha Feixing" [Jiang Zemin: The United States should stop reconnaissance flights in the airspace along China's coast], Lianhe Zaobao, April 3, 2001; Tang 2011, 334, 337.
246. Wu 2007a, 334.
247. Wu 2008a, 21.
248. The White House, Office of the Press Secretary, "Remarks by the President at American Society of Newspaper Editors Annual Convention," April 5, 2001, available at http://www.whitehouse.gov/news/releases/2001/04/20010405-5.html.
249. Willy Lam, "China Gains Leverage in U.S. Spy Plane Incident," CNN, April 6, 2001.
250. New York Times, April 7, 2001. Except for the phrase, "excuse me," Jiang's statement was in Chinese.
251. New York Times, April 7, 2001.
252. "Protesters Taken Away in Front of US Embassy in Beijing," Agence France-Presse, April 5, 2001, and Willy Lam, "China Gains Leverage in U.S. Spy Plane Incident," CNN, April 6, 2001; "Qianglie qianze Meizhenchaji zhuanghui wo junyong feiji qinfan wo zhuquan," Renmin Ribao, April 5, 2001, 4.
253. Blair and Bonfili 2006, 382.
254. Blair and Bonfili 2006, 382.
255. Keefe 2001, 10.
256. China Daily, April 16, 2001, accessed at http://www.china.org.cn/english/11181.htm.
257. Yang Dong, "Zhou Wenzhong: 40 nian waijiao chuanqi" [Zhou Wenzhong: 40-year diplomatic legend], Zhizheng Xinrui 11 (312) (2010).
258. Tang Jiaxuan, "Huiyi 2001 nian Zhong Mei Nan Hai 'zhuang ji shi jian'" [Remembering the 2001 South China Sea US-China plane collision], Wanxia, 2010, no. 6, 43, 44.
259. As Keefe noted: "The question in our mind was whether this pressure was real or induced. After all, Chinese state-controlled media was instrumental in misrepresenting facts and whipping up popular sentiment about the incident in the first place." Keefe 2001, 10.
260. Rice 2011, 46–47.
261. The term refers to the group of foreign policy advisors that George W. Bush picked during his presidential campaign, including Paul Wolfowitz, Condoleezza Rice, and Richard Armitage, in addition to Dick Cheney and Donald Rumseld.
262. Interview, no. 134, Washington, D.C., March 12, 2009.
263. Dana Milbank and Dan Balz, "Behind Scenes, Bush Played Vigorous Role," Washington Post, April 12, 2001, A1, quoted in Yee 2004, 59.
264. Yee 2004, 59.
265. Dana Milbank and Dan Balz, "Behind Scenes, Bush Played Vigorous Role," Washington Post, April 12, 2001, A1, quoted in Yee 2004, 59.
266. Zhang 2006.

267. See, for example, Larry Wortzel, "How to Respond to China's Coercive Behavior," Heritage Foundation, April 18, 2001, accessed at http://www.heritage.org/research/reports/2001/04/how-to-respond-to-chinas-coercive-behavior.

268. Robert Kagan and William Kristol, *Weekly Standard*, April 16, 2001.

269. Gries 2001.

270. Wasserstrom 1999.

271. As James Woolsey notes, "he weakened the position of those in China who would like to work with us." PBS NewsHour transcript, May 10, 1999, accessed at http://www.pbs.org/newshour/bb/europe/jan-june99/intelligence_5-10.html.

272. As Fewsmith notes, "with the U.S. bombing of the Chinese embassy in Belgrade, these voices became both strident and difficult to ignore. Jiang was, in the immediate aftermath of the embassy bombing, in a very difficult situation." Fewsmith 1999, 35; see also Shirk 2007.

273. Douglas Paal, PBS NewsHour transcript, May 10, 1999, accessed at http://www.pbs.org/newshour/bb/europe/jan-june99/intelligence_5-10.html.

274. Nathan and Gilley 2002, 170.

275. Mulvenon 2002.

276. Zheng 2000, 15.

277. Zhao 2003; interview with a researcher at the Chinese Academy of Social Sciences, a Party member and then-graduate student at People's University, no. 37, Beijing, China, July 19, 2006.

Chapter 4

1. Whiting 1989, 6.

2. Whiting 1989, 51, 195.

3. Barmé 2005, citing Liu Xinwu, *Wuyijiu Changjingtou* [Long camera lens on May 19] (1985).

4. Xu 2002, 118 n. 13.

5. Cherrington 1991, 73.

6. Chuan 1990, 101.

7. Quoted in "Ding Shisun's Reforms Began in Beijing University's Cafeterias," transcript of CCTV interview on *Da Jia*, March 24, 2006, available at http://news.sina.com.cn/c/2006-03-24/12419434078.shtml, last accessed April 14, 2007.

8. The following account draws primarily upon the following sources: Xu 2002; Chuan 1990; Whiting 1989; and Fang 2002.

9. In 1978, China adopted a new constitution that guaranteed the "four great freedoms," namely the right to speak out freely, air one's views fully, write big-character posters, and hold great debates. The new constitution presaged a brief period of political liberalization that resulted in the "Democracy Wall" movement, which the government suppressed in 1979. In 1980, the "four great freedoms" were repealed.

10. Chuan 1990, 104.

11. Chuan 1990, 105.

12. Chuan 1990, 107.

13. Chuan 1990, 110.

14. John Burns, *New York Times*, September 18, 1985; Xu 2002, 119.

15. Yang 2008.

16. Fang 2002, 29–30.

17. John Burns, *New York Times*, November 21, 1985; Whiting 1989, 7.

18. *Renmin Ribao*, September 20, 1985.

19. Whiting 1989, 69.

20. British Broadcasting Corporation, October 4, 1985; Kyodo News Agency, October 30, 1985.

21. Whiting 1989, 70.

22. Schell 1988, 130.
23. Daniel Southerland, "China Cracks Down on Students Posters Criticizing Japan, Calling for Freedoms Removed from University," *Washington Post*, October 10, 1985.
24. Kyodo News Agency, October 30, 1985.
25. Cai 2008, 413.
26. Tian et al. 1997, 233–36.
27. Although the anti-hegemony clause was largely directed against the Soviet Union, some Chinese scholars suggest that it was also meant to restrain Japan and even China. See Zhang 2002, 196.
28. He 2009, 195.
29. Nakanishi 2011, 117; Wan 2006, 95–96; Joint Communiqué of the Government of Japan and the Government of the People's Republic of China, September 29, 1972, available at http://www.mofa.go.jp/region/asia-paci/china/joint72.html.
30. Nakanishi 2011, 117.
31. Chung 2004, 36.
32. "1978 nian, ZhongRi 'Diaoyudao shijian' shimo," *Renmin Wang*, October 13, 2010.
33. Zhang 2000, 175.
34. Cheng 1985, 106.
35. Tretiak 1978, 1242.
36. Zhang 2000, 177.
37. Nakanishi 2011, 130.
38. "Deng fu zongli zai Dongjing jizhe zhaodaihui shang hui jizhe wen," *Renmin Ribao*, October 26, 1978, 5; Lin 1992, 239; Whiting 1989, 69. On the controversy over whether Japan ever agreed to this unofficial consensus, see Reinhardt Drifte, "The Senkaku/Diaoyu Islands Territorial Dispute between Japan and China: Between the Materialization of the 'China Threat' and 'Reversing the Outcome of World War II,'" UNISCI Discussion Paper no. 32 (May 2013), accessed at http://pendientedemigracion.ucm.es/info/unisci/revistas/UNISCIDP32-1DRIFTE.pdf.
39. Togo 2005, 138.
40. Zhao 1993, 165; Whiting 1989, 123.
41. Despite this widespread perception, Yinan He notes that "no official statement was ever made to explicitly link the aid programs to war reparations." He 2009, 196.
42. Nakanishi 2011, 132, 137.
43. Zhao 1993, 169.
44. Kokubun 1986, 20–21.
45. Liu 2007, 52; Johnson 1986, 419; Lee 1984; He 2009, 200.
46. He 2009, 200.
47. Whiting 1989, 123.
48. He 2009, 200; Whiting 1989, 121; Lee 1984, 74.
49. Murata 2011, 149.
50. Reilly 2012, 64; He 2009, 211; Johnson 1986.
51. Whiting 1989, 47; Reilly 2012, 64.
52. Rose 2005, 64; Ijiri 1990, 644.
53. Reuters, August 16, 1982; *New York Times*, September 23, 1982; Leung 2000, 224.
54. Lin 1992, 278.
55. Tian et al. 1997, 199.
56. Reuters, August 24, 1982.
57. Murata 2011, 149.
58. Japan Ministry of Foreign Affairs, Statement by Chief Cabinet Secretary Kiichi Miyazawa on History Textbooks, August 26, 1982, http://www.mofa.go.jp/policy/postwar/state8208.html.
59. Leng and Wang 2004, 856; Whiting 1989, 5.
60. Shin Kawashima, "The East Asian Textbook issue," Jiji Press, May 25, 2012, translated at http://www.nippon.com/en/in-depth/a00702/.
61. Nakanishi 2011, 114.

62. Tretiak 1978, 1244.
63. Murata 2011, 150; see also Kamiya 2002, 61.
64. Dan 1983, 5.
65. Liu 1986, 9.
66. Murata 2011, 150.
67. Particularly with George Shultz replacing Alexander Haig and "praising Japan's importance in Asia, over China." Murata 2011, 153; Rose 1998, 144.
68. "Wu Xueqian Tong Erjiejintang Juxing Huitan" [Wu Xueqian talks with Nakasone], *Renmin Ribao*, February 19, 1983; He 2009, 219. According to Kamiya Matake, Nakasone had "surprised Washington and the Japanese public" by increasing Japan's defense budget in December 1982 despite heated objections from the Ministry of Finance. Kamiya 2002, 70–71.
69. Dan 1982, 13.
70. Thornton 2003, 397.
71. Wu and Chen 2004, 47.
72. Wang and Wu 1998, 21.
73. Zhang 1984, 2; "Two 'Giants' Get Together," *Newsweek*, April 2, 1984, 9, cited in Cheng 1985, 91.
74. Wang and Wu 1998, 21; "Japanese Prime Minister in China," *Beijing Review*, April 2, 1984, cited in Cheng 1985.
75. Li 2008, 89; Cheng 1985, 100–101; Whiting 1989, 101, 121; He 2009, 224.
76. Ijiri 1990, 648.
77. Song 1993, 30.
78. Song 1993, 30.
79. Dan 1982, 12; see also Jia 2003.
80. Wang and Wu 1998, 23.
81. Hamrin 1983, 211.
82. Whiting 1983, 913; Hu Yaobang, "Create a New Situation in All Fields of Socialist Modernization: Report to the Twelfth National Congress of the Communist Party of China (September 1, 1982)," in *The Twelfth National Congress of the CCP* (Beijing: Foreign Languages Press, 1982), 55, cited in Cheng 1985.
83. Oksenberg 1982–83, 193.
84. "China Retracts Support for US-Japan Treaty," *Japan Times*, November 9, 1982, cited in Cheng 1985.
85. Quoted in Cheng 1985, 96.
86. Su 1989, cited in He 2009, 207.
87. Togo June 2006.
88. Rose 2005, 111–12; He 2009, 132.
89. Rose 2005, 111.
90. Shibuichi 2005; see also Hielscher 2004.
91. Xue 1985, 31.
92. Pyle 1998, 81.
93. Ijiri 1990, 649.
94. "Waijiaobu Xinwen Fayanren Shuo, Zhongzenggen Shouxiang Deng Canbai Jingguo Shenshe Hui Sunhai Shijie Geguo Renmin De Ganqing" [Ministry of Foreign Affairs spokesman says Prime Minister Nakasone's visit to Yasukuni will hurt the feelings of people around the world], *Renmin Ribao*, August 15, 1985.
95. Xiong 1989, 23, 26.
96. Whiting 1989, 54.
97. Rose 2005, 113, citing Nakajima 1986, 28.
98. "China Strongly Condemns Nakasone's War Shrine Visit," Associated Press, August 22, 1985.
99. Tian et al. 1997, 550.
100. Tian et al. 1997, 551; "Deng Makes Veiled Criticism of Nakasone," Kyodo News Agency, August 29, 1985.

101. Leng and Wang 2004, 1070–71; "Deng Makes Veiled Criticism of Nakasone," Kyodo News Agency, August 29, 1985.
102. Tian et al. 1997, 556.
103. Rose 1998, 113.
104. "Dongjing de 8.15," *Renmin Ribao*, August 16, 1985.
105. Kyodo News Agency, September 7, 1985.
106. Reilly 2012, 69.
107. "Yi pi fanying kangRi zhanzheng he shijie fanfaxisi zhanzheng de yingpian jin qi nei jiang zai quanguo luxu shangying," *Renmin Ribao*, August 17, 1985; "Balujun zhu Luoyang banshichu jiuzhi piwei jinianguan," *Renmin Ribao*, August 17, 1985.
108. Whiting 1989, 54–55; however, Chinese officials denied that this was intended to stoke anti-Japanese sentiment; see Reilly 2012, 68.
109. "Zhongzenggen ji qi neigeliao zhengshi canbai Jingguoshenshe, Ri zaiyedang he qunzhong tuanti biaoshi qianglie fandui," *Renmin Ribao*, August 16, 1985; "China Criticizes Nakasone's Visit to Shrine," Associated Press, August 17, 1985.
110. Xinhua News Agency, August 20, 1985, translated by BBC Summary of World Broadcasts, August 22, 1985.
111. Kyodo News Agency, August 29, 1985.
112. Reilly 2012, 69.
113. Xinhua, September 3, 1985.
114. Liao 2006, 163.
115. Reilly 2012, 69–70.
116. Although Chinese officials couched their warnings about the revival of Japanese militarism in language that also emphasized the importance of Sino-Japanese friendship, such mixed language is not incompatible with an intention to show resolve and press for concessions. Indeed, such an approach is a basic requirement of successful coercive diplomacy. If punishment is assured regardless of subsequent behavior, the target has little incentive to change course.
117. Whiting and Xin 1990, 117.
118. Reilly 2012, 74–75.
119. Shirk 2007, 163; see also Reilly 2012, 60.
120. Whiting 1989, 79; Zhang 1984, 2.
121. He 2009, 230–31.
122. On the dynamics of logrolling in foreign policy, see Snyder 1991.
123. Clyde Haberman, "Nakasone, Giving In, Will Shun Shrine," *New York Times*, October 9, 1985.
124. Kyodo News Agency, October 9, 1985.
125. Associated Press, October 10, 1985; Japan Economic Journal, October 6–12, 1985.
126. Leng and Wang 2004, 1086–1087.
127. Tian, Ji, and Jiang 1997, 564.
128. "Editorial Condemns Beating, Smashing and Looting," BBC Monitoring Service: Asia-Pacific, October 21, 1985.
129. Kyodo News Agency, October 17, 1985.
130. Kyodo News Agency, October 17, 1985; John Burgess, "War Memories Obstacle for Japan; Chinese, Recalling Occupation, Upset by Nakasone's Visit to Memorial," *Washington Post*, October 27, 1985.
131. Ijiri 1990, 650.
132. Xinhua News Agency in English, October 18, 1985; Zhang and Yang 1993, 463.
133. Kyodo News Agency, October 21, 1985.
134. Kyodo News Agency, November 5, 1985; Hielscher 2004, p. 203.
135. *Renmin Ribao*, November 9, 1985.
136. Nakasone 2006, 96; see also Nakasone 2004, 137.
137. John Burgess, "War Memories Obstacle for Japan; Chinese, Recalling Occupation, Upset by Nakasone's Visit to Memorial," *Washington Post*, October 27, 1985; Ijiri 1990, 650.

138. Wakamiya 1999, 177.
139. Shibuichi 2005, 206, citing *Asahi Shimbun,* August 3, 2001.
140. Central Intelligence Agency, Directorate of Intelligence, "Briefing Materials for the President's Meeting with Prime Minister Nakasone, 2 January 1985," December 1984, 21, Digital National Security Archive, JA01246, available at http://gateway.proquest.com/openurl?url_ver=Z39.88-2004&res_dat=xri:dnsa&rft_dat=xri:dnsa:article:CJA01246.
141. Lee 1984, 119.
142. Kokubun 1986, 30.
143. Leng and Wang 2004, 856.
144. Kawashima Shin, "The East Asian Textbook Issue," *Jiji Press,* May 25, 2012, translated at http://www.nippon.com/en/in-depth/a00702/.
145. Whiting 1989, 7.
146. Japan External Trade Organization (JETRO), *China Newsletter,* 32 (May–June 1981), quoted in Johnson 1986, 420.
147. Ijiri 1990, 660.
148. Whiting 1989, 57. The Chinese side otherwise exercised restraint, instructing the media to avoid the strident rhetoric used in the 1982 textbook controversy and 1985 war anniversary commemorations. According to Japanese officials interviewed by Whiting at the time, Chinese officials asked for Japan's " 'help' with dealing with internal divisions rather than 'making demands.' "
149. *Japan Times,* June 20, 1986, cited in Whiting 1989, 57.
150. "Statement by Chief Cabinet Secretary Masaharu Gotoda on Official Visits to Yasukuni Shrine by the Prime Minister and Other State Ministers on August 15 of this year," August 14, 1986, accessed at http://www.mofa.go.jp/policy/postwar/state8608.html; Clyde Haberman, "For Japan, Even the War Takes a Back Seat to Trade," *New York Times,* August 10, 1986.
151. Whiting 1989, 63.
152. Ijiri 1990, 652.
153. Clyde Haberman, "Japan's Education Chief Gets Lesson in Diplomacy," *New York Times,* September 10, 1986.
154. Whiting 1989, 62; "Hu Yaobang Stresses Importance of Sino-Japanese Ties," Xinhua News Service, September 15, 1986.
155. Leng and Wang 2004, 1135, 1141.
156. *Renmin Ribao,* October 27, 1985.
157. Schell 1988, 132.
158. Quoted in Whiting 1989, 73.
159. Whiting 1989, 74.
160. John Burns, *New York Times,* November 21, 1985; Kyodo News Agency, November 21, 1985.
161. See "New Minister Discusses Security Problems," *Beijing Review* 28 (52) (December 30, 1985): 15.
162. "Government Arrests Student Demonstrators," Confidential Cable, 27939, November 25, 1985, Digital National Security Archive, CH00755, available at http://gateway.proquest.com/openurl?url_ver=Z39.88-2004&res_dat=xri:dnsa&rft_dat=xri:dnsa:article:CCH00755, last accessed July 3, 2008.
163. Daniel Southerland, "Chinese Official Warns Students; Protesters Cautioned against Following 'Capitalist Road,' " *Washington Post,* December 9, 1985; see also Wiedemann 1986.
164. Jasper Becker, "Peking Alert for Student Protest," *Guardian,* December 6, 1985.
165. Jim Mann, "Student Protest Movement Spreads in China," *Los Angeles Times,* December 18, 1985.
166. Reuters, December 20, 1985.
167. Cherrington 1991, 84–85.
168. Reuters, December 20, 1985; Xu 2002, 120–21.
169. Schell 1988, 213.
170. Pepper 1987, 11.

171. Schell 1988, 241; Kwong 1988, 972 n. 8.
172. Kwong 1988, 970.
173. Wasserstrom 1991, 297.
174. Kelly 1987, 133.
175. Xu 2002, 124.
176. This was the third anti-bourgeois liberalism campaign since the end of the Cultural Revolution. The first took place in 1980–81; the second, termed an "anti-spiritual pollution" campaign, occurred in 1983. See Zhao 2004, 211.
177. Schell 1988, 269; see also Leng and Wang 2004, 1160–61.
178. Deng 2008, 198.
179. Deng 2008, 198.
180. Kyodo News Agency, January 14, 1987.
181. Kyodo News Agency, January 14, 1987.
182. Leng and Wang 2004, 1192; see also *Asahi Shimbun*, June 5, 1987, cited in Ijiri 1990, 642.
183. Translated in Whiting 1989, 164. Deng's remarks appeared in Chinese in *Cankao Xiaoxi* on June 30, 1987.
184. He 2009, 231.
185. Wan 2006, 107; Whiting 1989, 124.
186. Kokubun 2007, 153.
187. Kamiya 2002, 67–69.
188. Whiting 1989, 150. To the extent that conservative elements spurred the anti-Japanese protests in 1985 to undermine Hu Yaobang, they may have miscalculated in that anti-Japanese mobilization gave impetus and opportunity to pro-democratic stirrings among students and other participants.
189. Wan 2006, 107.
190. Kokubun and Liu 2004, 53.

Chapter 5

1. Quoted in Zhao 2004, 274.
2. Wan 2006, 128.
3. Chung 2004, 42–43.
4. "Senkaku Islands: A Sporting Effort," *Economist*, October 27, 1990.
5. Nicholas Kristof, "To Quiet Its Own Critics, China Aims at Japan," *New York Times*, November 21, 1990.
6. Downs and Saunders 1998, 131–32.
7. Lo Ping, "Bowing to Japanese Yen Has Angered the Masses," *Cheng Ming*, November 1, 1990, 6–7, quoted in Downs and Saunders 1998, 131.
8. Cui and Liu 2007, 2.
9. "Li Peng on Domestic and World Issues," *Beijing Review* 32 (49) (December 4–10, 1989): 12–14, cited in Zhao 1993, 177.
10. Murata 2006, 38.
11. Yokoi 1996, 145.
12. Kawashima 2003, 99.
13. Quoted in Tanaka 2007, 45.
14. Tanaka 2007, 45.
15. Lü 2009, 35.
16. Sarotte 2012, 177.
17. Mann 1999, 204–7.
18. Nicholas Kristof, "Strained U.S. Ties Reported in China," *New York Times*, October 5, 1989. See also Kluver 2010, 83.
19. Whiting and Xin 1990, 113.

20. Mann 1999, 223.
21. Lü 2009, 35.
22. Qian 2005, 150.
23. Whiting and Xin 1990, 113.
24. Li 2008, 397.
25. Togo 2008, 190.
26. Qian 2005, 150.
27. BBC Summary of World Broadcasts, "Other Reports on Jiang Zemin Interview; Japan Urged to 'Develop Its Relations with China Independently'—Xinhua News Agency," July 9, 1990; see also Whiting and Xin 1990, 114–15.
28. Wakamiya 1999, 270.
29. Downs and Saunders 1998, 128.
30. "China Demands That Japan Stop Installation of Lighthouse on Diaoyu Islands," Xinhua News Agency (BBC Summary of World Broadcasts), October 19, 1990.
31. Downs and Saunders also suggest that because the yen loans were not finalized until November 3, this delay may have given Japan additional leverage during the lighthouse crisis. Downs and Saunders 1998, 128.
32. Christensen 2011, 227 n. 10; Liu 2010, 398; Wiegand 2009; "Senkaku Islands: A Sporting Effort," *Economist*, October 27, 1990; "Islands of Contention," *Straits Times*, October 27, 1990. The peacekeeping bill failed to pass the Diet, but a revised bill with more restrictive conditions was proposed in September 1991 and ultimately passed. See Hook et al. 2012, 383–84.
33. Kyodo News Agency, October 24,1990; Steven Weisman, "Tempers Cool in Japan-China Island Dispute," *New York Times*, October 31, 1990; "Kaifu Will 'Act Prudently' in Diaoyutai Dispute," Japan News Agency (BBC Summary of World Broadcasts), October 23, 1990.
34. Green 2001, 85.
35. *New York Times*, January 15, 1990, cited in Zhao 1993, 175.
36. Wakamiya 1999, 271.
37. The Law of the People's Republic of China on the Territorial Sea and the Contiguous Zone, available at http://www.fdi.gov.cn/pub/FDI_EN/Laws/GeneralLawsandRegulations/BasicLaws/P020060620318668126917.pdf.
38. "China Shelves Claim over Senkaku Islands for Time Being," Japan Economic Newswire, March 17, 1992.
39. Drifte 2003, 50; Wakamiya 1999, 284.
40. Mineo Nakajima, "'Friendly Diplomacy' Gaffe," *Japan Times*, September 30, 2010, translated from a September 14 column in *Seiron* (*Sankei Shimbun*), accessed at http://www.japantimes.co.jp/text/eo20100930a1.html.
41. Rose 2005, 74.
42. "Ziliao: DuiRi minjian suopei de falv yiju," Zhong Ri Wang, December 11, 2004, accessed at http://www.sjhistory.org/site/newxh/yjzt5-4mb_a20041211533.htm, cited in Cui 2012.
43. "Qian Qichen Backs Demand for War Reparations," Japan Economic Newswire, March 23, 1992.
44. "Jiang Confirms Shelving of Claim over Senkaku Islands," Japan Economic Newswire, April 1, 1992.
45. Wakamiya 1999, 275–76.
46. "Japan-China Disputes Put Emperor's Visit in Doubt; Communist Leader Goes Home with No Commitment," *Nikkei Weekly*, April 18, 1992.
47. "Old Disputes Threaten to Cloud Chinese Leader's Visit; Recent Steps by Beijing Spark Concern in Tokyo," *Nikkei Weekly*, April 11, 1992.
48. "Japanese Emperor to Visit China in October," BBC Summary of World Broadcasts, August 26, 1992.
49. Wakamiya 1999, 270.
50. Murata 2006, 39; see also Wakamiya 1999, 283. When Japan prepared to send peacekeeping troops to Cambodia, Chinese officials refrained from strong objections. Michael Green even

suggests that the Chinese government "applauded" Japan's participation in the Cambodian mission. Green 2001, 89; David E. Sanger, "Japan's Parliament Votes to End Ban on Sending Troops Abroad," *New York Times*, June 16, 1992, A1.

51. Wakamiya 1999, 282.
52. Wakamiya 1999, 281–84.
53. Tanaka 2007, 143.
54. Tanaka 2007, 143.
55. Wakamiya 1999, 278.
56. Willy Lam, "Students Demand Akihito Apology," *South China Morning Post*, September 30, 1992; He 2009, 263–64.
57. S. Y. Yue and Susan Furlong, "Official Rules Out Akihito Apology," *South China Morning Post*, September 19, 1992.
58. Willy Lam, "Students to Mark Japan's Invasion," *South China Morning Post*, September 18, 1992.
59. "Concern at Protest Movement on Japan," *South China Morning Post*, October 9, 1992.
60. "Beijing Tightens Security for Emperor Akihito's Visit," *Ming Pao*, BBC Summary of World Broadcasts, October 23, 1992.
61. "Campaigners Ordered Out as Akihito Visits Peking," Central News Agency (Taiwan), October 23, 1992.
62. Kent Chen, "Activist to Continue Fight for Apology," *South China Morning Post*, November 5, 1992.
63. Kent Chen, "Liberal Parties in Joint Protest," *South China Morning Post*, October 24, 1992; Dennis Engbarth, "2,000 in Hong Kong Protest Emperor's Lack of Apology," Kyodo News Agency; Elaine Chan, "Marchers Call for Apology," *South China Morning Post*, October 26, 1992.
64. David E. Sanger, "Japan's Emperor Tells China Only of His 'Sadness' on War," *New York Times*, October 24, 1992; full text available at http://www.ioc.u-tokyo.ac.jp/~worldjpn/documents/texts/JPCH/19921023.O3J.html.
65. Li 2008, 600.
66. Qian 2005, 152.
67. He 2009, 240; Wakamiya 1999, 179.
68. David E. Sanger, "And Now for Another Japanese History Lesson," *New York Times*, May 8, 1994; Wakamiya 1999, 341.
69. John Kohut, "Beijing Defuses Protest outside Japan embassy," *South China Morning Post*, March 19, 1994.
70. *Ming Pao*, June 5, 1997, A12; "Bao Ge Released, Brother of Other Shanghai Dissidents Penalized," *Ming Pao*, June 5, 1997.
71. "Activist Bids for Vote on War Cash," *South China Morning Post*, March 10, 1993.
72. Goldman 2005, 81–82.
73. Interview with a Shanghai-based lawyer and academic who has worked with the compensation movement since the 1990s, no. 85, Shanghai, China, April 19, 2007.
74. Liu 2005, 36.
75. "Japanese 'Aggression' Victims Demand Compensation; Police 'Barged into' Conference," Kyodo News Agency, August 7, 1995; "Police Arrest War Reparations Activist," Agence France-Presse, August 9, 1995.
76. Zhang Weiguo, "Police Detain Dissident Ding Zilin, Husband; Tong Zeng Told to Leave," *South China Morning Post*, August 24, 1995; Chan Wai-Fong, "War Campaigner Refuses to Leave," *South China Morning Post*, August 26, 1995.
77. Amy Liu, "Police Surveil War-Reparation Activists," *Hong Kong Standard*, August 15, 1995; "4 Groups Mount Protest at H.K. Japanese Consulate," Kyodo News Agency, August 15, 1995.
78. According to Barry Naughton, "beginning around 1993, more than 30 million SOE workers were laid off, 38% of the entire labor force was laid off, and almost 50 million urban workers of all kinds" by the late 1990s. Naughton 2007, 184.
79. Tanner 2005; Chung et al. 2006, 6.

80. Wang 2012, 104–6.
81. Zhao 1998, 218–23.
82. Downs and Saunders 1998, 132.
83. Ya Yi, "Tuijin Zhongguo gongmin quanli yundong" [The movement to promote citizens' rights in China], *Beijing Spring* 57 (February 1998): 66–74, cited in Pei 2000, 29.
84. Naughton 2007, 99.
85. He 2009, 244–45.
86. Zhao 1998, 215.
87. Reilly 2012, 76.
88. By 1992, Deng Xiaoping was already eighty-eight years old. Deng died in 1997.
89. "Concern over Students' anti-Japanese Feelings Provoking Wider Unrest," *Ming Pao*, BBC Summary of World Broadcasts, September 17, 1996.
90. Downs and Saunders 1998, 133.
91. Murata 2006, 40.
92. Iokibe 2011, 185; Urayama 2000, 616.
93. Green 2001, 91.
94. Garrett and Glaser 1997, 385.
95. Wu 2005b, 119; Christensen 1999, 59.
96. Samuels 2007, 68; Liu 2007, 437.
97. Liu 2007, 439.
98. U.S.-Japan Joint Declaration on Security: Alliance for the 21st Century, April 17, 1996, available at http://www.mofa.go.jp/region/n-america/us/security/security.html.
99. Bush 2010, 17–18. Deputy Assistant Secretary of Defense for Asian Affairs Kurt Campbell later noted that "No one at any meeting—and I was in hundreds of meetings with the Japanese—conceptualized that the rationale for the U.S.-Japan revitalization had anything to do with the Taiwan Straits." Suettinger 2003, 269.
100. Christensen 1999, 61–62; Yoshihide 2001, 142–43; Green 2001, 90.
101. Liu 2007, 440.
102. Garrett and Glaser 1997, 387–88.
103. Tanaka 2007, 196–97; Garrett and Glaser 1997, 387–88.
104. Downs and Saunders 1998, 133.
105. Japanese officials protested in 1992 that the Chinese acquisition of a Ukrainian aircraft carrier would destabilize the region, and the lack of transparency in China's military modernization was a key item on Prime Minister Hosokawa's agenda during his 1994 visit. See Shambaugh 1996, 95.
106. Green 2001, 87.
107. "Japanese White Paper Names China as Primary Concern," Armed Forces Newswire Service, July 22, 1996.
108. Liu 2007, 218; He 2009.
109. Wakamiya 1999, 9–11; He 2009, 240.
110. Wakamiya 1999, 26.
111. Zhang 2002, 199.
112. "Japanese Maritime Zone to Become Controversial Reality," Agence France-Presse, July 19, 1996.
113. "China Hopes to Solve Senkaku Beacon Problem Calmly," Jiji Press, July 24, 1996; "China against Some Japanese Building Facilities on Diaoyu Islands," Xinhua News Agency, July 18, 1996.
114. "Japan's Claim to Senkaku Islands Triggers Protests," Japan Economic Newswire, July 22, 1996.
115. Sharon Cheung, "Cash Drive to Remove Island Lighthouse," *South China Morning Post*, September 5, 1996.
116. "Spokesman Says Government Will Continue to Consult Japan over Disputed Islands," Central News Agency (Taipei), via BBC Summary of World Broadcasts, July 18, 1996.
117. Daniel Kwan, "Beijing Backing for War Victims Urged," *South China Morning Post*, August 16, 1996.

118. "China's Nuclear Tests," Center for Nonproliferation Studies, Monterey Institute for International Studies, http://cns.miis.edu/archive/country_china/coxrep/testlist.htm; "China Urges Halt to War Shrine Visit by Japanese Premier," Agence France-Presse, September 10, 1996.

119. "Protesters Burn Japanese Imperial Flag as Ikeda Concludes Visit," Agence France-Presse, August 29, 1996.

120. "China Accuses Japan of Provoking Right-Wing Activity," Agence France-Presse, August 29, 1996.

121. "China Steers Sovereignty Row with Japan Away from Economic Ties," Agence France-Presse, September 3, 1996.

122. "Beijing Treads Warily on Islands Issue," *South China Morning Post*, September 7, 1996.

123. "China-Japan Island Row Flares after Fresh Landing," Agence France-Presse, September 10, 1996; "Japan Says Nationalists Legally on Disputed Islands," Agence France-Presse, September 10, 1996.

124. "Circulars Urge Moderate Steps during Protest," *South China Morning Post*, September 12, 1996.

125. Emily Ginsburg, "Students Warned to 'Cool' Their Outrage," *Hong Kong Standard*, September 16, 1996; "Diaoyu Protests Spread to Beijing University," *South China Morning Post*, September 14, 1996; "China Says Activist Studying, Not Banished," Associated Press, September 17, 1996; "Students' Protest Activities over Disputed Islands Die Down," *Ming Pao*, BBC Summary of World Broadcasts, September 19, 1996.

126. Maryloise Chan, "Jiang Issues Campus Gag Order," *Hong Kong Standard*, September 17, 1996.

127. Rodger Lee, "Online Site Shut Down by China College," *South China Morning Post*, September 18, 1996.

128. "Tong Zeng, Core Member of the Campaign to Defend the Diaoyu Islands, Ordered to Leave Beijing," Hong Kong *Ming Pao*, FTS19960913000031, September 13, 1996; "Campaigner against Japan Made to Leave Beijing Again," Associated Press, September 16, 1996.

129. "Campaigner against Japan Made to Leave Beijing Again"; see also "Tong Zeng: zai Diaoyudao shang fang fengzheng," China Youth Online, August 14, 2012, accessed at http://zqb.cyol.com/content/2004-01/05/content_799949.htm.

130. "Chinese Activists Set Up Group to Protect Diaoyu islands," Agence France-Presse, September 8, 1996; "Tong Zeng, Core Member of the Campaign to Defend the Diaoyu Islands, Ordered to Leave Beijing," Hong Kong *Ming Pao*, FTS19960913000031, September 13, 1996.

131. Charles Hutzler, "Activist under Chinese Pressure Abandons Anti-Japanese Protest," Associated Press, September 14, 1996. Tong Zeng's work unit, the Committee on Aging under the Ministry of Civil Affairs, sent him to Lanzhou in the far west of China for "research" activities during the anniversary period. *Wen Wei Po*, September 16, 1996; "China Says Activist Studying, Not Banished," Associated Press, September 17, 1996.

132. Ouyang 2003.

133. Richard K. Betts and Thomas J. Christensen, "China: Getting the Questions Right," *National Interest*, Winter 2000.

134. "Concern over Students' Anti-Japanese Feelings Provoking Wider Unrest," *Ming Pao*, BBC Summary of World Broadcasts, September 18, 1996.

135. "Beijing Students use Internet to Threaten Action over Disputed Islands," *Sing Tao Jih Pao*, BBC Summary of World Broadcasts, September 17, 1996.

136. "Circulars Urge Moderate Steps during Protest," *South China Morning Post*, September 12, 1996.

137. "Dissidents Call for Action on Disputed Islands," Agence France-Presse, September 30, 1996. Less than two weeks later, Liu Xiaobo was sentenced to three years of reform through labor. The letter had also expressed support for Tibetan self-determination. "Dissident Liu Xiaobo Sentenced to 3 years," Agence France-Presse, October 9, 1996.

138. Downs and Saunders 1998, 138.

139. "Chinese Activists Set Up Group to Protect Diaoyu islands," Agence France-Presse, September 8, 1996.

140. Charles Hutzler, "Activist under Chinese Pressure Abandons Anti-Japanese Protest," Associated Press, September 14, 1996.

141. "Beijing Treads Warily on Islands Issue," *South China Morning Post*, September 7, 1996.

142. Lao Ping, *Cheng Ming*, October 1, 1996, cited in Dreyer 2000, 170–71.

143. Linda Choy and Louis Won, "Let Grassroot Protesters Speak Freely, China Urged," *South China Morning Post*, September 14, 1996.

144. "Beijing Treads Warily on Islands Issue," *South China Morning Post*, September 7, 1996.

145. "Military Move Not Excluded, Official Reportedly Disclosed," *Hong Kong Economic Journal*, FBIS FTS19961001000033, October 1, 1996.

146. "Concern over Students' Anti-Japanese Feelings Provoking Wider Unrest," *Ming Pao*, September 18, 1996.

147. Chung 2004, 50.

148. Emily Ginsburg, "Students Warned to 'Cool' Their Outrage," *Hong Kong Standard*, September 16, 1996.

149. Rodger Lee, "Online Site Shut Down by China College," *South China Morning Post*, September 18, 1996.

150. "Foreign Minister Assures Chinese Counterpart of Efforts to Calm Island Row," Kyodo News Agency, September 25, 1996.

151. Downs and Saunders 1998, 140.

152. "Chinese Vice Premier Zhu Complains over Disputed Isles," Japan Economic Newswire, September 19, 1996.

153. Ibid.

154. Bao 2011, 81.

155. "Japan Urged to Draw Lessons from Cunning Chinese," Agence France-Presse, September 26, 1996.

156. Bush 2010, 72.

157. Green 2001, 85–86.

158. Tanaka 2007, 192.

159. "Foreign Ministry Spokesman Expresses Concern about Chinese Sentiment over Disputed Islands," Kyodo News Agency, September 17, 1996.

160. State Department Regular Briefing, Federal News Service, September 23, 1996.

161. "Japan Will Be 'Cautious' over Approving Lighthouse," Agence France-Presse, September 25, 1996.

162. "H.K. Protesters Break into Japan Consulate over Ties," Japan Economic Newswire, October 9, 1996.

163. Some international media speculated that a series of Chinese military exercises in late September were meant as a signal to Japan, although Chinese officials described the exercises as normal activity. For example, see "Chinese War Games Serve as Warning to Japan," Agence France-Presse, September 22, 1996.

164. "Li Peng Beats Nationalist Drum in Warning to Japan," Agence France-Presse, September 30, 1996.

165. Jasper Becker, "We're Too Scared to Protest, Say Students," *South China Morning Post*, September 26, 1996.

166. Chou Yu-chu, "Tong Zeng Writes Letter to Japanese Embassy in China, Warning It Not to Bully the Chinese," Hong Kong *Sing Tao Jih Pao*, FTS19961003000045, October 3, 1996; Chou Yu-chu, "Diaoyu 'Association' Member Cites Mainland Concern," Hong Kong *Ming Pao*, FTS19961005000057, October 5, 1996; "Military Move Not Excluded, Official Reportedly Disclosed," Hong Kong Economic Journal, FTS19961001000033, October 1, 1996.

167. Ada Yuen, "Diaoyu Activists Reportedly Hold Secret Meeting," *South China Morning Post*, November 12, 1996.

168. Zhao 1998, 163; Ma Shih-t'u, "Why Have the CPC Authorities Banned 'China Can Say No'? 'China Can Still Say No' Is Accused of Heterodoxy," *Hong Kong Economic Journal*, FTS19961029000161, October 29, 1996.

169. "Hashimoto Worried over Impact of H.K. Activist's Death," Japan Economic Newswire, September 26, 1996.

170. Ibid.

171. Tanaka 2007, 192–93; "Police Raid Rightist Group Involved in Island Dispute," Associated Press, October 3, 1996.

172. "Press Conference by the Press Secretary 4 October 1996," Ministry of Foreign Affairs of Japan, accessed at http://www.mofa.go.jp/announce/press/1996/10/1004.html.

173. "China Urges Halt to War Shrine Visit by Japanese Premier," Agence France-Presse, September 10, 1996.

174. "Hashimoto Offers to Shun Controversial War Shrine," Associated Press, October 4, 1996; "Hashimoto Says No More Yasukuni Visits," Xinhua News Agency, October 4, 1996.

175. According to Chinese government estimates, Japan left behind as many as two million chemical weapons across China, mostly mustard gas. The Chemical Weapons Convention, which went into force in April 1997, required all signatories to eliminate chemical weapons by 2007. Patrick Tyler, "In Chinese Village, Germ Warfare Is Remembered Nightmare," *New York Times*, April 2, 1997; "Japan to Dismantle Weapons at Plant," *South China Morning Post*, February 10, 1997.

176. Wan 2006, 25.

177. "Another Four Japanese Land on Disputed Island," Agence France-Presse, May 6, 1997; "Tokyo Says Japanese Landings on Disputed Islands Were Illegal," Agence France-Presse, May 7, 1997; Bao 2011, 81.

178. Agatha Ngai, "Activists Warned to Halt Diaoyu Protests," *South China Morning Post*, May 29, 1997.

179. "Japan Urged to Draw Lessons from Cunning Chinese," Agence France-Presse, September 26, 1996.

180. Mary Kwang, "We Don't Take Sides on Diaoyu: BG Lee," *Straits Times*, October 14, 1996.

181. Christensen 1999, 62–63.

182. Li 2008, 602–3.

183. Hook et al. 2012, 141.

184. He 2009, 284.

185. He 2009, 284.

186. "US Criticized for Sidestepping Island Dispute," Agence France-Presse, September 21, 1996.

187. Nicholas Kristof, "Treaty Commitments; Would You Fight for These Islands?" *New York Times*, October 20, 1996.

188. Nicholas Kristof, "An Asian Mini-tempest over Mini-island Group," *New York Times*, September 16, 1996.

189. Green 2001, 87.

190. Congressional Research Service, "Senkaku (Diaoyu) Islands Dispute: The U.S. Legal Relationship and Obligations," September 30, 1996.

191. Koichi Akaza, "U.S. Confirms Security Treaty Covers Senkakus," *Daily Yomiuri*, November 29, 1996.

192. Liu 2011b, 25.

193. Iokibe 2011, 188.

194. Wan 2006, 129.

195. He 2009, 282.

196. Zheng 1999, 133–34.

197. Hashimoto was also the first prime minister to visit the September 18 museum while in office, a symbolic gesture that pleased at least Li Peng, who wrote that "Hashimoto's attitude towards history and one China was good." Li 2008, 602–3.

198. Agence France-Presse, March 13, 1998.

199. Shirk 2007, 164.

200. Downs and Saunders 1998, 84.
201. After Prime Minister Keizo Obuchi gave South Korean president Kim Dae-jung a written apology for Japan's actions in World War II, Jiang may have believed that China could obtain one as well. Instead, the Japanese side only offered a verbal apology, concerned that China was not ready to put aside the history issue in exchange for a written apology. See Shirk 2007, 164; Noriko 2006, 60; Takahara 2004, 166.
202. Fewsmith and Rosen 2001, 163.

Chapter 6

1. In Chinese: *Mei pizhun, juedui mei pizhun, zhe shi zhengfu moren.*
2. Interview with Japanese foreign ministry official, no. 128, Tokyo, Japan, January 29, 2009.
3. "'Zheng Chang' Siguo Lianmeng Kaishi Jiti Chuzhao: Cuicu Lianda Qi Yuedi Qian Toupiao" [Four countries strive to become permanent members of UN Security Council and they request the General Assembly begin the vote before the end of July], *Wenhui Bao*, April 8, 2005.
4. Kim 1999.
5. "China's Japan Envoy Lodges Protest over Shrine Issue," Xinhua New Service, August 13, 2001; "Chinese Agency Says Koizumi's SHRINE visit to Damage Sino-Japanese Ties," BBC Worldwide Monitoring (Xinhua News Service), August 14, 2001.
6. "China Lodges Representations against Koizumi's Shrine Visit," Xinhua News Service, January 14, 2003.
7. On Chinese cybernationalism, see Wu 2007b.
8. Interview with senior Patriots Alliance Network organizer, no. 106, Beijing, China, July 6, 2007.
9. "Zhang Likun, Feng Jinhua, Lu Yunfei San Ren Tan Bao Diao Zhi Xing," *Renmin Wang*, June 27, 2003.
10. "Chinese Protesters leave after Nearing Isles Disputed with Japan." Kyodo News Agency, June 23, 2003.
11. "Japan's Lease of Disputed Senkaku Islands Fuels 'Ire' from China, Taiwan," *Mainichi Shimbun*, January 3, 2003; "China's Sovereignty over Diaoyu Islands Indisputable—Spokesman," Xinhua News Service, June 23, 2003.
12. "Determined to Defend Diaoyu Islands," *China Daily*, October 10, 2003.
13. "Expulsions at Diaoyus Could Sink China Claim," *South China Morning Post*, October 14, 2003.
14. "Japan Deported Chinese Protesters under Political Pressure," Japan Economic Newswire, April 1, 2004.
15. Ibid.
16. Ibid.
17. "Chinese Fans Block Streets, Harass Japanese Counterparts after Asia Cup loss," Kyodo News Agency, August 8, 2004.
18. "China Shuts Down Anti-Japan Website," Kyodo News Agency, August 31, 2004.
19. Ibid.
20. "China Admits Submarine Intruded into Japanese Waters," *Mainichi Daily News*, November 18, 2004.
21. "Waijiaobu Fayanren Da Jizhe Wen," *Renmin Ribao*, February 9, 2005.
22. "2.15 Kangyi Riben Zhengfu Qitu Jieguan Zhongguo Lingtu Diaoyudao Shang de Dengta," Patriots Alliance Network, February 15, 2005, accessed at http://bbs.54man.org/viewthread.php?tid=165478; "Chinese Protest against Tokyo's Move on Islands," *People's Daily*, February 16, 2005.
23. "Japan-U.S. Security Cooperation Breaches Bilateral Framework," Xinhua News Service, February 21, 2005.

24. Interview, no. 84, Shanghai, China, April 17, 2007.
25. Hong Kong *Ching Chi Yih Pao*, FBIS CPP20050418000140, April 18, 2005.
26. *Chengming*, May 2005, 7, citing the State Council General Office bulletin.
27. "Italy Urged Not to Count on US, China to Veto G4 UNSC Reform Proposal," *Corriere della Sera*, EUP20050411000073, FBIS, April 11, 2005.
28. Satoh 2001, 3.
29. Satoh 2001, 4.
30. Interview, no. 10, Tokyo, Japan, April 13, 2006.
31. Jiji Press, December 8, 2004; Agence France-Presse, March 7, 2005; see also Kitaoka 2005.
32. The statement was made by outgoing U.S. ambassador to Japan Howard Baker.
33. Agence France-Presse, March 7, 2005.
34. Kitaoka 2005, 12–17.
35. Agence France-Presse, March 19, 2005. Although Annan's sweeping announcement quickly eclipsed Rice's statement in the attention of the public and the media, some Chinese observers have concluded that her statement was one of the "true reasons" that the anti-Japanese protests "erupted" in China. See Zhang and Zhao 2005, 13.
36. Report of the Secretary-General, *In Larger Freedom: Towards Development, Security, and Human Rights for All*, March 21, 2005, 42–43, available at http://www.un.org/largerfreedom/.
37. Statement by Machimura upon publication of the report of Kofi Annan, March 21, 2005, available at http://www.us.emb-japan.go.jp/english/html/pressreleases/2005/032205b.htm.
38. FBIS, CPP20050322000209, March 22, 2005.
39. "Meiguo huaren fadong wangshang qianming fandui Riben jiaru anlihui," *Renmin Wang*, March 22, 2005, reposted at http://news.sina.com.cn/w/2005-03-22/06285425255s.shtml.
40. "Waitan huabao: baiwan wangmin qianming fandui Riben mouqiu changren," March 30, 2005, http://news.sina.com.cn/c/2005-03-30/20046243318.shtml.
41. Ibid.
42. *Yomiuri Shimbun*, April 4, 2005 and April 6, 2005; Hong Kong *Sing Pao*, April 4, 2005.
43. Interview, no. 106, Beijing, China, July 6, 2007.
44. Kitaoka 2005.
45. "Riben jiaokeshu jinu Zhong Chao," *Huanqiu Shibao*, April 6, 2005; "1000 wan qianming de quanliu cheng," *Nanfang Renwu Zhoukan*, April 6, 2005; "South Korean Lawmakers Work on Joint Resolution against Japan's UN Bid," Yonhap News Agency, April 1, 2005.
46. Tokyo Jiji Press, FBIS JPP20050405000020, April 5, 2005.
47. "Qianwan Qianming Ju Ji Riben," *Renmin Wang*, April 7, 2005, accessed at http://japan.people.com.cn/GB/35469/35478/3302180.html.
48. "Lianhe Zaobao: Zhongguo Ying Dui Riben 'Ru Chang' de Wu Hong Xuanze," *Renmin Wang*, April 8, 2005, accessed at http://japan.people.com.cn/GB/35464/35488/3305600.html.
49. Statement by Ambassador Shirin Tahir-Kheli, Senior Advisor to the Secretary of State on UN Reform, on the Secretary General's Report on UN Reform, in the General Assembly, April 7, 2005, http://www.usunnewyork.usmission.gov/05_063.htm or http://www.un.int/usa/05_063.htm.
50. "Riben 'Ru Chang' Zuli Jia Da," *Zhongguo Xinwen Zhoukan*, April 19, 2005, accessed at http://www.china.com.cn/chinese/HIAW/842131.htm.
51. "Mei Qian Guojia Anquan Guwen Ren Wei Riben 'Ru Chang' Ke Neng Xing Feichang Xiao," Xinhua New Service, April 8, 2005, accessed at http://news.sina.com.cn/w/2005-04-08/11346327744.shtml.
52. Kitaoka 2005.
53. Estimate by Beijing Public Security Bureau Public Order Department Chief Zhang Fengjie in "Quntixing Shijian de Weiji Guanli: Jiyu Beijingshi Anli de Shizheng Fenxi" [Crisis management of mass incidents: Analysis of evidence from Beijing], in *Jingcha Yujing yu Yingji Jizhi* [Police early warning and emergency mechanisms, ed. Yu Lingyun (China People's Public Security University Press, March 2007), 184.
54. Interview with Japanese official stationed at the Beijing embassy, no. 22, May 15, 2006.

55. "Secretary-General's Press Encounter," UN.org, Geneva, Switzerland, April 7, 2005, http://www.un.org/sg/offthecuff/index.asp?nid=711.

56. Ibid.

57. See, e.g., "Annan: Ri nengfou 'ruchang' yao you Yazhou guojia xian jueding" [Annan: Whether Japan joins the UNSC should first be decided by Asian countries], *Wenhui Bao*, April 10, 2005, reposted at http://news.xinhuanet.com/world/2005-04/10/content_2808942.htm.

58. Yoshikazu Shirakawa, *Yomiuri Shimbun*, April 13, 2005.

59. Qiangguo Luntan, "ZhongRi guanxi redian wenti yu sikao: Qinghua daxue guoji wenti yanjiusuo jiaoshou jian fusuozhang Liu Jiangyong," http://www.people.com.cn/GB/32306/32313/32330/3343159.html, April 22, 2005, last accessed July 26, 2012.

60. Kyodo News Agency, April 12, 2005.

61. Zhao Huanxin and Hu Qihua, "Japan Told to Face Up to History, Reflect on Protests," *China Daily*, April 13, 2005.

62. James Brooke, *New York Times*, April 14, 2005.

63. Agence France-Presse, April 12, 2005.

64. *Nihon Keizai*, April 14, 2005, FBIS, JPP20050414000020.

65. *Asahi Shimbun*, April 13, 2005, FBIS, JPP20050413000004.

66. Agence France-Presse, April 14, 2005; Xinhua Financial News, April 15, 2005.

67. "2005 Fan Ri Youxing Zhong Wangluo Shequ Zuoyong De Yidian Sikao," September 4, 2006, accessed at http://media.people.com.cn/GB/4777497.html#.

68. Xinhua News Service, April 16, 2005.

69. Kyodo News Agency, April 18, 2005.

70. *Mainichi Shimbun*, April 20, 2005.

71. Hong Kong *Zhongguo Tongxun She*, April 17, 2005.

72. Agence France-Presse, April 18, 2005.

73. Xinhua News Service, April 19, 2005, FBIS translation.

74. Josephine Ma and Shi Ting, *South China Morning Post*, April 22, 2005.

75. Zhang and Zhao 2005.

76. Kyodo News Agency, April 28, 2005.

77. Interview, no. 29, Beijing, China, June 2, 2006.

78. "Singapore Welcomes Koizumi Apology, sees Bigger Role for Japan," Japan Economic Newswire, April 22, 2005.

79. Naoko Aoki, Kyodo News Agency, April 23, 2005.

80. Associated Press, August 4, 2005.

81. http://usinfo.state.gov/xarchives/display.html?p=washfile-english&y=2005&m=July&x=20050712184505adynned0.5566522, July 12, 2005.

82. Wu Miaofa, "Siguo lianmeng zhengchang zhigu benguo liyi—ruchang mengxiang yi jiben pohui" [G4 nations seeking UNSC seat for own nation's interest—dream of joining UNSC already basically shattered], August 7, 2005, http://news.sohu.com/20050807/n226586688.shtml.

83. Ibid.

84. Interview with associate research professor at the China Institutes of Contemporary International Relations, no. 93, Beijing, China, May 24, 2007.

85. FBIS, CPP20040909000157, September 9, 2004. Ministry of Foreign Affairs of the People's Republic of China WWW-Text in Chinese.

86. E.g., http://news.tom.com/1002/20040909-1299026.html and http://news.xinhuanet.com/zhengfu/2004-09/10/content_1964696.htm, last accessed August 14, 2007.

87. In Chinese, "Zhongguo Waijiaobu ze mohu de duice biaoshi lijie." http://www.thechinapress.com/yaowen/ywimg/200409190066.htm, last accessed August 14, 2007.

88. Interview with a senior researcher at the China Institutes of Contemporary International Relations, no. 107, Beijing, China, July 9, 2007.

89. Liu 2005, 196–97, 261, 407–8.

90. Wu 2006c, 253.

91. Qiangguo Luntan, "ZhongRi guanxi redian wenti yu sikao: Qinghua daxue guoji wenti yanjiusuo jiaoshou jian fusuozhang Liu Jiangyong," http://www.people.com.cn/GB/32306/32313/32330/3343159.html, April 22, 2005, last accessed July 26, 2012.

92. "'Zheng Chang' Siguo Lianmeng Kaishi Jiti Chuzhao: Cuicu Lianda Qi Yuedi Qian Toupiao" [Four countries strive to become permanent members of UN Security Council and they request the General Assembly begin the vote before the end of July], *Wenhui Bao*, April 8, 2005.

93. The author would like to thank a source who wishes to remain anonymous for this information. For background on the role of the SCIO, see Shirk 2007, 92–96; Shambaugh 2007; and Xiao 2007.

94. http://news.xinhuanet.com/world/2005-03/25/content_2741791.htm.

95. "Ministry of Foreign Affairs Spokesman Liu Jianchao Answers Journalists' Questions at Routine News Conference on 24 March 2005," FBIS, CPP20050324000145.

96. FBIS, CPP20050329000169, March 29, 2005.

97. http://www.china-embassy.org/chn/zmgx/t189682.htm.

98. http://bbs.hzu.edu.cn/mainframe.php?tid=357245.

99. Interview with Beijing-based activist and senior Patriots Alliance Network organizer, no. 106, Beijing, China, July 6, 2007.

100. http://news.sina.com.cn/c/2005-03-31/20215520075s.shtml.

101. Interview with leading Bao Diao activist in Beijing, no. 43, July 27, 2006.

102. Josephine Ma and Shi Ting, *South China Morning Post*, April 22, 2005.

103. Interview, no. 92, Shenzhen, China, May 20, 2007.

104. "4.2 Chengdu Fasheng Za Dian Shijian Yu Women Wu Guan!" http://bbs.54man.org/viewthread.php?action=printable&tid=170610, April 3, 2005.

105. Transcript of PRC FM Spokesman News Conference on April 7, 2005, FBIS CPP20050407000218

106. *People's Daily*, April 6, 2005.

107. BBS post by Li Weixing, April 5, 2005.

108. Posted to the Patriots Alliance Network website on April 5, 2005.

109. Interview with Foreign Ministry policy planning official, no. 100, Beijing, China, June 26, 2007.

110. In Chinese: "Ruhe fangzhi shitai shikong, zhe shi rifang xuyao renzhen fansi de." PRC Foreign Ministry press conference, April 12, 2005, available at http://www.mfa.gov.cn/chn/gxh/tyb/fyrbt/jzhsl/t191219.htm, last accessed October 27, 2010; see also FBIS, CPP20050412000218, April 12, 2005.

111. *Ta Kung Pao*, FBIS, CPP20050603000054, June 3, 2005.

112. Interview, no. 81, Shanghai, China, April 16, 2007.

113. Leu Siew Ying, *South China Morning Post*, April 27, 2005.

114. Interview with a lifestyle magazine editor who participated in the April 16 Shanghai protest and holds a PhD from East China Normal University, no. 70, Shanghai, China, April 9, 2007.

115. Interview with Shanghai resident and high school student, no. 59, March 18, 2007.

116. Interview with Shanghai resident and high school student, no. 79, April 15, 2007.

117. Joseph Kahn, "China Is Pushing and Scripting Anti-Japanese Protests," *New York Times*, April 15, 2005.

118. Interview with activist and compensation lawyer, no. 85, May 19, 2007.

119. http://bbs.1931-9-18.org/viewthread.php?tid=170515&extra=&page=3, April 6, 2005.

120. E.g., http://tech.sina.com.cn/i/2005-04-02/1334569566.shtml.

121. Interview with senior journalist at *Huanqiu Shibao* who covers foreign affairs and Sino-Japanese relations, no. 103, Beijing, China, July 4, 2007.

122. Quoted in Shirk 2011, 230.

123. The data shown here were collected using the Chinese news search engine at http://news.baidu.com/advanced_news.html. I counted the number of unique articles (URLs) that mentioned "petition" (*qianming*) and "permanent UNSC member" (*changren lishiguo*) that were

posted each day to Sina.com.cn and People.com.cn. I chose Sina.com.cn because it is arguably the most popular of the three large portals among both citizens and officials. As one Foreign Ministry official told me, "I read the *People's Daily* when I have the time, when work is slow. But I read Sina all the time" (interview no. 100, June 2007).

124. Ching Cheong, "China Orders halt to Anti-Japanese Protests," *Straits Times*, April 5, 2005.

125. Interview with senior researcher at the Chinese Academy of Social Sciences Institute of Japanese Studies, no. 32, Beijing, China, July 12, 2006.

126. Interview, no. 42, Beijing, China, July 26, 2006.

127. Interview with Beijing-based activist and senior Patriots Alliance Network organizer, no. 106, Beijing, China, July 6, 2007.

128. "Riben zhengchang xianru kunjing," *Huanqiu Shibao*, April 11, 2005, reposted at http://www. people.com.cn/GB/paper68/14515/1290822.html; "Xifang yulun piping Riben," *Renmin Wang*, April 15, 2005, http://www.people.com.cn/GB/paper68/14541/1293017.html.

129. As one netizen wrote on the "Strong Nation Forum" of the People's Daily website: "Resolutely support Premier Wen Jiabao's remarks made in India on the large-scale anti-Japanese demonstrations in China, urging Japan to review its history of aggression and treat the issue correctly," FBIS, CPP20050413000141, April 13, 2005.

130. "Crackdown on Activists to Head Off Protests," *South China Morning Post*, April 16, 2005.

131. Josephine Ma and Leu Siew Ying, "Huge Police Presence Keeps Capital Quiet," *South China Morning Post*, April 17, 2005.

132. Interview with a Guangzhou-based artist, who had also participated in the demonstrations against the 1999 embassy bombing, no. 146, Guangzhou, China, January 7, 2010.

133. Interview with Tsinghua University professor of public policy and international affairs, no. 24, May 25, 2006. A professor at Renmin University in Beijing was given similar instructions. Interview with a Renmin University professor of sociology, no. 52, February 9, 2007.

134. Interview with Shenzhen People's Armed Police officer, no. 92, May 20, 2007.

135. "Phoenix TV Reports on Anti-Japanese Rallies in Shenzhen on 17 Apr," FBIS, CPP20050417000105, April 17, 2005.

136. Ibid.

137. BBS archive of the Shanghai Municipal Public Security Bureau, available at http://gaj.sh.gov. cn/webcases/zxzx/list.asp?deptid=2#, last accessed August 16, 2007.

138. "Crackdown on Activists to Head Off Protests," *South China Morning Post*, April 16, 2005.

139. Interview with Shanghai office worker in advertising who had never heard of the Bao Diao network, no. 74, April 11, 2007.

140. "Media Analysis: China Initiates Campaign to Rein in Anti-Japan Protests," April 21, 2005, FBIS, FEA20050421002681.

141. "China Holds Mass Meetings to Dampen Anti-Japan Sentiment," Kyodo News Agency, April 21, 2005.

142. Xinhua, "Boycotting Japanese Goods Makes No Good," April 23, 2005, reposted at http:// www.chinadaily.com.cn/english/doc/2005-04/23/content_436720.htm.

143. Wu 2006b, 356.

144. Qiangguo Luntan, "ZhongRi guanxi redian wenti yu sikao: Qinghua daxue guoji wenti yanjiusuo jiaoshou jian fusuozhang Liu Jiangyong," http://www.people.com.cn/ GB/32306/32313/32330/3343159.html, April 22, 2005, last accessed July 26, 2012.

145. Lu 2007, 20.

146. Interview, no. 146, Guangzhou, China, January 7, 2010.

147. Interview with anti-Japanese activist and website manager, no. 81, Shanghai, China, April 16, 2007.

148. Interview with Beijing-based activist and senior Patriots Alliance Network organizer, no. 106, Beijing, China, July 6, 2007.

149. Liu 2005, 407–8.

150. "Wei fan Ri jiangwen de yulun gongshi," *Guancha*, April 25, 2005, available at http://blog. boxun.com/hero/liuxb/290_1.shtml.

151. "Tang Ye he Shanghai dangju, shei zai weifa?" in Liu 2006, also available at http://blog.boxun. com/hero/liuxb/293_1.shtml.

152. "Ministry of Public Security Spokesman Makes Remarks on Recent Marches and Demonstration Activities Related to Japan in Some Localities," Xinhua News Service, April 21, 2005, FBIS, CPP20050421000171; see also http://news.sina.com.cn/c/2005-04-21/17385714946s.shtml.

153. Kyodo News Agency, May 16, 2005; Radio Free Asia, May 13, 2005, available at http://www. rfa.org/mandarin/shenrubaodao/2005/05/13/guofeixiong/.

154. "Chinese Dissident Gets 12 Years Jail," Reuters, December 26, 2005.

155. Kitaoka 2005.

156. Interview, no. 28, Beijing, China, June 2, 2006.

157. Interview with a Japanese cultural affairs officer, no. 21, Beijing, China, May 15, 2006.

158. April 17, 2005. Reported by FBIS on April 19, 2005.

159. Howard French, "China Allows More Protests in Shanghai against Japan," *New York Times*, April 17, 2005.

160. *Yomiuri Shimbun*, April 11, 2005.

161. *Sunday Project* talk show, Asahi TV, April 17, 2005, translated by FBIS, "PRC Anti-Japan Rallies, Gas Development Dispute Discussed on TV Talk Show," JPP20050418000069.

162. Agence France-Presse, April 12, 2005.

163. Howard French, "China Allows More Protests in Shanghai against Japan," *New York Times*, April 17, 2005.

164. Norimitsu Onishi, *New York Times*, April 11, 2005.

165. "Tang Jiaxuan Meets Japan's Kyodo News Agency President," Xinhua News Service April 15, 2005, FBIS, CPP20050415000193.

166. Interview with Japanese official stationed at the Beijing embassy, no. 22, May 15, 2006.

167. Interview, no. 20, Tokyo, Japan, April 18, 2006.

168. Satoshi Saeki and Masahiko Takekoshi, *Yomiuri Shimbun*, April 12, 2005.

169. Associated Press, April 12, 2005.

170. Interview, no. 137, Palo Alto, California, April 27, 2009.

171. *Sunday Project* talk show, Asahi TV, April 17, 2005, translated by FBIS, "PRC Anti-Japan Rallies, Gas Development Dispute Discussed on TV Talk Show," JPP20050418000069.

172. "Only Japan-China Cooperation Can Defuse Diplomatic Crisis," *Nihon Keizai Shimbun*, April 18, 2005, translated by FBIS, JPP20050418000039.

173. Togo 2008, 60.

174. *Sankei Shimbun*, FBIS, JPP20050424000002, April 24, 2005.

175. Ibid.

176. "Koizumi Apologizes for WWII Aggression; Japan's Premier Tries to Lower Tensions with China in Public Show of Remorse," *Straits Times*, April 23, 2005.

177. "China Wary: Beijing Now Awaits Koizumi's Next Move," *Straits Times*, April 25, 2005.

178. Ibid.

179. Ibid.

180. "Japanese PM Arrives in China for Official Visit; Holds Talks with Wen Jiabao," Xinhua News Service, October 8, 2006; Jiang Wenran, "China's Renewed Summit Diplomacy with Japan," Jamestown Foundation *China Brief* 6 (21) (October 25, 2006).

181. Jiji Press, April 12, 2005; *Yomiuri Shimbun*, April 14, 2005.

182. *Asahi Shimbun*, Apr 12, 2005, FBIS, JPP20050413000119.

183. *Mainichi Shimbun*, April 18, 2005, FBIS, JPP20050418000013.

184. "'Private Citizen' Koizumi's Visits to Yasukuni Shrine and Japanese Diplomacy: A Call for a New Nonreligious War Memorial," *Yomiuri Shimbun*, June 4, 2005; "China-Japan Relations and Koizumi's Yasukuni Visits," *Asahi Shimbun*, June 6, 2005; available at http://japanfocus. org/article.asp?id=302.

185. Togo June 2006.

186. Cui and Liu 2007, 2–3.

187. In hindsight, the failure of the G4 proposal to gain enough support for a General Assembly vote was probably overdetermined. Each of the G4 nations faced opposition within their respective regions: Italy opposed Germany, Mexico opposed Brazil, and Pakistan opposed India. In addition, the decision of African nations to press for two permanent seats with veto power meant that the G4 could not expect unified support from the 53-member African Union. The real question, then, was which governments would take the heat for opposing reform.
188. Interview, no. 128, Tokyo, Japan, January 29, 2009.
189. FBIS, JPP20050728000098, August 5, 2005.
190. Traub 2006, 371–72.
191. Interview, no. 134, Washington, D.C., March 12, 2009.
192. Interview, no. 128, Tokyo, Japan, January 29, 2009.
193. Interview, no. 127, Tokyo, Japan, January 27, 2009.
194. Kyodo News Agency, May 25, 2005.
195. Kyodo News Agency, June 24, 2005.
196. Ray Marcelo and Hugh Williamson, *Financial Times*, April 13, 2005.
197. Gries 2005b; Shirk 2007.
198. Okamoto and Tanaka 2005.
199. Reilly 2012, 155.
200. See *Cheng Ming*, No. 311, May 1, 2005; Justin McCurry and Jonathan Watts, "China's Angry Young Focus Their Hatred on Old Enemy," *Guardian*, December 30, 2004; and Tanner 2004, 150–51.
201. See Shimizu 2006.
202. Joseph Kahn, "State-Run Chinese Paper Lashes Anti-Japan Protests as 'Evil Plot,'" *New York Times*, April 27, 2005.

Chapter 7

1. "Baozhu feifa zifu" [Protect illegal characters], September 13, 2010, translation at http://www.danwei.org/nationalism/han_han_on_the_diaoyu_islands.php; original post at http://blog.sina.com.cn/s/blog_4701280b0100lcum.html, last accessed April 22, 2013.
2. Interview, no. 173, Washington, D.C., October 3, 2013.
3. Zou 2011, 79.
4. These episodes were not part of the theory-building process and are therefore useful for evaluating the theory's applicability to "out of sample" observations.
5. The restraint of anti-Japanese protests during this period contrasts with the tacit endorsement of an Internet campaign and street protests against Western organizations accused of supporting Tibetan independence, including Carrefour and CNN, in April 2008. See chapter 9.
6. Lu 2007, 20.
7. http://www.zhonghuahaiquan.com/bbs/dispbbs.asp?boardid=79&id=80, last accessed December 12, 2006.
8. http://bbs.1931-9-18.org/viewthread.php?tid=170126, last accessed August 14, 2006.
9. http://bbs.1931-9-18.org/viewthread.php?tid=211439&extra=page%3D1, last accessed October 8, 2006.
10. "Protesters in Sichuan Urge Boycott of Japan Goods," *Japan Times*, September 20, 2006.
11. "Protestors Slam Taiwan Separatist in Beijing," Reuters, June 18, 2007.
12. Kenji Minemura, "Activists in China Find It Harder to Stage Anti-Japan Protests," *Asahi Shimbun*, December 13, 2007.
13. Along with the sinking of a Taiwanese fishing boat in a collision with the Japanese Coast Guard. "Zuguo Tongyi Liyi Gao Yu Yi Qie—Changsha 6.18 Xuanchuan Huodong," http://www.cfdd.org.cn/bbs/thread-55213-1-1.html, June 18, 2008, last accessed March 4, 2009.
14. Minoura 2011; Daojiong Zha, "Calming Troubled Waters," *Beijing Review*, July 10, 2008.
15. Wu Hong, "A President Logs On," *Asia Times*, June 25, 2008.

16. Li Nan, "Bao Diao lianhehui luntan zui hou yi tie," CFDD.org.cn, June 26, 2008, last accessed July 21, 2008, reposted at http://www.cfdd.org.cn/bbs/viewthread.php?tid=55307.
17. "Chinese Protestors Oppose Gas Deal with Japan," Kyodo News Agency, June 18, 2008.
18. Mitoji Yabunaka, *Kokka No Meiun* [Fate of a nation] (Tokyo: Shincho Shinsho, 2010), 147, cited in Minoura 2011.
19. China Institute of International Studies 2008–09, 36–50.
20. Yang 2008.
21. The June 18 agreement stated that "the two sides will conduct cooperation in the transitional period prior to delimitation without prejudicing their respective legal positions." http://www. fmprc.gov.cn/eng/xwfw/s2510/t466632.htm, last accessed April 10, 2013.
22. Kristine Kwok, "CNOOC Official Defends Gas Deal with Japan," *South China Morning Post*, June 20, 2008.
23. Wu Hong, "A President Logs On," *Asia Times*, June 25, 2008.
24. Ibid.
25. Michael D. Swaine and M. Taylor Fravel, "China's Assertive Behavior Part Two: The Maritime Periphery," *China Leadership Monitor* 35 (2011): 10; Willy Lam, "Is China Afraid of Its Own People?" *Foreign Policy*, September 28, 2010.
26. "Gas Field Deal Signals China's PR challenge," *Nikkei Weekly*, July 7, 2008.
27. Chūgoku, "Ugoki Tomaru Nitchū Gasuden No Kaihatsu Gōi Kara 1 Nen" [China's moves stop 1 year after the Japan-China gas field development agreement],"*Asahi Shimbun*, June 17, 2009, cited in cited in Minoura 2011, 150; Julian Ryall, "Japanese Prime Minister Taro Aso Calls Off General election," *Telegraph*, October 28, 2008.
28. Wallace 2014.
29. Swaine and Fravel 2011.
30. Fravel 2010, 156; "China Denies Provoking Japan over Senkaku Islets," Kyodo News Agency, December 9, 2008; Bush 2010, 143.
31. James J. Przystup, "Japan-China Relations: New Year, Old Problems," Comparative Connections (2009).
32. China Institute of International Studies 2008–9, 53.
33. China Institute of International Studies 2008–9, 355.
34. China Institute of International Studies 2008–9, 54. Chinese commentators also commended the Aso administration for taking "resolute measures" to punish Chief of Staff for Japan's Air Self-Defense Force Tamogami Toshio, who had published an article denying Japanese aggression in World War II. "Riben hangkong ziweidui muliao chang zhuanwen fouren qinlve bei mianzhi," Zhongxinwang, October 31, 2008, accessed at http://news.163.com/08/1031/22/4PK9AJ4T0001121M.html; Norimitsu Onishi, "Japan: New Fallout from Essay on War," *New York Times*, November 4, 2008.
35. "Guan Yu '2009 Zhongguo Minjian Bao Diao Luntan—Changsha' Huiyi Bei Po Quxiao de Shuoming," January 15, 2009, reposted at http://www.cfdd.org.cn/bbs/redirect.php?fid=90&tid=58542&goto=nextoldset, last accessed April 10, 2013.
36. "China Protests Japan Premier's Remarks on Disputed Isles," Japan Economic Newswire, February 26, 2009; "Japan, China Agree Not to Let Isles Dispute Harm Overall Ties," Japan Economic Newswire, February 28, 2009.
37. "Protest Voyage from Taiwan to Senkakus Canceled, Protester Says," Japan Economic Newswire, May 4, 2009.
38. Reinhard Drifte, "Territorial Conflicts in the East China Sea—from Missed Opportunities to Negotiation Stalemate," *Asia-Pacific Journal* 22-3-09 (June 1, 2009); "H.K. Activists' Protest Voyage to Disputed Isles off Japan Stopped," Japan Economic Newswire, May 2, 2009; Chris Yeung, "Why Block on Diaoyus Trip Is Worrying," *South China Morning Post*, May 10, 2009; "City's Freedom at Risk, Diaoyu Activists Say," *South China Morning Post*, May 11, 2009; Yvonne Tsui, "Judge Allows Review over Diaoyus Protest," August 15, 2009.
39. "Cities Brace for Mass Anti-Japan Protests," *South China Morning Post*, September 18, 2010.

40. For example, http://www.cfdd.org.cn/bbs/forum-90-44.html, http://www.cfdd.org.cn/bbs/redirect.php?fid=90&tid=72164&goto=nextoldset; "China Breaks Up Anti-Japan Protests." *Al Jazeera*, September 18, 2010.

41. http://www.cfdd.org.cn/bbs/redirect.php?fid=90&tid=72170&goto=nextoldset, last accessed April 17, 2013.

42. http://www.cfdd.org.cn/bbs/thread-71855-1-1.html, last accessed April 17, 2013; "Activists Plan to Hold Protest at Disputed Islands," *South China Morning Post*, September 13, 2010.

43. For evidence that China did not uniformly restrict rare earth exports, see Johnston 2013.

44. The islands were not emphasized in the 2005 anti-Japanese demonstrations.

45. The emphasis on Chinese perceptions does not necessarily reflect agreement with these views and should not be construed as endorsement.

46. Johnston 2013, 22.

47. Bader 2012, 12.

48. China Institute of International Studies 2009–10, 39–43.

49. Sun 2010, 167.

50. "DPJ Win Will Settle 'Historical Issue' of Yasukuni: Chinese Experts," Japan Economic Newswire, August 28, 2009.

51. China Institute of International Studies 2009–10, 364.

52. "Chinese and Japanese Defence Departments' Joint Press Communique," Xinhua News Service, November 27, 2009.

53. "Premiers Answer Calls for Direct Hotline," *Global Times*, June 1, 2010; "China, Japan Resume Gas Talks; Two PMs Also Discuss Naval Concerns and North Korea; They Agree to Set Up Hotline," *Straits Times*, June 1, 2010.

54. As Sun writes, "Although the DPJ prepared to sort out Japan's relations with the United States and strengthen its Asia diplomacy, there is, however, no proof of Japan's anti-America position or Japan's intention to weaken its alliance with Washington." Sun 2010, 159. Likewise, Zhai Xin notes that "because the ruling party has [a] weak foundation and little experience, its China policy formulation and implementation is bound to encounter a lot of constraints after taking office." Zhai 2010, 95–101. See also Hu and Ai 2010.

55. "Japan PM Naoto Kan Vows Action on Debt and US ties," BBC, June 8, 2010, accessed at http://www.bbc.co.uk/news/10252301.

56. Shi Yinhong, quoted in Li Yang, "Is Hatoyama's Resignation 'Destined' or Will There Be a 'Power Vacuum' in Japanese Politics?" *Zhongguo Xinwenshe* (BBC Monitoring Asia Pacific), June 2, 2010.

57. "China, Japan Launch Prime Ministerial Hotline," Xinhua News Service, June 13, 2010.

58. Ministry of Foreign Affairs of the People's Republic of China, June 27, 2010, accessed at http://www.fmprc.gov.cn/eng/topics/hjtfwjnd4thG20/t712393.shtml.

59. Ministry of Foreign Affairs of Japan, June 28, 2010, accessed at http://www.mofa.go.jp/region/asia-paci/china/summit_meet1006.html.

60. "China Concerns with Japanese PM's 'Deterrent' Remarks: FM," Xinhua News Service, June 24, 2010, accessed at http://news.xinhuanet.com/english2010/china/2010-06/24/c_13367568.htm.

61. "Fenghuang guancha: Jianzhiren jiu Zhongguo junli fabiao kanfa bu he shiyi," June 24, 2010, http://news.ifeng.com/world/detail_2010_06/24/1667271_0.shtml.

62. Zhongguo Guoji Wenti Yanjiusuo 2010–11, 20.

63. See Chapter 6. Then, too, small-scale Chinese demonstrations had been permitted in front of the Japanese embassy.

64. "Japan Apologizes over Taiwan Boat Incident," Agence France-Presse, June 20, 2008; Jenny Hsu, "Japan Apologizes for Boat Collision," *Taipei Times*, June 21, 2008.

65. Johnston 2013, 22.

66. Zhongguo Guoji Wenti Yanjiusuo 2010–11, 27.

67. "Riben xunluochuan zai Diaoyudao fujin chongzhuang Zhongguo yuchuan," Xinhua News Service, September 7, 2010, accessed at http://news.xinhuanet.com/world/2010-09/07/c_12528283.htm.

68. "Waijiaobu fubuzhang yuejian zhu Hua dashi yaoqiu Rifang tingzhi feifa lanjie," *Huanqiu Shibao*, September 7, 2010, accessed at http://world.huanqiu.com/roll/2010-09/1081922.html.

69. "China Demands Japan Release Detained Fishing Boat, Guarantee Crew's Safety," Xinhua, September 8, 2010, accessed at http://news.xinhuanet.com/english2010/china/2010-09/08/c_13484605_2.htm.

70. "Chugokugyosen Sencho Taihoe [Captain of a Chinese trawler is to be arrested]," *Yomiuri Shimbun*, September 8, 2010.

71. Cabinet Secretariat, Cabinet Public Relations Office, September 8, 2010, accessed at http://www.kantei.go.jp/jp/tyoukanpress/201009/8_a.html; "JCG Arrests Chinese Capt. over Collisions," *Daily Yomiuri*, September 9, 2010.

72. "China Demands Japan Release Detained Fishing Boat, Guarantee Crew's Safety," Xinhua News Service, September 8, 2010, accessed at http://news.xinhuanet.com/english2010/china/2010-09/08/c_13484605_2.htm.

73. "40 Chinese Protest Near Japanese Embassy over Detention of Fishing Boat," *Renmin Wang*, September 9, 2010, accessed at http://english.cpc.people.com.cn/66102/7134801.html; see also "40 Chinese Protest Near Japanese Embassy over Detention of Fishing Boat," Xinhua News Service, September 8, 2010, accessed at http://news.xinhuanet.com/english2010/china/2010-09/08/c_13485520.htm.

74. http://www.cfdd.org.cn/bbs/thread-71574-1-1.html, http://www.wyzxsx.com/Article/Class4/201009/178369.html, last accessed November 26, 2010.

75. http://www.cfdd.org.cn/bbs/thread-71574-2-1.html, last accessed April 21, 2013.

76. "Diaoyu Islands Collision a Dangerous Game," *Global Times*, September 8, 2010, accessed at http://www.globaltimes.cn/opinion/editorial/2010-09/571138.html.

77. "Press Conference by Minister for Foreign Affairs Katsuya Okada," Ministry of Foreign Affairs of Japan," September 10, 2010, accessed at http://www.mofa.go.jp/announce/fm_press/2010/9/0910_01.html.

78. "Japan Gives 10-Day Detention to Chinese Skipper over Boat Incident," Kyodo News Agency, September 10, 2010.

79. "China's Dai Bingguo Urges Japan to Release Detained Crewmen," Xinhua News Service, September 12, 2010.

80. "China Postpones East China Sea Negotiation with Japan," Xinhua News Service, September 10, 2010.

81. "Beijing fenxi renshi: Tuichi yu Riben tanpan Zhongguo taidu wenhe," *Lianhe Zaobao*, reposted at http://club.mil.news.sina.com.cn/thread-257762-1-1.html, September 13, 2010.

82. "Senkakuoki Shototsu to Karameta Enki nara Ikan [Maehara calls it regrettable if China linked the collision with the decision to postpone gas field negotiation]," *Asahi Shimbun*, September 12, 2010.

83. "China Urges Japan to Make Wise Political Resolution, Release Fisherman Immediately," Xinhua News Service, September 12, 2010.

84. "Guanyu chexia 'dui Riben zhengfu gongkai xin' de shuoming," September 10, 2010, http://bbs.1931-9-18.org/viewthread.php?tid=251074&extra=page%3D1, last accessed September 10, 2010.

85. http://www.cfdd.org.cn/bbs/thread-71855-1-1.html, last accessed April 17, 2013. As Hong Kong activist Leung Kwok-hung told the *South China Morning Post*, "All three authorities across the straits have blocked us from going to the islands." Tanna Chong, "HK Activists Blocked From sailing," *South China Morning Post*, September 14, 2010.

86. "China Suppresses Anti-Japanese Protests, Bans Media Coverage," BBC Monitoring Asia-Pacific, September 13, 2010.

87. "Baozhu feifa zifu" [Protect illegal characters], September 13, 2010, translation by Julian Smisek at http://www.danwei.org/nationalism/han_han_on_the_diaoyu_islands.php; original post at http://blog.sina.com.cn/s/blog_4701280b0100lcum.html, last accessed April 22, 2013.

88. The group's petition called on Chinese at home and abroad to participate in anti-Japanese marches and protests, to boycott Japanese goods, and to prepare for war with Japan at any moment. "Zhongguo minjian kangRi lianmeng chengli gongao," September 12, 2010, http://www.shengfang.mo.cn/bbs/thread-53056-1-1.html, last accessed October 26, 2010.

89. "Jintian wo qu woguo shiguan le," September 11, 2010, http://www.cfdd.org.cn/bbs/thread-71712-1-57.html, last accessed April 22, 2013.

90. Foreign Ministry Spokesperson Jiang Yu's Remarks on the Chinese Government Taking Home 14 Fishermen, PRC Ministry of Foreign Affairs, September 13, 2010, accessed at http://www.fmprc.gov.cn/eng/xwfw/s2510/2535/t752270.htm.

91. Mari Yamaguchi, "China Postpones Official's Visit to Japan amid Row," Associated Press, September 14, 2010.

92. "China Enhances Law Enforcement Activities in Relevant Waters," Xinhua News Service, September 17, 2010; "China Brings Suspicious Machine to Gas Field," *Daily Yomiuri*, September 18, 2010.

93. "Police Snuff Out Anti-Japanese Protests," *South China Morning Post*, September 18, 2010.

94. "Shanghai de jin, 9.18 huodong," September 14, 2010, http://www.cfdd.org.cn/bbs/thread-71967-1-1.html, last accessed September 23, 2010; "Shanghai de yi shiqu lianxi, jiuji!" September 15, 2010, http://www.cfdd.org.cn/bbs/viewthread.php?tid=72100, last accessed September 23, 2010.

95. "Dalu baodiao xingdong xiaozu 9.15 zui xin xiaoxi," September 15, 2010, http://www.bd2010.org/?p=130, last accessed September 16, 2010.

96. "Don't Believe the Protest Hype," ChengduLiving, September 17, 2010, http://www.chengduliving.com/dont-believe-chengdu-protest-hype/, last accessed May 8, 2013.

97. "Baodiao lianhehui QQ qun yijing bei feng, jinhou you hua shang luntan fatie," September 12, 2010, http://www.cfdd.org.cn/bbs/thread-71807-1-54.html, last accessed April 22, 2013; "Minjian baodiao zongqun yijing jia man 500 ren de qun bei feng," September 13, 2010, http://www.cfdd.org.cn/bbs//thread-71913-1-48.html, last accessed May 9, 2013.

98. "OSC Report: Prominent PRC Activist Bloggers' Postings, 16–22 Sept 2010," CPP20100922715027.

99. In Chinese: *kebu keyi ba fanri youxing biancheng fan qiangchai youxing? Shi youxing wo dou hui canjia de.* http://twitter.com/aiww/status/24584033411 and http://twitter.com/aiww/status/24627611938, last accessed September 15, 2010.

100. "The Meaning of Protests," available at http://www.bullogger.com/blogs/twocold/archives/366539.aspx, last accessed March 29, 2011.

101. "China Should Not Be Easily Irritated," *Global Times*, September 16, 2010, accessed at http://opinion.globaltimes.cn/editorial/2010-09/573563.html.

102. "Youguan bumen kaiche lai jie wo, qing wo qu he cha," September 16, 2010, http://www.cfdd.org.cn/bbs/viewthread.php?tid=72172, last accessed September 22, 2010.

103. *South China Morning Post*, September 17, 2010.

104. In 2003, for example, the Patriots Alliance Network organized an Internet signature campaign demanding Japanese compensation for victims of poison gas bombs left near Qiqihar in northeastern China. In announcing the start of the petition campaign, the official declaration read: "We firmly support the Ministry of Foreign Affairs' stern negotiations with Japan on August 8 and August 12 [and] hope that this campaign will help the government put pressure on Japan." http://bbs.1931-9-18.org/viewthread.php?tid=22454, last accessed March 16, 2011.

105. This date, "Victory over Japan Day," is commemorated in the United States on September 2, 1945, due to the difference in time zone.

106. "Jintian, 2010.9.3 shi weida de Zhonghua minzu kangRi zhanzheng shengli 65 zhou nian jini-anri," http://www.cfdd.org.cn/bbs/thread-71399-1-1.html, September 3, 2010, last accessed May 6, 2013.

107. "Four Chinese Protest at Foreign Ministry over China-Japan Gas Deal," *Ming Pao*, BBC Monitoring Asia Pacific, September 4, 2010.

108. Li Nan, "Bao Diao lianhehui luntan zui hou yi tie," CFDD.org.cn, June 26, 2008, last accessed July 21, 2008, reposted at http://www.cfdd.org.cn/bbs/viewthread.php?tid=55307; see also Baodiao lianhe hui wang zhan guanli yuan (web administrator), "Zhongguo minjian baodiao lian he hui huyu jiu donghai xieyi zhixun waijiaobu," June 17, 2008, http://www.cfdd.org.cn/bbs/thread-55139-1-1.html, last accessed May 6, 2013.

109. Communication with a CFDD associate of Li Yiqiang, June 9, 2007.

110. The Xiamen PX protest was one of the first large-scale mass incidents to be mobilized via online social media. See Xiao 2011.

111. Flickr photos by "Cloudswander," available at http://www.flickr.com/photos/78205250@N00/524460512/in/set-72157600293959345/, http://www.flickr.com/photos/78205250@N00/524460954/in/set-72157600293959345/, last accessed May 2, 2013.

112. http://bbs.china918.cn:81/showtopic.aspx?topicid=28156&page=end, last accessed March 12, 2011; Tanna Chong, "HK Activists Blocked from Sailing," *South China Morning Post*, September 14, 2010; http://www.cfdd.org.cn/bbs/thread-71855-1-1.html, last accessed April 17, 2013.

113. Post by "Zhongguo chengguan," September 15, 2010, http://www.cfdd.org.cn/bbs/viewthread.php?tid=72100, last accessed September 23, 2010.

114. Comment by *da jiang you*, http://www.cfdd.org.cn/bbs/viewthread.php?tid=72172, September 16, 2010, last accessed September 22, 2010.

115. "Baodiao lianhehui QQ qun yijing bei feng, jinhou you hua shang luntan fatie," September 12, 2010, http://www.cfdd.org.cn/bbs/thread-71807-1-54.html, last accessed April 22, 2013.

116. "Jintian baodiao de zuixin xiaoxi: 9.13 wanshang gengxin," http://www.cfdd.org.cn/bbs/thread-71899-1-53.html, last accessed April 22, 2013.

117. "OSC Report: Prominent PRC Activist Bloggers' Postings, 16–22 Sept 2010," CPP20100922715027.

118. http://twitter.com/wenyunchao/status/24765420508, September 17, 2010.

119. Shi Tianjian, "Bao Diao Bushi Danxiaogui Youxi" [Protecting Diaoyu Islands is not a game for cowards], *Phoenix Weekly*, October 15, 2010, 40–41, also at http://blog.sina.com.cn/s/blog_5214b1d80102dxok.html.

120. "China Federation for Defending Diaoyu Islands Denies Organizing Beijing Protests," Hong Kong *Feng Huang Wei Shih Tzu Hsun Tai* in Mandarin, CPP20100920715001, September 16, 2010.

121. "Jing baodiao gu gan zao jiankong nan chu men," *Ming Pao*, September 21, 2010, http://news.mingpao.com/20100921/caa4.htm.

122. "Shanghai Shenyang deng di dou chuxian fanRi shiwei," *Lianhe Zaobao*, September 18, 2010.

123. "Police Snuff Out Anti-Japanese Protests," *South China Morning Post*, September 18, 2010.

124. "Chinese, HK Citizens Stage Protests over Isle Dispute with Japan," Japan Economic Newswire, September 18, 2010.

125. "Police Snuff Out Anti-Japanese Protests," *South China Morning Post*, September 18, 2010.

126. "Poor Judgment Lit Initial Fuse," *Nikkei Weekly*, October 4, 2010.

127. "Illegal Detention of Chinese Trawler's Captain Harms Chinese Public's Trust in Japan," *People's Daily*, September 21, 2010.

128. "Sea Row Putting Chinese Tourists Off Trips to Japan," Xinhua News Service, September 21, 2010.

129. "China and Japan Spat Mars Youth Expo Visit," *Financial Times*, September 20, 2010.

130. "Japan Extends Detention of Chinese Skipper to Sept. 29," Xinhua News Service, September 19, 2010.

131. "Sea Row Putting Chinese Tourists Off trips to Japan," Xinhua News Service, September 21, 2010.
132. "Public Outrage Flares Up Again over Japan's Detention of Chinese Trawler Captain," *People's Daily*, September 21, 2010.
133. Ibid.
134. "Premier Wen Urges Japan to Release Captain," *China Daily*, September 22, 2010.
135. "Japan Warns against Extreme Nationalism," *Nation*, September 22, 2010.
136. "China Will Never Waiver on Sovereignty Issues—Experts," Xinhua News Service, September 23, 2010.
137. "Clinton Tells Maehara Senkakus Subject to Japan-US Security Pact," Kyodo News Agency, September 23, 2010.
138. Translated from "Kongo mo Nippon no genri gensoku o mamoru," *Chūō Kōron*, December 2010, 106–11, accessed at http://www.japanechoweb.jp/jew0403/.
139. Peter Lee, "High Stakes Gamble as Japan, China and the U.S. Spar in the East and South China Seas," *Asia-Pacific Journal* 43-1-10 (October 25, 2010).
140. Special Assistant to the President and Senior Director for Asian Affairs Jeff Bader, White House Press Briefing, September 23, 2010, accessed at http://www.whitehouse.gov/the-press-office/2010/09/23/press-briefing-press-secretary-robert-gibbs-special-assistant-president-; U.S. State Department Spokesman Philip J. Crowley, Remarks to the Press, September 23, 2010, accessed at http://www.state.gov/r/pa/prs/ps/2010/09/147836.htm.
141. Agence France-Presse, October 28, 2010.
142. Cheng Gang, "Diaoyudao xunhang riji yi: wo chuanyuan zhi dou Riben xunluo jian," September 23, 2010, http://world.huanqiu.com/roll/2010-09/1130288.html, last accessed May 9, 2013. "Two Chinese Patrol Boats Leave Waters off Senkakus," *Daily Yomiuri*, October 7, 2010.
143. "Japan Retreats with Release of Chinese Boat Captain," *New York Times*, September 24, 2010.
144. "Remarks to the Press from UNGA," U.S. Department of State, September 24, 2010, accessed at http://www.state.gov/p/af/rls/spbr/2010/147922.htm.
145. "Ganxie Zuguo renmin Rifang zhuakou feifa," *Nanfang Dushibao*, September 26, 2010.
146. "China Demands Apology, Compensation from Japan over Boat Row," Xinhua News Service, September 25, 2010.
147. "Japan Says China's Demand for Apology 'Totally Unacceptable,'" Kyodo News Agency, September 25, 2010.
148. "Boat Row: Japan Seeks Payment for Damage," *Straits Times*, September 28, 2010.
149. "China Softens Its Remarks in Dispute with Japan," *New York Times*, September 29, 2010.
150. "Tokyo, Beijing Defusing Their Feud," *Nikkei Weekly*, October 4, 2010.
151. Chico Harlan and William Wan, "Japan to Release Chinese Boat Captain," *Washington Post*, September 24, 2010.
152. Zhongguo Guoji Wenti Yanjiusuo 2010–11, 21–23.
153. Zhongguo Guoji Wenti Yanjiusuo 2010–11, 23.
154. Mark Landler, "Offering to Aid Talks, U.S. Challenges China on Disputed Islands," *New York Times*, July 23, 2010.
155. "Biden: US-China Ties Must Go through Tokyo," Agence France-Presse, September 20, 2010.
156. Bao 2011, 82; Yang 2011, 149.
157. Teng 2011, 75–76.
158. Lian Degui, "Jianxi Meiguo zai Diaoyudao wenti shang de mohu zhengce," Xinhua News Service, November 9, 2012, available at http://www.siis.org.cn/Lunwen_View.aspx?lid=10000533.
159. Liu Jiangyong, "A Change in Japan's US policy," *China-US Focus*, March 11, 2013.
160. "China Issues Japan Travel Warning," *Straits Times*, October 2, 2010.
161. Shigeru Ishiba, "Kita Chōsen, Chūgoku, Roshia ni azawarawareru Nihon" [The laughing-stock of East Asia], *Chūō Kōron*, January 2011, 94–101, translated at Japan Echo Web, No. 4 (December 2010–January 2011), http://www.japanechoweb.jp/jew0412/2/.

162. "Parties Unite in Demanding Senkaku Video," *Japan Times*, October 1, 2010.
163. "Japan and China Agree to Improve Ties Despite Row," Reuters, October 5, 2010.
164. "China's Wen Tells Japan PM Disputed Islands Are Chinese territory," Xinhua News Serevice, October 5, 2010.
165. "Hawkish Mainlanders Back Wen's Claims of Diaoyus Sovereignty," *South China Morning Post*, October 6, 2010.
166. "Japanese Navy Ship Cancels China Visit," Kyodo News Agency, October 14, 2010.
167. "Four Japanese Lawmakers Inspect Disputed Islands from Plane," Kyodo News Agency, October 9, 2010.
168. Foreign Ministry Spokesman's regular press conference, October 12, 2010, http://www.fmprc.gov.cn/eng/xwfw/s2510/2511/t761429.shtml.
169. "Japan's Okinawa Adopts Resolution over Disputed Islands row," Kyodo News Agency, September 28, 2010; "Japanese Mayor Urges Enhanced Security Near Islands Disputed with China," Kyodo News Agency, October 4, 2010.
170. "Japan Asks Google to Delete Chinese Names of Disputed Islets," Kyodo News Agency, October 14, 2010.
171. "China Issues Japan Travel Warning," *Straits Times*, October 2, 2010.
172. For example, http://zhidao.baidu.com/question/186851526.html, last accessed May 9, 2013. The CFDD website remained largely inaccessible following allegedly Japanese hacking attacks that had paralyzed the website on September 17. It was not until October 12 that CFDD members reported being finally able to log on to the forum. "Zhongguo baodiao zuzhi wang zhan bei hei, fuze ren cheng 'Ribenren gan de,' " *Huanqiu Wang*, September 18, 2010, accessed at http://news.cn.yahoo.com/ypen/20100918/26800.html; "Wang zhan you keyi dengji le, zhandou jiezhe jinxing," October 12, 2010, http://www.cfdd.org.cn/bbs/thread-72189-1-47.html, last accessed May 9, 2013.
173. "Japan Protests China's Diaoyu Patrols," *South China Morning Post*, October 25, 2010.
174. "10.3, Changsha juxing dizhi Rihuo huodong," October 15, 2010, http://www.cfdd.org.cn/bbs//thread-72267-1-47.html, last accessed June 4, 2013.
175. For example, "Riben youyi zuzhi zai 18 ge chengshi faqi fanhua youxing," http://war.163.com/10/1004/10/6I5647CL00011MTO.html, October 4, 2010; "Zutu: Xianchang muji Riben youyi fanhua youxing naoju," http://news.qq.com/a/20101007/000738.htm, October 7, 2010.
176. "Thousands Join Anti-Japan Protests in Several Chinese Cities," Xinhua News Service, October 16, 2010.
177. "Thousands in China, Japan Rally over Island Claims," Associated Press, October 16, 2010.
178. "Bufen zai rong gaoxiao daxuesheng zai tianfu guangchang juji, wei fasheng guoji xingwei," Sichuan Xinwen wang, October 16, 2010.
179. Barbara Demick, "Thousands in Chinese Provinces Stage Anti-Japan Protests," *Los Angeles Times*, October 18, 2010.
180. Xiaohua99, October 16, 2010, http://www.cnni.com.cn/bbs/dispbbs.asp?boardid=65&id=76886, last accessed November 25, 2010.
181. Ibid.
182. "FM Spokesman Comments on Demonstrations over Diaoyu Islands," *China Daily*, October 17, 2010.
183. "More Anti-Japan Protests Take Place in China for Second Day," Kyodo News Agency, October 17, 2010; "China-Japan Row Simmers as Protests Enter Third Day," Agence France-Presse, October 18, 2010.
184. "Ji Sichuan Shaanxi Henan Wuhan baofa fan Ri youxing," *Aozhou Ribao*, reposted at http://dailynews.sina.com/gb/chn/chnnews/ausdaily/20101018/18051917210.html, October 18, 2010; "Anti-Japan Protests Go into 3rd Day, Violence Reported in Wuhan," Japan Economic Newswire, October 18, 2010.
185. On September 24, former ambassador Wu Jianmin again cautioned Chinese citizens against boycotting Japanese goods in a widely reposted interview, e.g., "Qian zhu Fa dashi Wu Jianmin

xu lixing aiguo, wu dizhi Rihuo,"http://news.163.com/10/0924/05/6HAR9HER0001124J. html.

186. Associated Press, October 18, 2010.
187. "Shi Yinhong: ZhongRi guanxi jiegouxing wenti yuan shengyu qinggan yinsu," *Phoenix News*, October 19, 2010, http://news.ifeng.com/mainland/special/zrczdydxz/content-0/ detail_2010_10/19/2829181_0.shtml.
188. "Eda, Yang Vow to Build Sound Japan-China Ties Despite Senkaku Row," October 19, 2010.
189. "China-Japan Row Simmers as Protests Enter Third Day," Agence France-Presse, October 18, 2010.
190. "China 'Shocked' by Japan FM's Comments as Two Sides Meet," Agence France-Presse, October 19, 2010.
191. "Japan Promises to Talk to China Despite Protests," Associated Press, October 19, 2010.
192. Press conference by Minister for Foreign Affairs Seiji Maehara, October 19, 2010, http:// www.mofa.go.jp/announce/fm_press/2010/10/1019_01.html.
193. "China Strictly Controls Media Reports on Anti-Japan Protests," Japan Economic Newswire, October 20, 2010.
194. Priscilla Jiao, "Cover Story on China Hawk Breaks Media Mould," *South China Morning Post*, October 23, 2010.
195. "Wangmin wangshang huyu fanRi shiwei, Shenzhen dangju jietou yanmi jingjie," *Radio Free Asia*, October 20, 2010, http://www.rfa.org/cantonese/news/china_diaoyu-10202010104158.html.
196. "Many Chinese Set to Stage Anti-Japan Protests This Weekend," Japan Economic Newswire, October 22, 2010.
197. "'78 Senkaku Accord Unrecognized," Kyodo News Agency, October 22, 2010, available at http://www.japantimes.co.jp/text/nn20101022a4.html. Whether the two sides ever reached such a consensus became controversial again in 2012. E.g., Taylor Fravel, "Something to Talk About, Again," *Diplomat*, October 10, 2012, accessed at http://thediplomat.com/2012/10/ something-to-talk-about-again.
198. "'78 Senkaku Accord Unrecognized," Kyodo News Agency, October 22, 2010, available at http://www.japantimes.co.jp/text/nn20101022a4.html.
199. "Shaanxi he Gansu shubai ren fanRi youxing," October 25, 2010, www.cfdd.org.cn/bbs/ thread-72429-1-45.html, last accessed May 9, 2013.
200. "Anti-Japan Protests Spread in Chinese Cities," Associated Press, October 26, 2010.
201. "Chinese Criticize Japan, Gov't in Protest in Shaanxi," Japan Economic Newswire, October 24, 2010.
202. "Beijing Now Worried That Anti-Japan Protests Could Backfire," *Christian Science Monitor*, October 26, 2010.
203. "Kongzhi fanRi youxing Zhongguo bufen daxue 'feng xiao,'" *Voice of America*, October 23, 2010, http://www.voanews.com/chinese/news/20101023-school-anti-japan-105593108. html.
204. "More Anti-Japan Protests in China," *Japan Times*, October 24, 2010; "Police Curb Anti-Japanese Protesters in Sichuan City," *South China Morning Post*, October 24, 2010.
205. "Changsha de kangri huodong canyu renyuan bei jingcha kongzhi," October 23, 2010, http:// www.cfdd.org.cn/bbs/thread-72391-1-1.html, last accessed November 25, 2010.
206. Guo Xin, "Yi fa li xing biaoda aiguo reqing," *Renmin Ribao*, October 24, 2010, accessed at http://opinion.people.com.cn/GB/70240/13033100.html.
207. "China Urges Order as Anti-Japan Protest Flares," Reuters, October 26, 2010.
208. "Thousands Join Anti-Japan Protests in China's Chongqing," Xinhua News Service, October 26, 2010.
209. Forum moderator "Qi kai de sheng," in reply to "Ming ri Chongqing chaotianmen" thread, October 25, 2010, http://www.cfdd.org.cn/bbs//thread-72436-1-46.html, last accessed June 4, 2013.
210. "Anti-Japan March in Chongqing," *Radio Free Asia*, October 26, 2010.

211. Liu 2011a, 10.

212. "Shi Yinhong: Zhongguo ying hui ying Riben jiang Diaoyudao wenti guojihua," Phoenix Television, September 30, 2010, http://news.ifeng.com/mainland/special/zrczdydxz/content-0/detail_2010_09/30/2678047_0.shtml#.

213. Ministry of Foreign Affairs of the People's Republic of China, "Yang Jiechi Meets with His Japanese Counterpart, Reaffirming China's Solemn Position on the Issue concerning the Diaoyu Islands," October 29, 2010.

214. "Japan PM Airs Concern over China's Stance on Island Dispute," Kyodo News Agency, October 30, 2010.

215. "China, Japan Ties Strained over Islands at Summit," Reuters, October 29, 2010.

216. "Japan Protests China's Diaoyu Patrols," *South China Morning Post*, October 25, 2010.

217. "Expansion of Fleet to Safeguard Sea Rights," *China Daily*, October 28, 2010.

218. "Yang Jiechi duncu Meifang zai Diaoyudao wenti shang jin yan shen xing," *Renmin Wang*, October 30, 2010, http://world.people.com.cn/GB/13087168.html. State media criticized Hillary Clinton's statement, saying that U.S. "interference" would not solve the dispute. Xinhua News Service, November 3, 2010, http://news.xinhuanet.com/world/2010-11/03/c_13589573.htm, last accessed July 26, 2012.

219. "Yao xiang baodiao bi xian mie Tengxun," http://www.cfdd.org.cn/bbs//thread-72493-1-45.html, October 29, 2010; see also http://www.cfdd.org.cn/bbs//thread-72513-1-45.html, October 30, 2010.

220. https://twitter.com/ranyunfei/status/27524083833, October 16, 2010, 1:32 a.m.

221. "Henan Authorities Order One-Year Reeducation through Labor Sentence for Activist's Satirical Tweet," December 10, 2010, http://cecc.gov/pages/virtualAcad/index.phpd?showsingle=150989.

222. "Chinese Hold Anti-Japan Protests over Boat row," Kyodo News Agency, September 18, 2010.

223. "Chinese Protests "Sporadic" Thanks to Beijing's Efforts—Japanese FM," Kyodo News Agency, September 19, 2010.

224. "Press Conference by Minister for Foreign Affairs Katsuya Okada," Ministry of Foreign Affairs of Japan, September 10, 2010, accessed at http://www.mofa.go.jp/announce/fm_press/2010/9/0910_01.html.

225. "Gyomin Ikari to Rakutan" [Fishermen are upset and disappointed], *Yomiuri Shimbun*, September 25, 2010.

226. "Kokkosho Yoso Koeta Shogeki" [Maehara says his visit was more shocking than expected], *Asahi Shimbun*, September 16, 2010.

227. "Clinton Urges Dialogue to Resolve China-Japan Row," Agence France-Presse, September 24, 2010.

228. "Nihon no Shihouseido Chugokuni Rikaiwo" [Promoting China's understanding of the Japanese judiciary], *Asahi Shimbun*, September 21, 2010.

229. "China Shouldn't Stir Up Anti-Japanese Sentiment," *Daily Yomiuri*, September 17, 2010.

230. "Chinese Fishing Boat Captain's Arrest Reasonable," *Daily Yomiuri*, September 10, 2010.

231. "Wen Weighs In on Row over Captain," *Daily Yoimuri*, September 23, 2010.

232. "Chinese Scholar: Nationalism Gives Beijing Little Wiggle Room in Japan Dispute," Kyodo News Agency, September 23, 2010.

233. "Poor Diplomacy Inflamed China Row," *Asahi Shimbun*, September 27, 2010.

234. "China's Row with Japan Threatens to Escalate," *Sidney Morning Herald*, September 21, 2010.

235. Ibid.

236. Press conference by Minister for Foreign Affairs Seiji Maehara, October 19, 2010, http://www.mofa.go.jp/announce/fm_press/2010/10/1019_01.html.

237. Translated from "Kongo mo Nippon no genri gensoku o mamoru," *Chūō Kōron*, December 2010, 106–11, accessed at http://www.japanpolicyforum.jp/en/archive/no4/000195.html.

238. "Protests Triggered by Anger of China's Young," *Daily Yomiuri*, October 19, 2010.

239. "Chinese Leaders Must Calm Anti-Japan Rallies," *Daily Yomiuri*, October 19, 2010.

240. Ibid.

241. "Poor Judgment Lit Initial Fuse," *Nikkei Weekly*, October 4, 2010. Other Japanese commentators were more wary of labeling Xi either a moderate or a hawk. As Jiji Press noted: "Some diplomatic experts in Beijing speculate that Xi's appointment to the key military post may give hardliners a stronger voice against Japan. However, various sources pointed out that Xi is not necessarily a hardliner against Japan," citing assurances that Xi had given past prime minister Tomiichi Murayama in April 2008. "China's Xi Has Strong Interest in Foreign Policy," Jiji Press, October 19, 2010.

242. Shiraishi Takashi, "Chinese Motives behind the Senkaku Incident," November 2, 2010, accessed at http://www.japanechoweb.jp/jewb014/.

243. "Government Alarmed Tensions Could Worsen," *Daily Yoimuri*, September 22, 2010.

244. Ibid.

245. "Anti-Japan March in Chongqing," *Radio Free Asia*, October 26, 2010.

246. "Kongzhi fanRi youxing Zhongguo bufen daxue 'feng xiao,'" *Voice of America*, October 23, 2010, http://www.voanews.com/chinese/news/20101023-school-anti-japan-105593108.html.

247. "Nationalist Protest in China: Doth We Protest Too Much?" *Economist*, September 21, 2010.

248. "China 'Shocked' by Japan FM's Comments as Two Sides Meet," Agence France-Presse, October 19, 2010.

Chapter 8

1. Michael Green, "Japan Is Back: Unbundling Abe's Grand Strategy," Lowy Institute Analysis, December 17, 2013, available at http://www.lowyinstitute.org/publications/japan-back-unbundling-abes-grand-strategy.

2. "Japanese Prime Minister Noda Admits 'Miscalculation' over Diaoyus," *South China Morning Post,* September 21, 2012.

3. Including wishful thinking or other motivated biases. Jervis 1976.

4. The emphasis on Chinese perceptions reflects the research design and does not imply endorsement.

5. "China 'Overbearing' over Maritime Disputes: Japan Defense Paper," Japan Economic Newswire, August 2, 2011.

6. "Minister Lodges Protest over Chinese Boats' Approach Near Senkakus," Japan Economic Newswire, August 25, 2011.

7. "Noda's Potential Foreign Policy Pitfalls," *Wall Street Journal*, August 29, 2011, accessed at http://blogs.wsj.com/japanrealtime/2011/08/29/nodas-potential-foreign-policy-pitfalls/.

8. Ibid.

9. Feng Zhaokui, "Constant Parade of Leaders," *China Daily*, August 31, 2011, http://usa.chinadaily.com.cn/china/2011-08/31/content_13339702.htm.

10. James Przystup, "Japan-China Relations: Another New Start," Comparative Connections, January 2012, http://csis.org/files/publication/1103qjapan_china.pdf.

11. "Chinese Premier Greets Noda on Election as Japanese PM," Xinhua News Service, August 30, 2011, http://news.xinhuanet.com/english2010/china/2011-08/30/c_131084430.htm.

12. "Japan's New PM Needs to Respect China's Core Interests, Development Demands," Xinhua News Service, August 30, 2011, http://english.peopledaily.com.cn/90883/7583349.html.

13. "Japanese PM Noda Vows Not to Visit Yasukuni Shrine during Tenure," Xinhua News Service, September 2, 2011, http://news.xinhuanet.com/english2010/world/2011-09/02/c_131094599.htm.

14. "Japan Premier Talks Tough on China's Military," *China Daily*, September 15, 2011, http://usa.chinadaily.com.cn/china/2011-09/15/content_13690549.htm.

15. "Chinese President Meets Japanese PM on Advancing Bilateral Ties," Xinhua News Service, November 13, 2011, http://news.xinhuanet.com/english2010/china/2011-11/13/c_122271164.htm.

16. "Noda Calls for Early Resumption of Gas Treaty Talks with China," *Japan Times*, November 14, 2011, http://www.japantimes.co.jp/news/2011/11/14/national/noda-calls-for-early-resumption-of-gas-treaty-talks-with-china/#.UWD4B1txsVk.

17. "Japan PM Visit, Military Exchanges Show Warming Ties," *China Daily*, December 15, 2011.

18. "Japan Arrests China Boat Captain for Illegal Fishing," *Asahi Shimbun*, December 20, 2011.

19. "China, Japan Keen to Improve Ties," *China Daily*, December 27, 2011, http://usa.chinadaily.com.cn/world/2011-12/27/content_14331920.htm.

20. Ibid.

21. "China Proposes Environment Protection Projects with Japan in E. China Sea," Japan Economic Newswire, April 2, 2012.

22. "Japanese Politicians Land on Disputed Isles," Agence France-Presse, January 3, 2012.

23. "Guoji Luntan: Zhongguo Weihu Lingtu Zhuquan de Yizhi Bu Rong Shitan," *Renmin Ribao*, January 17, 2012, accessed at http://military.people.com.cn/GB/16895368.html.

24. "China Now Calls Senkaku Islands 'Core Interest,'" *Asahi Shimbun*, February 3, 2012, https://ajw.asahi.com/article/asia/china/AJ201202030018.

25. "China Rejects Japan Protest over Gas Exploration," Associated Press, February 3, 2012.

26. Martin Fackler, "Chinese City Severs Ties after Japanese Mayor Denies Massacre," *New York Times*, February 22, 2012, http://www.nytimes.com/2012/02/23/world/asia/chinese-city-severs-ties-after-japanese-mayor-denies-massacre.html; "Nagoya Mayor Sticks to 'Nanking Massacre' Denial," *Asahi Shimbun*, February 28, 2012, http://ajw.asahi.com/article/behind_news/social_affairs/AJ201202280033.

27. "Japan Names 39 Uninhabited Islands to Cement Economic Zone," Japan Economic Newswire, March 3, 2012; "Beijing Names Disputed Isles in East China Sea," Jiji Press, March 3, 2012. Although Japan had placed 23 other uninhabited islands under state control the previous year, the Diaoyu/Senkaku Islands had not been included, leading Japanese media to speculate that the government had sought to avoid provoking China. "Japan Makes 23 Remote Islands State Property," Jiji Press, March 7, 2012.

28. "Chinese Indicted over 2010 Ship Collision Near Senkaku," Jiji Press, March 15, 2012.

29. "China Vessels Hold Drill Near Gas Fields," *Daily Yomiuri*, March 19, 2012.

30. "China Seeks to 'Break' Japan's Control over Senkaku through Patrols," Japan Economic Newswire, March 21, 2012.

31. "Chinese FM Urges Japan to 'Fully Recognize' Sensitivity of History, Diaoyu Islands Issues," March 6, 2012, accessed at http://www.gov.cn/misc/2012-03/06/content_2084431.htm.

32. "DPJ, Chinese Communist Party Calling on the Hotline," *Asahi Shimbun*, March 26, 2012, http://ajw.asahi.com/article/behind_news/politics/AJ201203260 http://ajw.asahi.com/article/behind_news/politics/AJ201203260012012.

33. "Press Conference by the Chief Cabinet Secretary (Excerpt)," March 26, 2012, accessed at http://www.kantei.go.jp/foreign/tyoukanpress/201203/26_p.html.

34. Yang Jingjie, "China Slams Japan's Move over Diaoyu Islands," *Global Times*, March 28, 2012, accessed at http://english.peopledaily.com.cn/90780/7771782.html.

35. Ibid.

36. "Ri Cheng 2 Sou Zhongguo Yuzhengchuan Shi Ru Diaoyudao Pilin Qu, Chudong Feiji Jianshi," *Huanqiu Wang*, April 5, 2012, accessed at http://world.huanqiu.com/roll/2012-04/2584457.html.

37. Yoshitaka Unezawa, "Ishihara, Citing Chinese Moves, Plans to Buy Senkaku Islands," *Asahi Shimbun*, April 17, 2012, accessed at http://ajw.asahi.com/article/behind_news/politics/AJ201204170071.

38. "Tokyo Govt to Establish 'Senkaku Team,'" *Daily Yomiuri*, April 29, 2012.

39. "Foreign Ministry Spokesperson Liu Weimin's Remarks on the Issue of Diaoyu Islands," PRC Ministry of Foreign Affairs, April 19, 2012, accessed at http://www.fmprc.gov.cn/eng/xwfw/s2510/t924272.htm.

40. Yoshitaka Unezawa, "Ishihara, Citing Chinese Moves, Plans to Buy Senkaku Islands," *Asahi Shimbun*, April 17, 2012, accessed at http://ajw.asahi.com/article/behind_news/politics/AJ201204170071.

41. "Tree Planting Commemorates China, Japan Ties Anniversary," Xinhua News Service, April 21, 2012, http://news.xinhuanet.com/english/china/2012-04/21/c_131542292.htm.

42. "Japan–People's Republic of China Summit Meeting (Summary)," Ministry of Foreign Affairs of Japan, May 31, 2012, accessed at http://www.mofa.go.jp/announce/jfpu/2012/05/0531-01.html.

43. Yoshitaka Unezawa, "Ishihara, Citing Chinese Moves, Plans to Buy Senkaku Islands," *Asahi Shimbun*, April 17, 2012, accessed at http://ajw.asahi.com/article/behind_news/politics/AJ201204170071.

44. Li Tao, "Riben Toupiao Xianshi 92% Riben Wangmin Zhichi Dongjing Goumai Diaoyudao," *Huanqiu Wang*, April 30, 2012, accessed at http://world.huanqiu.com/roll/2012-04/2674845.html.

45. CCTV, "Dongjing Du Zhengfu Shengcheng 'Goumai Diaoyudao': Kuang Yan! Huaji Xi!" Xinhua Net, May 1, 2012, accessed at http://news.xinhuanet.com/world/2012-05/01/c_111867245_4.htm.

46. Interview with senior Japanese diplomat, no. 172, Beijing, China, June 27, 2013.

47. "Chinese State Media Stokes Senkaku Islands Dispute," *Daily Yomiuri*, May 15, 2012.

48. Mure Dickie, "Tokyo Warned over Plans to Buy Islands," *Financial Times*, June 6, 2012.

49. Ibid.

50. "Fenghuang Quanqiu Lian Xian: Riben Dashi Diaoyudao Wenti Shang: 'Jiang Zhen Hua Tian Mafan,'" Phoenix Television, June 8, 2012, accessed at http://dailynews.sina.com/gb/news/int/phoenixtv/20120608/23273454628.html.

51. "Riben Youyi Diaoyudao Fujin Bisai Diaoyu, Haishang Bao'anting Tigong Hu Hang," Xinhua Net, June 11, 2012, accessed at http://news.xinhuanet.com/world/2012-06/11/c_123262144.htm.

52. "Ri Youyi Fenzi Deng Diaoyudao Fushu Daoyu," Xinhua News Service, July 7, 2012, accessed at http://news.163.com/12/0707/03/85PI1MEE00014AED.html.

53. Zhang Zhe, "Tai Xunluo Jianting Quan Cheng Hu Hang Baodiao Chuan," *Dongfang Zaobao*, July 5, 2012, accessed at http://www.dfdaily.com/html/51/2012/7/5/819781.shtml.

54. "Ri Xiao Dang Gudong Diaoyudao Zhu Jun," *Huanqiu Shibao*, July 6, 2012, accessed at http://news.xinhuanet.com/world/2012-07/06/c_123380781.htm.

55. Foreign Minister of Japan Koichiro Gemba, "Japan-China Relations at a Crossroads," *International Herald Tribune*, November 21, 2012.

56. "Central Government Plans to Buy Senkaku Islands," *Asahi Shimbun*, July 7, 2012, accessed at http://ajw.asahi.com/article/behind_news/politics/AJ201207070062.

57. "Japan Tried but Failed to Avert Disaster in China Dispute," *Asahi Shimbun*, September 26, 2012.

58. "ZhongRi Guanxi: Sishi Hen Nan Bu Huo," *CCTV*, July 11, 2012, accessed at http://world.people.com.cn/n/2012/0711/c1002-18494645.html.

59. "Xinhua Shiping: Riben Zhengfu 'Gou Dao' Naoju Wu Yi Yu 'Wan Huo,'" Xinhua News Service, July 8, 2012, accessed at http://news.xinhuanet.com/world/2012-07/08/c_112386058.htm.

60. "Zhongguo Baodiao Renshi 'Qi Qi Shi Bian' Jinian Huodong Zao Jingfang Quan Cheng Jiankong," Radio France Internationale, July 8, 2012, accessed at http://www.chinese.rfi.fr/中国/20120708-中国保钓人士"七七事变"纪念活动遭警方全程监控.

61. "Lugouqiao Jinian 'Qi Qi' Jing Quan Cheng Jiankong," *Ming Pao*, July 8, 2012, accessed at http://www.iask.ca/news/china/2012/0708/144386.html.

62. Ibid.

63. "Genba, Yang Tread Carefully around Senkaku Islands Issue," *Asahi Shimbun*, July 12, 2012.

64. Akihisa Nagashima, member of the House of Representatives and former aide to Noda, writes that some Japanese media, particularly the *Asahi Shimbun*, inappropriately used the English term "nationalization" to describe the government's repurchase of islands sold by the Japanese government in 1932. "'Diaoyudao Guoyouhua' Zhi Shuo Shi Riben Meiti de 'Wu Dao'?" Radio France Internationale, October 27, 2013, accessed at http://www.chinese.rfi.fr/中国/20131027-"钓鱼岛国有化'之说是日本媒体的'误导.'"

65. Ibid.
66. "ZhongRi Waizhang Cuoshang Diaoyudao Wu Jieguo, Tan Ji Donghai Youqitian," *Dongfang Net*, July 12, 2012, accessed at http://news.qq.com/a/20120712/000467.htm.
67. Michael Swaine, "Chinese Views Regarding the Senkaku/Diaoyu Islands Dispute," *China Leadership Monitor* 41 (June 2013): 5.
68. "ZhongRi Guanxi: Sishi Hen Nan Bu Huo," *CCTV*, July 11, 2012, accessed at http://world.people.com.cn/n/2012/0711/c1002-18494645.html.
69. Luo Guoqiang, "Riben 'Gou Dao' Zhi Ju De Guojifa Xiaoli Jiexi," *Xiandai Guoji Guanxi*, no. 10, 2012.
70. Zhang Zhe, "ZhongRi Waizhang Cuoshang Diaoyudao Wu Jieguo," *Oriental Morning Post*, July 12, 2012, accessed at http://www.dfdaily.com/html/51/2012/7/12/823583.shtml. CASS Japan expert Jiang Lifeng uses the same "money laundering" metaphor to describe the "true motive" behind Japan's nationalization plan. Jiang 2012, 35.
71. "Press Release: Position of Japan on the Senkaku Islands," Embassy of Japan in the Netherlands, October 10, 2012, accessed at http://www.nl.emb-japan.go.jp/e/policy/response%20senkaku.html.
72. Zhang Jianshu, "Huo Yun Zai Diaoyudao Juxing 'Wei Ling Ji' Riben Zhengfu Xiao Dongzuo Buduan," *China Youth Daily*, July 12, 2012, accessed at http://zqb.cyol.com/html/2012-07/12/nw.D110000zgqnb_20120712_1-04.htm; Press Conference by the Chief Cabinet Secretary, July 25, 2012, accessed at http://www.kantei.go.jp/foreign/tyoukanpress/201207/25_p.html.
73. "Riben Chaodangpai Guohui Yiyuan Jin Ri Shenqing Deng Diaoyudao," *Xinhua News Service*, August 3, 2012, accessed at http://news.xinhuanet.com/yzyd/world/20120803/c_112613646.htm.
74. Zhai 2012, 29.
75. http://www.ciis.org.cn/english/2013-06/04/content_6002574.htm.
76. Zhai 2012, 29.
77. Wu 2012, 9–10.
78. For example, Hu 2013, 85.
79. "Ri Waixiang Cheng Diaoyudao Shiyong 《RiMei An Bao Tiaoyue》," *Renmin Ribao*, July 25, 2012, accessed at http://paper.people.com.cn/rmrb/html/2012-07/25/nw.D110000renmrb_20120725_5-03.htm.
80. "Noda Hints at Using SDF to Defend Senkaku Islands," *Asahi Shimbun*, July 27, 2012, accessed at http://ajw.asahi.com/article/behind_news/politics/AJ201207270060.
81. "Foreign Ministry Spokesperson Hong Lei's Remarks on Japanese Leader's Comments on the Diaoyu Islands," PRC Ministry of Foreign Affairs, July 27, 2012, accessed at http://www.fmprc.gov.cn/eng/xwfw/s2510/2535/t956958.htm.
82. Interview with senior Chinese Foreign Ministry official, no. 171, Beijing, China, June 26, 2013; "Michael Swaine: Long-Term Study Suggests Sino-Japanese Tensions Likely to Increase," *Asahi Shimbun*, June 7, 2013.
83. Jiang 2012, 4, 35.
84. Zhu Wenzheng, "2009 Bao Diao ri ji," May 6, 2009, accessed at http://forum.diaoyuislands.org/viewtopic.php?t=2636.
85. "Jia Fazhi Zhi Ming Canshi Ziyou, Xianggangren Jiben Quanli Wei Yi," *Ming Pao*, May 9, 2009, accessed at http://forum.tvb.com/viewtopic.php?f=20&t=32481.
86. Maggie Chen, "Something Fishy about Boat Incident; Some People Believe Local Authorities' Moves to Stop Diaoyu Activists Are Motivated by Political Reasons," *South China Morning Post*, October 7, 2010.
87. Ibid.
88. Wei Yingyin and Zhou Yan, "Bao Diao Chuan Xianggang Chufa Fu Diaoyudao Bei Shui Jing Jiecha Hou Zhefan," *Renmin Wang*, January 3, 2012, accessed at http://news.ifeng.com/mainland/detail_2012_01/03/11731246_0.shtml.

89. "Taiwan Baodiao Xiehui Tuidong Chengli Quanqiu Huaren Bao Diao Da Lianmeng [Taiwan Bao Diao Association helps establish the World Chinese Alliance for the Defense of the Diaoyu Islands]," Radio France Internationale May 2, 2010.

90. Zhang Zhe, "Tai Xunluo Jianting Quan Cheng Hu Hang Baodiao Chuan," *Dongfang Zaobao*, July 5, 2012, accessed at http://www.dfdaily.com/html/51/2012/7/5/819781.shtml.

91. Song Ruxin, "Huang Xilin Huiying Baodiao Dai Wuxingqi, Cheng Liang An Hezuo Mei Cuo," *DWNews*, July 8, 2012, accessed at http://china.dwnews.com/news/2012-07-08/58779608-all.html.

92. "Fang Qu Di Yi Ma," *Apple Daily*, August 13, 2012, accessed at http://hk.apple.nextmedia.com/international/art/20120813/16598867.

93. Nojima Tsuyoshi, "'Fan Dui Meiguo Liyong Riben' Zhuan Fang Bao Diao Huodong Jia Liang Guo Xiong," *Asahi Shimbun*, November 19, 2012, accessed at http://asahichinese.com/article/news/AJ201211190008?imgIX=0&page=1.

94. Ibid.

95. "Fang Xiaosong: Lin Chufa Guo An Zhao Shang Men," *Ming Pao*, August 19, 2012.

96. "Mainland, Taiwan Activists Pull out of Diaoyu Trip," *Global Times*, August 15, 2012, http://www.globaltimes.cn/content/727023.shtml.

97. "Yang Shi Leng Zhuan Re, Miji Zhi Ji Qiangtan, Waijiaobu Ji Zhao Ri Shi, Cu Liji Wu Tiaojian Fang Ren," *Ming Pao*, August 16, 2012.

98. Ibid.

99. "A Role to Play for HK," *South China Morning Post*, August 17, 2012.

100. "815 Beijing Fan Ri Shiwei, Song Dao Cu Ye Tian Xie Zui," Kdnet, August 16, 2012, accessed at http://club.kdnet.net/dispbbs.asp?boardid=1&id=8549359; http://www.cfdd.org.cn/bbs/viewthread.php?tid=82881, August 15, 2012.

101. Many papers obscured the image of the ROC flag. David Bandurski, "The Flag That Launched 1,000 Headaches," http://cmp.hku.hk/2012/08/16/26013/.

102. "Zhongguo Minjian Baodiao Lianhehui Huizhang: Haijianchuan Xunhang Pinci Ying Zengjia," *Beijing News*, August 16, 2012, reposted at http://www.21cbh.com/HTML/2012-8-16/zMNjUxXzQ5OTEzMw.html, last accessed November 13, 2012.

103. E.g., http://www.cfdd.org.cn/bbs/viewthread.php?tid=82919; http://www.cfdd.org.cn/bbs/viewthread.php?tid=82911, last accessed July 19, 2013.

104. "Zhongguo Wangmin 'Fa Qi Duo Ge Chengshi Fan Ri Youxing,'" BBC, August 16, 2012, accessed at http://www.bbc.co.uk/zhongwen/simp/chinese_news/2012/08/120816_china_japan_protest.shtml; "Net Postings Ready Protests in China," *Japan Times*, August 18, 2012; "Japan Report Says Internet Messages in China for Protests 'Deleted,'" BBC Monitoring (Kyodo News Agency), August 17, 2012.

105. "Noda Team Moves Swiftly to Curtail Senkaku Controversy," *Asahi Shimbun*, August 17, 2012, accessed at http://ajw.asahi.com/article/behind_news/politics/AJ201208170043.

106. Emily Wang, "Japan Activists Land, Raise Flags on Disputed Isle," Associated Press, August 19, 2012, accessed at http://bigstory.ap.org/article/japan-activists-land-raise-flags-disputed-isle.

107. Wallace and Weiss 2013. Data were gathered using keyword searches of Chinese news media, online forums, activist websites, individual blogs, and Weibo, among others. At least two independent sources were required to verify the occurrence of an anti-Japanese protest. Between August 15 and September 18, 208 of China's 287 prefectural-level cities had at least one anti-Japanese protest. See http://ssrn.com/abstract=2406056.

108. "Zhongguo Ge Di Minzhong Xiangying Canyu Fan Ri Youxing," BBC, August 19, 2012, accessed at http://www.bbc.co.uk/zhongwen/simp/chinese_news/2012/08/120819_china_diaoyu_protest.shtml; "掀车、砸店、烧旗 深圳反日游行失控," *United Daily News*, August 19, 2012, accessed at http://dailynews.sina.com/gb/chn/chnoverseamedia/udn/su/20120819/18213688548.html.

109. Ibid.

110. "Protests Erupt at Diaoyu Arrests," *South China Morning Post*, August 17, 2012.

111. Mai Yanting, "Bao Diao Renshi Jinwan Fan Gang, Zhongguo Jiajin Daya Fan Ri Shiwei," Radio France Internationale, August 17, 2012, accessed at http://www.chinese.rfi.fr/中国/20120817-保钓人士今晚返港中国加紧打压反日示威.

112. Ibid.

113. Cao Lin, "Hehu Aiguo Reqing, Yancheng Da Za Baoxing," *China Youth Daily*, August 20, 2012, accessed at http://zqb.cyol.com/html/2012-08/20/nw.D110000zgqnb_20120820_5-01.htm.

114. "Zhongxuanbu Ling Chuanmei Danhua Fan Ri Shiwei, Jin Deng Da Za Zhao Pian, Zhi Zhun Yong Xinhuashe Gao," *Ming Pao*, August 21, 2012, accessed at http://hk.news.yahoo.com/中宣部令傳媒淡化反日示威-禁登打砸照片-只准用新華社稿-211503290.html.

115. "Jian Riben Che Ji Za, Cu Zhengfu Chubing Diaoyudao," *Ming Pao*, August 20, 2012.

116. Press Conference by the Chief Cabinet Secretary, August 20, 2012, accessed at http://www.kantei.go.jp/foreign/tyoukanpress/201208/20_a.html.

117. "Noda in Quandary as Hong Kong Activists Plan Return Landing on Disputed Isles," *Asahi Shimbun*, August 21, 2012, accessed at http://ajw.asahi.com/article/behind_news/politics/AJ201208210092. Nagashima's role as go-between was later reported by Japanese media. "Senkaku Snafu Laid to Broad Miscalculation," Kyodo News Agency, November 20, 2012, accessed at http://www.japantimes.co.jp/text/nn20121120a9.html.

118. Press Conference by Prime Minister Yoshihiko Noda, August 24, 2012, accessed at http://www.kantei.go.jp/foreign/noda/statement/201208/24kaiken_e.html.

119. Ibid.

120. "US-Japan Drill 'Raises Regional Tension,'" *China Daily*, August 22, 2012; Chang Liu, "U.S. Should Cease to Stoke Tensions over Diaoyu Islands," Xinhua News Service, August 21, 2012.

121. "Zhongguo Minjiang Bao Diao Lianhehui Huizhang Tong Zeng," *Renmin Wang*, August 23, 2012, accessed at http://t.people.com.cn/talk/243-2.html.

122. "Diaoyu Solution Lies in Strength and Unity," *Global Times*, August 20, 2012, accessed at http://www.globaltimes.cn/content/727852.shtml.

123. "Shandong Qian Ren Fan Ri Za Canguan, Wangmin Haozhao 25 Ri Guangdong Hainan Youxing," *Sinchew Daily*, August 25, 2012, accessed at http://news.sinchew.com.my/node/258757.

124. "Zhongguo Lianxu Lianzhou You Fan Ri Youxing Jiefangjun Yanlian Shiwei," Radio France Internationale, August 27, 2012, accessed at http://www.chinese.rfi.fr/中国/20120827-中国连续两周有反日游行解放军演练示威.

125. "Ri Mei: Zhongguo Duo Ci Jiu Diaoyudao Wenti Jinggao Riben," *Cankao Xiaoxi*, September 4, 2012, accessed at http://www.chinanews.com/mil/2012/09-04/4157259.shtml.

126. "Noda Sends Letter to Beijing amid Tension," *Asahi Shimbun*, August 28, 2012, accessed at http://ajw.asahi.com/article/behind_news/politics/AJ201208280099.

127. "Senkaku Snafu Laid to Broad Miscalculation," Kyodo News Agency, November 20, 2012, accessed at http://www.japantimes.co.jp/text/nn20121120a9.html.

128. Chen Jianjun, "Tang Jiaxuan: 'Gou Dao' Yinfa De Chongtu Yanzhong Ganrao Zhong Ri Liangguo Guanxi," *Renmin Wang*, August 29, 2012, accessed at http://japan.people.com.cn/35469/7928587.html.

129. "Ri Mei Cheng Zhongguo Jiang Dui Ri Tichu Diaoyudao Wenti Jiejue 'San Bu' Yuanze," Phoenix Television, August 29, 2012, accessed at http://news.ifeng.com/mainland/special/diaoyudaozhengduan/content-3/detail_2012_08/29/17172751_0.shtml.

130. "Fu Ying Hui Jian Shan Kou Zhuang, Yaoqiu Ri Fang Shenzhong Chuli You Guan Diaoyudao Wenti," Xinhua, August 31, 2012, accessed at http://news.ifeng.com/mainland/special/diaoyudaozhengduan/content-3/detail_2012_08/31/17260250_0.shtml.

131. Han Xiaoqing, director of the *People's Daily* Japan bureau, provoked an online outcry by writing that Bao Diao activism detracted from the nation's economic development and destabilized Sino-Japanese relations. She later apologized and emphasized her respect for the Bao Diao activists who landed on August 15. Han Xiaoqing, "Renzhen Fansi Ri Zhong Guanxi, Lengjing Pingpan Xianggang Bao Diao Zhe Xingdong," *Sina*, August 28, 2012, accessed at http://news.

sina.com.cn/pl/2012-08-28/094525051069.shtml; "Ri Zhong Xinwenshe Shezhang Jiu 'Bao Diao Hai Guo' Lun Zhi Qian: Wo Shi Aiguozhe," *Huanqiu Wang*, September 3, 2012, accessed at http://world.people.com.cn/n/2012/0903/c1002-18906859.html.

132. "Japanese Flag Incident Not Premeditated, Chinese Authorities Say," *Asahi Shimbun*, September 3, 2012, accessed at http://ajw.asahi.com/article/asia/china/AJ201209030070; Andrew Chubb, "Internet Censors Step In to Protect Tang Jiaxuan?" September 2, 2012, http://south-seaconversations.wordpress.com/2012/09/02/internet-censors-step-in-to-protect-tang-ji axuan/#KIR.

133. "Commentary: Japan's Buying Diaoyu Islands Is Flagrant Move," Xinhua News Service, September 5, 2012.

134. "Dangerous Waters: China-Japan Relations on the Rocks," Crisis Group Asia Report No. 245, April 8, 2013, 8.

135. "Japan Tries to Break Ice with Neighbors on Fringes of APEC," *Asahi Shimbun*, September 10, 2012; "Tokyo 'Must Realize This Is Serious,'" *China Daily*, September 10, 2012.

136. "Hu States China's Stance on Japan Ties, Diaoyu Islands," Xinhua News Service, September 9, 2012.

137. "Ribao Cheng Ye Tian Zhengquan Ji Ji Ke Wei," Xinhua News Service, August 8, 2012, accessed at http://news.xinhuanet.com/world/2012-08/08/c_123544389.htm.

138. "Japan Upper House Passes Noda Censure in Bid to Force Election," Bloomberg, August 29, 2012, accessed at http://www.bloomberg.com/news/2012-08-29/japan-upper-ho use-passes-noda-censure-in-bid-to-force-election.html.

139. Shinji Hijikata, "Tokyo Facing Donation Quandary," *Daily Yomiuri*, September 7, 2012.

140. "Noda, Ishihara Prime Senkaku Movers," *Daily Yomiuri*, September 7, 2012.

141. Conversation with professor of international relations and leading expert on Sino-Japanese relations, Beijing, June 16, 2013.

142. Yoshihiko Noda, "Ketsudan koso Waga Shimei" [Decision-making is my mission], *Bungeishunju* (文藝春秋), January 2013, 134–43. The article originally appeared on December 10, 2012.

143. Junya Hashimoto, "Govt Drew Up Multiple Plans for Senkaku Use; Ideas Ranked according to Likelihood of Provoking China, Taiwan Included SDF Deployment," *Daily Yomiuri*, September 13, 2012.

144. Ibid.

145. Kazuhiko Togo, "Help Beijing Step Back from Hegemonism," *Wall Street Journal*, December 23, 2012.

146. "Dangerous Waters: China-Japan Relations on the Rocks," Crisis Group Asia Report No. 245, April 8, 2013.

147. E.g., "Hu Jintao Jiu Dang Qian Zhong Ri Guanxi Huo Diaoyudao Wenti Biaoming Lichang," Xinhua News Service, September 9, 2012, accessed at http://news.xinhuanet.com/world/2012-09/09/c_113010420.htm.

148. Katsuji Nakazawa, "Anti-Japan Protests May Have Finished, but Diligence Still Needed," *Nikkei Weekly*, October 22, 2012.

149. "Japan Tried but Failed to Avert Disaster," *Asahi Shimbun*, September 26, 2012.

150. Statement of the Ministry of Foreign Affairs of the People's Republic of China, September 10, 2012, accessed at http://www.fmprc.gov.cn/eng/topics/diaodao/t968188.shtml.

151. Jane Perlez, "China Accuses Japan of Stealing after Purchase of Group of Disputed Islands," *New York Times*, September 11, 2012.

152. "Riben 'Gou Dao' Tiaozhan Fan Faxisi Zhanzheng | Diaoyudao," *Renmin Ribao*, September 11, 2012, accessed at http://news.sina.com.cn/c/2012-09-11/025925143576.shtml.

153. "Japan Must Bear Serious Consequences of Breaking Promises," *People's Daily*, October 26, 2012, accessed at http://english.peopledaily.com.cn/90883/7992334.html. On the interpretation of Zhong Sheng columns and other semiauthoritative sources "intended to convey the view of an important PRC organization," see, for example, Michael Swaine, "Chinese Leadership and Elite Responses to the U.S. Pacific Pivot," *China Leadership Monitor* 38 (August 6, 2012).

154. Fu Ying, "Diaoyu Islands Belong to China," *China Daily*, September 21, 2012. Fu Ying's remarks were originally given in an interview with Japanese media on September 14, 2012.

155. "Dangerous Waters: China-Japan Relations on the Rocks," Crisis Group Asia Report No. 245, April 8, 2013; Stephanie Kleine-Ahlbrandt, "China: New Leaders, Same Assertive Foreign Policy," CNN, March 8, 2013, accessed at http://www.cnn.com/2013/03/08/opinion/china-foreign-policy-kleine-ahlbrandt.

156. "Ri Mei: Zhongguo 6 Sou Haijianchuan Fu Diaoyudao 'Qian Suo Wei You,'" *Cankao Xiaoxi*, September 14, 2012, accessed at http://world.cankaoxiaoxi.com/2012/0914/92726.shtml.

157. Mure Dickie and K. Hille, "Japan Risks China's Wrath over Senkaku," *Financial Times*, September 10, 2012.

158. http://www.ciis.org.cn/english/2013-06/04/content_6002574.htm.

159. "Si Wei Zhengzhiju Changwei Xian Hou Jiu Diaoyudao Wenti Biaotai," Sina.com, September 12, 2012, accessed at http://news.sina.com.cn/c/2012-09-12/060925153612.shtml.

160. "'Absolutely No Concession' on Diaoyu Islands, Says Chinese Premier," Xinhua News Service, September 10, 2012, http://news.xinhuanet.com/english/china/2012-09/10/c_131841113.htm; "Ri Mei: Zhongguo Dui Riben Gou Dao Kangyi Lidu Chu Hu Yi Liao," *Cankao Xiaoxi*, September 14, 2012, http://china.cankaoxiaoxi.com/2012/0914/92619.shtml.

161. "China Brings Up Japan's Past Militarism in Senkaku Dispute," *Asahi Shimbun*, September 14, 2012.

162. Fu Ying, "Diaoyu Islands Belong to China," *China Daily*, September 21, 2012.

163. "Japan Must Bear Serious Consequences of Breaking Promises," *People's Daily*, October 26, 2012, accessed at http://english.peopledaily.com.cn/90883/7992334.html.

164. This demand was first raised by the Foreign Ministry on September 10 and repeated subsequently, e.g., PRC Ministry of Foreign Affairs, Foreign Ministry Spokesperson Hong Lei's Regular Press Conference, September 21, 2012, accessed at http://www.fmprc.gov.cn/eng/xwfw/s2510/t973323.htm.

165. Stephanie Kleine-Ahlbrandt, "China: New Leaders, Same Assertive Foreign Policy," CNN, March 8, 2013, accessed at http://www.cnn.com/2013/03/08/opinion/china-foreign-policy-kleine-ahlbrandt.

166. "Anger is also smoldering among the general public in China, with anti-Japanese demonstrations taking place Tuesday," Xinhua reported. "China Voice: Japan shouldn't underestimate severity of Diaoyu Islands issue," Xinhua News Service, September 11, 2012; the protests were also reported in Chinese, e.g. http://news.sina.com.cn/c/2012-09-12/031925152619.shtml.

167. Foreign Ministry Spokesperson Hong Lei's Regular Press Conference, September 11, 2012, accessed at http://www.fmprc.gov.cn/eng/xwfw/s2510/2511/t969123.shtml.

168. Louisa Lim, "Second Day of Anti-Japan Protests Rock China," NPR, September 16, 2012.

169. E.g. "Anqing Fan Ri Qingxu Gaozhang, Laobing Minzhong Jixu Kangyi!" September 26, 2012, accessed at http://www.yjqfy.gov.cn/a/tupianrensheng/2012/0917/2484.html; "Fuyang Minjian Zuzhi Faqi Kang Ri Bao Diao Huodong," September 14, 2012, accessed at http://www.fun68.cn/zt/71358.html; "Wo Gongsi Canyu Fan Ri Youxing, Kangyi Riben Qinzhan Wo Guo Diaoyudao," September 18, 2012, accessed at http://www.216611.com/mod_article-article_content-article_id-365.html.

170. "Duo Di Minzhong Wenming 'Bao Diao,'" *Cankao Xiaoxi*, September 16, 2012, http://china.cankaoxiaoxi.com/2012/0916/93400_2.shtml; "Jiu Yue Shiliu Ri: Wuhu Fanchang Juxing Fan Ri Aiguo Youxing," September 16, reposted at http://blog.sina.com.cn/s/blog_6b271e38010186nn.html; "Suizhou 9.16 Bao Diao Fan Ri Da Youxing," September 17, 2012, http://www.szqhnet.com/News/Company_News/839.html.

171. Conversation with Peking University professor and department chair, Beijing, China, June 16, 2013.

172. "Qiqihar Daxue Daya Xuesheng Bao Diao Aiguo Xingwei, Dajia Dou Lai Weiguan!" reposted to http://blog.sina.com.cn/s/blog_53162eab010165rm.html, September 21, 2012.

173. "Anti-Japan Protests Turn Violent in Shenzhen, Guangzhou and Qingdao," *South China Morning Post*, September 17, 2012.

174. Ibid.

175. Yoree Koh, "Shanghai Consulate Details Accounts of Japanese Harassed in China," *Wall Street Journal*, September 14, 2012, accessed at http://blogs.wsj.com/japanrealtime/2012/09/14/shanghai-consulate-details-accounts-of-japanese-harassed-in-china/.

176. Louisa Lim, "Second Day of Anti-Japan Protests Rock China," NPR, September 16, 2012; "Fan Ri Youxing Bian Da Za Shao Qiang, Shei Zai Dianwu Aiguo Qingjie," *Caixun Wang*, September 15, 2012, accessed at http://economy.caixun.com/content/20120915/NE037g1a.html.

177. "Xi'an Rixi Chezhu Bei Fan Ri Youxingzhe Yong Gang Suo Za Chuan Lugu," *Beijing Youth Daily*, September 21, 2012, accessed at http://news.qq.com/a/20120921/000756_1.htm.

178. Retweeted by former Google China president Kaifu Lee, September 15, 2012, http://www.weibo.com/1197161814/yC6fLq8O1, last accessed September 16, 2012.

179. Han Han, "Tiao Chu Qipan De Qizi," September 17, 2012, accessed at http://www.weibo.com/1191258123/yCijNeXo7; see also Han Han, "My Feelings about the Recent Anti-Japan Protests," *South China Morning Post*, September 18, 2012.

180. "Meiti Huyu Lixing Aiguo Xu Xiang 'Da Za Qiang' Shuo Bu, Bu Neng Qinzhe Tong Chouzhe Kuai," *Renmin Wang*, September 16, 2012, accessed at http://opinion.people.com.cn/n/2012/0916/c1003-19021171.html.

181. "Beijing Du Cha Ju Xunsu Zhaokai Quanti Renyuan Huiyi Chuanda Xuexi Liang Ban Tongzhi Jingshen Zuo Hao Wei Wen Gongzuo," http://bjdc.mlr.gov.cn/dcyw_2043/dckx/201209/t20120917_1141640.htm, September 17, 2012; "Panjin Zhaokai Tuoshan Chuli Kangyi Riben Feifa 'Gou Dao' Wei Wen Huiyi," September 17, 2012, http://www.ln.chinanews.com/html/2012-09-18/536089.html; "Shangwu Ting Dangzu Chuanda Guanche Zhongyang Ji Zizhiqu Guanyu Tuoshan Chuli Bufen Qunzhong Kangyi Riben Feifa 'Gou Dao' Huodong Tongzhi Jingshen Jiji Weihu Shehui Wending," September 18, 2012, http://www.xjftec.gov.cn:7001/DataSupport/Family/Jingmaojianbao/4028c283380ebdd00139d79359ef5b2d.html; "Sanya Shi Fagaiwei Xunsu Zhaokai Quanti Renyuan Huiyi Chuanda Xuexi 'Liang Ban' Wei Wen Tongzhi He Jiang Shuji Zai Shiwei Lilun Yantaohui De Jianghua Jingshen," September 18, 2012, http://fg.sanya.gov.cn/business/htmlfiles/fgwsite/ggl/201209/39133.html.

182. "Guizhou Sheng Gong Shang Lian Chuanda Xuexi Zhong Ban Fa Dian 【2012】 21 Hao Wenjian Jiji Zuo Hao Jiguan Ganbu Zhigong Wei Wen Gongzuo," http://www.acfic.org.cn/publicfiles/business/htmlfiles/qggsl/gz_gzdt/201209/35928.html, last accessed September 28, 2012.

183. "Panjin Zhaokai Tuoshan Chuli Kangyi Riben Feifa 'Gou Dao' Wei Wen Huiyi," September 17, 2012, http://www.ln.chinanews.com/html/2012-09-18/536089.html.

184. "Chinese Ships Enter Waters around Diaoyu Islands," *South China Morning Post*, September 18, 2012.

185. "9 Yue 18 Ri Wo Guo 180 Duo Ge Chengshi Lixing Kangyi Riben Gou Dao," *Global Times*, September 20, 2012, accessed at http://news.sina.com.cn/c/2012-09-20/012325210587.shtml.

186. Ian Johnston, "More Protests in China over Japan and Islands," *New York Times*, September 18, 2012, accessed at http://www.nytimes.com/2012/09/19/world/asia/china-warns-japan-over-island-dispute.html?_r=0.

187. "Japan Tried but Failed to Avert Disaster," *Asahi Shimbun*, September 26, 2012.

188. "Cong Yigong Dao Baotu De Na Yi Bu," *China Youth Daily*, October 17, 2012, accessed at http://zqb.cyol.com/html/2012-10/17/nw.D110000zgqnb_20121017_3-10.htm.

189. "Beijing Vows More Measures on Islands," *China Daily*, September 27, 2012.

190. "Japanese Vessels Expelled from Diaoyu Islands Waters," Xinhua News Service, October 30, 2012, accessed at http://news.xinhuanet.com/english/china/2012-10/30/c_131939991.htm.

191. "Beijing Stores Suspend Sales of Japanese Books," *Japan Times*, September 24, 2012, accessed at http://www.japantimes.co.jp/text/nn20120924a6.html; "Novelist Murakami Weighs In

on Japan Territorial Rows," WSJ Japan Real Time report, accessed at http://blogs.wsj.com/japanrealtime/2012/09/28/novelist-murakami-weighs-in-on-japan-territorial-rows/.

192. State Council Information Office, "Diaoyu Dao, an Inherent Territory of China," September 25, 2012, accessed at http://news.xinhuanet.com/english/china/2012-09/25/c_131872152.htm.

193. Keiko Yoshioka, "Even Chinese Criticize Top Officials Boycotting IMF Meet," *Asahi Shimbun*, October 14, 2012, accessed at http://ajw.asahi.com/article/asia/china/AJ201210140051. In September, a researcher affiliated with the Ministry of Commerce also proposed that China employ "economic sanctions" against Japan, using the WTO's "security exceptions" clause. Baisong Jin, "Consider Sanctions on Japan," *China Daily*, September 17, 2012, accessed at http://www.chinadaily.com.cn/opinion/2012-09/17/content_15761435.htm.

194. "Senkaku Snafu Laid to Broad Miscalculation," Kyodo News Agency, November 20, 2012, accessed at http://www.japantimes.co.jp/text/nn20121120a9.html.

195. "Chinese State Media Stokes Senkaku Islands Dispute," *Daily Yomiuri*, May 15, 2012.

196. "Avoiding Confrontation Is Beneficial for Both Nations," *Asahi Shimbun*, August 20, 2012.

197. "Beef Up Measures to Prevent Future Senkaku Intrusions," *Daily Yomiuri*, August 17, 2012.

198. Yuriko Koike, "China's Expanding Core," *Project Syndicate*, May 24, 2012, accessed at http://www.project-syndicate.org/commentary/china-s-expanding-core.

199. "Fan Ri Qingxu Daodi Shi Shenme?" *Nikkei Shimbun*, August 29, 2012, accessed at http://cn.nikkei.com/columnviewpoint/column/3437-20120829.html.

200. "Beijing Should Ensure Safety of Japanese in China," *Daily Yomiuri*, August 21, 2012.

201. Quoted in "Yu Zhongguo Wei Lin, Shi Riben de Bu Xing Ma?" *Jiefang Ribao*, August 23, 2012, accessed at http://news.xinhuanet.com/world/2012-08/23/c_123618011.htm.

202. Mo Zhixu, August 16, 2012, 3:49 a.m., accessed at https://twitter.com/mozhixu/status/236006849646821376.

203. "Diaoyudao Weiji Jiaju Zhongguo Minjian Fan Ri Qingxu," BBC, August 16, 2012, accessed at http://www.bbc.co.uk/zhongwen/simp/chinese_news/2012/08/120816_iv_diaoyudao.shtml.

204. "Nicchu Mondai wo Kangaeru" [Thinking about issues between Japan and China], *Nikkei Shimbun*, September 30, 2012.

205. "Japan Tried but Failed to Avert Disaster," *Asahi Shimbun*, September 26, 2012.

206. "Dangerous Waters: China-Japan Relations on the Rocks," International Crisis Group Asia Report no. 245, April 8, 2013, 8.

207. "China's Hu Shows Firm Opposition to Japan's Senkaku Nationalization," Jiji Press, September 9, 2012.

208. "Japan Tried but Failed to Avert Disaster," *Asahi Shimbun*, September 26, 2012.

209. Email correspondence, September 24, 2012.

210. "Gogatsu Jyuhachinichi Senkaku Konyu ni Fumidashita" [The national government began to undertake the plan to purchase the Senkaku Islands on May 18], *Asahi Shimbun*, September 26, 2012.

211. "Japan, US, EU Launch WTO Complaint against China's Rare-Earth Export Curbs," BBC, March 13, 2012; "China to Face Japan, EU, U.S. WTO Suit; Trio to Seek Fair Distribution of Rare Earths," *Daily Yomiuri*, March 14, 2012.

212. "Nicchu Mondai wo Kangaeru" [Thinking about issues between Japan and China], *Nikkei Shimbun*, September 30, 2012.

213. "China's Other Land Disputes Show It Can Compromise," *Asahi Shimbun*, September 28, 2012.

214. Conversation with U.S. consulate official, June 20, 2013.

215. "Anti-Japan Protests May Have Finished, but Diligence Still Needed," *Nikkei Weekly*, October 22, 2012.

216. Shiroyama Hidemi, "Hannichi demo no shakai kōzō chūgoku shakai no 'bunretsu' to sono haikei," *Kokusai Mondai* 620 (April 2013): 29–33.

217. Ian Johnston, "More Protests in China over Japan and Islands," *New York Times*, September 18, 2012, accessed at http://www.nytimes.com/2012/09/19/world/asia/china-warns-japan-over-island-dispute.html?_r=0.

218. "Mao References in Anti-Japan Protests a Concern for Chinese Authorities," *Asahi Shimbun*, September 18, 2012, accessed at http://ajw.asahi.com/article/asia/china/AJ201209180053.

219. "China Struggles to Curb Anger as Protesters Denounce Japan," Reuters, September 16, 2012, accessed at http://www.reuters.com/article/2012/09/16/us-china-japan-idUSBRE88F00H20120916.

220. "Beijing Both Encourages and Reins in Anti-Japan Protests, Analysts Say," *Washington Post*, September 17, 2012.

221. Heyan Wang, "Closer Look: How a Protest in Beijing Stuck to the Script," *Caixin*, September 17, 2012, accessed at http://english.caixin.com/2012-09-17/100438867.html.

222. "Japanese Jets 'Disturb Routine Island Patrols,'" *China Daily*, January 12, 2013, accessed at http://www.chinadaily.com.cn/world/2013-01/12/content_16107398.htm.

223. Liu Jiangyong, "Zhongguo De Dui Ri Zhengce Ji Qi Guonei Beijing," *Northeast Asia Forum* 5 (2012): 6.

224. Foreign Minister of Japan Koichiro Gemba, "Japan-China Relations at a Crossroads," *International Herald Tribune*, November 21, 2012.

225. "Abe's Questionable Sincerity in Mending Ties with China," Xinhua News Service, December 18, 2012, accessed at http://news.xinhuanet.com/english/indepth/2012-12/18/c_132048969.htm.

226. Abe Shinzo, "Atarashii Kunie" [Toward a new country], *Bungeishunju* (文藝春秋) January 2013, 124–33.

227. "Transcript of Interview with Japanese Prime Minister Shinzo Abe," *Washington Post*, February 20, 2013, available at http://www.washingtonpost.com/world/transcript-of-interview-with-japanese-prime-minister-shinzo-abe/2013/02/20/e7518d54-7b1c-11e2-82e8-61a46c2cde3d_print.html.

228. Ibid.

229. "China Military Officials Admit Radar Lock on Japanese Ship, Says Report," *South China Morning Post*, March 18, 2013.

230. "From Beijing, Hatoyama Tells Tokyo to Admit Row," *Japan Times*, January 18 2012, cited in http://www.japanfocus.org/-Gavan-McCormack/3947#sthash.RTrsb4c3.dpuf

231. Kyodo News Agency, "China's Trust Can Be Won with Diplomacy: Kono," *Japan Times*, January 18, 2013, accessed at http://www.japantimes.co.jp/news/2013/01/18/national/chinas-trust-can-be-won-with-diplomacy-kono/#.UdIDSvmceRM.

232. Kazuhiko Togo, "Help Beijing Step Back from Hegemonism," *Wall Street Journal*, December 23, 2012, accessed at http://online.wsj.com/article/SB10001424127887324660404578196932041909170.html.

233. "Editorial: Japan, China Should Pursue Best Way to Settle Senkaku Islands Dispute," *Mainichi Shimbun*, June 12, 2013, accessed at http://mainichi.jp/english/english/perspectives/news/20130612p2a00m0na008000c.html.

234. Hitoshi Tanaka, "A Reset for East Asia-Managing Risks under New Leadership," *East Asia Insights* 8 (1) (March 2013), accessed at http://www.jcie.or.jp/insights/8-1.html.

235. Shigeru Ishiba, "Kita Chōsen, Chūgoku, Roshia ni azawarawareru Nihon" [The laughing-stock of East Asia], *Chūō Kōron*, January 2011, 94–101, translated in *Japan Echo* 4 (December 2010–January 2011), available at http://www.japanechoweb.jp/jew0412/2/.

236. Shigeru Ishiba, "Kokka Anzen Hosho Kihonho no Seitei wo Isoge [Japan should promptly enact the National Security Act], *Voice*, December 2012, 102–3.

Chapter 9

1. Keefe 2001, 10.
2. Stanley Roth, Testimony before the Senate Committee on Foreign Relations Subcommittee on East Asian and Pacific Affairs, May 27, 1999, available at http://www.usembassy-china.org.cn/press/release/1999/roth.html.
3. Ross 2011; Shirk 2007.
4. "Genron Studio: Senkaku Issue and Future of Japan-China Relations," October 2012, translated at http://www.japanpolicyforum.jp/en/archive/no12/000369.html#kiji.
5. "Frenemies: U.S.-China Relations," Carnegie Endowment for International Peace, November 9, 2010, available at http://carnegieendowment.org/publications/index.cfm?fa=view&id=41907, last accessed February 23, 2011.
6. Shaun Tandon, "Obama Aide Criticizes Romney Tough Talk on China," Agence France-Presse, October 25, 2012.
7. Johnston 2013, 37.
8. John Pomfret, "The U.S. Interest in an Asian Island Dispute," *Washington Post*, February 5, 2013, accessed at http://www.washingtonpost.com/opinions/japan-and-chinas-island-argument-is-a-us-concern/2013/02/05/fbc7ed62-6999-11e2-af53-7b2b2a7510a8_story.html.
9. Perry Link, "Beijing's Dangerous Game," *New York Review of Books*, September 20, 2012, accessed at http://www.nybooks.com/blogs/nyrblog/2012/sep/20/beijings-dangerous-game/.
10. On Chinese Internet censorship, see King et al. 2013.
11. E.g., C. Custer, "China's Anti-Japan Riots Are State-Sponsored. Period." September 17, 2012, http://chinageeks.org/2012/09/chinas-anti-japan-riots-are-state-sponsored-period/.
12. In fact, a situation in which protests actually destabilize the regime is an unlikely outcome. Because the government can placate protesters by taking a tough foreign policy stance, we will rarely see evidence of the full range of risks and costs posed by antiforeign protests. Moreover, the government is more likely to allow nationalist protests when it is prepared to satisfy them with a tough diplomatic stance and other "countermeasures" to demonstrate the government's resolve.
13. Mercer 1996.
14. Evan Osnos, "A Billion Stories," *New Yorker*, July 5, 2013, accessed at http://www.newyorker.com/online/blogs/evanosnos/2013/07/a-billion-stories.html.
15. Wallace 2013; Mimi Lau, "Police Stop Anti-Japan Protests in Bigger Guangdong Cities," *South China Morning Post*, September 16, 2012.
16. Not all efforts to guide online opinion are done under the cover of anonymity. See, for example, comments by former Foreign Ministry counselor Zou Jianhua: "Some government departments, now beginning to recognize the importance of the Internet and the importance of guiding online sentiments, have started to establish Internet spokesmen, who can immediately respond to miscomprehensions and rumors and calm discontent." Zou 2011, 79.
17. Susan Shirk, "China: Fragile Superpower," remarks at the Center for National Policy, May 7, 2008, accessed at http://www.cnponline.org/ht/a/GetDocumentAction/i/5249.
18. Perry Link, "Beijing's Dangerous Game," *New York Review of Books*, September 20, 2012, accessed at http://www.nybooks.com/blogs/nyrblog/2012/sep/20/beijings-dangerous-game/.
19. Barmé 2006; Wang 2012, 113.
20. On media marketization and government control, see Stockmann 2013.
21. On whether China's behavior and interests can be said to be "revisionist" or supportive of the status quo, including the international "rules of the game" and the balance of power, see Johnston 2003.
22. "How Should Japan Deal with a Rich, Strong China?" *Japan Echo* 3 (October–November 2010), translated from "Yutaka de tsuyoi Chūgoku to dō mukiau ka," *Sekai*, September 2010, 102–9, accessed at http://www.japanpolicyforum.jp/en/archive/no3/000146.html.

23. Yoshihide Soeya, "Tokyo's China Problem: Claiming the High Ground," *Japan Echo* 4 (December 2010–January 2011), accessed at http://www.japanpolicyforum.jp/en/archive/no4/000197.html#kiji.

24. Wang 2011. In another example, Dikötter 1992 notes that a nationalist journal published by Chinese students in 1903 stated that nationalism "erects borders against the outside and unites the group inside."

25. Interview with anti-Japanese activist and website manager, no. 81, Shanghai, China, April 16, 2007.

26. Liu Ning, "Zhongguo Minzu Zhuyi: Wu Bi Jian Nan de Yan Shuo," *Chinese Review Weekly*, October 2003, no. 4, available at http://www.chubun.com/modules/article/view.article.php/2722.

27. Tan 2006, 467

28. Interview with leading Bao Diao activist in Beijing, no. 43, July 27, 2006.

29. http://bbs.china918.cn:81/showtopic.aspx?topicid=28156&page=end, last accessed March 12, 2011.

30. Interview with anti-Japanese activist and website manager, no. 121, Beijing, China, January 17, 2009.

31. Barmé 2005.

32. Barmé 2005; Calhoun 1994, 100.

33. Zhao 1997, 728–29.

34. Wasserstrom 1999, 60.

35. Whiting 1989, 67.

36. Agence France-Presse, October 3, 1985.

37. "Update on Arrests in China," *Asia Watch*, January 30, 1991, accessed at http://www.hrw.org/reports/pdfs/c/china/china911.pdf.

38. Pepper 1987, 11.

39. O'Brien 1996.

40. "Bao Ge released, Brother of Other Shanghai Dissidents Penalized," *Ming Pao*, June 5, 1997; "Activist Bids for Vote on War Cash," *South China Morning Post*, March 10, 1993.

41. Fewsmith 2008, 226.

42. Hvistendahl 2009; Ma 2002.

43. http://history.qikoo.com/article/q7112127,8fb9b2,s5570_38089.html, translated by Danwei.org, http://www.danwei.org/nationalism/godfathers_of_todays_angry_you.php.

44. http://www.cfdd.org.cn/bbs/viewthread.php?tid=72100, last accessed November 23, 2010.

45. Interview, no. 146, Guangzhou, China, January 7, 2010.

46. Interview with lawyer and compensation activist, no. 85, Shanghai, China, April 19, 2007.

47. Interview with anti-CNN.com founder, no. 120, Beijing, China, January 15, 2009.

48. "Zhongguo Minjian Kang Ri Lianmeng Chengli Gonggao," September 12, 2010, http://www.shengfang.mo.cn/bbs/thread-53056-1-1.html, last accessed March 8, 2011.

49. Quoted in He 2007a, 9.

50. Wang Xizhe and Liu Xiaobo, "Views on Several Major State Issues Concerning China Today," FTS19961010000032 Hong Kong *Ming Pao*, in Chinese, October 10, 1996.

51. Liu Ning, "Zhongguo Minzu Zhuyi: Wubi Jiannan de Yan Shuo," *Riben Zhongwen Daobao* [Japan China Herald], October 2003, no. 4.

52. Jim Yardley, "Chinese Police Head Off Anti-Japan protests," *New York Times*, May 5, 2005.

53. "Shijie Huaren Bao Diao Lianmeng Mishuzhang Li Yiqiang: Jujiao Diaoyudao Wenti," http://t.people.com.cn/talk/239.html, August 20, 2012.

54. http://bbs.1931-9-18.org/viewthread.php?tid=22454, last accessed March 16, 2011.

55. Interview with leading Bao Diao activist in Beijing, no. 43, July 27, 2006.

56. http://qun.qq.com/#search/cnum/0/st/0/c1/0/c2/0/c3/0/pg/1/tx/%E7%88%B1%E5%9B%BD%E8%80%85, last accessed September 16, 2010.

57. Mulvenon 2009.

58. Interview, no. 44, Beijing, China, July 28, 2006.

59. Liu Xiaobo, "Wei Fan Ri Jiangwen De Yulun Gongshi, April 24, 2005, accessed at http://blog. boxun.com/hero/liuxb/290_1.shtml.

60. Guo Feixiong was detained in April 2005 after applying for permission to organize a protest march against Japan's UN Security Council bid. See *Radio Free Asia*, May 13, 2005, available at http://www.rfa.org/mandarin/shenrubaodao/2005/05/13/guofeixiong/.

61. Jie Yu, "The Anti-Japanese Resistance War, Chinese Patriotism and Free Speech. How Can We Forgive Japan?" July 16, 2007, *Japan Focus*, available at http://www.japanfocus. org/-yu-jie/2654.

62. Li Chengpeng, "Yi Ge Maiguozei De Zi Bai," September 17, 2012, translated at http:// www.tealeafnation.com/2012/09/prominent-chinese-writers-viral-confession-i-am-a-traitor/#sthash.f2guM6Fb.dpuf.

63. "Ai Weiwei Calls Anti-Japan Protests 'Prepared by Officials,'" *South China Morning Post*, September 20, 2012.

64. Still, my count of protests in mainland China is likely to understate the actual number. Using Lexis-Nexis, FBIS databases as well as several anti-Japanese activist websites, I counted an incident as an antiforeign protest if it met the following criteria: two or more people were involved; the primary target was Japan; and the activity sought to attract the attention and/or participation of bystanders in a public location.

65. Gries 2005a.

66. *New York Times*, April 17, 2008.

67. Johnston and Stockmann 2007, 193; see also Johnston 2006, 367.

68. Han and Zweig 2010.

69. Interview, no. 150, London, United Kingdom, June 19, 2010.

70. "Mapping the Hurt Feelings of the Chinese People," Danwei.org, December 11, 2008, accessed at http://www.danwei.org/foreign_affairs/a_map_of_hurt_feelings.php.

71. "Fen Nu Bushi Chuli Nanhai Wenti De Zhengdao," June 9, 2011, *Huanqiu Shibao*, http:// opinion.huanqiu.com/roll/2011-06/1744966.html, last accessed at May 9, 2012.

72. "Quanqiu Huaren Qianming Baowei Huangyandao," QQ, May 16, 2012, accessed at http:// w2h.3g.qq.com/g/s?p=http://infoapp.3g.qq.com/g/s%3Ficfa%3Dnews_zfhyd%26aid% 3Dexpress_index%26action%3D1%26.

73. "Protest over Huangyan Island Dispute Held in Beijing," Xinhua News Agency, May 12, 2012, accessed at http://www.china.org.cn/china/2012-05/12/content_25367605.htm.

74. Johnston 2013, 19; Fravel 2011; "Stirring Up the South China Sea," International Crisis Group Asia Report no. 223, April 23, 2012.

75. E.g., Shen and Breslin 2010; Shen 2011; Gries 2005c.

76. Gries 2005a, 847.

77. Johnston and Stockmann 2007, 177. Stockmann notes that on a 100-point feeling thermometer, Beijing residents surveyed in 2004 felt about 39 degrees toward the United States, 10 degrees warmer than toward Japan. Stockmann 2013, 213.

78. "Patriotic Chinese Venting on Internet," *Daily Yomiuri*, July 19, 2008.

79. Wang Zhongguo, "H7N9 Qinliugan Shi Meiguo Yu Riben Zhizao Zai Zhongguo Sanbu," http://www.cfdd.org.cn/bbs/viewthread.php?tid=83962, last accessed April 10, 2013.

80. Shirk 2007, 185–186.

81. Interview with international relations expert, no. 24, May 25, 2006.

82. Interview with research analyst at the CICIR Institute of American Studies, no. 93, Beijing, May 2007.

83. "Taiwan's Fading Independence Movement," *Foreign Affairs*, March–April 2006.

84. See Shirk 2007, 188.

85. Sheng 2001, 34; "Wo Liu Mei Xuesheng Kangyi Lee Teng-hui Fang Mei," *Renmin Ribao*, June 10, 1995; Fang Yuan, "Beijing Has No Scruples about Resorting to Use of Force or Breaking Off Diplomatic Ties with U.S. to Safeguard Sovereignty, Territorial Integrity," *Ming Pao*, FTS19950710000125, July 10, 1995.

86. Swaine 2001, 326.

87. Tung Cheng-Yuan, "Liang An Jingmao Jiaoliu Dui Liang An Guanxi Hudong De Yingxiang," PhD dissertation, Johns Hopkins University School of Advanced International Studies, April 5, 2002, 33, accessed at www3.nccu.edu.tw/~ctung/Documents/W-B-b-3.doc; see also "Zheng Chiyan: A-Bian Yi Shi Ji Qi Qian Chong Lan," March 23, 2000, accessed at http://www.china-week.com/html/116.htm.

88. "Dalu Wangmin Lianming Fan Dui Tai Du," Xinhua News Service, November 28, 2003, accessed at http://www.people.com.cn/GB/shizheng/1026/2216716.html; "Aiguozhe Tongmengwang Zhengji Toupiao Yu Liang Wan Wangmin Qianming Fan Dui Tai Du," *Xinjing Bao*, November 29, 2003, accessed at http://it.sohu.com/2003/11/29/26/article216232621.shtml.

89. Wu 2004, 13.

90. Chen-Yuan Tung, "Cross-Strait Relations after Taiwan's 2004 Presidential Election," Paper presented at the Japanese Association for Taiwan Studies, Tokyo, August 4, 2004, 18.

91. Interview, no. 101, Beijing, China, June 27, 2007.

92. Xi'an Jiaotong University News Web, http://xjtunews.xjtu.edu.cn/xinghuo/llxx/2007-05-31/1180600546d14620.html, last accessed June 27, 2007.

93. "3 Yue2 Ri Beijing Gongyi Gequ 'Taiwan, Wo De Xiongdi' Xinwen Fabuhui Xianchang Zhaopian," http://bbs.1931-9-18.org/viewthread.php?action=printable&tid=81769, March 2, 2004.

94. "Dalu Nianqing Ren Wangluo Da Qianming Huhuan 'Taiwan, Wo De Xiongdi,'" *Lianhe Zaobao*, March 3, 2004, accessed at http://www.gznf.net/thread-1468-1-1.html.

95. "3 Yue7 Ri, Shi Anhui Wangyou Yuan Ding De Juxing 'Taiwan, Wo De Xiongdi' Xianchang Qianming Huodong De Rizi," http://bbs.1931-9-18.org/viewthread.php?tid=83597, March 9, 2004, last accessed July 30, 2008.

96. Ibid.

97. "Aiguo Renshi Zai Riben Zhu Hua Shiguan Kangyi Li Denghui Fang Ri," *Xinjing Bao*, December 31, 2004, http://news.sina.com.cn/c/2004-12-31/02555381341.shtml, last accessed December 3, 2009.

98. Sohu, QQ and *Global Times* (the nationalistic subsidiary of *People's Daily*) jointly sponsored the Internet petition. "Chinese Netizens Strongly Condemn the American Arms Sale to Taiwan," *Global Times*, January 31, 2010, http://china.huanqiu.com/roll/2010-01/705232.html, last accessed March 30, 2010.

99. Comment by netizen "Yongheng Nuoyan" on *Tiexue* forum, January 30, 2010, last accessed March 30, 2010, http://bbs.tiexue.net/post_4072556_1.html.

100. Kokubun and Liu 2004.

101. Swaine and Zhang 2006, 18.

102. Interview, no. 134, Washington, D.C., March 12, 2009.

103. Paris LCI Television in French, FBIS, EUP20080325950056, March 25, 2008.

104. Agence France-Presse, April 23, 2001.

105. Victor Cha, "Beijing's Olympic-Sized Catch-22," *Washington Quarterly*, Summer 2008.

106. "Darfur Collides with Olympics, and China Yields," *New York Times*, April 13, 2007.

107. Interview, no. 132, Washington, D.C., March 11, 2009.

108. "UK diplomat: China Risks Weakening Reputation over Handling of Unrest in Tibet," Associated Press, March 17, 2008.

109. FBIS, EUP20080322499014, March 22, 2008; FBIS, EUP20080326950013, March 26, 2008. Kouchner himself was opposed to a boycott, suggesting that "It would be fantastic if we could come up with a common position" but arguing that "boycotting the games would not be effective in the least."

110. FBIS, EUP20080322499014 Frankfurt am Main *Frankfurter Allgemeine* (Internet Version-WWW) in German, Mar 22, 2008.

111. FBIS, EUP20080329072002 Paris AFP (North European Service) in English, 1246 GMT, Mar 29, 2008.

112. FBIS, EUP20080325950066 Paris AFP (Domestic Service) in French, 1425 GMT, March 25, 2008.
113. FBIS, EUP20080325950056 Paris LCI Television in French, 1400 GMT, March 25, 2008.
114. JPP20080327969100 Tokyo Kyodo World Service in English, 1631 GMT, March 27, 2008.
115. http://www.anti-cnn.com/forum/cn/thread-124384-1-1.html, last accessed February 16, 2009.
116. Aside from a journalist from the *Economist* who happened to be in Tibet at the time, no foreign journalists were allowed to cover the events locally. When this was pointed out by Chang Ping, an influential commentator and then-senior editor at the liberal *Southern Metropolis Weekly*, nationalist netizens denounced him and his newspaper as "race traitors."
117. Xinhua News Service, "'Anti-CNN' Website Reflects Chinese People's Condemnation," March 27, 2008, available at http://www.china-embassy.org/eng/zmgx/zmgx/Political%20Relationship/t418923.htm.
118. "Quanqiu Huaren Da Qianming Kangyi Xi Fang Meiti Waiqu Baodao Lasa 3-14Da Za Qiang Shao Shijian," March 30, 2008, http://hi.news.sina.com.cn/news/fanfenlie/index.php?dpc=1; "Fan Fenlie Hu Shenghuo Quanqiu Huaren Da Qianming," April 3, 2008, http://hi.news.sina.com.cn/news/fanfenlie/index.php?page=408423&dpc=1.
119. Interview, no. 111a, Beijing, China, May 27, 2008.
120. Interview, no. 111b, Beijing, China, May 27, 2008.
121. "Interview with Torchbearer Jin Jing," Sohu.com, April 10, 2008, accessed at http://torchrelay.beijing2008.cn/en/torchbearers/headlines/n214299940.shtml.
122. "China demands apology from Cafferty," CNN, May 1, 2008, http://edition.cnn.com/2008/WORLD/asiapcf/04/15/cnn.china/.
123. Kitty Shelley, "Jintian Rang Hong Se Chuan Bian Zhongguo," Shui Mu She Qu, April 13, 2008, reposted at http://blog.sina.com.cn/s/blog_3f487373010095ch.html.
124. http://news.163.com/08/0415/18/49JFLASB0001124J.html, April 17, 2008.
125. "CNN Apologises to China over 'Thugs and Goons' Comment by Jack Cafferty," *The Times*, April 16, 2008. In May, CNN president Jim Walton formally apologized for the remarks by Jack Cafferty in a letter to China's ambassador to the United States.
126. Xinhua News Service (English), May 1, 2008.
127. Interview with senior Tsinghua University professor of international relations, no. 112, Beijing, China, January 10, 2009.
128. Interview, no. 110, Shanghai, China, May 26, 2008.
129. Interview, no. 112, Beijing, China, January 10, 2009.
130. JPP20080327969100 Tokyo Kyodo World Service in English, 1631 GMT, March 27, 2008.
131. *International Herald Tribune*, April 21, 2008.
132. "MOC: China Welcomes Carrefour's Statement against Tibet Independence," Xinhua, April 23, 2008, accessed at http://english.people.com.cn/90001/90776/90883/6397235.html.
133. http://bbs.9jjz.com/dispbbs.asp?boardid=169&id=59104&star=1&page=1, last accessed April 30, 2008; see also "Be Patriotic? First Be Cool!" *China Digital Times*, April 30, 2008, http://chinadigitaltimes.net/2008/04/be-patriotic-first-be-cool/.
134. Mark Magnier, "China Tries to Limit Internet Vitriol toward the West," *Los Angeles Times*, April 19, 2008.
135. http://www.anti-cnn.com/forum/cn/announcement.php?id=19#19, April 19, 2008, last accessed April 20, 2008.
136. "Protests Erupt at Carrefour Stores in Four Chinese Cities," *International Herald Tribune*, May 1, 2008.
137. Associated Press, June 30, 2008.
138. Interview, no. 137, Palo Alto, California, April 27, 2009.
139. Interview with former senior White House official, no. 135, Washington, D.C., March 12, 2009.
140. "Lishi Hui Ji Zhu 2008 Nian De 'Si Yue Qingnian,'" *China Youth Daily*, October 20, 2008, accessed at http://news.xinhuanet.com/theory/2008-10/20/content_10221407.htm.

141. Interview, no. 111b, Beijing, China, May 27, 2008.

142. Telhami 1993.

143. Lynch 1999, 163; Shulman 2008, 124.

144. Lynch 2006, 75; see also Roscoe Suddarth, "Take Account of Arab Opinion and Keep a Cool Watch on Saddam," *Washington Post*, December 9, 1997.

145. Steven Greenhouse, "War in the Gulf: The Arabs; War Puts Strain on North Africa," *New York Times*, February 6, 1991.

146. Bush and Scowcroft 1998, 489.

147. See Snyder and Borghard 2011; and Snyder and Diesing 1977, 215.

148. Note that the domestic benefits of nationalist protest require evidence of diplomatic success or victory.

149. Kissinger 2001.

150. "Xuezhe Cheng Yunan He Feilvbin Fangren Fanhua Qingxu Jiang Rang Ziji Shoushang," June 24, 2011, *Huanqiu Shibao*, http://mil.news.sina.com.cn/2011-06-24/0806653716.html, last accessed March 26, 2013. On anti-China protests in the Philippines and Vietnam, see Ciorciari and Weiss 2014.

151. "Feilvbin De QinMei FanHua Jiyin, Wenhua Shou Mei Lao Yin, Wai Zhang Shou Mei Jiaoyu," Xinhua News Service, October 28, 2011, http://news.xinhuanet.com/mil/2011-10/28/c_122208416.htm, last accessed March 26, 2013.

152. Xinhua News Service, December 11, 2007, quoted in Ian Storey, "Trouble and Strife in the South China Sea: Vietnam and China," *China Brief*, Jamestown Foundation, 8 (8) (April 2008).

Appendix

1. *Ming Pao*, October 21, 1992.

2. Patrick E. Tyler, "Olympics; There's No Joy in Beijing as Sydney Gets Olympics," *New York Times*, September 24, 1993.

3. John Kohut, "Beijing defuses protest outside Japan embassy," *South China Morning Post*, March 19, 1994; Daniel Kwan, "Activists freed after questioning," *South China Morning Post*, March 14, 1994.

4. Kyodo News Agency, August 1, 1995; Kyodo News Agency, August 7, 1995.

5. Hong Kong *Sing Tao Jih Pao*, Foreign Broadcast Information Service, FTS19950929000001, September 29, 1995.

6. *Hong Kong Standard*, Foreign Broadcast Information Service, FTS19961001000034, October 1, 1996; *South China Morning Post*, September 14, 1996; Associated Press, September 14, 1996.

7. "新闻资料：保钓人士曾于1996 年登钓鱼岛插旗," Phoenix Television, August 16, 2012, http://news.ifeng.com/mainland/special/diaoyudaozhengduan/content-4/detail_2012_08/16/16852035_0.shtml.

8. CASS, "历年保钓事件记载," June 16, 2008, accessed at http://jds.cass.cn/Item/7454.aspx; "國民運-1996年10月份新聞摘要," http://www.alliance.org.hk/info/news/wp/?p=1673.

9. CASS, "历年保钓事件记载," June 16, 2008, accessed at http://jds.cass.cn/Item/7454.aspx.

10. Kyodo News Agency, September 6, 1997.

11. No Kwai-Yan and Genevieve Ku, "Nanjing tribute group turned back; Shunned Diaoyu activists told protest plans make them unwelcome at massacre memorial," *South China Morning Post*, December 13, 1997.

12. Dingxin Zhao, "Problems of Nationalism in Contemporary China: Student-Government Conflicts during Nationalist Protests," in C.X. George Wei and Xiaoyuan Liu, eds. *Exploring Nationalisms of China: Themes and Conflicts*. Westport, Conn: Greenwood Press, 2002, 106–7.

13. "Futile gesture," *South China Morning Post*, June 25, 1998; CASS, "历年保钓事件记载," June 16, 2008, accessed at http://jds.cass.cn/Item/7454.aspx.

14. Associated Press, August 14, 2001; *South China Morning Post*, August 15, 2001; Kyodo News Agency, August 16, 2001; "清华学子聚集日本使馆 抗议小泉参拜靖国神社," http://news.sina.com.cn/w/2001-08-15/330128.html, August 15, 2001.

15. http://bbs.1931-9-18.org/viewthread.php?tid=4950, last accessed March 15, 2011.

16. Willy Wo-Lap Lam, "Beijing curbs antiwar protests," CNN.com, March 30, 2003, http://edition.cnn.com/2003/WORLD/asiapcf/east/03/30/sprj.irq.china.protests.

17. "Chinese, Hong Kong activists abandon Diaoyu Islands protest," *South China Morning Post*, June 24, 2003.

18. "More than one million sign petition on gas bombs," *South China Morning Post*, September 18, 2003.

19. CASS, "历年保钓事件记载," June 16, 2008, http://jds.cass.cn/Item/7454.aspx.

20. "Activists ditch Diaoyu landing plan," *South China Morning Post*, October 10, 2003.

21. "《反对'台独', 网络大签名》的联合声明," November 27, 2003, http://bbs.1931-9-18.org/dispbbs.asp?boardID=30&ID=59838.

22. "首都各界, 保钓勇士共祭遇难同胞," *Jinghua Shibao*, http://news.sina.com.cn/c/2003-12-14/04221334997s.shtml, December 14, 2003; http://bbs.1931-9-18.org/viewthread.php?tid=59993, last accessed March 15, 2011.

23. "靖国阴魂引发中国民间'抗战'", China News, January 12, 2004, http://www.chinanews.com/n/2004-01-12/26/390538.html.

24. CASS, "历年保钓事件记载," June 16, 2008, accessed at http://jds.cass.cn/Item/7454.aspx; "Anti-Japanese protests push Beijing to take a hard line," *Daily Yomiuri*, March 28, 2004.

25. "Activists Protest Attack on Osaka Chinese Consulate," *South China Morning Post*, April 24, 2004.

26. http://www.thechinapress.com/yaowen/ywimg/200409190066.htm, last accessed August 14, 2007.

27. "爱国人士在日本驻华使馆抗议李登辉访日," *Xinjingbao*, December 31, 2004, http://news.sina.com.cn/c/2004-12-31/02555381341.shtml, last accessed December 3, 2009.

28. CASS, "历年保钓事件记载," June 16, 2008, accessed at http://jds.cass.cn/Item/7454.aspx.

29. Kyodo News Service, July 13, 2005.

30. Kyodo News Service, August 10, 2005.

31. "北京网友10月17号在日本领事馆抗议小泉参拜靖国神社活动照片," http://bbs.1931-9-18.org/viewthread.php?action=printable&tid=186332, October 17, 2005.

32. Xinhua, "Taiwan politicians sail to waters near Diaoyu Islands to protest Japan's harassment," *Renmin Wang*, June 22, 2005, accessed at http://english.peopledaily.com.cn/200506/22/eng20050622_191602.html.

33. The original petition proposed four candidates: June 17, the anniversary of the 1972 Agreement Between the United States of America and Japan Concerning the Ryukyu Islands and the Daito Islands, wherein the United States transferred administrative rights over the islands to Japan; October 7, to commemorate the 1996 landing of Taiwan and Hong Kong activists; September 26, to commemorate the 1996 death of Hong Kong activist David Chan who drowned trying to reach the island; and March 24, to commemorate the landing of 7 mainland activists on the main island.

34. Author observation, July 7, 2006.

35. http://blog.voc.com.cn/blog_showone_type_blog_id_71901_p_1.html and http://blog.ifeng.com/article/294390.html, last accessed May 10, 2012.

36. "Anti-Japan protest in China's Shenyang after cab driver beaten," *South China Morning Post*, August 25, 2006.

37. On BBS closure, see http://bbs.1931-9-18.org/viewthread.php?tid=170126, last accessed August 15, 2006; "深圳3000军警严防反日示威," Nextmedia, August 20, 2006, http://hk.apple.nextmedia.com/international/art/20060820/6235944, last accessed on instructions not to hold large protests, see "Anti-Japan groups in China agree not to stage protests over Koizumi's

Yasukuni visit," *Mainichi Shimbun*, August 21, 2006; BBC Chinese, August 19, 2006, accessed at http://news.bbc.co.uk/chinese/simp/hi/newsid_5260000/newsid_5265700/5265778.stm.

38. "Protesters in Sichuan urge boycott of Japan goods," *Japan Times*, September 20, 2006.

39. Feng Jinhua, "日相访华的今天是中国的什么日子？看看日本媒体的报道吧," http://bbs.1931-9-18.org/viewthread.php?tid=211439, last accessed October 8, 2006.

40. "Chinese make rare protest at Japanese embassy," Reuters, May 31, 2007; "Chinese slam Japan WWII payment denial," *China Post*, June 1, 2007.

41. Author observation; see also http://junshi.blog.china.com/200706/548331.html, http://news.phoenixtv.com/taiwan/3/200706/0618_353_137210.shtml, last accessed June 18, 2007, http://www.cfdd.org.cn/html/90/n-90.html, last accessed May 14, 2012.

42. http://www.cfdd.org.cn/html/89/n-89.html, last accessed May 14, 2012.

43. http://www.cfdd.org.cn/html/50/n-50.html, last accessed May 16, 2012.

44. http://blog.sina.com.cn/s/blog_4a1ea099010009sv.html, http://ido.3mt.com.cn/Article/200709/show823663c12p1.html, last accessed May 14, 2012.

45. "浙江网友国庆爱国活动实录," http://www.cfdd.org.cn/html/89/n-289.html, November 20, 2007.

46. "保钓湘军祭奠南京大屠杀70周年," http://www.cfdd.org.cn/html/80/n-480.html, December 18, 2007.

47. "保钓联合会在日使馆抗议日本军舰撞沉我渔船," http://www.cfdd.org.cn/html/42/n-1142.html, June 10, 2008.

48. "华人保钓大事记," *163 News* (网易新闻), 2012, accessed at http://news.163.com/special/baodiaojianshi/.

49. "萨科齐见达赖中国网民吁抵制法货；法政客不以为然," http://www.china.com.cn/tech/txt/2008-12/08/content_16917070.htm, December 8, 2008; "第二次'抵制法货'?萨科齐会见达赖惹怒中国," http://www.infzm.com/content/20921, December 9, 2008.

50. Zhu, Wenzheng, "2009 保钓日记," May 6, 2009, accessed at http://forum.diaoyuislands.org/viewtopic.php?t=2636.

51. "民间保钓人士在日驻华使馆前抗议 要求日本道歉," September 8, 2010, http://news.163.com/photoview/00AN0001/10800.html; "北京日使馆外大批市民聚集抗议," *Lianhe Zaobao*, September 18, 2010, http://realtime.zaobao.com/2010/09/100918_12.shtml; "上海沈阳等地都出现反日示威," *Lianhe Zaobao*, September 18, 2010, http://realtime.zaobao.com/2010/09/100918_13.shtml; "重庆2000余名市民聚会步行街高唱抗日歌曲," iFeng News, September 18, 2010, http://news.ifeng.com/mainland/detail_2010_09/18/2548128_0.shtml.

52. "水警阻撓釣魚台二號出海經過," *Taiyang Bao*, September 24, 2010, accessed at http://the-sun.on.cc/cnt/news/20100924/00407_006.html.

53. "台湾保钓船在钓鱼岛海域与日舰对峙5小时," *Huanqiu Wang*, September 14, 2010, accessed at http://taiwan.huanqiu.com/news/2010-09/1100657.html.

54. "世界華人保釣聯盟首征釣魚島," *Hong Kong Bao Diao Forum* (香港保釣論壇), June 29, 2011, accessed at http://forum.diaoyuislands.org/viewtopic.php?p=5350&sid=b27ef352b2044c40ef559c59d40892cd.

55. "关于我国南海卖国外交文件的请愿书," July 29, 2011, http://www.cfdd.org.cn/bbs/viewthread.php?tid=75679.

56. "918日本侵华80周年 中共低调悼念 禁止民間紀念," Aboluo Wang, September 19, 2011, http://tw.aboluowang.com/news/2011/0919/219200.html.

57. "保钓船香港出发赴钓鱼岛被水警截查后折返," Phoenix Television, January 3, 2012, http://news.ifeng.com/mainland/detail_2012_01/03/11731246_0.shtml.

58. "腾讯网保卫南海中国人万人签名," QQ.com, May 11, 2012, http://tieba.baidu.com/p/1582601705.

59. "Protest over Huangyan Island dispute held in Beijing," Xinhua News Agency, May 12, 2012, http://www.china.org.cn/china/2012-05/12/content_25367605.htm.

60. "民间'保钓'的感人往事," *CPPCC News Network* (人民政协新闻网), August 23, 2012, accessed at http://cppcc.people.com.cn/n/2012/0823/c34948-18813110.html.

61. "中国保钓人士'七七事变'纪念活动遭警方全程监控," Radio France Internationale, July 8, 2012, http://www.chinese.rfi.fr/print/114046?print=now.

62. "中国多地口号'打倒日本帝国主义'举行反日大游行," *Xingming Wang*, August 19, 2012, http://xmwww.com/fj/shidian/32349.html; "大陆网民继续号召举行反日大示威," BBC News, August 18, 2012, http://www.bbc.co.uk/zhongwen/simp/chinese_news/2012/08/120818_china_protest_japan.shtml.

REFERENCES

Acemoglu, Daron, and James A. Robinson. 2006. *Economic Origins of Dictatorship and Democracy.* New York: Cambridge University Press.

Bader, Jeffrey A. 2012. *Obama and China's Rise: An Insider's Account of America's Asia Strategy.* Washington, D.C.: Brookings Institution Press.

Banks, Arthur S. 2010. "Cross-National Time Series Archive." Jerusalem, Israel: Databanks International.

Bao, Xiaqin. 2011. "Zhongri Diaoyudao Lingtu Zhengduan de Yanbian yu Xianzhuang- Yi 'Gezhi Zhengyi' Yuanze wei Zhongxin." *Riben Yanjiu* 3.

Barmé, Geremie. 2005. "Mirrors of History: On a Sino-Japanese Movement and Some Antecedents." *Japan Focus,* May 11. http://www.japanfocus.org/site/make_pdf/1713.

———. 2006. "A Year of Some Significance." *Australian Financial Review,* March 31.

Baum, Matthew A. 2004. "Going Private: Public Opinion, Presidential Rhetoric, and the Domestic Politics of Audience Costs in U.S. Foreign Policy Crises." *Journal of Conflict Resolution* 48 (5): 603–31.

Blair, Dennis C., and David V. Bonfili. 2006. "The April 2001 EP-3 Incident: The U.S. Point of View." In *Managing Sino-American Crises: Case Studies and Analysis,* ed. M. D. Swaine, T. Zhang, and D. F. S. Cohen, 377–90. Washington, D.C.: Carnegie Endowment for International Peace.

Brand, L. A. 1991. "Liberalization and Changing Political Coalitions: The Bases of Jordan's 1990–91 Gulf Crisis Policy." *Jerusalem Journal of International Relations* 13 (4): 1–46.

Breuilly, John. 1994. *Nationalism and the State.* Chicago: University of Chicago Press.

Bueno de Mesquita, Bruce, James D. Morrow, Randolph M. Siverson, and Alastair Smith. 1999. "An Institutional Explanation of the Democratic Peace." *American Political Science Review* 93 (4): 791–807.

Bush, George, and Brent Scowcroft. 1998. *A World Transformed.* New York: Knopf; distributed by Random House.

Bush, Richard C. 2010. *The Perils of Proximity: China-Japan Security Relations.* Washington, D.C.: Brookings Institution Press.

Cai, Yongshun 2008. "Power Structure and Regime Resilience: Contentious Politics in China." *British Journal of Political Science* 38 (3): 411–32.

Callahan, William A. 2010. *China: The Pessoptimist Nation.* New York: Oxford University Press.

Calhoun, Craig C. 1994. "Science, Democracy, and the Politics of Identity." In *Popular Protest and Political Culture in Modern China,* ed. Jeffrey Wasserstrom and Elizabeth Perry. 2nd ed., 93–124. Boulder, CO: Westview Press.

Campbell, Kurt M., and Richard Weitz. 2006. "The Chinese Embassy Bombing: Evidence of Crisis Management?" In *Managing Sino-American Crises: Case Studies and Analysis,* ed. M. D.

Swaine, T. Zhang, and D. F. S. Cohen, 327–50. Washington, D.C.: Carnegie Endowment for International Peace.

Chang, Gordon G. 2006. "China in Revolt." *Commentary* 122 (5): 31–36.

Cheng, Joseph Y. S. 1985. "China's Japan Policy in the 1980s." *International Affairs* (Royal Institute of International Affairs) 61 (1): 91–107.

Cherrington, Ruth. 1991. *China's Students: The Struggle for Democracy*. New York: Routledge.

China Institue of International Studies 2008–9. *The CIIS Blue Book on International Situation and China's Foreign Affairs*. World Affairs Press.

———. 2009–10. *The CIIS Blue Book on International Situation and China's Foreign Affairs*. World Affairs Press.

Christensen, Thomas J. 1999. "China, the U.S.-Japan Alliance, and the Security Dilemma in East Asia." *International Security* 23 (4): 49–80.

———. 2011. *Worse Than a Monolith: Alliance Politics and Problems of Coercive Diplomacy in Asia*. Princeton, NJ: Princeton University Press.

Christensen, Thomas J., Alastair I. Johnston, and Robert S. Ross. 2006. "Conclusions and Future Directions". In *New Directions in the Study of China's Foreign Policy*, ed. A. I. Johnston and R. S. Ross, 379–420. Stanford, CA: Stanford University Press.

Chuan, Fu. 1990. *Shinian Xuechao Jishi: 1979–1989* [Ten years of student upheaval: *1979–1989*]. Beijing: Beijing Press.

Chung, Chien-Peng. 2004. *Domestic Politics, International Bargaining, and China's Territorial Disputes*. New York: Routledge.

Chung, Jae Ho, Hongyi Lai, and Ming Xia. 2006. "Mounting Challenges to Governance in China: Surveying Collective Protestors, Religious Sects and Criminal Organizations." *China Journal* 56: 1–31.

Ciorciari, John D. and Jessica Chen Weiss. 2014. "Nationalist Protests, Government Responses, and The Risk of Escalation in Interstate Disputes."

Coser, Lewis A. 1956. *The Functions of Social Conflict*. Glencoe: IL: Free Press.

Cui, Liru and Junhong Liu. 2007. "Xinshiqi de ZhongRi guanxi: Cong sikao zouxiang goujian." *Xiandai Guoji Guanxi* 10.

Cui, Shunji. 2012. "Problems of Nationalism and Historical Memory in China's Relations with Japan." *Journal of Historical Sociology* 25 (2): 199–222.

Dan, Dong. 1982. "Riben xin shouxiang Zhongzenggen Kanghong." *Shijie Zhishi* 24.

———. 1983. "Zhongzenggen fang Mei: Tuchu junshi fangmian." *Shijie Zhishi* 4.

Debs, Alexandre, and Jessica Chen Weiss. Forthcoming. "Circumstances, Domestic Audiences, and Reputational Incentives in International Crisis Bargaining." *Journal of Conflict Resolution*.

Deng, Xiaoping. *Deng Xiaoping Wen Xuan*. 2008. 3 vols. Vol. 3. Beijing: Renmin Chubanshe.

Dikötter, Frank. 1992. *The Discourse of Race in Modern China*. Stanford, CA: Stanford University Press.

Ding, Xiaowen. 2004. "Zhongmei Chuli Liangguo Waijiao Weiji de Tedian Bijiao" [Comparing the characteristics of U.S.-China diplomatic crisis management]. *Guoji Wenti Yanjiu* 6.

Downes, Alexander B., and Todd S. Sechser. 2012. "The Illusion of Democratic Credibility." *International Organization* 66 (3): 457–89.

Downs, Erica Strecker, and Phillip C. Saunders. 1998. "Legitimacy and the Limits of Nationalism: China and the Diaoyu Islands." *International Security* 23 (3): 114–46.

Dreyer, June Teufel. 2000. "China and Its Neighbors." In *What If China Doesn't Democratize? Implications for War and Peace*, ed. E. Friedman and B. L. McCormick, 163–94. Armonk, NY: M.E. Sharpe.

Drifte, Reinhard. 2003. *Japan's Security Relations with China since 1989: From Balancing to Bandwagoning?* New York: Routledge.

Eyerman, Joe, and Robert A. Hart. 1996. "An Empirical Test of the Audience Cost Proposition: Democracy Speaks Louder Than Words." *Journal of Conflict Resolution* 40 (4): 597.

Fang, Ning. 2002. *Chengzhang de Zhongguo: Dangdai Zhongguo Qingnian de Guojia Minzu Yishi Yanjiu* [Maturing China: Research on the national consciousness of contemporary Chinese youth]. Renmin Chubanshe.

Fearon, James D. 1992. "Threats to Use Force: Costly Signals and Bargaining in International Costs." PhD dissertation, Department of Political Science, University of California, Berkeley.

———. 1994a. "Domestic Political Audiences and the Escalation of International Disputes." *American Political Science Review* 88 (3): 577–92.

———. 1994b. "Signaling versus the Balance of Power and Interests: An Empirical Test of a Crisis Bargaining Model." *Journal of Conflict Resolution* 38 (2): 236.

———. 1995. "Rationalist Explanations for War." *International Organization* 49 (3): 379–414.

———. 1997. "Signaling Foreign Policy Interests: Tying Hands versus Sinking Costs." *Journal of Conflict Resolution* 41 (1, New Games: Modeling Domestic-International Linkages): 68–90.

Fewsmith, Joseph. 1999. "The Impact of the Kosovo Conflict on China's Political Leaders and Prospects for WTO Accession." *NBR Briefing* 6 (July).

———. 2001. *China since Tiananmen: The Politics of Transition*. New York: Cambridge University Press.

———. 2008. *China since Tiananmen: From Deng Xiaoping to Hu Jintao*. New York: Cambridge University Press.

Fewsmith, Joseph, and Stanley Rosen. 2001. "The Domestic Context of Chinese Foreign Policy: Does 'Public Opinion' Matter?" In *The Making of Chinese Foreign and Security Policy in the Era of Reform, 1978–2000*, ed. D. Lampton, 151–87. Stanford, CA: Stanford University Press.

Fong, Vanessa L. 2007. "SARS, a shipwreck, a NATO attack, and September 11, 2001: Global Information Flows and Chinese Responses to Tragic News Events." *American Ethnologist* 34 (3): 521–39.

Fravel, M. Taylor. 2010. "Explaining Stability in the Senkaku (Diaoyu) Islands Dispute." In *Getting the Triangle Straight: Managing China-Japan-US Relations*, ed. G. Curtis, R. Kokubun, and J. Wang, 144–64. Washington, D.C.: Brookings Institution Press.

———. 2011. "China's Strategy in the South China Sea." *Contemporary Southeast Asia* 33 (3): 292–319.

Garrett, Banning, and Bonnie Glaser. 1997. "Chinese Apprehensions about Revitalization of the US-Japan Alliance." *Asian Survey* 37 (4): 383–402.

Geddes, Barbara. 1991. "A Game Theoretic Model of Reform in Latin American Democracies." *American Political Science Review* 85 (2): 371–92.

George, Alexander L. 1991. "A Provisional Theory of Crisis Management." In *Avoiding War: Problems of Crisis Management*, ed. A. L. George, 22–30. Boulder, CO: Westview Press.

Goemans, Hein E. 2000a. "Fighting for Survival: The Fate of Leaders and the Duration of War." *Journal of Conflict Resolution* 44 (5): 555–79.

———. 2000b. *War and Punishment: The Causes of War Termination and the First World War*: Princeton, NJ: Princeton University Press.

Goemans, Hein E., Kristian Skrede Gleditsch, and Giacomo Chiozza. 2009. "Introducing Archigos: A Dataset of Political Leaders." *Journal of Peace Research* 46 (2): 269–83.

Goldman, Merle. 2005. *From Comrade to Citizen: The Struggle for Political Rights in China*. Cambridge, MA: Harvard University Press.

Gonganju, Beijing, ed. 2002. *Beijing Gongan Nianjian*. Beijing: Zhongguo Dang'an Chubanshe.

Gourevitch, P. 1978. "2nd Image Reversed: International Sources of Domestic Politics." *International Organization* 32 (4): 881–911.

Green, Michael J. 2001. *Japan's Reluctant Realism: Foreign Policy Challenges in an Era of Uncertain Power*. New York: Palgrave.

Gries, Peter Hays. 2001. "Tears of Rage: Chinese Nationalist Reactions to the Belgrade Embassy Bombing." *China Journal* 46: 25.

———. 2004. *China's New Nationalism: Pride, Politics, and Diplomacy*. Berkeley: University of California Press.

———. 2005a. "China's 'New Thinking on Japan'." *China Quarterly* 184.

———. 2005b. "Chinese Nationalism: Challenging the State?" *Current History* 104 (683): 251.

———. 2005c. "The Koguryo Controversy, National Identity, and Sino-Korean Relations Today." *East Asia* 22 (4): 3–17.

Guisinger, Alexandra, and Alastair Smith. 2002. "Honest Threats: The Interaction of Reputation and Political Institutions in International Crises." *Journal of Conflict Resolution* 46 (2): 175.

Haas, Ernst B. 1986. "What is Nationalism and Why Should We Study it?" *International Organization* 40 (3): 707.

Hamrin, Carol Lee. 1983. "China Reassesses the Superpowers", *Pacific Affairs* 56 (2): 209–31.

Han, Donglin, and David Zweig. 2010. "Images of the World: Studying Abroad and Chinese Attitudes towards International Affairs." *China Quarterly* 202: 290–306.

Harris, Sheldon. 1991. "Japanese Biological Warfare Experiments and Other Atrocities in Manchuria, 1932–1945, and the Subsequent United States Cover Up: A Preliminary Assessment." *Crime, Law and Social Change* 15 (3): 171–99.

He, Yinan. 2007a. "History, Chinese Nationalism and the Emerging Sino–Japanese Conflict." *Journal of Contemporary China* 16 (50): 1–24.

———. 2007b. "Remembering and Forgetting the War: Elite Mythmaking, Mass Reaction, and Sino-Japanese Relations, 1950–2006." *History and Memory* 19 (2): 43–74.

———. 2009. *The Search for Reconciliation: Sino-Japanese and German-Polish Relations since World War II.* New York: Cambridge University Press.

Hielscher, Gebhard. 2004. "The Yasukuni Jinja Debate: Dealing with Symbols of the Past." In *Japan in the 1990s: Crisis as an Impetus for Change,* ed. G. Foljanty-Jost. Munster: Lit; distributed in North America by Transaction.

Hook, Glenn D., Julie Gilson, Christopher W. Hughes, and Hugo Dobson. 2012. *Japan's International Relations: Politics, Economics, and Security.* 3rd ed. New York: Routledge.

Horowitz, Michael, Rose McDermott, and Allan C. Stam. 2005. "Leader Age, Regime Type, and Violent International Relations." *Journal of Conflict Resolution* 49 (5): 661–85.

Hsueh, Roselyn. 2011. *China's Regulatory State: A New Strategy for Globalization.* Ithaca, NY: Cornell University Press.

Hu, Lingyuan. 2013. "Riben Minzhudang Zhengquan yu ZhongRi Guanxi." *Guoji Wenti Yanjiu* 1.

Hu, Lingyuan and Jing Ai. 2010. "Riben Zhengju de Kunju." *Guoji Wenti Yanjiu* 5: 42–48.

Hvistendahl, Mara. 2009. "The Great Forgetting: 20 Years after Tiananmen Square." *Chronicle of Higher Education,* May 19.

Ijiri, Hidenori. 1990. "Sino-Japanese Controversy since the the 1972 Diplomatic Normalization." *China Quarterly* 124: 639–61.

Iokibe, Makoto. 2011. "Japanese Diplomacy after the Cold War." In *The Diplomatic History of Postwar Japan,* ed. M. Iokibe and R. D. Eldridge, 173–209. New York: Routledge.

Jervis, Robert. 1976. *Perception and Misperception in International Politics.* Princeton, NJ: Princeton University Press.

Jia, Dan. 2003. "Lengzhanhou Riben xin baoshou zhuyi de fazhan ji qi yingxiang." *Guoji Luntan* 5 (5).

Jiang, Lifeng. 2012. "Diaoyudao Wenti yu ZhongRi Guanxi." *Riben Xuekan* 5.

Jiang, Zemin. 2006. *Jiang Zemin wen xuan.* 3 vols. Beijing: Ren min chu ban she.

———. 2010. *Selected Works of Jiang Zemin.* 3 vols. Beijing: Foreign Language Press.

Johnson, Chalmers. 1986. "The Patterns of Japanese Relations with China, 1952–1982." *Pacific Affairs* 59 (3): 402–28.

Johnston, Alastair Iain. 2003. "Is China a Status Quo Power?" *International Security* 27 (4): 5–56.

Johnston, Alastair Iain. 2006. "The Correlates of Beijing Public Opinion toward the United States, 1998–2004." In *New Directions in the Study of China's Foreign Policy,* ed. A. I. Johnston and R. S. Ross, 340–77. Stanford, CA: Stanford University Press.

———. 2013. "How New and Assertive Is China's New Assertiveness?" *International Security* 37 (4): 7–48.

Johnston, Alastair Iain, and Daniela Stockmann. 2007. "Chinese Attitudes toward the United States and Americans." In *Anti-Americanisms in World Politics*, ed. P. J. Katzenstein and R. O. Keohane, 157–95. Ithaca, NY: Cornell University Press.

Kamiya, Matake. 2002. "Japanese Politics and Asia-Pacific Policy." In *The Golden Age of the U.S.-China-Japan Triangle, 1972–1989*, ed. E. F. Vogel, M. Yuan, and A. Tanaka, 52–75. Cambridge, MA: Harvard University Asia Center; distributed by Harvard University Press.

Kan, Shirley A., Richard Best, Christopher Bolkcom, Robert Chapman, Richard Cronin, Kerry Dumbaugh, Stuart Goldman, Mark Manyin, Wayne Morrison, Ronald O'Rourke, and David Ackerman. 2001. "China-U.S. Aircraft Collision Incident of April 2001: Assessments and Policy Implications." Congressional Research Service Report no. RL30946.

Kawashima, Yutaka. 2003. *Japanese Foreign Policy at the Crossroads: Challenges and Options for the Twenty-First Century*. Washington, D.C.: Brookings Institution Press.

Keefe, John. 2001. *Anatomy of the EP-3 Incident, April 2001*. Alexandria, VA: CNA Corporation.

Kelly, David A. 1987. "The Chinese Student Movement of December 1986 and its Intellectual Antecedents." *Australian Journal of Chinese Affairs* 17: 127–42.

Kim, Samuel S. 1999. "China and the United Nations." In *China Joins the World: Progress and Prospects*, ed. E. Economy and M. Oksenberg, 42–89. New York: Council on Foreign Relations Press; distributed by Brookings Institution Press.

King, Gary, Jennifer Pan, and Margaret E. Roberts. 2013. "How Censorship in China Allows Government Criticism but Silences Collective Expression." *American Political Science Review* 107 (2): 326–43.

Kissinger, Henry. 2001. *Does America Need a Foreign Policy? Towards a Diplomacy for the 21st Century*. New York: Simon & Schuster.

Kitaoka, Shinichi. 2005. "Answering China's Japan Bashers." *Japan Echo* Special Issue (June): 12–17.

Kluver, Randolph. 2010. "Rhetorical Trajectories of Tiananmen Square." *Diplomatic History* 34 (1): 71–94.

Kokubun, Ryosei. 1986. "The Politics of Foreign Economic Policy-Making in China: The Case of Plant Cancellations with Japan." *China Quarterly* 105: 19–44.

———. 2007. "Changing Japanese Strategic Thinking toward China." In *Japanese Strategic Thought toward Asia*, ed. G. Rozman, K. Togo, and J. P. Ferguson, 149–51. New York: Palgrave.

Kokubun, Ryuosei, and Jie Liu. 2004. "The Danger of China's Disaffected Masses." *Japan Echo* 31 (6): 51–55.

Kuran, Timur. 1991. "Now Out of Never: The Element of Surprise in the East European Revolution of 1989." *World Politics* 44 (1): 7–48.

Kurizaki, Shuhei. 2007. "Efficient Secrecy: Public versus Private Threats in Crisis Diplomacy." *American Political Science Review* 101 (3): 543–58.

Kwong, Julia. 1988. "The 1986 Student Demonstrations in China: A Democratic Movement?" *Asian Survey* 28 (9): 970–85.

Kydd, Andrew H. 2005. *Trust and Mistrust in International Relations*. Princeton, NJ: Princeton University Press.

Laitin, David D. 1998. *Identity in Formation: The Russian-Speaking Populations in the Near Abroad*. Ithaca, NY: Cornell University Press.

Lam, Willy Wo-Lap. 2006. *Chinese Politics in the Hu Jintao Era: New Leaders, New Challenges*. Armonk, NY: M.E. Sharpe.

Lardy, Nicholas R. 2002. *Integrating China into the Global Economy*. Washington, D.C.: Brookings Institution Press.

Lee, Chae-Jin. 1984. *China and Japan: New Economic Diplomacy*. Stanford, CA: Hoover Institute Press.

Leeds, Brett Ashley. 1999. "Domestic Political Institutions, Credible Commitments, and International Cooperation." *American Journal of Political Science* 43 (4): 979–1002.

Leng, Rong and Zuoling Wang, eds. 2004. *Deng Xiaoping Nian Pu, 1975–1997*. Beijing: Zhong yang wen xian chu ban she.

Leung, Benjamin K. P. 2000. "The Student Movement in Hong Kong: Transition to a Democratizing Society." In *The Dynamics of Social Movement in Hong Kong*, ed. S. W.-k. Chiu, D. Lü, and T.-l. Lui, 209–26. Hong Kong: Hong Kong University Press.

Levendusky, Matthew S., and Michael C. Horowitz. 2012. "When Backing Down Is the Right Decision: Partisanship, New Information, and Audience Costs." *American Journal of Political Science* 74 (2): 323–38.

Leventoglu, Bahar, and Ahmer Tarar. 2005. "Prenegotiation Public Commitment in Domestic and International Bargaining." *American Political Science Review* 99 (3): 419–33.

Li, Peng. 2008. *He ping fa zhan he zuo: Li Peng wai shi ri ji.* 2 vols. Beijing: Xin hua chu ban she.

Li, Xiguang. 2005. "Yinyan: Shenme Shi Quanqiu Chuanbo." In *Ruan Liliang Yu Quanqiu Chuanbo*, ed. X. Li and Q. Zhou, 12–13. Beijing: Tsinghua University Press.

Liao, Kuang-Sheng. 1976. "Linkage Politics in China: Internal Mobilization and Articulated External Hostility in the Cultural Revolution, 1967–1969." *World Politics* 28 (4): 590–610.

———. 1990. *Antiforeignism and Modernization in China*. 3rd ed. Hong Kong: Chinese University Press.

Liao, Xuanli. 2006. *Chinese Foreign Policy Think Tanks and China's Policy towards Japan*. Hong Kong: Chinese University Press.

Lin, Daizhao. 1992. *Zhan hou Zhong Ri guan xi shi, 1945–1992*. Beijing: Beijing da xue chu ban she.

Liu, Jiangyong. 1986. "Lun Riben dui wai zhanlue de fazhan." *Riben Yanjiu* 1: 6–11.

———. 2007. *Zhongguo yu Riben: bianhua zhong de "zheng leng jing re" guanxi*. Beijing: Renmin chubanshe.

———. 2010. "Sixty Years of PRC Research on Sino-Japanese Relations (1949–2009)." *Japanese Journal of Political Science* 11 (Special Issue 3): 389–400.

———. 2011a. "Meiguo junshi jieru Diaoyudao jiang mianling liang nan kun jing." *Guoji Wenti Yanjiu* 3: 10–18.

———. 2011b. "Zhongri Diaoyudao zhizheng zhong de Meiguo yinsu." *Shijie Zhishi* 9: 24–26.

Liu, Ning. 2005. *Bingqi "zhong-ri youhao" de xiang chou* [Giving up the nostalgia of "Sino-Japanese friendship"]. Hong Kong: Tidetime Publishing.

Liu, Xiaobo. 2006. *Dan ren du jian: Zhongguo min zu zhu yi pi pan*. Taipei: Bo da chu ban she.

Lohmann, Susanne. 1994. "The Dynamics of Informational Cascades: The Monday Demonstrations in Leipzig, East Germany, 1989–91." *World Politics* 47 (1): 42–101.

———. 2003. "Why Do Institutions Matter? An Audience-Cost Theory of Institutional Commitment." *Governance* 16 (1): 95–110.

Lü, Congmin. 2009. *Wai jiao ren sheng: wo de hui yi he gan wu*. Beijing: Zhong xin chu ban she.

Lu, Yi. 2007. "ZhongRi guanxi: Cong Xiao Quan dao An Bei." *Riben Yanjiu* 4.

Lynch, Marc. 1999. *State Interests and Public Spheres: The International Politics of Jordan's Identity*. New York: Columbia University Press.

———. 2006. *Voices of the New Arab Public: Iraq, Al-Jazeera, and Middle East Politics Today*. New York: Columbia University Press.

Ma, Ying. 2002. "China's America Problem." *Policy Review* 111, February 1. http://www.hoover.org/publications/policy-review/article/7914.

Mann, James. 1999. *About Face: A History of America's Curious Relationship with China from Nixon to Clinton*. New York: Alfred Knopf.

Mansfield, Edward D., Helen V. Milner, and B. Peter Rosendorff. 2002. "Why Democracies Cooperate More: Electoral Control and International Trade Agreements." *International Organization* 56 (3): 477.

Martin, Lisa L. 1993. "Credibility, Costs, and Institutions: Cooperation on Economic Sanctions." *World Politics* 45 (3): 406–32.

Masuda, Hajimu. 2012. "The Korean War through the Prism of Chinese Society: Public Reactions and the Shaping of "Reality" in the Communist State, October–December 1950." *Journal of Cold War Studies* 14 (3): 3–38.

Mayhew, David R. 1974. *Congress: The Electoral Connection*. New Haven: Yale University Press.

Mercer, Jonathan. 1996. *Reputation and International Politics*. Ithaca, NY: Cornell University Press.

Miller, Joanne M., and Jon A. Krosnick. 2000. "News Media Impact on the Ingredients of Presidential Evaluations: Politically Knowledgeable Citizens Are Guided by a Trusted Source." *American Journal of Political Science* 44 (2): 301–15.

Minoura, Haruna. 2011. "Energy Security and Japan-China Relations: Competition or Cooperation." Master's thesis, Elliott School of International Affairs, George Washington University.

Mitter, Rana. 2004. *A Bitter Revolution: China's Struggle with the Modern World*. Oxford: Oxford University Press.

Morrow, James D. 1989. "Capabilities, Uncertainty, and Resolve: A Limited Information Model of Crisis Bargaining." *American Journal of Political Science* 33 (4): 941.

Mueller, John E. 1973. *War, Presidents, and Public Opinion*. New York: Wiley.

Mulvenon, James. 2002. "Civil-Military Relations and the EP-3 Crisis: A Content Analysis." *China Leadership Monitor* (1), 1–11, January 30. http://www.hoover.org/publications/china-leadership-monitor/article/6646.

———. 2009. "PLA Computer Network Operations: Scenarios, Doctrine, Organizations, and Capability." In *Beyond the Strait: PLA Missions Other Than Taiwan*, ed. R. Kamphausen, D. Lai, and A. Scobell, 253–85. Carlisle, PA: Defense Technical Information Center.

Murata, Koji. 2006. "Domestic Sources of Japanese Policy towards China." In *Japan's Relations with China: Facing a Rising Power*, ed. P. E. Lam, 37–49. New York: Routledge.

———. 2011. "Japanese Diplomacy in the 1980s." In *The Diplomatic History of Postwar Japan*, ed. M. Iokibe and R. D. Eldridge, 143–72. New York: Routledge.

Nakajima, M. 1986. "Chugoku ni jubaku sareta Nihon" [Japan spellbound by China]. *Shokun*, March, 26–42.

Nakanishi, Hiroshi. 2011. "Japanese Diplomacy in the 1970s." In *The Diplomatic History of Postwar Japan*, ed. M. Iokibe and R. D. Eldridge, 108–142. New York: Routledge.

Nakasone, Yasuhiro. 2004. *Jiseiroku: rekishi hōtei no hikoku to shite*. Tokyo: Shinchōsha.

———. 2006. *Meditations: On the Nature of Leadership*. Tokyo: PHP Institute.

Nathan, Andrew J. 2002. "Guest Editor's Introduction." *Chinese Law and Government* 35 (2): 3–13.

Nathan, Andrew J., and Bruce Gilley. 2002. *China's New Rulers: The Secret Files*. New York: New York Review of Books.

Naughton, Barry. 2007. *The Chinese Economy: Transitions and Growth*. Cambridge, MA: MIT Press.

Noriko, Kamachi. 2006. "Japanese Writings on Post-1945 Japan-China Relations." In *Japan's Relations with China: Facing a Rising Power*, ed. P. E. Lam, 50–68. New York: Routledge.

O'Brien, Kevin J. 1996. "Rightful Resistance." *World Politics* 49 (1): 31–55.

O'Donnell, Guillermo A., and Philippe C. Schmitter. 1986. *Transitions from Authoritarian Rule: Tentative Conclusions about Uncertain Democracies*. Baltimore: Johns Hopkins University Press.

Okamoto, Yukio, and Akihiko Tanaka. 2005. "The Dangerous Surge of Chinese 'Patriotism.'" *Japan Echo* 32 (4) 10–11.

Oksenberg, Michel. 1982. "A Decade of Sino-American Relations." *Foreign Affairs* 61: 175–95.

———. 1986. "China's Confident Nationalism." *Foreign Affairs* 65 (3): 501–23.

Ouyang, Bin. 2003. "Zhongguo Minjian Fanri Shili Yanshao" [Anti-Japan sentiment rises in China]. *Phoenix Weekly*, September 4.

Partell, Peter J., and Glenn Palmer. 1999. "Audience Costs and Interstate Crises: An Empirical Assessment of Fearon's Model of Dispute Outcomes." *International Studies Quarterly* 43 (2): 389–405.

Pearson, Margaret. 2001. "The Case of China's Accession to GATT/WTO." In *The Making of Chinese Foreign and Security Policy in the Era of Reform, 1978–2000*, ed. D. Lampton, 337–70. Stanford, CA: Stanford University Press.

Peceny, Mark, Caroline C. Beer, and Shannon Sanchez-Terry. 2002. "Dictatorial Peace?" *American Political Science Review* 96 (1): 15–26.

Pei, Minxin. 2000. "Rights and Resistance: The Changing Contexts of the Dissident Movement." In *Chinese Society: Change, Conflict, and Resistance*, ed. E. J. Perry and M. Selden, 20–40. New York: Routledge.

Pepper, Suzanne. 1987. *Deng Xiaoping's Political and Economic Reforms and the Chinese Student Protests*. Vol. 1986, no. 30. Indianapolis, IN: Universities Field Staff International.

Perry, Elizabeth J. 2001. "Challenging the Mandate of Heaven—Popular Protest in Modern China." *Critical Asian Studies* 33 (2): 163–80.

———. 2002. *Challenging the Mandate of Heaven: Social Protest and State Power in China*. Armonk, NY: M.E. Sharpe.

Pevehouse, Jon C. 2002. "With a Little Help from My Friends? Regional Organizations and the Consolidation of Democracy." *American Journal of Political Science* 46 (3): 611–26.

Pickering, Jeffrey, and Emizet F. Kisangani. 2010. "Diversionary Despots? Comparing Autocracies' Propensities to Use and to Benefit from Military Force." *American Journal of Political Science* 54 (2): 477–93.

Pool, Ithiel de Sola. 1973. "Communication in Totalitarian Societies." In *Handbook of Communication*. Chicago: Rand McNally.

Powell, Robert. 1990. *Nuclear Deterrence Theory*. New York: Cambridge University Press.

Putnam, Robert. 1988. "Diplomacy and Domestic Politics: The Logic of 2-Level Games." *International Organization* 42 (3): 427–60.

Pyle, Kenneth B. 1998. "In Pursuit of a Grand Design: Nakasone betwixt the Past and the Future." In *Showa Japan: Political, Economic and Social History, 1926–1989*. Vol. 4: 1973–1989, ed. S. S. Large, 64–89. London: Routledge.

Qian, Qichen. 2005. *Ten Episodes in China's Diplomacy*. New York: HarperCollins.

Ramsay, Kristopher W. 2004. "Politics at the Water's Edge: Crisis Bargaining and Electoral Competition." *Journal of Conflict Resolution* 48 (4): 459–86.

Reilly, James. 2006. "China's History Activism and Sino-Japanese Relations." *China: An International Journal* 4 (2): 189–216.

———. 2012. *Strong Society, Smart State: The Rise of Public Opinion in China's Japan Policy*. New York: Columbia University Press.

Rice, Condoleezza. 2011. *No Higher Honor: A Memoir of My Years in Washington*. New York: Crown Publishers.

Roeder, Philip G. 1993. *Red Sunset: The Failure of Soviet Politics*: Princeton, NJ: Princeton University Press.

Rose, Caroline. 1998. *Interpreting History in Sino-Japanese Relations: A Case Study in Political Decision-Making*. New York: Routledge.

———. 2005. *Sino-Japanese Relations: Facing the Past, Looking to the Future?* New York: RoutledgeCurzon.

Ross, Robert S. 1986. "International Bargaining and Domestic Politics: Conflict in U.S.-China Relations since 1972." *World Politics* 38 (2) (January): 255–87.

———. 2011. "Chinese Nationalism and Its Discontents." *National Interest*, November–December.

Ruan, Cishan. 2004. *Leng he: Zhong Mei shi ji zhi huo*. Beijing: Shi jie zhi shi chu ban she.

Rubin, Barry. 2002. "The Real Roots of Arab Anti-Americanism." *Foreign Affairs*, November–December.

Samuels, Richard J. 2007. *Securing Japan: Tokyo's Grand Strategy and the Future of East Asia*. Ithaca, NY: Cornell University Press.

Sarotte, M. E. 2012. "China's Fear of Contagion: Tiananmen Square and the Power of the European Example." *International Security* 37 (2): 156–82.

Sartori, Anne E. 2002. "The Might of the Pen: A Reputational Theory of Communication in International Disputes." *International Organization* 56 (1): 121.

Satoh, Yukio. 2001. "Step by Step toward Permanent Membership: Japan's Strategy for Security Council Reform." *Gaiko Forum: Japanese Perspectives on Foreign Affairs* 1 (2).

Schell, Orville. 1988. *Discos and Democracy: China in the Throes of Reform*. New York: Pantheon Books.

Schelling, Thomas C. 1960. *The Strategy of Conflict*. Cambridge, MA: Harvard University Press.

———. 1966. *Arms and Influence*. New Haven: Yale University Press.

———. 1978. *Micromotives and Macrobehavior*. New York: Norton.

Schultz, Kenneth A. 1999. "Do Democratic Institutions Constrain or Inform? Contrasting Two Institutional Perspectives on Democracy and War." *International Organization* 53 (2): 233–66.

———. 2001a. *Democracy and Coercive Diplomacy*. New York: Cambridge University Press.

———. 2001b. "Looking for Audience Costs." *Journal of Conflict Resolution* 45 (1): 32–60.

Shambaugh, David L. 1996. "China and Japan towards the Twenty-First Century: Rivals for Pre-eminence or Complex Interdependence?" In *China and Japan: History, Trends, and Prospects*, ed. C. Howe, 83–96. New York: Oxford University Press.

———. 2007. "China's Propaganda System: Institutions, Processes and Efficacy." *China Journal* 57: 25–58.

Shen, Simon. 2004. "Nationalism or Nationalist Foreign Policy? Contemporary Chinese Nationalism and Its Role in Shaping Chinese Foreign Policy in Response to the Belgrade Embassy Bombing." *Politics* 24 (2): 122–30.

———. 2011. "Exploring the Neglected Constraints on Chindia: Analysing the Online Chinese Perception of India and Its Interaction with China's Indian Policy." *China Quarterly* 207: 541–60.

Shen, Simon, and Shaun Breslin. 2010. *Online Chinese Nationalism and China's Bilateral Relations*. Lanham, MD: Lexington Books.

Sheng, Lijun. 2001. *China's Dilemma: The Taiwan Issue*. London: I. B. Tauris.

Shibuichi, Daiki. 2005. "The Yasukuni Shrine Dispute and the Politics of Identity in Japan: Why All the Fuss?" *Asian Survey* 45 (2): 197.

Shimizu, Yoshikazu. 2006. *Chuugoku ga "han-nichi" o suteru hi* [The day China abandons "anti-Japan"]. Kodansha Alpha Plus New Books.

Shirk, Susan L. 1993. *The Political Logic of Economic Reform in China*. Berkeley: University of California Press.

———. 2007. *China: Fragile Superpower*. Oxford: Oxford University Press.

———, ed. 2011. *Changing Media, Changing China*. New York: Oxford University Press.

Shulman, Debra Lois. 2008. "Regime Strategy and Foreign Policy in Autocracies: Egypt, Jordan, and Syria in the Gulf Wars." PhD dissertation, Yale University, 2008.

Signorino, Curtis S. 1999. "Strategic Interaction and the Statistical Analysis of International Conflict." *American Political Science Review* 93 (2): 279–97.

Slantchev, Branislav L. 2005. "Military Coercion in Interstate Crises." *American Political Science Review* 99 (4): 533.

———. 2006. "Politicians, the Media, and Domestic Audience Costs." *International Studies Quarterly* 50 (2): 445–77.

Smith, Alastair. 1996. "To Intervene or Not to Intervene: A Biased Decision." *Journal of Conflict Resolution* 40 (1): 16–40.

———. 1998. "International Crises and Domestic Politics." *American Political Science Review* 92 (3): 623–38.

Snyder, Glenn Herald, and Paul Diesing. 1977. *Conflict Among Nations: Bargaining, Decision Making, and System Structure in International Crises*. Princeton, N.J.: Princeton University Press.

Snyder, Jack. 1991. *Myths of Empire: Domestic Politics and International Ambition*. Ithaca, N.Y.: Cornell University Press.

———. 1993. "Nationalism and the Crisis of the Post-Soviet State." *Survival* 35 (1): 5–26.

Snyder, Jack, and Erica D. Borghard. 2011. "The Cost of Empty Threats: A Penny, Not a Pound." *American Political Science Review* 105 (3): 437–56.

Song, Chengyou. 1993. "Riben de daguo mubiao zhuiqiu yu ZhongRi guanxi." *Riben Xuekan* 1: 25–39.

Spence, Jonathan D. 1999. *The Search for Modern China*. 2nd ed. New York: W.W. Norton.

Stockmann, Daniela. 2013. *Media Commercialization and Authoritarian Rule in China*. New York: Cambridge University Press.

Su, Chi. 1989. "Sino-Soviet Relations of the 1980s: From Confrontation to Conciliation." In *China and the World: New Directions in Chinese Foreign Relations*, ed. S. S. Kim, 109–27. Boulder, CO: Westview Press.

Suettinger, Robert L. 2003. *Beyond Tiananmen: The Politics of U.S.-China Relations, 1989–2000.* Washington, D.C.: Brookings Institution Press.

Sun, Cheng. 2010. "An Analysis on the Politics and Diplomacy of the Hatoyama Cabinet". *China International Studies*, March–April.

Swaine, Michael D. 2001. "Decision-Making Regarding Taiwan: 1979–2000." In *The Making of Chinese Foreign and Security Policy in the Era of Reform*, ed. D. Lampton, 316–17. Stanford, CA: Stanford University Press.

Swaine, Michael D., and M. Taylor Fravel. 2011. "China's Assertive Behavior, Part Two: The Maritime Periphery." *China Leadership Monitor* 35.

Swaine, Michael D., and Tuosheng Zhang, eds. 2006. *Managing Sino-American Crises: Case Studies and Analysis.* Washington, D.C.: Carnegie Endowment for International Peace.

Takahara, Akio. 2004. "Japan's Political Response to the Rise of China." In *The Rise of China and a Changing East Asian Order*, ed. J. Wang and R. Kokobun, 157–74. Tokyo: Japan Center for International Exchange; Washington, D.C.: Brookings Institution Press.

Tan, Ruirui. 2006. "Dui Quntixing Shijian Chuzhi Gongzuozhong Ruogan Wenti de Sikao" [Reflections on certain working problems in the management of mass incidents]. In *Xin Shiqi Quntixingshijian Yanjiu* [Research on mass incidents in the new era], ed. G. Hu and W. Lin, 475–85. China People's Public Security University Press.

Tanaka, Akihiko. 2007. *Ajia no naka no Nihon.* Tokyo: NTT Shuppan.

Tang, Jiaxuan. 2010. "Huiyi 2001 nian Zhong Mei Nan Hai 'zhuang ji shi jian' " [Remembering the 2001 South China Sea US-China plane collision]. *Wanxia* 6.

———. 2011. *Heavy Storm and Gentle Breeze: A Memoir of China's Diplomacy.* New York: HarperCollins.

Tanner, Murray Scot. 2004. "China Rethinks Unrest." *Washington Quarterly* 27 (3): 137–56.

———. 2005. Hearing of the Testimony Presented to the US-China Economic and Security Review Commission, April 14. "Chinese Government Responses to Rising Social Unrest."

Tarrow, Sidney G. 1998. *Power in Movement: Social Movements and Contentious Politics.* New York: Cambridge University Press.

Telhami, Shibley. 1993. "Arab Public Opinion and the Gulf War." *Political Science Quarterly* 108 (3): 437–52.

———. 2002. *The Stakes: America and the Middle East. The Consequences of Power and the Choice for Peace.* Boulder, CO: Westview Press.

Teng, Jianqun. 2011. "The Third-Party Factors in China-U.S. Relations." *China International Studies*, January–February.

Thornton, Richard C. 2003. *The Reagan Revolution: Rebuilding the Western Alliance.* Victoria, B.C.: Trafford.

Tian, Huan, Chaoqin Ji, and Lifeng Jiang. 1997. *Zhan hou Zhong Ri guan xi wen xian ji, 1971-1995.* Di 1 ban. ed. Beijing: Zhongguo she hui ke xue chu ban she.

Togo, Kazuhiko. 2005. *Japan's Foreign Policy, 1945–2003: The Quest for a Proactive Policy.* 2nd ed. Leiden: Brill.

———. 2008. *Rekishi to gaiko: Yasukuni, Ajia, Tokyo saiban.* Tokyo: Kodansha.

———. 2006. "A Moratorium on Yasukuni Visits." *Far Eastern Economic Review,* June.

Tomz, Michael. 2007. "Domestic Audience Costs in International Relations: An Experimental Approach." *International Organization* 61 (4): 821–40.

Tong, James. 2002a. "Anatomy of Regime Repression in China: Timing, Enforcement Institutions, and Target Selection in Banning the Falungong, July 1999." *Asian Survey* 42 (6): 795–820.

———. 2002b. "An Organizational Analysis of the Falun Gong: Structure, Communications, Financing." *China Quarterly* 171: 636–60.

Trager, Robert F., and Lynn Vavreck. 2011. "The Political Costs of Crisis Bargaining: Presidential Rhetoric and the Role of Party." *Journal of Politics* 55 (3): 526–45.

Traub, James. 2006. *The Best Intentions: Kofi Annan and the UN in the Era of American World Power.* New York: Farrar, Straus and Giroux.

Tretiak, Daniel. 1978. "The Sino-Japanese Treaty of 1978: The Senkaku Incident Prelude." *Asian Survey* 18 (12): 1235–49.

Urayama, Kori J. 2000. "Chinese Perspectives on Theater Missile Defense: Policy Implications for Japan." *Asian Survey* 40 (4): 599–621.

van Evera, Stephen. 1994. "Hypotheses on Nationalism and War." *International Security* 18 (4): 5-39.

Wakamiya, Yoshibumi. 1999. *The Postwar Conservative View of Asia: How the Political Right Has Delayed Japan's Coming to Terms with Its History of Aggression in Asia.* 1st English ed. Tokyo: LTCB International Library Foundation.

Waldron, Arthur. 1999. "A Regime in Crisis." *Weekly Standard*, May 24.

Wallace, Jeremy L. 2013. "Cities, Redistribution, and Authoritarian Regime Survival." *Journal of Politics* 75 (3): 632–45.

———. 2014. *Cities and Stability: Urbanization, Redistribution, and Regime Survival in China.* New York: Oxford University Press.

Wallace, Jeremy L., and Jessica Chen Weiss. 2013. "The Political Economy of Nationalist Protests in China: A Subnational Approach." Paper presented at the Annual Meeting of the Midwest Political Science Association. Chicago, IL.

Waltz, Kenneth. 1979. *Theory of International Politics.* New York: McGraw-Hill.

Wan, Ming. 2006. *Sino-Japanese Relations: Interaction, Logic, and Transformation.* Washington, D.C.: Woodrow Wilson Center Press; Stanford University Press.

Wang, Jianwei, and Xinbo Wu. 1998. "Against Us or with Us? The Chinese Perspective of America's Alliances with Japan and Korea." Institute for International Studies: Stanford University Asia / Pacific Research Center.

Wang, Jisi. 2011. "China's Search for a Grand Strategy." *Foreign Affairs*, March–April.

Wang, Jisi, and Hui Xu. 2006. "Pattern of Sino-American Crises: A Chinese Perspective." In *Managing Sino-American Crises: Case Studies and Analysis*, ed. M. D. Swaine and T. Zhang, 133–48. Washington, D.C.: Carnegie Endowment for International Peace.

Wang, Mingming (王鸣鸣). 2002. "Gongzhong Yulun yu Meiguo Duiwai Zhengce" [Public opinion and US foreign policy]. *Shijie Jingji yu Zhengzhi* 5.

Wang, Zheng. 2012. *Never Forget National Humiliation: Historical Memory in Chinese Politics and Foreign Relations.* New York: Columbia University Press.

Wasserstrom, Jeffrey N. 1999. "Student Protests in Fin-de-Siècle China." *New Left Review* 237: 52–76.

———. 1991. *Student Protests in Twentieth-Century China: The View from Shanghai.* Stanford, Calif.: Stanford University Press.

Weeks, Jessica L. 2008. "Autocratic Audience Costs: Regime Type and Signaling Resolve." *International Organization* 62 (1): 35–64.

———. 2012. "Strongmen and Straw Men: Authoritarian Regimes and the Initiation of International Conflict." *American Political Science Review* 106 (2): 326–47.

Weiss, Jessica Chen. 2013. "Authoritarian Signaling, Mass Audiences, and Nationalist Protest in China." *International Organization* 67 (1): 1–35.

Whiting, Allen S. 1983. "Assertive Nationalism in Chinese Foreign Policy." *Asian Survey* 23 (8): 913–33.

———. 1989. *China Eyes Japan.* Berkeley: University of California Press.

Whiting, Allen S., and Jianfei Xin. 1990. "Sino-Japanese Relations: Pragmatism and Passion." *World Policy Journal* 8 (1): 107–35.

Wiegand, Krista E. 2009. "China's Strategy in the Senkaku/Diaoyu Islands Dispute: Issue Linkage and Coercive Diplomacy." *Asian Security* 5 (2): 170–93.

Wilkenfeld, Jonathan. 2006. "Concepts and Methods in Crisis Management." In *Managing Sino-American Crises: Case Studies and Analysis*, ed. M. D. Swaine, T. Zhang, and D. F. S. Cohen, 103–32. Washington, D.C.: Carnegie Endowment for International Peace.

Wong, John, and Yongnian Zheng. 2000. "Nationalism and Its Dilemma: Chinese Responses to Embassy Bombing." In *Reform, Legitimacy and Dilemmas: China's Politics and Society*, ed. G. Wang and Y. Zheng, 321–44. Singapore: Singapore University Press, World Scientific.

Wu, Baiyi. 2005a. "Zhongguo dui 'Zhaguan' Shijian de Weiji Guanli [China's crisis management during the embassy bombing]." *Shijie Jingji yu Zhengzhi* 3: 22–29.

———. 2006a. "Chinese Crisis Management during the 1999 Embassy Bombing Incident." In *Managing Sino-American Crises: Case Studies and Analysis*, ed. M. D. Swaine, T. Zhang, and D. F. S. Cohen, 351–75. Washington, D.C.: Carnegie Endowment for International Peace.

Wu, Jian. 2004. "Taiwan Xuanju yu Haixia Junshi Xingshi." *Guoji Zhanwang* 4.

Wu, Jianmin. 2006b. *Waijiao yu Guojiguanxi: Wu Jianmin de Kanfa yu Sikao*. Beijing: Zhongguo Renmin Daxue Chubanshe.

———. 2007a. *Waijiao Anli* [Case studies in diplomacy]. Beijing: Zhongguo Renmin Daxue Chubanshe.

Wu, Ji'nan. 2012. "Shixi Diaoyudao Zhengduan de Riben Guonei Zhengzhi Bei Jing." *Guoji Guancha* 6.

Wu, Ji'nan and Hongbin Chen. 2004. *Zhong Ri guan xi "ping jing" lun*. Beijing Shi: Shi shi chu ban she.

Wu, Miaofa. 2006c. "Lianheguo Gaige Yu Zhongguo De Fanglue." In *Shijie Dashi Yu Heping Fazhan*, ed. D. Xu, 245–60. Beijing: World Affairs Press.

Wu, Xinbo. 2005b. "The End of the Silver Lining: A Chinese View of the U.S.-Japanese Alliance." *Washington Quarterly* 29 (1): 117–30.

———. 2008a. Managing Crisis and Sustaining Peace between China and the United States. Washington, D.C.: United States Institute of Peace Press.

———. 2008b. "Understanding Chinese and U.S. Crisis Behavior." *Washington Quarterly* 31 (1): 61–76.

Wu, Xu. 2007b. *Chinese Cyber Nationalism: Evolution, Characteristics, and Implications*. Lanham, MD: Lexington Books.

Xia, Liping. 2006. "Crisis Management in the Relationship between China and the United States." *International Review* (Shanghai Institute for International Studies) 45 (Winter): 61–86.

Xiao, Gongqin. 2001. "Kesuowo Weiji yu Ershiyi Shiji Zhongguo de Minzuzhuyi [The Kosovo crisis and 21st century Chinese nationalism]." *Dangdai Zhongguo Yanjiu* 1.

Xiao, Qiang. Hearing of the U.S.-China Economic and Security Review Commission. July 31, 2007.

———. 2011. "The Rise of Online Public Opinion and Its Political Impact." In *Changing Media, Changing China*, ed. S. L. Shirk. New York: Oxford University Press.

Xiong, Dayun. 1989. "Lun Zhongzenggen Kanghong qi zhengzhi." *Riben Xuekan* 1: 21–29.

Xiong, Zhiyong. 2006. *Bai Nian Zhong Mei Guan Xi*. Beijing Shi: Shi jie zhi shi chu ban she.

Xu, Dunxin. 2006. "Zhongri Guanxi He Zhongguo Duiri Zhengce" [Sino-Japanese relations and China's strategy towards Japan]. In *Shijie Dashi Yu Heping Fazhan* [World trends and China's peaceful development], ed. X. Dunxin, 388–89. Beiing: Shijie Zhishi Chubanshe.

Xu, Luo. 2002. *Searching for Life's Meaning: Changes and Tensions in the Worldviews of Chinese Youth in the 1980s*. Ann Arbor: University of Michigan Press.

Xue, Fang. 1985. "Jingguo Shenshe." *Shijie Zhishi* 19.

Yan, Xuetong. 2000. *Meiguo Ba Quan Yu Zhongguo An Quan*. Tianjin Shi: Tianjin ren min chu ban she.

Yang, Bojiang. 2011. "Riben minzhudang duiwai zhanlue tiaozheng." *Zhongguo Guoji Zhanlue Pinglun* 4: 145–53.

———. Jul./Aug. 2008. "Zhongri Guanxi: 'Nuan Chun' Shi Jie de Xing Shi yu Ren Wu [Implications of a 'Warm Spring' in China-Japan Relations]." *Xiandai Guoji Guanxi* 18 (4): 1–5.

Yang, Zhongxu. 2008. "Hei Se 5.19: Nan Yi Chengshou Zhi Zhong" [Black 5.19: An unbearable burden]. *Zhongguo Xinwen Zhoukan*, June 24.

Yee, Albert S. 2004. "Semantic Ambiguity and Joint Deflections." *China: An International Journal* 2 (1): 53–82.

Yokoi, Yoichi. 1996. "Plan and Technology Contracts and the Changing Pattern of Economic Interdependence Between China and Japan." In *China and Japan: History, Trends, and Prospects*, ed. C. Howe, 127–45. New York: Oxford University Press.

Yoshihide, Soeya. 2001. "Taiwan in Japan's Security Considerations." *China Quarterly* 165: 130–46.

Yu, Zhiyuan, and Dingxin Zhao. 2006. "Differential Participation and the Nature of a Movement: A Study of the 1999 Anti-U.S. Beijing Student Demonstrations." *Social Forces* 84 (3): 1755–77.

Zhai, Xin. 2010. "An Analysis of DPJ's China Policy." *China International Studies*, January–February.

———. 2012. "Riben Minzhudang Zhengquan 'Guoyouhua' Diaoyudao de Dongyuan." *Guoji Wenti Yanjiu* 5.

Zhang, Baijia. 2009. "The Evolution of China's Diplomacy and Foreign Relations in the Era of Reform, 1976–2005." In *Challenges to Chinese Foreign Policy: Diplomacy, Globalization, and the Next World Power*, ed. Y. Hao, C. X. G. Wei, and L. Dittmer, 15–33. Lexington: University Press of Kentucky.

Zhang, Ping. 2000. *Diaoyu Dao Feng Yun*. Beijing Shi: Guo ji wen hua chu ban she.

Zhang, Tuosheng. 2002. "China's Relations with Japan." In *The Golden Age of the U.S.-China-Japan Triangle, 1972–1989*, ed. E. F. Vogel, M. Yuan, and A. Tanaka, 191–208. Cambridge, MA: Harvard University Asia Center; distributed by Harvard University Press.

———. 2006. "The Sino-American Aircraft Collision: Lessons for Crisis Management." In *Managing Sino-American Crises: Case Studies and Analysis*, ed. M. D. Swaine, T. Zhang, and D. F. S. Cohen, 391–421. Washington, D.C.: Carnegie Endowment for International Peace.

Zhang, Xiangshan. 1984. "Hu Yaobang zong shuji de fangRi chengguo." *Shijie Zhishi* 2–3.

Zhang, Xuan and Zhengguang Yang. 1993. "Dang dai Zhong Ri guan xi si shi nian, 1949–1989." In *Zhong Ri Guan Xi Shi Cong Shu 2*. Beijing: Shi shi chu ban she.

Zhang, Yu and Junfeng Zhao. 2005. "Meiguo meiti dui Zhongguo fanri youxing baodao de pianjian fenxi" [The American media's biased analysis of anti-Japanese protests in China]. *Xinwen Zhishi* [Journalism knowledge] 6.

Zhao, Dingxin. 2003. "Nationalism and Authoritarianism: Student-Government Conflicts during the 1999 Beijing Student Protests after the Belgrade Embassy Bombing." *Asian Perspective* 27 (1): 5–34.

Zhao, Quansheng. 1993. *Japanese Policymaking: The Politics behind Politics. Informal Mechanisms and the Making of China Policy*. Westport, CT: Praeger.

Zhao, Suisheng. 1997. "Chinese Intellectuals' Quest for National Greatness and Nationalistic Writing in the 1990s." *China Quarterly* 152: 725–45.

———. 1998. "A State-Led Nationalism: The Patriotic Education Campaign in Post-Tiananmen China." *Communist and Post-Communist Studies* 31 (3): 287–302.

———. 2004. *A Nation-State by Construction: Dynamics of Modern Chinese Nationalism*: Stanford, CA: Stanford University Press.

Zheng, Yongnian. 1999. *Discovering Chinese Nationalism in China: Modernization, Identity, and International Relations*. New York: Cambridge University Press.

———. 2000. "China's Politics in 1999: Neiyou Waihuan." In *China's Politics and Economy in 1999: Coping with Crises*, ed. Y. Zheng and J. Wong, 1–26. Singapore: World Scientific, Singapore University Press.

Zhongguo Guoji Wenti Yanjiusuo. 2010–11. *Guoji Xingshi he Zhongguo Waijiao Lanpishu*. Beijing: Shishi Chubanshe.

Zhu, Rongji. 2011. *Zhu Rongji Jiang Hua Shi Lu*. 4 vols. Beijing: Ren min chu ban she.

Zong, Hairen. 2002. *Zhu Rongji zai 1999*. Xianggang: Ming jing chu ban she.

Zou, Jianhua. 2011. *Zou Jin Waijiaobu Fayanren: Xinwen Fayanren Miandui Meiti de Zhan Lue Yu Jiqiao*. Beijing Shi: Zhongguo zhongyang dangxiao chubanshe.

INDEX

R

Ran Yunfei, 171, 184

Reagan, Ronald, 90, 97

reassurance: and credibility, 30, 224; observational implications, 33t, 44; and resolve, balance of, 27–28, 35, 44, 248; as signaled by repression of nationalist protests, 25; in Sino-Japanese relations, 110, 123–25, 216, 271. *see also* repression; Sino-U.S. relations (EP-3 incident, 2001)

Reilly, James, 39, 94

repression: cost of, 4, 17, 20–23, 49, 71, 119, 128, 171, 220, 260*n*38; defined, 10; fear of, among protesters, 55; of nationalist protest in China, 9, 46, 112, 125; resentment at, among protesters, 230, 231; as signal of reassurance, 6, 30, 33, 38, 71, 77, 114, 123, 221. *see also* self-censorship

resolve: and audience costs, 17–19; foreign misperception of, 190, 199, 210, 248; observable implications, 32t; and protest management, 24–30, 46, 58–59, 61, 65, 108, 138, 161, 166, 217, 220, 223, 246; reputation for, 28, 224; signaling of, 4, 5, 45, 62, 66, 72, 170, 175, 180, 189, 199, 215–16, 225, 235–36; and state incapacity, 37; tests of, 52–53, 192; utility of, 27–28, 221

resource mobilization, defined, 19

Rice, Condoleezza, 77–78, 132, 139, 142

River Elegy (TV show), 228

Rose, Caroline, 93

Rosen, Stanley, 39, 126

Ross, Robert S., 38, 236

Roth, Stanley, 63–64, 222

Ruan Cishan, 50

Russia, 15, 60–61, 132, 136

S

Saiki, Akitaka, 169

Sakajiri, Nobuyoshi, 212

Sarkozy, Nicolas, 9, 239, 240, 242–43

Sasser, James, 47, 48, 54, 58

Satoh, Yukio, 131–32

Saunders, Phillip C., 113, 116, 120

Schell, Orville, 56

Schelling, Thomas, 17, 24, 25, 45

Schmitt, Gary, 79

Schultz, Kenneth A., 18, 261*n*68

Scowcroft, Brent, 107, 134

selection effects, 20, 35, 37, 261*n*68

self-censorship, 225, 231, 232

Sengoku, Yoshito, 169, 185

Shanghai Public Security Bureau, 144, 148

Shen, Simon, 40

Shen Guofang, 117

Shi, Tianjian, 173–74

Shi Guangsheng, 63, 64

Shirk, Susan: on elite divisions in China, 95, 262*n*77; on internet nationalism, 224; on Jiang's consolidation of power, 126; on WTO negotiations, 61, 65

Shi Yinhong, 130, 142, 180, 183

signaling. *see* diplomatic signaling; resolve

Sina.com.cn, 133, 139, 142, 240–41, 287*n*123

Singapore, 155, 156–57

Sino-Japanese relations (1980s), 82–103; anti-Japanese protests (1985), 82–86; from anti-Japan to pro-democracy protests, 82, 85–86, 99–103; China's independent foreign policy, 89–92; China's reaction to Nakasone's visit to Yasukuni Shrine, 92–95; diplomatic impact of protests and Japanese concessions, 95–99; economic assistance and Japanese concessions, 87–89; mutual compromise, 86–87; student mobilization and government response, 83–86; summary conclusion, 103, 227–234

Sino-Japanese relations (1990s), 104–26; diplomatic objectives and protest management, 104–5; patriotic education and repression of anti-Japanese protests, 105, 112–14; reshelving East China Sea issues, 120–25; stifling of anti-Japanese protest (1990) and lighthouse controversy, 105–8, 114–15, 116; stifling of anti-Japanese protest (1992) and Emperor Akihito's visit to China, 109–12; stifling of anti-Japanese protest (1996) and lighthouse controversy, 114–120; summary conclusion, 125–26

Sino-Japanese relations (2000–2005), 127–159; anti-Japanese protests as diplomatic asset and negotiations over UNSC expansion, 138–142; challenges of curtailing anti-Japanese protests, 146–150; diplomatic impact, 154–57; escalation of anti-Japanese mobilization, 142–46, 143f, 145f; foreign perceptions, 150–54; summary conclusion, 157–59, 220–22. *see also* Koizumi, Junichiro

Sino-Japanese relations (2006–2010), 160–188; continued tension and protests in both countries, 178–184; demonstrating resolve, 175–78; diplomatic impact, Japanese perceptions, 184–87; gas agreement and protest containment, 162–64, 172–73, 193; instability risk and cost of repression, 171–78; summary conclusion, 187–88, 221; trawler incident, and anti-Japanese protests, 165–171, 175–76, 177, 178, 185, 193, 199, 212, 216–17

Sino-Japanese War (1894–95), 7, 235

Sino-U.S. relations (embassy bombing, 1999): overview, 42–44; bombing event, 46–48; first phase, spontaneous, volatile protests, 54–57; protest management motivations, 44–46, 49–51; second phase, stage management, diminished risk